AF835129

SAUDI ARABIA: RUSH TO DEVELOPMENT

SAUDI ARABIA
Rush to Development

Profile of an Energy Economy and Investment

RAGAEI EL MALLAKH

CROOM HELM
London & Canberra

UNIVERSITY LIBRARY
10 JUN 1982
LANCASTER

© 1982 Ragaei El Mallakh
Croom Helm Ltd, 2-10 St John's Road, London SW11

British Library Cataloguing in Publication Data

El Mallakh, Ragaei
Saudi Arabia.
1. Saudi Arabia - Economic conditions
I. Title
330.953 HC497.A6

ISBN 0-7099-0905-5

Printed and bound in Great Britain by
Biddles Ltd, Guildford and King's Lynn

81 008669

CONTENTS

TABLES

FIGURES

To my brother Kamal El Mallakh, in recognition of his many and ongoing contributions to the history of science, archaeology, journalism, art and Arabic literature – truly a modern 'renaissance' man.

FOREWORD

This book culminates close to seven years of research, data collection and interviews with leaders in the public and private sectors in Saudi Arabia carried out during numerous visits to that country. A study of the economic development in the Kingdom came as a logical extension of the more than two decades of academic and applied interest and work in Middle Eastern economics, developmental economics and planning, and allied fields in energy, investment, international trade and finance.

For much of this century, many people have connected Saudi Arabia with the mysterious and adventurous aura exemplified by such writers and personalities as Richard Haliburton and Lawrence of Arabia. Its religious significance to a large portion of the world's population has given it a further special meaning that transcended its earlier poverty and harsh geographic and climatic conditions. Overwhelmingly imprinted in the Western mind has been the nomadic tradition which, until recently, has marked much of Saudi life.

Yet today, and in common with many states in the Gulf region and the Middle East, Saudi Arabia is undergoing rapid economic growth. The challenge facing the Kingdom's planners has been to channel this relatively sudden and unprecedented growth into stabilizing, orderly and self-sustaining development. One way to gauge the manner in which this challenge is being met is through the evolution of the nation's development plans. In this volume the first in-depth analysis is offered of the recently published *Third Development Plan, 1400-1405 AH/1980-1985 AD*, its development and economic targets and policies.

Moreover, Saudi Arabia's internal economic growth has been matched by its expanding international stature in global investment, aid and trade. In trade, the Kingdom is the world's largest single exporter of petroleum and the holder of the world's largest oil reserves. Its role in the Organization of the Petroleum Exporting Countries (OPEC) is frequently a pivotal one as is its stance in pursuing moderate-pricing policies and devising a long-term energy strategy, both of which exhibit a sensitivity to worldwide economic interdependence. Saudi Arabia is a major source of funding for the World Bank and International Monetary Fund (IMF). In March 1981, the Fund concluded a $10 billion loan from the Kingdom which led to an increase in Saudi Arabia's voting strength to sixth place among the 141-member IMF and a permanent seat on the 22-member board of directors. Aside from this multilateral agency, foreign economic aid from the Kingdom, itself a developing country, is extended through a number of other international and national bodies. Saudi assistance to the developing nations in 1980 was estimated at upwards of $5 billion.

In preparing a study on the Kingdom, there are two obstacles: (1) the lag in publication of statistical data and (2) the extremely dynamic economic conditions obtaining in the country and in the fluctuations in supply, demand, and pricing of petroleum. Yet, while some figures are subject to change and revision, the overall trends discerned in this book should retain their validity. Moreover, an attempt has been made to be as comprehensive as possible in order to meet a wide range of needs and interests not only in the academic world but for those concerned with industry, finance and commerce. The approach has been both quantitative and qualitative, the latter bolstered from extensive first-hand interviews. Finally, this book benefits from the long-term and ongoing research carried out in energy, Middle Eastern and development economics either individually or collectively as, for example, the major study under my direction at the International Research Center for Energy and Economic Development (ICEED) on 'New Constraints in Absorptive Capacity and the Optimum Rate of Petroleum Output' supported by the Rockefeller Foundation and the volume in the 1980s Project of the Council on Foreign Relations, *The Middle East in the Coming Decade*: *From Wellhead to Well-Being*?

Special acknowledgement and appreciation is due to Saudi officials and specialists who have granted interviews and supplied data: Sheikh Ahmed Zaki Yamani, Dr Ghazi Algosaibi, Dr Mohammed Abduh Yamani, Sheikh Mohammed Abalkhail, Hisham Nazer, Dr Abdul Hady Taher, Abdul Aziz Al-Quraishi, Dr Farouk Akhdar, Dr Mansour Al-Turki, Dr Fouad Al-Farsy, Dr Ahmed A. Al-Malik, Dr Abdelaziz Khodja, Sheikh Fahd Sudairy, Abdel Aziz Al-Turki, Dr Faisal Al-Bashir, Dr Abdulaziz Al-Sowayyegh, Dr M.A. Hassainain, Dr Yusuf Nimatallah, Abdulaziz Al-Zamil, Dr Rida Obaid, Dr Ibrahim Obaid, Dr Bakr Abdullah Bakr, Dr Abdullah Naseef, Farouk Al-Husseini, Osama Tarabulsi, Ibrahim A. Khaberi, Suleiman Al-Harbash, Dr Osama Adbulrahman, Dr Hossein Alawi, Mohammed Sabbagh, Khalil Gindy, Dr Faiz Al-Habeeb, Suleiman Mandeel, Ali Al-Sugair, Mansour A. Sehaimi, Dr Abdulrahman A. Al-Said, Dr Abdullah E. Dabbagh, Mukhlis Hammouri, Ahmed Al-Khatani and Saud Ounallah.

My present and former students from Saudi Arabia have provided knowledge, insights, and linkages: Dr Ali D. Johany, Dr Talal Hafiz, Abdullah Taher Dabbagh, Dr Alawi Al-Khayal, Dr Moheddin Al-Khayal, Dr Abdulwahab H.A. Mansouri, Dr Jobara Al-Suraisry, Dr Saud Al-Barkan, Dr Abdulrahman M. Al-Naiem, Dr Zain Barry, Dr Mohammed Raddady, Turki Al-Saud, Ibrahim Abouleila, Eid Abdullah Al-Juhani, Faisal Al-Kadi, Saiyed Al-Khouli, Abdolaziz Al-Noaim, Yousef Al-Saadon, Mohammed Al-Sabban, Mohammed Al-Sheikh, Abdul-Aziz As Sudais, Abdulla A. Ibrahim, Shehab Jamaladdeen, Yahya M.E. Mahboob, Yousef A. Zamel, Dr Abdulaziz S. Al-Jarbou, Abdullah A. Al-Tabaib, Sabry Abu Al-Hamail, Abdullah Al-Saba'i, Yahya Al-Zaid – a partial listing given a professor's habitual problem in remembering names!

In the private sector within Saudi Arabia and in the United States, a number of individuals have always been helpful and encouraging: Sheikh Ali Shobokshi, Sheikh Fahd Shobokshi, Mohammed Al-Tayib, Faisal Al-Bassam, James Balog, Christopher Beirn, Roy E. Brakeman, John R. Hayes, Charles Hedlund, James V. Knight, Weldon Kruger, William Lindenmuth, Rajai R. Masri, Donald Snook, Norman Tanber and William D. Witter.

In preparing the manuscript, certain of the ICEED's staff have contributed to tabulation, econometric analysis and up-dating, including Dr Murad Aseil, Dr Mihssen Kadhim, Dr Jacob Atta, Dr Mohammed Akacem, Jon Richards and Dennis Miller. My colleagues in the Department of Economics at the University of Colorado have been both a sounding board and a source of ideas: Professors Malcolm Dowling, Fred Glahe, Carl McGuire, Robert McNown, Barry Poulson, and John Powelson. Glenda Bolin, Cindy Harrison, Nancy Nachman Hunt, Kathleen O'Brien and Suzanne F. Young of the ICEED staff have handled typing, proofing and indexing chores with accuracy and a consistently cheerful manner. The final eye over the entire process from idea to manuscript to book has been that of my wife Dr Dorothea H. El Mallakh. Without the assistance of the persons acknowledged above and many others over the years, this volume could not have been completed.

Ragaei El Mallakh
Director, International Research Center for Energy and Economic Development and Professor of Economics
University of Colorado
Boulder, Colorado

ABBREVIATIONS, ACRONYMS AND CONVERSION EQUIVALENTS

ADB	Agricultural Development Bank; also known as the Saudi Arabian Agricultural Bank (SAAB)
AH	Anno Hijra (dates in the Hijra lunar year)
Aramco	Arabian American Oil Company
b/d	barrels per day
CDS	Central Department of Statistics
CPO	Central Planning Organization; in 1975 was elevated to the Ministry of Planning
GDP	gross domestic product
GNP	gross national product
GSFMO	Grain Silos and Flour Mills Organization
ha	hectare
IMF	International Monetary Fund
ISDC	Industrial Studies and Development Centre; in 1979 became the Saudi Consulting House (SCH)
km	kilometre
km^2	square kilometre
KW	kilowatt
kWh	kilowatt-hour
m	metre
m^2	square metre
m^3	cubic metre
milliard	10^9 cubic metres used to quote production and sales of natural gas annually; also widely used is millions of cubic feet daily
MMcf/d	millions of cubic feet per day
MOAW	Ministry of Agriculture and Water
MOMRA	Ministry of Municipal and Rural Affairs
mrd m^3/yr	milliard
MW	megawatt
Petromin	General Petroleum and Mineral Organization
REDF	Real Estate Development Fund
SAAB	Saudi Arabian Agricultural Bank; also known as the Agricultural Development Bank (ADB)
Sabic	Saudi Basic Industries Corporation

SAMA	Saudi Arabian Monetary Agency
SANCST	Saudi Arabian National Centre for Science and Technology
SAUDIA	Saudi Arabian Airlines Corporation
SCH	Saudi Consulting House; formerly the Industrial Studies and Development Centre (ISDC)
SDF	Saudi Development Fund; also called the Saudi Fund for Development (SFD)
SFD	Saudi Fund for Development; also called the Saudi Development Fund (SDF)
SIDF	Saudi Industrial Development Fund
SR	Saudi riyal; annual average rate of the riyal to 1 Special Drawing Right (SDR) of the International Monetary Fund has been: 4.248 (1974); 4.272 (1975); 4.076 (1976); 4.115 (1977); 4.282 (1978); 4.312 (mid-year 1979). The variation in the value of the riyal to the US dollar for the second and fourth quarter averages have been: 1978 – second quarter, 3.445 SR to $1/fourth quarter, 3.315 SR to $1; 1979 – second quarter, 3.375 SR to $1/ fourth quarter, 3.365 SR to $1; 1980 – second quarter, 3.325 SR to $1/fourth quarter, 3.325 SR to $1; 1981 – as of April, 3.355 SR to $1.
SWCC	Saline Water Conversion Corporation

Conversion equivalents:

1 ton (metric) = 1.1 short tons
1 cubic foot (ft^3) = 0.028317 cubic metres (m^3)
1 kilogram (kg) = 2.20462 pounds (lbs)
1 metre (m) = 3.281 feet (ft) and 1.095 miles
1 kilometre (km) = 0.6214 mile
1 square metre (m^2) = 10.764 square feet (ft^2)
1 square kilometre (km^2) = 0.3861 square mile ($mile^2$)
1 hectare (ha) = 2.471 acres and 0.01 square kilometres (km^2)
1 milliard (mrd m^3/yr) = 100 million cubic feet per day (MMcf/d)

1 AN OVERVIEW

Introduction

For as far back as most residents of Yanbu and Jubail can remember, their small villages have remained largely unchanged. Each lies near a body of water – Yanbu on the Red Sea and Jubail on the Arabian Gulf. The inhabitants are involved primarily in fishing and some maritime trading on a small scale; the villages are dusty and far from the mainstream of the major commercial and governmental centres within Saudi Arabia. Today Yanbu and Jubail are even dustier with the nearly ceaseless comings and goings of trucks and equipment, and the noise-level of the once sleepy towns has risen so quickly and to such a pitch that it would be understandable if the local people were beset with a feeling of unreality.

Saudi Arabia is involved not in a move or thrust, but a stampede toward economic development; the transformation taking place in Yanbu and Jubail perhaps best epitomizes this almost cataclysmic restructuring of an economy on an unprecedented scale and with dizzying speed. The construction of industrial complexes at these Red Sea and Gulf sites is the most massive new undertaking of its kind worldwide. The impact of the vast Yanbu and Jubail facilities will first be felt in the 1980s when some production will begin.

The larger complex is being established at Jubail, which lies some 55 miles to the northwest of Dhahran, the headquarters of the Saudi oil industry; its cost could run as high as $70 billion (US) for the basic infrastructure and industrial plants. Both sites will have petrochemical facilities, refineries, smaller-scale industrial plants and permanent housing; Jubail, in addition, is scheduled for an aluminium smelter, steel mill, international airport, two deepwater ports, power-generating units, telecommunications, as well as the largest desalination plant existing globally. Once a community of about 4,000, Jubail is now swarming with workers from, literally, all over the world. Obviously, Saudi Arabia is rich in two of the most critical elements required for such industrial development – capital funds and access to sufficient cheap energy and petrochemical feedstocks in oil and natural gas.

The development of Yanbu and Jubail falls under the authority of a Royal Commission created specifically to handle this major enterprise. In its annual report for 1977 the Commission delineated the prevailing thinking within the country on the projects and, in fact, on the objectives of the development process itself.

> To continue exporting our oil wealth in its crude form, to the point of total depletion, would have adverse economic effects in the not-too-distant future. For then the Kingdom would find itself with no economic basis to rely on.
>
> Thus our industrialization strategy aims at the long-term objective of diversifying the Kingdom's industrial base, thus enabling Saudi Arabia to realize a greater measure of economic self-sufficiency and allowing it to reap the benefits of local production.[1]

Whether the Yanbu and Jubail project targets can be met on schedule, and indeed, those of the $142-billion Second Development Plan (1975-80) and the $235-billion Third Development Plan (1980-85), depends not only on the availability of capital and energy. There exist a number of relatively severe constraints in physical and supporting infrastructure and especially in human resources, both quantitative and qualitative. Thus, the drive for industrialization must be long term in that the transfer of technology is time consuming. To this end, the Saudi policy in education has been to train as many citizens as quickly as possible. By the opening of the 1980s as many as 13,000 Saudis may be in the United States alone for university and specialized training. Within the Kingdom 20 per cent of the population was enrolled in some form of education, with 1.24 million enrolled full time. Some 44,000 of these students were attending universities, intermediate colleges, or post-graduate institutions. The projected figure for the end of the Third Plan period (1985) was some 69,000 students in higher education with 10,090 graduates. Considering the population of Saudi Arabia (in the neighbourhood of 7 million), the enrolment and education statistics carry great importance for the coming years and for the development process.

The construction boom is not limited to the industrial centres, as in Yanbu and Jubail. The skylines of Riyadh, Jeddah and other cities are clouded with cranes and rising steel skeletons. If one can be excused a pun, then the national bird of Saudi Arabia certainly should be the crane. In fact, about the only non-Saudi city where the hustle and bustle of a boom-town can be seen on the same scale as Riyadh is in Casper, Wyoming (USA), where the building and overall feeling of barely contained vigour are generated from the oil, coal, and uranium activities and associated growth in this American energy centre.

In recent years much world attention has riveted on Saudi Arabia, heretofore largely ignored but destined now to retain its new prominence throughout the 1980s and 1990s. There are many causes, but a brief listing would include: (1) that country has been a leading ally of the USA and the West in holding down increases in world oil prices since 1975; (2) more than any other producer, Saudi Arabia, possessing the world's largest reserves of this resource, has been instrumental in meeting the incremental demand for oil; (3) it is the number-one supplier of petroleum to the United States; (4) the Kingdom has the second highest monetary reserves in the world; (5) in terms of gross national product, Saudi economic aid is one of the highest proportions extended by any donor nation; (6) the country has been a major moderating influence not only within the Organization of the Petroleum Exporting Countries (OPEC), but within the politics of the Middle East; and (7) Saudi Arabia is the fastest-growing market in the world.

Until the beginning of the 1970s, when the Arab oil embargo catapulted the Kingdom of Saudi Arabia to the apex of the world energy market, little had been written about the economy of that nation and its people. Tales about the land, its inhabitants and ancient heroes, such as those retold in the *Arabian Nights*, have existed of course for generations. Also, Saudi Arabia has been regarded as the guardian of the Islamic religion by all Muslims, many of whom strive to make a pilgrimage to the holy places in Mecca and Medina at least once in their lifetimes.[2] Interest in the holy land has increased in recent years beyond the level of religious belief. Saudi Arabia is now called upon to play strategic roles in the world of energy, specifically in the activities of OPEC and OAPEC (Organization of the Arab Petroleum Exporting Countries), and in international monetary arrangements. The share of the Kingdom in total world oil exports and reserves and its large investments in OECD countries (particularly the USA) all add up to make Saudi Arabia a very critical country, or a kind of a super oil power, not only to policy-makers but also to the people of developed market economy nations, whose life-styles could be changed by decisions in Saudi Arabia. One should not forget Saudi contributions to development aid to needy countries, Arab economic co-operation, and the Middle East war and peace efforts by serving increasingly as a vital source of finance.

A study on the economy of Saudi Arabia is not just an academic exercise. It must necessarily seek to analyse the domestic development programmes, policies, and political, social, financial and economic structures, with a view to drawing implications for the vital roles which the Kingdom has come to play in the international economic scene. Such is the objective of the analysis contained in this volume.

At the risk of sounding apologetic, the author observes that this study is first and foremost constrained by the paucity of data which, therefore, has generated a host of non-quantifiable magnitudes. Yet there has been an attempt to provide as detailed an analysis of the various sectors of the country as possible. Before a turn is made to detailed analysis, a brief overview of the land, the people and the economy should set the stage.

The Land

The Kingdom of Saudi Arabia comprises the bulk of what is commonly known as the Arabian peninsula and has a land area of about 2.3 million square kilometres.

Saudi Arabia is bounded on the north by Jordan, Iraq, and Kuwait; on the south by North and South Yemen; on the west by the Red Sea and the Gulf of Aqaba; and on the east by Oman, Qatar, the United Arab Emirates, and the Arabian Gulf (Figure 1.1). The Red Sea washes a narrow strip of low land whose width varies from 10 to 40 miles. These western coastal plains which are called 'Tihamats' are unique in their extensive marshlands and lava fields. To the east of these plains a range of mountains runs, broken here and there by wadis or valleys. Among the wadis, most of which have oases, the most important are Al-Himdh, Yanbu, Fatima, and Itwid and Bisha in the Asir region. The mountain ranges decline towards the coastal plains (i.e. to the west), enabling flood waters to wash silt onto the plains; thus, the soil in this region is kept more fertile than that of any other part of the Kingdom.

The Asir region has the highest peaks in the country, rising to over 2,743 metres. The Mecca region follows with about 2,438 metres declining to 1,219 metres above sea-level in the western Mahd Adh-Dhahab and to 914 metres in the Medina region. The mountain range also extends to the northern part of the country. The Najd plateau lies directly to the east of the northern section of the mountain range. The plateau which continues southwards to Wadi Ad-Dawaser and runs parallel to the Rub al-Khali has an average elevation ranging from 1,219 to 1,829 metres. The northern portion of the Najd plateau consists of plains which extend about 1,448 kilometres beyond Hail to join the Iraqi and Jordanian borders. The sandy hills of Nafud are dry and have no vegetation until rainfall changes the land into

Figure 1.1: Physical Features of Saudi Arabia

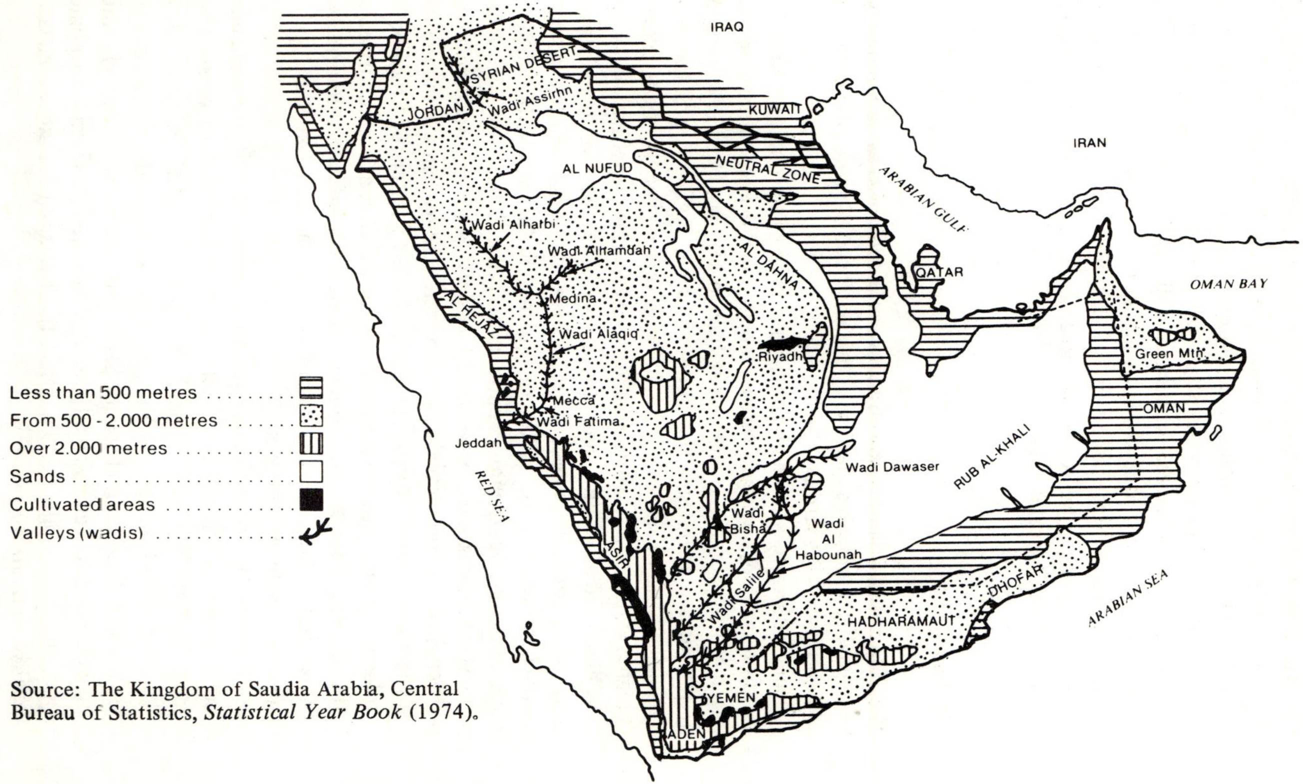

Source: The Kingdom of Saudia Arabia, Central Bureau of Statistics, *Statistical Year Book* (1974).

temporary grazing pastures.

Only after the discovery of oil in Saudi Arabia did attention shift to geological studies, which seek to discover the mineral wealth of the land other than oil; only recently a geological survey of 65 per cent of the Precambrian Arabian Shield (located in the western part of the country) was completed. The study has revealed substantial deposits of other minerals. Therefore, in addition to oil, the Kingdom may have respectable assets in copper, lead, zinc, gold, silver, iron, phosphates, uranium, and potash; major efforts are required to develop the metallic minerals to reach operational stage. There is, however, commercialization of non-metallic minerals such as cement, gypsum, lime, marble, and salt. Figure 1.2 shows the distribution of mineral deposits in the Precambrian Arabian Shield of the Kingdom.

Most of the land is desert, and water is the most scarce input in both production and consumption activities. Since the land comes under the influence of a subtropical high-pressure system, rainfall is generally very sparse. Summers are hot and dry, while during the winter the occasional inflow of a cold system from the Siberian region cools the temperatures across the country. The winter is thus mostly cold and dry during this time of the year. An exception to this climate picture is the coastal plains which are also unlike the interior regions that experience extreme high temperatures with large daily variations, especially during the summer. Most of the rainfall occurs in the form of thunderstorms resulting from the low-pressure system in the Mediterranean region, which moves into the northern province in the winter. Summer rains are common over the intertropical Covergence Zone.

Saudi Arabia has no overland free-flowing fresh water, except that when it rains some valleys fill with water. Many dams have been constructed to impound this important source of water for irrigation and other purposes. Other natural sources of water consist of confined and free-flowing aquifers and springs. Confined aquifers are underground water under pressure and the free-flowing aquifers are the type not under any source of pressure.

The climate and soil converge to determine cultivable agricultural lands. Areas where such natural conditions intersect to create arable lands include Al-Hasa, Al-Qatif, Al-Qasim, Al-Aflaj, Al-Kharj, Jizan, Tihamah, Wadi Fatima Al-Medina, Taif, Abha, and Hail. In addition there exists a substantial area of Saudi land which can be brought under cultivation given an adequate supply of water, contrary to popular opinion and despite the fact that the Kingdom has little vegetation relative to its size.

Figure 1.2: Major Mineral Deposits: Metalliferous Minerals

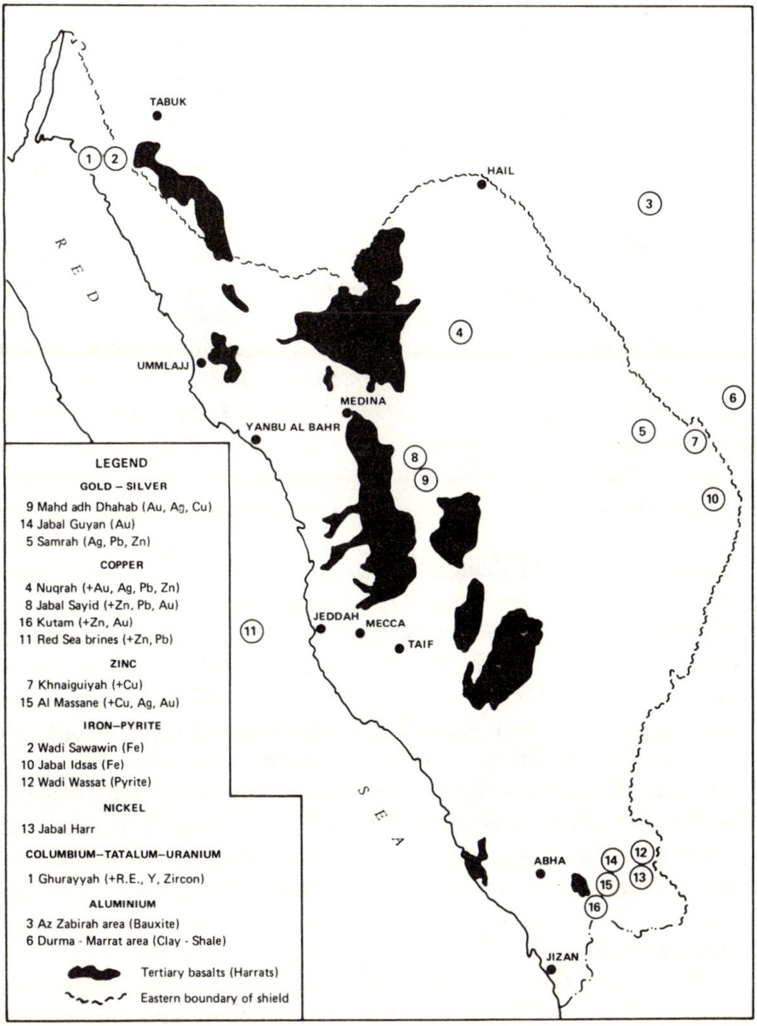

Source: Kingdom of Saudi Arabia, *Third Development Plan, 1400-1405/ 1980-1985,* Chapter4, p. 209

The geophysical constraints which confront Saudi Arabia are not as binding as those with which some of the other oil-producing countries in the area must contend. Even though Saudi Arabia has limited agricultural potential, this sector can still be expanded significantly beyond its present traditional level. In addition, the presence of exploitable deposits of other minerals will allow the Saudis to broaden the resource base on which their economy now depends.

Perhaps the most significant feature of the land is its geo-political importance. Saudi Arabia dominates the Arabian peninsula, the land mass being between Asia and Africa. Most of the oil fuelling the industrial economies of Europe, Japan and the USA is transported in the waters surrounding this peninsula. If in pumping the life-blood of industrial economies Saudi Arabia is characterized as the heart, then these sea routes, the Suez Canal, the Bab al Mandab Straits and the Strait of Hormuz are as vital as the aorta in bringing oil to the Western world. It is of no surprise that Western observers are concerned. Whereas Saudi Arabia does not directly border any of these crucial sea lanes, it is centrally located and a leading political force in the region.

The Population and Labour Force

Prior to the 1974 population census, estimates of the size of the Saudi population ranged from 3 million to 15 million. The preliminary results of the census put the population at some 7,012,642.[3] Throughout this study the official Saudi figures are utilized in computations for which population and other demographic data are necessary.

About 27 per cent of the population of Saudi Arabia are nomads. Nomadic agglomerations are unevenly distributed among administrative areas, but in no area except Jizan did the census results indicate that the nomadic population was below 10 per cent of total population. Indeed, only five administrative areas have a nomadic/total-population ratio below 30 per cent, and in some cases, such as Hail and the frontiers, nomadic population are in the majority. Table 1.1 gives further details about the distribution of population among administrative regions.

Thirty-nine per cent of the population in Saudi Arabia lives in towns having 30,000 inhabitants or more (see Table 1.2 for major urban-centre statistics). This obviously cannot be used to measure the extent of urbanization in the Kingdom, since it will tend to underestimate it *vis-à-vis* other countries, for example, the United States, where urban population may include areas with 2,500 inhabitants or more. If the

Table 1.1: Population of Saudi Arabia by Administrative Area

Administrative area	Number of demographic units[a]	Number of families	Population			
			Sedentary	Nomadic	Percentage of nomadic to total population	Total
Riyadh	1,992	198,936	965,805	306,470	24	1,272,275
Mecca	4,088	325,789	1,513,634	240,474	13.7	1,754,108
Eastern Province	667	120,684	690,188	79,460	10.3	769,648
Asir	4,597	127,131	434,884	246,477	36.2	681,361
Medina	1,742	98,835	282,195	237,099	45.7	519,294
Jizan	4,537	85,483	387,161	15,945	4.0	403,106
Qasim	509	48,724	215,447	101,193	32.0	316,640
Hail	504	45,338	117,210	142,719	54.9	259,929
Tabuk	472	33,642	105,388	88,375	45.6	193,763
Al-Baha	1,296	34,323	156,997	28,908	15.5	185,905
Najran	242	26,569	91,555	56,415	38.1	147,970
Northern Frontiers	130	19,345	42,666	86,079	66.9	128,745
Jawf	85	10,243	34,093	31,401	47.9	65,494
Qurayyat	98	5,873	18,432	12,972	41.3	31,404
Frontier Nomads	–	30,000	–	210,000	–	210,000
Saudis resident abroad at time of census	–	–	73,000	–	26.8	73,000
Total	20,995	1,210,915	5,128,655	1,883,987		7,012,642

Note: a. Demographic units: consisting of towns, villages, settlements, farms, water wells and nomad agglomerations.
Source: Abdel R. Al-Madani and Muhamed Al-Fayez, *Population Bulletin of the United Nations Commission for Western Asia*, nos. 10 and 11 (1976), p. 186.

entire land area of Saudi Arabia is taken into consideration, the population density is very low, not more than three persons per square kilometre. However, to the extent that large expanses of sandy lands, such as the Rub al-Khali desert region, are virtually inhospitable, the inhabited areas are densely populated. The skewness in the population distribution tends to put pressure on the economic resources of the country; but for the oil, the pressure would have taken the form of extremely low real-income per capita. Since labour is one of the most-needed resources in the Kingdom, it cannot be said that Saudi Arabia is overpopulated, despite the social, economic and cultural problems which the rapid rate of urbanization has created in the country.

Table 1.2: Principal Towns in Saudi Arabia with a Population of over 30,000

Town	Administrative area	Number of families	Population
Riyadh	Riyadh	101,506	666,840
Jeddah	Mecca	97,363	561,104
Mecca	Mecca	67,947	366,801
Taif	Mecca	30,877	204,857
Medina	Medina	35,390	198,186
Dammam	Eastern Province	21,513	127,844
Hofuf	Eastern Province	14,551	101,271
Tabuk	Northern Province	10,696	74,825
Buraida	Qasim	8,774	69,940
Mubarraz	Eastern Province	7,775	54,325
Khamis Mushayt	Asir	9,142	49,581
Khobar	Eastern Province	9,023	48,817
Najran	Najran	9,149	47,501
Hail	Hail	6,065	40,502
Jizan	Jizan	5,648	32,812
Abha	Asir	5,413	30,150

Source: Abdel R. Al-Madani and Muhamed Al-Fayez, *Population Bulletin*, p. 187.

Even with the 1974 census, the Saudi Central Bureau of Statistics is still uncertain about the natural rate of growth of the Saudi population owing to inadequate report of births and deaths throughout the nation, especially in rural areas. It is estimated to be in the range of 2.8 to 3 per cent per annum. Net immigration then increases the estimated population growth to an annual rate of 4 per cent which, it is felt, if maintained, would raise the population of Saudi Arabia to 10 million in 1985 and almost double the 1974 figure by 1990.

Given that overpopulation is not an immediate problem, the Saudi

Figure 1.3: Municipalities and Regions

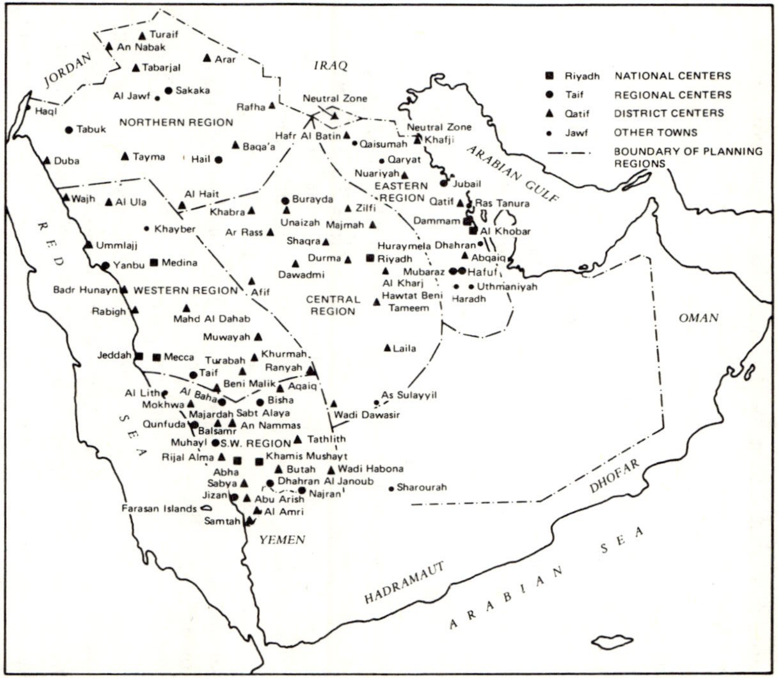

Source: Kingdom of Saudi Arabia, *Third Development Plan, 1400-1405 / 1980-1985*, p. xxxv.

government has had a relaxed attitude towards population control. Nevertheless, Saudi Arabia shares with most emerging nations the problem of rural-to-urban migration. Consequently, and especially in the 1970s, depopulation of the countryside has been faster than the rate at which technological advancement in the agricultural sector could release labour to the other sectors of the economy. Hence, agricultural production has not been able to keep pace with the rest of the economy, and its contribution to the gross domestic product has been falling, as the discussion in the chapter on agriculture will show.[4] Also, the rural-urban migration has created all but one of the problems which usually accompany rapid urbanization: housing shortages, pressure on social infrastructure, inflation and the like. The single exception is that unemployment is not yet a problem in the urban centres. There is as well the question of grouping the population in small villages and settling the nomads who constitute over a quarter of the population. The problems, formidable as they are, have recently received the serious attention of the government, which has made several efforts at least to reduce their adverse impacts on the social and economic welfare of the population.

Saudi Arabia has a youthful population. Persons under 15 years of age constitute 44 per cent of the total, according to the United Nations estimates.[5] This youthful feature of the population is a characteristic shared by most developing countries. Further, the proportion of women in the labour force is very low, about 6 per cent during the Second Plan period (1975-80). As a result, although the share of population 65 years and over is relatively small, the economic participation rate of Saudi males 12 years and older was about 65 per cent in 1980, down from 69 per cent five years earlier. In large part this is attributable to the longer span of formal education for those 12 years of age and older. It would appear that population size alone cannot be held responsible for the scarcity of both skilled and unskilled manpower with the resultant constraint on economic development. On the contrary, the literacy rate, inadequate training, the high proportion of unsettled nomadic population, attitudes towards female labour and female education, and the youthfulness of the population, all are responsible for keeping the proportion of the population actively engaged in economic activities at such a low level. In recognition of these factors which constrict the supply of labour, the government has in all of the three development plans, made efforts at devising more progressive educational programmes and changing the attitude of the society towards female labour so that it can assume a more important place in the process of economic development. Like most attempts to change behavioural parameters, however, the process is going to be a long, time-consuming one. Labour, therefore, is going to remain a constraint on the drive toward diversification of the economy to the extent envisaged by the government for a considerable period to come. It was with this constraint in mind that planners designated manpower development as a primary area of concern in the Third Development Plan.

The distribution of employment by economic activity in Saudi Arabia experienced structural changes between 1975 and 1980. However, unlike the usual pattern of such changes during the development process, although there has been a shift of manpower from the agricultural sector, it has not been only toward construction but also toward utilities, commerce (trade), finance and business services, and community and social services. Table 1.3 offers the distribution of employment among economic activities for 1975 and 1980. It will be noted that the labour force engaged in manufacturing accounted for 4.2 per cent, unchanged between 1975 and 1980. However, in view of the diversification policy of the government, which essentially means increased industrialization of the economy, a relative shift of the labour force toward the manufacturing sector could be expected in the future. Only if this occurs and productivity of the overall Saudi working population continues to grow at a reasonable rate, will the diversification programmes be successful in the face of these noted manpower constraints.

Social and Political System of Saudi Arabia

Almost all Saudis are Arab Muslims, brought together into a form of statehood in 1932 by HM Abd al Aziz ibn Abd ar Rahman al Saud after 25 years of tribal conquest and diplomatic efforts. Since then the Kingdom of Saudi Arabia has been ruled by the house or line of Saud. The king is both the symbol of political and religious power, although the extent of the power of each ruler depends on his personality and ability. Also, since leaders differ in administrative capabilities, Saudi rulers have had varied successes in managing the economy, especially since the exploitation of oil brought an infiltration of Western socio-economic values into the social fabric of the country. Fortunately, most of the Saudi rulers were able to accept the modernization which oil wealth bestowed upon the country, but without drastic changes in

Table 1.3: Employment by Economic Activity, 1975 and 1980

Economic activity	Employment 1975 (thousands)	Employment 1975 (per cent)	Employment 1980 (thousands)	Employment 1980 (per cent)	Average annual growth rate 1975-80 (per cent)
1 Producing sectors					2.2
Agriculture	695.0	39.8	598.8	24.2	–2.9
Mining	3.4	0.2	7.3	0.3	16.5
Oil and refineries	27.4	1.6	36.0	1.5	5.6
Manufacturing	74.4	4.2	104.2	4.2	7.0
Utilities	16.1	0.9	31.5	1.3	14.4
Construction	172.3	9.9	330.1	13.4	13.9
	988.6	56.6	1,107.9	44.8	
2 Services sectors					15.3
Trade	153.6	8.8	310.6	12.6	15.1
Transport	114.5	6.6	214.6	8.7	13.4
Finance and business services	13.1	0.8	34.8	1.4	21.6
Community and social services	230.0	13.2	482.3	19.5	16.0
	511.2	29.3	1,042.3	42.2	
3 Government[a]	246.7	14.1	321.0[b]	13.0	5.4
Total (1+2+3)	1,746.5	100.0	2,471.2	100.0	7.2

Notes: a. Civilian employment only. b. This government figure includes an estimated 49.6 thousand daily workers not classified as civil servants.
Source: Ministry of Planning estimates for the Third Development Plan (1980-5).

the social values of the population. But whereas social values for some time have remained relatively stable, education and wealth are changing the living patterns of many Saudis.

The legal system also has not reflected much influence from Western culture. Saudi Arabia is among the few countries in the world which bases its judicial system on the Shari'a (Islamic Jurisprudence, the body of laws contained in the Quoran, the Sunna, Ijma and the qiyas).[6]

Although to the non-Saudi the traditional set-up of the legal and social systems of the Kingdom may seem strange, the country has so far exhibited an unusual ability to maintain most of its social values and institutions and still develop at considerably rapid rates. Whereas increased oil revenues have contributed to this growth, an important reason is perhaps the capability of the institutional framework of the country to circumvent traditional rules which appear to restrain the growth process. An example of such flexibility in the social structure is the charging of a 'commission' instead of interest in Saudi banking practices, when it was found that Islamic teachings do not permit interest to be earned or charged on money or loans.

The social and cultural framework of Saudi Arabia will undoubtedly be influenced by the country's rapid development. To gain a perspective of the enormity of the Yanbu and Jubail construction projects, together valued at over $80 billion, one may compare them to the Alaskan pipeline which cost $9 billion. Combining the magnitude and rapid pace of such industrialization projects with the socio-demographic aspects of Saudi Arabia is a unique experiment.

Thousands upon thousands of workers from Asia, Europe, North America and other Arab countries have converged upon Saudi Arabia to alleviate the shortage of labour and specialists. Not only must the government cope with such an influx of foreigners, it must also screen its own society from the different attitudes prevalent in these other cultures.

The Economy

The Structural Features

Saudi Arabia has a single-commodity economy. The dominance of oil in the country's foreign exchange earnings, government revenue, and as a source of growth of the national income, is the most obvious characteristic of the economic system. It is of interest to note, once again, that the oil sector is not an important source of employment, which is perhaps not so negative an aspect for an economy in which labour is scarce. There is a catch here, however. To the extent that the technology in the oil industry requires a very high calibre of manpower, this sector, if defined broadly to include oil-related forms of economic activities like petrochemical industries, may be found to shortchange the rest of the economy so far as employment of top-level manpower is concerned. It is in this level of labour, however, that the country suffers a dearth.

A convenient methodology for carrying out structural analysis of the economy is to look at the distribution of its gross national product (GNP) according to economic activities. The analysis can be done either at a point in time or, from a more dynamic view, by looking at the way the shares of various economic activities have been behaving over time. Both approaches are adopted here.

During the 13-year period from 1965 to 1978 there were significant structural changes in the economy of Saudi Arabia so far as industrial origin of the gross domestic product (GDP) was concerned. To illustrate the changing composition of economic activity, let us consider the contrast between 1965 and 1978, as contained in Table 1.4. One can discern a number of major characteristics of this period. There was a relative shift to crude petroleum and gas whose share of nominal GDP peaked in 1974 and declined through the rest of the decade. The dramatic price rise for oil in 1973-4 resulted in significant reductions in the relative contributions of all non-oil activities in the economy in favour of crude oil and gas production. Notable between 1975 and 1978 were the increased shares to construction (from 5.5 to 14.3 per cent), to government services (from 3.6 to 6.8 per cent), and to transport, storage and communications (from 1.7 to 4.5 per cent). This, however, has been only in the case of current price evaluations. In terms of real GDP (i.e. GDP at constant prices), the structural shift appears to be less prominent. Indeed, as Table 1.4 shows, the following economic activities all increased their shares of real GDP between 1965 and 1978: (1) manufacturing other than petroleum refining; (2) electricity, gas and water; (3) construction; (4) commerce, restaurants and hotels; (5) services; and (6) other minerals. This occurred not only at the expense of crude-oil and natural-gas production, but also at the cost of reduced shares of other non-oil activities, such as agriculture, government services, and transport, storage and communications.

The fact still remains that the Saudi economy's structure shifted in the 13-year period in favour of crude-oil and gas production and construction and away from some important sectors of the economy, especially agricultural activity.

Table 1.4: Saudi Arabia's Gross Domestic Product by Economic Activity (per cent)

Type of economic activity	Current prices				Constant prices			
	1965	1975[a]	1976[a]	1978[b]	1965	1975[a]	1976[a]	1978[b]
Agriculture, forestry and fishing	8.5	1.0	0.9	1.0	8.3	3.7	3.5	3.2
Mining and quarrying:	44.2	75.2	66.9	56.9	44.2	54.9	51.1	47.3
Crude petroleum and natural gas	44.0	75.0	66.6	56.4	43.9	54.6	50.8	46.9
Other minerals	0.2	0.2	0.3	0.5	0.3	0.3	0.3	0.4
Manufacturing:	8.3	5.2	4.9	4.4	8.0	6.3	6.2	6.4
Petroleum refining	6.4	4.1	3.6	2.6	6.2	4.1	3.8	3.8
Other manufacturing	1.9	1.1	1.3	1.8	1.8	2.3	2.4	2.6
Electricity, gas and water	1.3	0.1	0.1	0.1	1.1	1.0	1.0	1.3
Construction	4.9	5.5	9.6	14.3	5.2	7.8	9.6	10.9
Commerce, restaurants and hotels	7.0	2.8	3.8	4.9	7.1	6.0	6.8	8.5
Transport, storage and communications	7.2	1.7	2.5	4.5	6.9	4.1	4.6	5.6
Services:	4.8	3.9	5.1	5.7	4.8	7.0	7.6	8.3
Ownership of dwellings	4.2	2.5	3.2	3.4	4.2	5.2	5.6	6.1
Other[c]	0.6	1.4	1.9	2.3	0.6	1.8	2.0	2.2
Community services	5.5	0.9	1.2	1.5	5.7	1.0	1.1	1.1
Less bank charges		–0.2	–0.3	–0.7		–0.2	–0.2	–0.3
Subtotal (GDP) of population	91.7	96.1	94.7	92.6	91.3	91.7	91.4	92.3
Government services	8.3	3.9	5.3	7.4	8.7	8.3	8.6	7.7
GDP in a factor cost	100.0	100.0	100.0	100.0	100.0	100.0	100.0	100.0

Notes: a. Revised estimates. b. Preliminary estimates. c. Less imputed bank service charges.
Source: Computed from SAMA, *Statistical Summary*, 1st issue (Riyadh, 1977), Tables 27 and 28, and 2nd issue (1977), Tables 28 and 29; SAMA, *Annual Reports* (1977), Tables 28 and 29, pp. 146-9 and (1979), Tables 19 and 30, pp. 165-8.

The 1978 situation could be described as follows. Crude-oil and natural-gas production generated 56.4 per cent of the GDP at factor cost (current prices) in Saudi Arabia. At constant prices, however, the share of oil and gas was reduced to 46.9 per cent. Of the nominal GDP, manufacturing (including refining) contributed only 4.4 per cent, construction some 14.3 per cent, transport and communications 4.5 per cent, commerce 4.9 per cent, and services 5.7 per cent. Such was the structure of the economy of Saudi Arabia during 1978.

For some time, Saudi governmental policy has been to restrict oil output to 8.5 million barrels per day unless special circumstances dictate otherwise. There, in view of this general policy not to expand the production of crude oil and to diversify the economy, it is also unlikely that the share of this sector in real income will show the same upward trend of the last five years or so in the future. Indeed, as the bottlenecks presently existing in the economy are reduced, the non-oil sectors may be able to catch up. There is, of course, the outside chance that even in terms of real income the dominance of crude oil and gas will continue to grow, especially if plans to market all associated gas, most of which is currently flared, succeed on a continuing basis.

Expenditure Patterns

Production is not an end in itself, but a means to the ultimate objective of all economic activities – consumption. It is important after discussing production (or the supply side of the economy) to shift attention to the analysis of the manner in which goods and services produced in Saudi Arabia are utilized. The objective of such an analysis, which involves expenditure composition of national income, is to ascertain how much private consumption, government consumption, capital formation, and foreign accumulation of savings have been taking place in Saudi Arabia in the period 1963 to 1978. Tables 1.5 and 1.6 will aid in this analysis.

As can be found in most developing countries, the share of the private sector *vis-à-vis* that of the government in total consumption has been predictable. The share of government consumption increased consistently over the decade. This is not surprising in Saudi Arabia, where the traditional system requires that the government shares with the whole populace the wealth of the country, and therefore subsidies, provision of social services and increased employment become mechanisms through which wealth is redistributed. This means that private consumption alone is not a sufficient measure of the economic welfare of the population.

Table 1.5a: Gross Domestic Product of Saudi Arabia by Expenditure Categories, 1963-70 (SR (Saudi riyals) millions)

	1963	1964	1965	1966	1967	1968	1969	1970
Consumption expenditures								
Private	2,742	2,835	2,910	3,026	3,177	4,585	5,360	5,859
Government	1,244	1,430	1,654	1,915	2,437	2,747	3,026	3,421
	3,986	4,265	4,564	4,941	5,614	7,332	8,386	9,280
Gross capital formation	1,076	1,094	1,499	1,987	2,418	3,127	3,354	2,806
Net foreign sector	3,611	3,961	4,341	5,011	5,196	4,197	4,235	5,312
Expenditure on GDP	8,673	9,320	10,404	11,939	13,228	14,656	15,975	17,398

Table 1.5b: Gross Domestic Product of Saudi Arabia by Expenditure Categories, 1971-8 (SR millions)

	1971	1972	1973	1974	1975[a]	1976[a]	1977[a]	1978[b]
Consumption expenditures								
Private	6,412	6,914	7,896	9,827	17,897	23,738	34,148	50,995
Government	3,798	4,285	5,335	9,864	15,911	28,883	41,033	47,034
	10,210	11,199	13,231	19,691	33,808	52,621	75,181	98,029
Gross capital formation	2,727	2,498	5,694	8,400	17,841	33,705	51,416	67,136
Net foreign sector	9,984	13,559	21,740	70,389	87,204	77,421	77,622	57,688
Expenditure on GDP	22,921	28,256	40,552	99,315	139,600	164,526	205,056	223,747

Notes: a. Revised estimates. b. Preliminary estimates.
Sources: SAMA, *Statistical Summary* (December 1970), Table 25 and 2nd issue (1977), Table 30; SAMA, *Annual Reports 1977*, Table 30, p. 150 and 1979, Table 31, p. 169.

Table 1.6a: Rate of Growth of Important Economic Variables in the Saudi Arabian Economy, 1964-71 (per cent)

	1964	1965	1966	1967	1968	1969	1970	1971
Consumption expenditures	7.0	7.0	8.3	13.6	30.6	14.4	10.7	10.0
Private	3.4	2.7	4.0	5.0	44.3	17.0	9.3	9.4
Government	15.0	15.7	15.8	27.3	12.7	10.2	13.1	11.0
Gross capital formation	1.7	37.0	32.6	21.7	29.3	7.3	−16.3	−2.8
Net foreign sector	9.7	9.6	15.4	3.7	−19.2	0.9	25.4	88.0
GDP (current prices)	7.5	11.6	14.8	10.8	10.8	9.0	8.9	31.7
Population growth rate	3.0	3.0	3.0	3.0	3.0	3.0	3.5	3.5
Rate of inflation	2.8	0.4	1.6	2.1	1.6	3.5	0.2	4.9
GDP (constant prices)	4.7	11.2	13.2	8.7	9.2	5.5	8.7	26.8
Real GDP *per capita*	1.7	8.2	10.2	5.7	6.2	2.5	5.2	23.3
Real total consumption *per capita*	1.2	3.6	3.7	8.5	26.0	7.9	7.0	1.6
Real private consumption *per capita*	−2.4	−0.7	−0.6	−0.1	39.7	10.5	5.8	1.0

Source: Computed from Table 1.5; see note 8 for explanation of population growth rates; rate of inflation computed from Table 9.9.

Table 1.6b: Rate of Growth of Important Economic Variables in the Saudi Arabian Economy, 1972-8 (per cent)

	1972	1973	1974	1975	1976	1977	1978	1964-9	1970-8	1964-78
Consumption expenditures	9.7	18.1	48.5	72.1	55.6	42.9	30.4	13.5	31.9	24.5
Private	7.8	14.2	24.5	82.1	32.6	43.9	49.3	12.8	30.3	23.3
Government	12.8	24.5	–8.8	61.3	81.5	42.1	14.6	16.1	28.0	23.2
Gross capital formation	28.3	127.9	47.5	112.4	88.9	52.5	30.6	21.6	52.1	39.9
Net foreign sector	35.8	60.3	223.8	23.9	–11.2	0.3	–25.7	3.4	46.7	29.4
GDP (current prices)	23.2	43.5	40.6	17.9	40.6	24.6	9.1	10.8	26.7	20.3
Population growth rate	3.5	3.5	3.5	3.5	3.5	3.5	3.5	3.0	3.5	3.3
Rate of inflation	4.2	16.0	21.5	34.6	31.6	11.4	–1.6	2.0	13.6	9.0
GDP (constant prices)	19.1	27.5	15.1	0.3	8.6	15.1	15.6	8.8	14.1	12.0
Real GDP *per capita*	15.6	24.0	11.6	–3.2	5.1	11.6	2.1	5.8	12.1	10.0
Real total consumption *per capita*	2.0	–1.4	23.5	13.3	23.4	38.6	26.4	8.5	9.9	9.2
Real private consumption *per capita*	0.1	–5.3	–1.5	2.6	1.8	39.5	44.8	7.8	0.6	4.2

Sources: Computed from Table 1.5; see note 8 for explanation of population growth rates; rate of inflation computed from Table 9.9.

From the point of view of growth, the amount which the country devotes to capital formation is significant. A critical feature of the expenditure composition of the GDP in Saudi Arabia is the size of the foreign sector's net contribution. The importance of these two expenditure categories is more pronounced when we look at the rate of growth of nominal GDP and its components, given in Tables 1.6a and 1.6b, which also offer the growth rates of other major variables in the Saudi economy, such as the rate of inflation, population growth rate, rate of growth of real income *per capita*, rate of growth of real consumption *per capita*, and the like.

The Performance of the Saudi Economy, 1974-8

The performance of the Saudi economy has been uneven over the years. Available data allow for an evaluation of how well the economy has been doing since 1964; a 15-year period, 1964-78, is taken as the basis of analysis. Nominal GDP on the average has grown at the dramatically rapid rate of 20.3 per cent per annum. For the purpose of comparison, the 15-year period may be divided into: period 1 (Table 1.6a), which covers the non-oil boom era of 1964-9; and period 2 (Tables 1.6a and 1.6b), which starts in 1971 and ends in 1978 – what might be called the modern period. In terms of nominal GDP the Saudi economy can be said to have performed remarkably well in the modern period, growing at an annual rate of 26.7 per cent, compared with only 10.8 per cent in the earlier segment before the oil boom in the 1970s. The explanation for the high performance of the economy in this period is simply the increased oil revenues, as the growth of net foreign contribution to GDP (Net foreign sector, Tables 1.6a and 1.6b) indicates.[7] However, it is during the 1970-5 span that inflation accelerated, and consequently the real rate of growth of GDP (i.e. GDP at constant prices) was very much lower than the nominal rates. Thus, if the rate of inflation in the entire period is taken into account, real GDP is found to have grown at 8.8 per cent, 14.1 per cent, and 12.0 per cent for period 1, period 2, and the entire 1964-78 span, respectively. (See GDP, the last three columns of Table 1.6b.)

Output per head is a better measure of the average income in Saudi Arabia. The rate of growth of real GDP *per capita* (last three columns, Real GDP Table 1.6b) indicates that the average Saudi income recorded impressive increases, although much of the increase was generated from the net foreign sector in the modern period. But even during the 1960s, the real income *per capita* grew at an annual rate of 5.8 per cent, which is quite a satisfactory rate and one at which the standard of living of a country should be rising.

While economic welfare is an amorphous concept from a purely pragmatic point of view, one could allow consumption *per capita* to be a measure of how well off the Saudi population is becoming. Since 1964 the average citizen has been enjoying a better and better standard of living as shown by the growth of real *per capita* consumption at an annual rate of at least 8 per cent. It may be added that if the alternative definition of welfare, real private consumption *per capita*, is used, the rate of growth of welfare falls considerably to 4.2 for the span 1964-78 and to an astonishing 0.6 per cent per annum during the 1970-8 period.[8] This is a private-consumption performance which is not consistent with the oil boom. Whereas the low rate of growth of private consumption in the 1960s may be attributed to the increased government consumption at the expense of private consumption, the 1970-6 decline is due to the high rate of inflation, which dissipated whatever gains were made in nominal private consumption *per capita*.

The seemingly low rate of growth of consumption expenditures in Saudi Arabia is compensated for by the very high rate at which the country added to capital stock. Gross capital formation grew at the rate of 39.9 per cent, a growth rate surpassed by no other sector in the period under discussion. Even the first period (1964-9) recorded a 2.16 per cent rate of growth of capital formation, and although in 1970 and 1971 capital formation decreased, the modern period overall recovered quickly to maintain a 52.1 per cent growth rate for the period, thanks to the increased oil revenues after 1972 and development emphasis on infrastructure construction. The rapid rate at which capital continues to be accumulated in the nation *vis-à-vis* consumption expenditures, suggests that greater emphasis is placed on the welfare of future generations with the realization that oil resources are finite.

The Role of the Government in Saudi Economic Development

The role of the Saudi government in the development process of the country has essentially been to undertake policies which would diversify the economy and improve the standard of living of the population, without sacrificing the freedom of the individual and the private sector's ability to respond to the government's incentives within a free market system.

But although it is the policy of the government to interfere as little as possible in the working of the market system in particular, and in the economy as a whole in general, its actions, as may be expected from the government of any country at the threshold of development, encompass more than what would normally be expected in a free-enterprise system in an economically advanced nation. Thus, the government of Saudi Arabia over the years has sought to influence the economy by means of several measures such as fiscal policies, participation in the oil industry in co-operation with other OPEC countries, and lastly, planning. It is not clear whether monetary policies which are independent of fiscal measures have been effective in the Kingdom. As Chapter 9 will show, it appears that the two policies – monetary and fiscal – are intertwined in an intricate manner. It is, however, through several quasi-governmental financial institutions that most of the assistance and incentives which the government renders to the private sector are disbursed. Through these institutions, therefore, the government can undertake selective monetary policies.

It is indeed through government expenditure appropriations that one sees the greatest influence of the government on the levels of economic activities.[9] The annual budget serves both as a means to appropriate government expenditures and as platforms on which to outline the government's tax, trade, financial and other policies. Budgets also serve as the medium through which development plans are executed.

Economic Planning

Saudi Arabia has had three five-year plans.[10] The First Plan covered the period 1970-5, the Second was for the span 1975-80, and the Third Plan was launched in 1980. With a few exceptions, the first two programmes have been implemented successfully. During 1970-5 GDP at constant prices grew at the rate of 13.5 per cent or some 3.7 points above the target.[11] Between the half decade from 1975 to 1980, growth in the GDP was around 8 per cent, somewhat below the projected rate of approximately 10 per cent annually. However, actual expenditures were almost 200 per cent more than planned expenditures in the First Plan and well over once again in the second. The level of productivity is, therefore, somewhat uncertain. The large expenditures made during the 1970s were made possible due to the substantial amount of oil revenues which removed any financial constraints that might have existed. Both the Second and Third Plans were thus conceived in a time when, for all practical purposes, no financial limitations existed. As a result, the second programme was almost nine times larger than the first in terms of total planned expenditures (in 1974-5 constant prices); the Third Plan was better than half again what its predecessor had been.

The structural features of the three plans differed. The primary purpose of the first was to lay down a firm infrastructural foundation for future development; consequently, physical infrastructure was stressed. The Second Plan, with the virtual elimination of financial constraints, was more ambitious in accelerating the development of physical infrastructure while allowing for more overall development. The Third Plan signalled a rather dramatic change in that a consolidation of growth was projected in order to curtail the amount of expatriate labour employed. Development of Saudi manpower and diversification of the economy were earmarked to receive primary attention during the 1980-5 period.[12]

Developed planning in Saudi Arabia has been plagued by all the problems – with the exception of financial constraints – which traditionally face attempts to successfully implement plans in developing countries. In the Saudi case, the main bottlenecks have been inadequate administrative capacity, manpower shortages, and the inability of physical infrastructure to absorb the increased expenditures. Peculiar to the Second Development Plan period was an additional problem generated by the high rate of inflation. Inflation forced the government to freeze budgetary appropriations for 1976/7 at the 1975/6 level of SR 110.9 billion. The slowdown in government expenditure for the first two years of the Second Plan abated the high rate of inflation and allowed expenditure appropriations to return to SR 130 billion and SR 160 billion in the final two years of that plan period. The adjustment of expenditure levels, however, resulted in the first year of the Plan recording the highest rate of growth of the entire 1975-80 period.[13]

With the waiting time at Saudi ports dropped to nil, and with most of the physical bottlenecks which prevailed during the early years of the Second Plan reduced, major objectives of that plan relating to the movement of goods were met.

The problem of high inflation that beset the Saudi economy at the end of the First Plan and beginning of the Second was eliminated largely as a result of prudent government fiscal policies. However, the higher oil revenues garnered by the 1979 and 1980 price increases could set off another substantial round in the inflationary spiral. According to the official statistics in the *Annual Report, 1978 (1398)* of the Saudi Arabian Monetary Agency, the per annum increase in the cost-of-living index for 1977/8 was estimated at –1.6 per cent, compared to 11 per cent, 32 per cent, and 35 per cent for the earlier years 1976/7 to 1974/5, respectively.[14] If restrained fiscal policies are extended through the early 1980s, estimates indicate that the high inflation rates of the 70s (reaching upwards of 50 per cent in some years) can be avoided, settling in at about 10 to 12 per cent annually.

The gap between actual and allocated expenditures in the government budget, i.e. budgetary surplus, has been a distinctive feature. However, the trend recently has been toward a closer balance between the real and budgeted; in 1977/8 the surplus was practically eliminated. Government spending has risen seventeenfold from the initial years of the First Development Plan (1970/1), with an implied compounded growth rate of 50 per cent annually.[15] The gap between budgeted and actual expenditures, which had been 21 per cent during the span of the First Plan, was not only filled in the Second Plan with the accelerated rise in absorptive capacity, but in fact actually exceeded the original appropriations due largely to supplementary allocations during the course of the fiscal years. More significant as an indicator of the rapidly rising absorptive capacity of the government machinery is that the budget surplus between real and allocated expenditures in each of the first three years of the Second Plan has exceeded the total budgeted outlay of the full five years of the First Plan.[16]

As the 1980s open, the lessons to be gained from the Second Development Plan are critical to the success of the Third Plan (1980-5). Sufficient labour remains a massive problem. Imported labour requirements in the Second Plan to 1980 (812,600) were so inadequate that a 60 per cent overrun was recorded in 1979. This was exacerbated by the limited response of the indigenous population to meet the labour needs. A major thrust of the Second Plan, and now the Third Plan, has been to upgrade local labour skills through vocational training programmes; the disappointing participation in such programmes can be traced to the lure of immediate financial rewards available in trade, real estate and lower levels of government bureaucracy. Yet another problem arising from the Second Plan's implementation was the near-saturation of construction in public infrastructure projects – hospitals, schools, government buildings – while the petrochemical projects remained behind schedule. And petrochemicals form a vital component in the development schemes of any oil-based economy. One should keep in mind that the delay in petrochemicals did not result in a major negative impact, in part because the international market in petrochemicals had been depressed. With the decline in the world petroleum supply emanating from the Iranian situation in 1978-9 and other factors, the market may show improvement.

The Third Development Plan (1980-5) is given adequate examination elsewhere in this study. Briefly, it will emphasize the social aspects of development, particularly in labour resources and training, and it will have to pick up the tab for the major problems of maintenance, still high-priced and largely imported because the Saudi economy lacks sufficient back-up in this activity. Areas to be stressed in the 1980-5 span will include the productive and service industries, manufacturing and agriculture, the latter selective and limited to sites having water and soil of a quality already evaluated as good.

Saudi Arabia in the International Scene

In this era of complex interrelationships among nations, no country wants to adopt a purely isolationist policy. Even nations which try to follow such a policy of one kind or another do not wish to be branded isolationists. The world is indeed becoming increasingly interdependent.

Nevertheless, this has not generated equitable sharing of benefits and responsibilities among all states. An economic expression of such inequity has tended to create a dichotomization of the world into two groups: the developed and the developing countries. The nations in the latter group generally supply primary products to feed the industries of the former, with little or no influence on both political and economic issues affecting even their own destinies. Developed countries, however, have a larger voice in world affairs, in part because they supply manufactured and sophisticated capital goods which have the characteristics conducive for attaining favourable terms of trade. More importantly, advanced nations have stronger bargaining power since they are more developed. With time, hitherto non-influential countries like Japan may acquire the characteristics which make a nation of world importance, apart from waging war. But until the 1970s, when the oil-price increases catapulted oil-producing countries into the limelight of the international economic scene, no supplier of raw materials from the developing world, no matter how vital its primary product was to industrialization, had received the recognition consistent with the importance of that primary product. The reason for this was simply that these countries remained comparatively poor and lacked bargaining strength.

The unilateral hike in oil prices, the general primary-commodity price boom of 1972-4, and the fear of imminent exhaustion of the world's natural resources have been seen as the symptoms of a major shift in the power relationship between the industrialized and developing countries.[17] However, this new power has become almost permanent only for the oil-producing countries, because of the nature of this raw material which makes multilateral, organized actions on the part of the suppliers possible. Thus, the Organization of the Petroleum Exporting

Countries (OPEC) nations were able to take actions which have varied their terms of trade due to the nature of demand and supply in the oil industry and to the essentiality of oil.[18]

There has been some fear that policies based on the new power which oil-exporting countries have obtained, while sharply boosting revenues and prestige, might be somewhat retaliatory toward the industrial bloc because of past treatment from that grouping toward the developing nations. Yet, Saudi Arabia has shown a considerable degree of moderation in the role of manipulating the worldwide influence which oil wealth has brought to the country.[19] The main policy on oil resources has been to utilize them in a manner which will promote the economic development of the nation without disrupting the global economic and political order. Consequently, fiscal management has been partly based on the desire of the Kingdom to fulfil its international obligations and to promote international co-operation and monetary stability.[20] In practice, despite the limited absorptive capacity, the country has been attempting to translate its oil wealth into tangible renewable assets, investing a good portion of the surplus in Western advanced economies. In this manner, the stability of the international monetary system is not jeopardized.

So far as the balance of payments between Saudi Arabia and the advanced bloc is concerned, there is no reason for alarm about the rate at which Saudis are accumulating international reserves. Theoretically at least, there should be no apprehension about potential monetary crisis since the current-account deficit balances in advanced countries (i.e. current-account surplus for Saudi Arabia) is balanced by the capital flow from Saudi Arabia in the form of capital account surpluses (i.e. deficit for Saudi Arabia), plus or minus current-account balance and the capital flow between Saudi Arabia and other countries. There exists, however, the potential for crisis in the international monetary arrangement if the foreign reserves portfolio of Saudi Arabia is juggled too often and the amounts involved are substantial. Such changes in reserve composition need not be undertaken by Saudi Arabia with the intent of destabilizing the existing international monetary order, but instead with the genuine motive of maximizing the rate of return on the country's foreign investment. But even in this connection, when faced with the choice of either accepting possible future losses of earnings on its investment or undertaking policies which would destabilize the world economic system, the Saudi government has shown a remarkable degree of mature judgment and a knack for a quick decision in the right direction. A case in point is the minor crisis which the dollar almost faced at the close of 1977 and throughout 1978. In January 1978 the Saudi Finance Minister issued a statement to emphasize the Kingdom's commitment to continue to use the dollar as the currency unit in which payments for its oil exports are made.[21] Thus, the Minister reaffirmed his country's confidence in the dollar and might have averted a possible world monetary crisis.

Even in the area where the country is most influential (negotiations at OPEC meetings on price increases), Saudi Arabia has been an effective 'barometer', a partner generally advocating moderation, as evidenced by the stand taken in concert with Iran and the United Arab Emirates at the Caracas, Venezuela, OPEC meeting in December 1977; the result was a freeze in oil prices for the moment. The policy-makers in this oil-powerful country have been cautious because they are vividly aware that the economic health of the rest of the world is intricately tied to that of their own nation.

But for how long can Saudi Arabia work to keep down the prices of crude oil? The instability of the US dollar and the resultant substantial revenue and foreign exchange losses which OPEC members have incurred, have put great pressures on the Kingdom.[22] The extent of these pressures were evident at the Abu Dhabi OPEC conference in December 1978. Although the so-called 'radical' members did not completely have their way, the 10 per cent (average) oil-price hike agreed upon for 1979 is an ample demonstration that the moderating influence of Saudi Arabia has its limits. It stands to reason, however, that the influence was still at work, although it was not as dominant as at Caracas earlier (December 1977).

However, 1979 brought an energy crisis which, while not as severe as that of 1973-4, was none the less a serious blow to the world economy. At the OPEC sessions held in Geneva near the end of June 1979, an attempt was made to stabilize prices which had been increasing in an *ad hoc* manner since early in that year. Again, Saudi Arabia played a major and moderating role by managing to set the 'marker crude' (Saudi Arabian Light 34° API) at \$18 per barrel as a floor price (up from \$13.33 per barrel); the ceiling was placed at \$23.50 per barrel for high-grade crude. Due to the Saudi influence, that June OPEC price-setting resulted in keeping the overall 1979 increment to about 50 per cent. Saudi Arabia was joined in this effort by Qatar and the United Arab Emirates; these three countries account for no less than one-third of OPEC's total production.

Oil prices had been in growing disarray as the Iranian crisis brought first, cutbacks and stoppages which translated into a supply shortage in the international oil market and second, a free-for-all in bidding on the crude available. Moreover, the new government in Iran quickly adopted a maximalist stance on oil prices, in contrast to that of moderation adhered to for several years after 1974. 'Spot' prices, that is, the price paid for short-term, low-volume contracts, rose to as high as $40 per barrel in the first half of 1979.

Saudi Arabia moved in July 1979 to further stabilize the world oil market by announcing an increase in its production on a temporary basis, above its self-imposed output ceiling of 8.5 million barrels per day (b/d). The addition of approximately 1 million b/d more of Saudi crude, while unable to solve the energy problem, served to take the sharp edge off it and to calm the market. This came at a strategic moment: disruptions again in Iranian production; alarms within the OECD and particularly the USA as witnessed at the Tokyo summit of the major industrialized nations; the United States was confronting shortages in gasoline and looking ahead to possible fuel oil shortfalls in the 1979-80 winter months. The rationale for the Saudi policy of increased production was explained as the need to meet revenue requirements for the five-year development plan, which coincided with a 1978-9 budget deficit. Of course, other factors played a part in both the timing of the decision and the decision itself. Saudi Arabia had raised its production to above 10 million b/d near the close of 1978 to diminish the massive and harmful effects of Iranian export cutbacks, and again in October 1980 as a result of the Iran-Iraq conflict which affected world oil supply. Again, political elements were coupled with concern for the health of the international economy in the most recent output decision. It should be noted the increased Saudi output would seem to be tied to the industrialized bloc's renewed commitment to conservation in consumption.

It is also in the light of the acknowledgement of global interdependence that the Kingdom has contributed increasingly substantial amounts of aid to 'fourth world' countries.[23] Saudi foreign aid has risen from $220.9 million (or 2.7 per cent of its GDP in 1972) to $5.664 million (or 13.8 per cent of its GDP) in 1975. While the majority of the assistance goes to non-oil Arab countries, considerable amounts are distributed to other members of the 'fourth world' through such institutions as the Arab Bank for Economic Development in Africa, among other agencies.[24]

The influence of Saudi Arabia in the international scene is not limited to economic matters. For one thing, the nation has been the custodian of two of the holiest places of the Islamic faith; its religious influence is consequently not to be taken lightly. The oil wealth, on the other hand, has enabled the Kingdom to give practical backing to this influence in the form of funding the construction of mosques throughout the Islamic countries and as a prime mover in the Islamic Development Bank. Further, it is not at all clear whether aid requests from predominantly Muslim states are not received and reviewed more sympathetically.

As a 'moderate' Arab nation (politically speaking), Saudi Arabia is realizing the need to use its wealth in Arab and Pan-Islamic causes. Although the government of Saudi Arabia has been careful not to interfere in the internal affairs of fellow Arab countries, it was instrumental in convening the Riyadh Summit which resulted in a process towards the cease-fire in Lebanon.

Saudi Arabia has sought actively to consolidate its position in the Arabian peninsula through greater co-ordination and co-operation with its smaller Arab neighbours. The settlement of disputed boundaries with Kuwait and the United Arab Emirates reduced the potential for friction and apprehension. The Saudi linkages with North Yemen have been close for a number of years; and now, despite ideological differences, the Kingdom has relations with South Yemen. Perched across the Red Sea from the Yemens is the Horn area of Africa where the Somali-Ethiopian conflict has brought this heretofore largely unknown area into the spotlight of world affairs. The clash between Soviet and American interests in the Horn has found Saudi Arabia supporting the USA and Western positions with an eye to keeping the oil transport lanes through the Red Sea open.

To sum up, Saudi Arabia, thanks to oil, has received world recognition within a relatively short span of time. The Kingdom is presently important not only because it controls the world's largest reserves of oil, or that it has the second-largest foreign exchange reserves and is the principal exporter of petroleum globally, but also because it has been supporting actively the developing bloc of countries, Arab and non-Arab alike. Saudi Arabia has shown a considerable amount of maturity and moderation in the utilization of this rapidly acquired power and prestige emanating directly from its oil wealth.

Notes

1. *New York Times*, 13 February 1978.
2. Mecca is the city which has the holiest shrine of Muslims, the Kaabah,

whereas Medina is the city in which the Prophet of Islam, Muhammad, first established the Islamic religion.

3. Saudi Arabian Monetary Agency, *Statistical Summary* (1975/76), 1st issue (Riyadh, Saudi Arabia), p. 18. (Hereafter the Saudi Arabian Monetary Agency will be cited as SAMA.) See also Abdel R. Al-Madani and Muhamed Al-Fayez, 'The Demographic Situation in the Kingdom of Saudi Arabia,' *Population Bulletin of the United Nations Commission for Western Asia*, nos. 10 and 11, January and July 1976 (Amman, Jordan), pp. 185-9. The census results referred to in the remainder of the discussion in this chapter are those in this UN publication.

4. During the Second Development Plan (1975-80), the agricultural sector grew at approximately 5 per cent annually compounded, only one-third as fast as the total non-oil sector.

5. United Nations, Department of Economic and Social Affairs of the Secretariat, *Selected World Demographic Indicators by Countries, 1950-2000* ESA/P/W, p. 55.

6. The Quoran, the holy book of the Islamic religion, contains 200 legal verses, constituting the primary source of Saudi law. The Sunna is the recorded statements and actions of the Prophet Muhammad, while Ijma is the consensus of the ulama, the high-priests of the faith in Saudi Arabia. Thus, the Ijma are decisions of the ulama which serve as legal precedents. The last source of law in the Kingdom, qiyas, is simply the use of analogies in reaching decisions when the other three sources cannot be of any help. This aspect of Saudi law, as would be expected, is by nature very controversial. Richard F. Nyrop *et al.*, *Area Handbook for Saudi Arabia*, 3rd edn (Washington, DC, American University, Foreign Area Studies, 1977), p. 186.

7. The contributions remained significant in absolute amounts (1976-8), but began to fall in 1976.

8. The *per capita* rates of growth were computed upon the basis of the population growth rates assumed in Tables 1.6a and 1.6b. Although the results of the 1964 population census, as reported by A.R. Al-Madani and M. Al-Fayez in *Population Bulletin*, estimate the population growth of Saudi Arabia at 4 per cent, it is likely to be an overestimation. Therefore, population growth rates of 3.5 for the 1970s and 3 per cent for the 1960s have been assumed and that net immigration and natural rate of growth were not as high as in the 1970s.

9. See Chapter 8 for further analysis of the Saudi Arabian government finance.

10. See Chapters 5, 6 and 7.

11. The growth rate given here differs from 34.5 in Table 1.6b because the methods used in accounting for inflation differ. The 13.7 per cent growth rate is based on GDP at constant prices calculated in SAMA, *Statistical Summary* (various issues). It is felt that these rates underestimate the oil sector GDP in the Saudi economy; hence, the method employed here of deflating nominal GDP by the consumer price index, the results of which are shown in Tables 1.6a and 1.6b.

12. See Chapters 6 and 7 for a comparative analysis of the plans.

13. 'Nazer Outlines Two Years' Progress on Plan,' *Middle East Economic Digest*, 27 January 1978, p. 29. (Hereafter *Middle East Economic Digest* will be cited as MEED.)

14. Also, SAMA, *Annual Report, 1979 (1399)*, p. 161.

15. SAMA, *Annual Report, 1978 (1398)*, p. 11.

16. Ibid., p. 17.

17. E. Stearn and W. Tims, 'The Relative Bargaining Strengths of the Developing Countries,' in Ronald G. Ridler (ed.), *Changing Resource Problems of the Fourth World* (Washington, DC, Resources for the Future, 1976), p. 7.

18. See ibid., for fuller discussion of these characteristics which have contributed to the increased bargaining strength of oil-producing developing countries.

19. Such a concern has been expressed by Fred Bergaten, 'The Response to the Third World', *Foreign Policy*, Winter 1974-5, p. 6.

20. See Chapter 10, which also discusses the details of direction and composition of Saudi trade with the rest of the world.

21. *Middle East Economic Survey*, 23 January 1978, p. 1. (Hereafter *Middle East Economic Survey* will be cited as MEES.)

22. For a succinct delineation of the impact of dollar weakness and inflation on the purchasing power of OPEC, see Mansoor Dailami, 'Inflation, Dollar Depreciation, and OPEC's Purchasing Power', *Journal of Energy and Development*, Spring 1979, pp. 336-43.

23. The 'fourth world' group of developing countries has been recently coined to describe the non-oil developing countries, 'the poorest of the poor.' Ronald G. Ridler, *Changing Resource Problems*, p. 1.

24. Chapter 11 analyses in greater detail the assistance which the Kingdom extends to developing countries. From 1977 to the close of the decade, Saudi aid was in the order of 5 per cent of GDP.

2 THE ECONOMICS OF OIL

Introduction

With the basic foundations of the Saudi Arabian economy sketched, a sectoral analysis offers greater detail. The first step towards this analysis unquestionably involves the economics of the petroleum industry in general, as well as the more specific role of the oil industry in Saudi Arabia. While it is not within the scope of this chapter to present the multi-faceted complexities of the world petroleum industry, it is helpful to present at least a brief overview of the more relevant work that has already been done in this area and into which the predominant role of Saudi Arabia can be fitted. In so doing, the characteristics and structural features of this industry will be examined as well as the nature of supply and demand for energy. Certain institutional characteristics of the economics of oil, most notably the OPEC, are not only critical as fundamental structural changes in the industry, but also as channels through which the Kingdom of Saudi Arabia operates. Finally, and most importantly, the discussion of the Saudi Arabian petroleum industry must be presented in a context of global and domestic economic development.

A Brief Overview of the World Petroleum Industry[1]

The international oil industry has a special character that inevitably affects everything it touches. The very nature of the industry is highly conducive to extremely large capital expenditure. Every process leading to oil production, from the initial geologic surveys, through drilling, well completion and the extraction process itself, requires sophisticated machinery and highly skilled personnel. Once the oil is on stream, extensive systems of gathering, storage and transportation are necessary to move the petroleum to refineries and ultimately to the market.

The industry itself has been affected in varying degrees with regard to time and place, by certain 'fundamental determinants'.[2] Perhaps most basic to these determinants has been the existence of an extremely high degree of investment risk. Many oil deposits are in inaccessible locations, as the so-called 'frontier' areas of Alaska or the North Sea, and concessions granted by the host governments are often quite extensive. Unforeseen problems can occur at almost any point in the exploration and production processes; the most precise geologic study cannot determine the presence or absence of petroleum with certainty, leaving the possibility of a 'dry-hole' rather significant. Furthermore, pervasive and complex government regulations can make these risks political as well as technical.

Although the postwar petroleum industry has developed into an effectively competitive one, relatively high barriers to entry remain due to the substantial capital investments required. A final determinant of the industry lies in its need for a 'continuity of operations'. This is primarily due to the fact that petroleum has relatively substantial storage costs, and maximum efficiency dictates that the oil continues to flow smoothly. This point alone provides a rather strong incentive for vertical integration within the industry, which leads to a closer examination of the firm itself.

In general terms, major firms within the industry tend to be large, vertically integrated and multinational in nature to take advantage of the sizable economies of scale. Because of the expense and complexity involved, projects are usually planned many years in advance. By operating with other companies under joint-venture agreements and by investing in several countries to diversify capital investment, firms attempt to spread the inherent economic and political risks noted earlier.

A rather significant aspect of the petroleum industry is that it is highly *capital*-intensive. It has been estimated that the average gross investment per employee in the US petroleum industry in 1973 was $567,000 compared to an average of $36,000 per employee for all manufacturing operations.[3] (This can reasonably be assumed to be an acceptable proxy for the investment/labour ratio in the foreign oil industry as well.) Due to this heavy capital investment, the average cost per barrel of oil, including depreciation and a normal return on investment, is much greater than marginal cost. This and the previously mentioned factors have contributed, over time, to a high degree of concentration in the foreign petroleum industry.

A final element of the industry which should be noted is the ever increasing influence of *government* on production and pricing decisions.[4] Furthermore, government regulation in the 1970s evolved into 'supranational' regulation of the industry, the most obvious of which is OPEC. The critical role of petroleum with respect to economic growth as well as national security have been the major reasons for government intervention on the part of consuming and producing states alike. While the oil-importing countries are only now realizing the importance of developing comprehensive national oil policies, the oil exporters have made long-standing commitments to this end. Further attention to the issue of government intervention will be given following an examination of the demand for and supply of petroleum.

The Nature of Demand

An overall picture of the oil industry today can perhaps best be seen by examining present supply-and-demand trends. It must first of all be pointed out that the demand for oil is derived and generally considered to be price inelastic.[5] This is due to the fact that oil is a basic input for numerous products, such as gasoline and fertilizer, many of which have inelastic demand schedules themselves. A second reason is that while oil is an important component of many products, its proportion of total cost is often relatively low. Third, and most critical, is the lack of close substitutes for oil as a primary commodity. Furthermore, demand inelasticity holds only for a given time period, as substitutes for certain uses of petroleum will most likely be found in the long run. The length of this period is a function of the current price level; a higher price will provide a greater incentive for oil users to find substitutes and alternative sources of supply. At a higher price, more expensive substitutes become competitive with petroleum.

The elasticity of demand may actually differ from one country to another, according to the urgency of their needs and the quantities consumed from each of the petroleum products. These needs may be affected by factors such as technical progress, growth of GNP, certain policy measures including taxes and import duties, and even weather conditions.[6] The inelasticity of demand for crude oil with respect to price means that changes in the price level will lead to a relatively smaller change in the demand for oil. Referring to Table 2.1, one may examine the effects of the 1973/4 rises in the price of oil on levels of world consumption, as well as for selected countries. While these substantial increases in price (in addition to a persistence of global recession and an extremely mild winter) resulted in decreased demand in the 1974-5 period, the 1976 demand for petroleum returned to the pre-1974 levels. Since then, however, the growth rate of demand has fallen significantly from the pre-1973 levels. It will be noted, however, that much of the reductions in demand were effected by Western Europe. During the 1972-7 period, the US average growth rate of oil consumption

Table 2.1: Oil Consumption (thousands barrels per day)

	1974	1975	Per cent change	1976	Per cent change	1977	Per cent change	1978	Per cent change	1979	Per cent change
United States	16,150	15,875	–1.7	16,980	+7.0	17,945	+5.7	18,365	+2.3	17,930	–2.4
Japan	5,270	5,020	–4.7	5,190	+3.4	5,345	+3.0	5,420	+1.4	5,495	+1.4
West Germany	2,760	2,665	–3.8	2,885	+8.7	2,855	–1.0	2,960	+3.7	3,045	+2.9
France	2,460	2,255	–8.3	2,430	+7.8	2,350	–3.3	2,445	+4.0	2,430	–0.6
Italy	2,015	1,895	–6.0	2,065	+9.0	1,940	–6.1	2,015	+3.9	2,045	+1.5
Total Western Europe	14,180	13,505	–4.8	14,465	+7.1	14,235	–1.6	14,630	+2.8	14,870	+1.6
Total World[a]	46,210	45,155	–2.3	48,090	+6.5	49,430	+2.8	51,015	+3.2	51,280	+0.5

Note: a. Excluding USSR, Eastern Europe and China.
Source: British Petroleum Company Ltd, *BP Statistical Review of the World Oil Industry* (London, 1975), p. 8 (1976), p. 8 (1977), p. 8, and (1979), p. 8.

has been positive *vis-à-vis* a negative growth rate for Western Europe. Hence the accusation by European countries that the USA has not done enough in the area of energy conservation. The dissatisfaction with US energy policy was voiced at the May 1979 summit meeting of consuming countries in Japan.

Over the decade 1967-77, the world has experienced a growth in demand for oil at the rate of 5.3 per cent per annum.[7] It appears that the most significant determinant of these levels of consumption will continue to be the rate of real GNP growth of the industrialized countries, while the effects of energy conservation measures established by the oil-consuming nations will become increasingly important in determining future levels of consumption.

In spite of the increased efforts on the part of the oil consumers to restrain consumption and stimulate domestic production, demand for Saudi Arabian oil rose steadily after 1974 until 1978 when it began to slacken. This has been primarily a result of depleting domestic supplies of oil on the part of the Western industrialized nations, precisely at a time when demand levels have been attaining record proportions. For example, US demand for Saudi crude has increased from 9 per cent of total oil imports in 1974 to an unprecedented 16.4 per cent in 1976 (see Table 2.2). Furthermore, US demand for all OPEC sources of crude has increased an average of 7.3 per cent annually between 1974 and 1978.

The Nature of Supply

Before a discussion of the pricing of crude oil in Saudi Arabia, the supply of that commodity should be evaluated. While Saudi Arabia remains the third largest producer of oil, supplying 13.8 per cent of the world's total in 1978, it is now the world's largest exporter of crude. Furthermore, the Kingdom supplied some 29, 27 and 31 per cent of all OPEC crude in 1977, 1978 and 1979, respectively, clearly establishing itself as a highly influential member in that decision-making body, as shown in Table 2.3.

Saudi Arabia's reserve of oil is now estimated at about 170 billion barrels, or over one-fourth of the world's probable-proved petroleum reserves (Table 2.4). Although precise reserves figures are difficult to obtain, the country is generally regarded as having the highest level of reserves in the world, as well as possessing the greatest future potential. Even at 1979 production levels, proven reserves were expected to last

Table 2.2: US Imports of Foreign Oil (thousand of barrels per day)

	1974		1975		1976		1977[a]		1978	
	Volume	Per cent of total	Volume	Per cent of total	Volume	Per cent of total	Volume	Per cent of total	Volume	Per cent of total
Saudi Arabia	675.2	9.0	891.6	12.4	1,365.8	16.4	1,377.4	15.8	1,132.2	13.8
Nigeria	912.2	12.1	837.8	11.7	1,119.2	13.5	1,135.3	13.0	902.6	11.0
Venezuela	1,457.8	19.4	1,030.1	14.3	972.2	11.7	686.8	7.9	630.5	7.7
Iran	731.0	9.7	524.8	7.3	546.5	6.6	530.3	6.1	544.1	6.6
Total *OPEC*	4,669.3	62.1	4,753.0	66.1	6,079.9	73.1	6,148.5	70.3	5,607.4	68.5
Canada	1,067.6	14.2	845.2	11.8	599.3	7.2	515.7	6.0	460.5	5.6
Total *non-OPEC*	2,852.4	37.9	2,435.4	33.9	2,234.0	26.9	2,592.7	29.7	2,577.1	31.5
Total imports[b]	7,521.7	100.0	7,188.4	100.0	3,313.9	100.0	8,741.2	100.0	8,184.5	100.0

Notes: a. Figures computed based on 1978 figures and percentage changes. b. Includes total direct and non-direct US petroleum imports.
Source: US Bureau of Mines and Federal Energy Administration; *Petroleum Intelligence Weekly*, 24 October 1977 and 23 April 1979, p. 11.

approximately 36 to 50 years. However, as domestic Saudi consumption increases as a result of economic growth, and as the pressures of global demand influence future production levels, this reserve/production ratio is likely to diminish in spite of the fact that annual discoveries of new reserves in the Kingdom outpaced total production levels in the past.

Table 2.3: Percentage Share of Saudi Arabia in Crude Oil Production of the Middle East, the OPEC Countries and the World (Saudi Arabia's production as per cent of respective totals)

			World total	
	Middle East[a]	OPEC[b]	Excl. Sino-Soviet area	Incl. Sino-Soviet area
1960	24.8	15.1	7.5	6.3
1965	26.3	15.4	8.9	7.3
1970	27.3	16.2	10.0	8.3
1971	29.3	18.8	11.9	9.9
1972	33.4	22.2	14.3	11.9
1973	36.0	24.5	16.3	13.5
1974	38.9	27.6	18.6	15.1
1975	36.3	26.1	17.1	13.4
1976	38.3	27.5	18.1	14.4
1977	41.2	29.2	19.0	15.0
1978	39.3	27.7	17.8	13.8
1979[c]	44.5	31.0	19.6	15.1

Notes. a. Excluding North African countries. b. Includes the 13 members of OPEC at the end of 1975. c. Provisional.
Sources: International Monetary Fund, *Saudi Arabia – An Economic and Financial Survey* (26 March 1976), p. 1; British Petroleum Company, Ltd, *BP Statistical Review of the World Oil Industry* (1976), p. 6 and (1977), p. 6; *Oil and Gas Journal*, 25 December 1979, pp. 102-3; Ministry of Petroleum and Mineral Resources, Economics Department, *Petroleum Statistical Bulletin, 1979*, p. 21.

The exploitation of these reserves has understandably become a source of policy debate. A number of analysts believe that stable or even decreased levels of production are in the best interest of Saudi Arabia for a variety of reasons.

The arguments for limited production have been categorized as the 'price-revenue effect', the 'absorptive capacity effect', the 'surplus-capital effect', and the 'resource-exhaustion effect'.[8] The price-revenue effect is based upon the inelasticity of demand for oil as briefly discussed earlier in this chapter. Policy-makers using this argument note that since revenue can be increased by raising price without increasing production, price increases, rather than expanded production, should be used to generate additional revenue.

Table 2.4: Saudi Arabian Oil Reserves (millions of barrels)

Year end	Aramco production	Aramco reserves Proved	Aramco reserves Probable	Total proved reserves	Reserves in years of current production Proved	Reserves in years of current production Probable
1960	456	45,598	n.a.	n.a.	100	n.a.
1965	739.1	63,707	n.a.	n.a.	86	n.a.
1970	1,295.3	135,000	123,908	138,700	107	96
1971	1,641.6	134,720	127,497	138,260	81	78
1972	2,098.4	133,830	156,393	137,070	65	75
1973	2,677.1	133,680	164,520	136,830	51	62
1974	2,996.5	136,850	172,529	141,040	47	58
1975	2,491.8	141,250	175,800	144,580	58	71
1976	3,053.9	147,850	177,500	151,410	49	58
1977	3,291.2	165.680	n.a.	169,480	51	n.a.
1978	2,944.1	163,350	n.a.	167,060	57	n.a.
1979	3,376.6	164,770	n.a.	168,390	49	n.a.

Note: n.a. = not available.
Sources: For 1960-74, Aramco, *Annual Report*, various issues; for 1975, *Middle East Economic Survey*, 26 April 1976, p. 8; for 1976, *Petroleum Intelligence Weekly*, 2 May 1977, p. 11; *Oil and Gas Journal*, 25 December 1979, p. 102; Ministry of Petroleum and Mineral Resources, Economics Department, *Petroleum Statistical Bulletin, 1979*, p. 16.

The absorptive capacity effect relates to the inability of some oil-rich nations to invest their net oil revenues productively. This is an especially important consideration in Saudi Arabia. According to this argument, if financing long-term development is the ultimate goal of oil production policy, current production levels should not generate more net revenue than the country can currently invest domestically. For oil-producing nations such as Saudi Arabia this implies steady current production levels, if not a reduction in output. Closely related to this constraint is the surplus-capital effect. Countries which have capital funds in excess of their domestic absorptive capacity often turn to foreign investment of these surplus funds. It is frequently asserted that the increasing risks associated with these growing numbers and sizes of investment make it more prudent to curtail production.

The resource-exhaustion effect is a further recognition of the fact that petroleum is a non-renewable resource. This is perhaps a restatement of the obvious fact that oil produced today will not be available in the future, and therefore also suggests curtailed production levels. 'The meaning of these problems for the Saudi economy may be that the best place for investing a surplus is in the ground in the form of larger oil reserves instead of cash'.[9]

Table 2.5 presents the annual levels of crude oil production in Saudi

Arabia from 1938 to 1979. The annual data have been indexed based on 1970 levels of oil production to indicate the accelerated growth of oil production in Saudi Arabia since 1970. While pre-1970 increases in yearly production were approximately 5 per cent, increased global demand and subsequent price increases have provided the stimulus for a rise in production levels of approximately 15 per cent per annum since 1970. However, in view of the fact that Saudi production capacity now approaches 12 million b/d,[10] the central source of debate with respect to the global balance of energy supply and demand has focused upon whether or not Saudi Arabia will choose to exploit this surplus output capacity. To a certain extent, the country has already become the 'swing producer' among OPEC, acting to control the price-level through output. But it remains questionable whether or not it is in the best interests of future generations for Saudi Arabia to become the 'supplier of first resort' to meet the inevitable rise in world energy demand.[11] This question has led one analyst to conclude: 'The most important single energy issue over the next 15 years . . . is whether the level of Saudi Arabia's output will be that dictated by its own needs or that dictated by the needs of its customers.'[12] It would appear that the Kingdom has chosen to strike a balance between these conflicting interests. As of early 1978 the government announced that it planned to continue an 8.5 million b/d ceiling on the production of crude oil in the near future.[13] While this level of output may not meet the projected demand requirements of the importers of Saudi crude, it remains significantly higher (estimated anywhere between 2 million to 4 million b/d) than was needed for domestic revenue to meet allocations for domestic spending in the late 1970s.

Basically, what are these needs that will influence future production decisions in Saudi Arabia? First and foremost is the necessity of economic development as outlined by the Third Development Plan (described in Chapter 7). Production must be maintained at a level to generate sufficient revenue to finance the Plan. Second, as was previously mentioned, a production policy of long-run consequence must be established to take into account an assurance of economic prosperity for the citizenry of the Kingdom in the future. And finally, in the eyes of the Saudi Arabian government, it is in the nature of enlightened self-interest to maintain a production policy that will not disrupt the international economy in general.

Table 2.5: Saudi Arabia: Annual Production of Crude Oil (millions of US barrels)

Year	Aramco	Getty Oil Co.	Arabian Oil Co.	Total	Average production (million b/d)	Index (1970 = 100)
1938	0.5	–	–	0.5	a	–
1946	59.6	–	–	59.6	a	4.3
1950	199.5	–	–	199.5	a	14.4
1955	352.2	4.4	–	356.6	a	25.7
1956	360.9	5.8	–	366.7	1.00	26.5
1957	362.1	11.6	–	373.7	1.02	27.0
1958	370.5	14.7	–	385.2	1.06	27.8
1959	399.8	21.2	–	421.0	1.15	30.4
1960	456.4	24.9	–	481.3	1.32	34.7
1961	508.3	28.7	3.7	540.7	1.48	39.0
1962	555.0	33.7	11.0	599.7	1.64	43.3
1963	594.6	33.1	24.1	651.8	1.79	47.0
1964	628.1	34.4	31.8	694.3	1.90	50.1
1965	739.1	33.0	32.8	804.9	2.21	58.1
1966	873.3	30.2	46.1	950.0	2.60	68.5
1967	948.1	25.1	50.0	1,023.8	2.80	73.9
1968	1,035.8	23.2	54.7	1,114.1	3.04	80.3
1969	1,092.3	22.7	58.9	1,173.9	3.22	84.7
1970	1,295.3	28.6	62.6	1,386.7	3.80	100.0
1971	1,641.6	33.7	65.3	1,740.6	4.77	125.6
1972	2,098.4	28.5	75.0	2,201.0	6.01	158.8
1973	2,677.1	23.6	71.9	2,772.6	7.60	200.0
1974	2,996.5	29.8	68.7	3,095.1	8.48	223.2
1975	2,491.8	31.2	59.5	2,582.5	7.08	186.2
1976	3,053.9	29.7	55.7	3,139.3	8.58	226.4
1977	3,291.2	32.0	34.8	3,358.0	9.20	242.2
1978	2,944.1	29.5	56.3	3,029.9	8.30	218.5
1979	3,376.7	30.1	72.6	3,479.4	9.53	250.9

Note: a. Less than 1 million b/d.
Sources: Saudi Arabian Monetary Agency (SAMA), *Annual Reports* (1969), p. 83 and (1979), p. 137; Ministry of Petroleum and Mineral Resources, Economics Department, *Petroleum Statistical Bulletin, 1979*, pp. 17-20.

OPEC, Pricing, and the Role of Oil Revenues

The pricing of crude oil has long been a subject of controversy between governments of producing countries, such as Saudi Arabia, the multinational oil corporations and the consuming countries alike. To understand the petroleum-pricing policies of Saudi Arabia, one should first evaluate the role of OPEC as a fundamental determinant of the world oil economy and its relationship to Saudi Arabia.

Briefly, OPEC was established in September 1960 'as a direct response to the challenge posed by the multinational oil companies in arbitrarily and unilaterally reducing the posted prices of crude oil in February of 1959 and again in August of 1960.'[14] Shortly after its foundation the Organization began an in-depth study of oil prices to determine a 'just' pricing formula supported by a study of international prorationing. In April of 1962 the Organization recommended that its member countries should immediately enter into negotiations with the oil companies in order that oil produced in member countries be paid for upon the basis of posted prices not below those applying prior to 1960. It also directed the Board of Governors of OPEC to prepare a comprehensive study on a rational price structure to guide their long-term pricing policy, a critical element of which was the linking of crude-oil prices to an index of imported manufactured goods.

This system of pricing was later to evolve into the June 1968 Declaratory Statement of Petroleum Policy, which recommended, in part, that the posted (i.e. tax-reference price) ought to be determined by the government, such that it is consistent with the prices of manufactured goods which enter into international trade.

By 1970 a 'seller's market' for petroleum had emerged as a result of the overwhelming increase in oil consumption in the Western industrialized countries. This factor, coupled with and reinforced by the temporary shutdown of the Trans-Arabian Pipeline which moved Saudi oil to points of export on the Mediterranean, and the closure of the Suez Canal between 1967 and 1974, encouraged the producing countries to enter into negotiations with the major oil companies. At the Caracas, Venezuela, meeting in December of 1970, OPEC was to adopt several objectives, including the establishment of a uniform general increase in the posted prices in all member countries. This increase reflected the general improvement of conditions in the global petroleum market. This conference ultimately resulted in the February 1971 Teheran Agreement, which provided for long-sought financial rewards. A separate agreement between Saudi Arabia and its major concessionaires[15] was concluded, incorporating the basic provisions of the parent document, in addition to other benefits reflecting locational features.[16]

A further objective of OPEC was to insure the price of oil against potentially damaging fluctuations of exchange rates. This effort culminated in the January 1972 Geneva Agreement which stipulated that 'postings of future oil prices would be determined according to changes in exchange rates on a quantity basis in accordance with an agreed index.'[17] It thus appeared that, as a result of these two agreements, Saudi Arabia would no longer be as vulnerable as it once was to the imported inflation and price changes that precipitated the balance-of-payments crisis in the late 1950s.[18]

OPEC, from a modest beginning, has now become a vital force in the world oil industry. It has worked hard not only to gain the confidence of its members, but also to make its views acceptable to both the general public in producing countries and world general opinion at large. The initial years, as would be expected, were rough, espccially given the suspicion of the Arab League about the intentions of the Organization. The absence of concrete results during the first decade of its existence prompted some of its member countries to question the viability of the body. The post-1970 image of OPEC is obviously different from that of the early years. Yet there remain elements of strain and stress within this international group of oil-producing countries. These, however, should be expected in an organization composed of states with divergent domestic policies and international political orientations.

The first sign of disagreement among member countries emerged with the implementation of the Caracas resolution of December 1970. The resolution, among other things, sought to establish a minimum income tax of 50 per cent and a general increase in posted prices. Libya, Venezuela, Indonesia and Algeria broke away from the Gulf countries which later negotiated for the Teheran agreement. Since then, however, although OPEC has found it increasingly more difficult to arrive at a consensus with regard to oil price, the division within the Organization has taken a different turn; there is no more the case of Gulf countries versus the rest of OPEC. Both Geneva I and II price revisions were effected within intense disunity among member countries. After the October 1973 oil embargo and the unilateral price hike on the 16th of that month, a measure of agreement prevailed within OPEC, except that the price agreed upon was considered by some members (the so-called 'high absorbers') as not high enough. This cleavage prevails even today.

It has become customary in the analysis of OPEC pricing policies and the conflicts which they generate to divide the member countries into two groups. The first is the 'high absorbers' referred to above, sometimes called 'spender countries'. The second group is labelled as 'low absorbers' or 'saver countries'.[19] Members of the latter group, consisting of Saudi Arabia, Kuwait, Qatar and the United Arab Emirates (UAE), have the common characteristic that they are surplus-funds countries, in the sense of being unable to spend all the oil revenues accruing, owing to manpower and physical constraints on their development efforts. The spender nations, it is believed, are capable of utilizing all the oil revenues they can earn; these countries are Iran, Iraq, Nigeria, Venezuela and Libya. It so happens that high absorbers have low reserves *per capita* while low absorbers have high *per capita* oil reserves. Consequently, the former put a higher value on current production than do the latter, and thus have the tendency of demanding higher prices for oil.

This implication for OPEC pricing policy has been succinctly explained by Professor Pindyck of MIT:

> This division of OPEC's membership leads to a clear-cut conflict over what is the best pricing strategy. Spender countries would prefer somewhat higher prices than would saver countries, first because they wish to conserve their more limited reserves, and second because they prefer larger revenues today, even if that means much smaller revenues five or ten years later as residual demand falls. Part of the OPEC bargaining process involves the reconciliation of this conflict . . .[20]

However, in practice, the support for or against moderate pricing policy by member countries has not split along the lines of the above categorization. Usually, it is Saudi Arabia plus one or two other countries against the rest of OPEC members, with low-absorber countries like Kuwait and Qatar sometimes voting for high prices of oil.

Examples of conflicts on pricing at OPEC conferences abound. At the June 1974 (Quito) and September 1974 (Vienna) meetings, Saudi Arabia exempted itself from the decision to raise royalty and tax paid by oil companies although it reserved the right to effect the increases at a later date. Then at the Doha conference in December 1976, Saudi Arabia and the UAE decided to hold the 1977 price increase at only 5 per cent instead of the 10 per cent favoured by the other eleven members. A showdown between the moderate and non-moderate members of OPEC occurred at the 20 December 1977, Caracas conference at which Iran joined Saudi Arabia and the UAE to freeze prices in the face of serious opposition from other members of the organization.

The Abu Dhabi Conference of December 1978 provided another

forum for testing the solidarity of OPEC and its responsiveness to global economic issues. The Organization resolved the conflicts at that meeting by introducing an ingenious system of graduated price increases in response to heavy demand pressures forecasted for 1979. Later events in Iran made even this price system obsolete, precipitating the Geneva meeting of March 1979. The change of government in Iran removed that country from the moderate camp on oil pricing which had existed since 1977. This, in turn, made it more difficult for nations such as Saudi Arabia and the UAE to set pricing policy in OPEC due to the shift of Iran from the 'moderate' to the 'radical' camp. In addition, the Iranian crisis created excess demand for oil, a situation further exacerbated by excessive competition among oil companies panicking for supply.

Thus, the Iranian political change was the immediate factor causing the multi-tier price structure introduced at the Geneva Extraordinary Meeting of March 1979. Apart from the fact that the price for the marker crude which was to have become effective in the last quarter of 1979 was drawn closer to 1 April 1979, the March 1979 meeting for the first time did not set a ceiling price. A floor was set at $14.54 per barrel, while the ceiling was ripped open by the provision allowing members to append surcharges to the floor price. Saudi Arabia, therefore, did not succeed in obtaining a ceiling on the price of crude oil.

The continuous tightness of global crude-oil supply in 1979 and the subsequent competition in the spot market, gave rise to what happened at the second Geneva meeting in June of that year. This session also introduced a multi-price system for crude oil, but this time a ceiling was provided. The price of the crude marker was raised by 25 per cent from $14.54 to $18.00 per barrel. The new price was, however, only the floor price, since member countries once again had the liberty to surcharge up to a crude-oil price ceiling of $23.50. Saudi Arabia, the UAE and Qatar as usual decided to charge the floor price, while the other member countries (including notably Iran) announced they would take advantage of the surcharge provision.

The question which could be asked on 28 June 1979, when the meeting ended, was whether Saudi Arabia had the capability to maintain the $23.50 ceiling price on a barrel of oil. An answer came barely a month later when the Kingdom announced a decision to raise its crude oil production from 8.5 million b/d to 9.5 million b/d. This move could be interpreted as having two objectives: (1) to take some of the pressure off world demand resulting from dislocations caused by Iranian cutbacks and (2) to shore-up the OPEC price ceiling.

The stresses and strains which have characterized the activities of OPEC during approximately two decades of its existence need not be construed as signifying a weakness of that organization. Instead, the disagreements and their resolutions have tended to increase the awareness of members about the need to close their ranks, thereby strengthening the bargaining power of the body. In this regard, the view of Saudi Arabia has served as the catalyst, harmonizing the aspirations of OPEC within the Organization and in relation to the policies of consuming countries, despite some weakening in 1979 and 1980 of the moderate influence on pricing policy because of Iran's shift on pricing (which has been offset partially by a more flexible Iraqi stance on output and price levels).

The significance of oil revenue goes far beyond its being a source of finance. The contribution of oil-sector revenues, both direct and indirect, is vital to the development programme in general, as well as to investment, balance of payments, foreign exchange earnings, currency and price stabilization, and especially regional development and co-operation.

Considering the prevailing contractual agreements between the OPEC members and the operating companies, the major determinants of oil revenue for the government are considered to be the following: (1) price of crude oil, especially posted prices or tax-reference prices; (2) the level of crude-oil production; (3) the extent of government participation in the oil companies and/or government share as related to the nature and terms of concession and royalty payments;[21] and (4) costs of production. Additionally, there are two other conditions of import often overlooked, at least in formal discussions: (5) the ownership, operation and management of the activity in relation to the distribution of benefits, including all the direct and indirect impacts of the oil operation on the socio-economic and political conditions of the countries concerned; and (6) the bargaining power of the parties involved, particularly between the oil-producing countries and the foreign operating firms, either individually or collectively.

Taking these factors into consideration, the establishment of OPEC in 1960 was a major step towards the achievement of stronger and more collective bargaining power by the oil-producing member countries. Given the international, vertically integrated character of the major oil companies and their affiliates, and the dominance of production, transportation, marketing and distribution of oil business activities by these companies, the negotiations which were initiated and the actions taken by OPEC since its inception have definitely proved beneficial to the member states. With oil as a wasting asset and predominant within the economies of these countries, issues such as reforms in the structure of concessions and royalty payments, price stabilization and adjustment to current international conditions, production programming, multilateralism, negotiations on taxes and discounts, producer-government participation and the like, were all bound to have deep effects on the oil-producing economies.

In Saudi Arabia, government income from the oil sector consists of: (1) oil royalties from the operating companies; (2) income tax collected from these companies; (3) to a much lesser extent, an oil-product tax which is levied on consumption of locally produced or imported oil products;[22] (4) tapline fees; and more recently, (5) payments received by the government in respect of the 60 per cent participation interest in Aramco's production facilities.

As seen in Table 2.5, crude-oil production in Saudi Arabia increased rapidly in the 1970s, from about 1.4 billion barrels in 1970 to close to 3.5 billion barrels per annum nine years later. Oil revenues have shown a considerable growth both within the decade of the 1960s and during the early 1970s (evidenced in Table 2.6). Whereas, with 1970 as the base year, the 1965 crude-oil production index was 58.1, the index for revenues which originate from oil was 54.7. This trend has undergone a reversal from 1972 throughout the remainder of the decade; oil revenues by 1976 increased more than 25 times the 1970 level, while oil output had more than doubled in the same span. The enormous leap came in 1974, when revenues rose more than 400 per cent within a year, reflecting the quadrupling in OPEC prices.

As a result of the Teheran and Geneva Agreements' provisions for increases in the posted prices and tax rates, the growth in the value of Saudi exports as well as revenues exceeded significantly the growth in the volume of exports in the last three years. Exports increased by 29 per cent from 1,722.1 million barrels in 1971 to 2,195.2 million barrels in 1972. However, this was accompanied by a rise in the posted prices: first by about 10 cents a barrel (approximately 5 per cent) as of June 1971 in pursuance of the Teheran Agreement, and then by a further 18 to 19 cents per barrel, or nearly 8.5 per cent, in February of 1972 due to the Geneva Agreement following the currency realignment of December 1971. These two increments in the posted prices led to a rise of 43 per cent in the value of exports of crude oil and refined products, from $3,838.8 million in 1971 to $5,491.5 million in 1972. The Teheran Agreement provision for an increase in the tax rates from 50 to 55 per cent reflected itself in a significantly higher rate of growth of 45 per cent in oil revenues. As a result of the combined effects of sharp increases in production, exports and changes in posted price and tax rates, the revenues from oil more than doubled in a period of only three years, from $1,214 million in 1970 to $2,744.6 million in 1972.

Table 2.6: Saudi Arabia: Oil Revenue by Source (US $ millions)

Year	Aramco[a]	Getty Oil Co.	Arabian Oil Co.	Other cos.	Total	Index (1970 = 100)
1939	3.2	–	–	–	3.2	0.26
1946	10.2	–	–	–	10.4	0.86
1950	56.7	–	–	–	56.7	4.67
1955	338.2	2.6	–	–	340.8	28.07
1960	312.8	18.4	2.5	–	333.7	31.10
1961	352.2	22.9	2.5	–	377.6	–
1962	381.7	25.0	3.0	–	409.7	33.75
1963	571.1	23.0	13.6	–	607.7	50.06
1964	482.1	23.7	17.4	–	523.2	43.10
1965	618.7	23.8	20.4	1.2	664.1	54.70
1966	745.8	20.6	21.4	2.1	789.0	65.07
1967	859.2	17.8	31.8	0.8	903.6	74.43
1968	872.0	13.6	34.3	6.5	926.4	76.31
1969	895.1	15.2	37.1	1.7	949.2	78.19
1970	1,148.4	17.2	40.3	8.1	1,214.0	100.00
1971	1,806.4	20.6	44.2	13.7	1,884.9	155.26
1972	2,643.2	28.0	68.7	4.7	2,744.6	226.08
1973	4,195.0	22.0	91.4	31.7	4,340.0	357.50
1974	22,375.0	53.3	113.6	31.6	22,573.5	1,859.43
1975	24,838.6	191.1	642.7	3.8	25,676.2	2,115.01
1976	29,937.3	254.7	559.2	3.6	30,754.9	2,533.35
1977	35,703.8	263.4	571.6	1.2	36,540.1	3,009.89
1978	31,609.0	286.6	338.2	–	32,233.8	2,655.17
1979	47,590.1	277.8	575.2	–	48,443.1	3,990.37

Note. a. Including the value of royalty oil payments in kind and Saudi Arabian government's share in the Abu Sa'fah oilfield.
Sources: SAMA, *Annual Reports* (1969), p. 84 (1977), p. 140, and (1979), p. 138; Ministry of Petroleum and Mineral Resources, Economics Department, *Petroleum Statistical Bulletin, 1979*, p. 44.

Three other developments during 1973 contributed to a further rise in government revenues in the 1970s. The increase of approximately 11 cents in posted prices as of 1 January 1973, occurred in pursuance of the Teheran Agreement provision for an annual increase of 2.5 per cent in posted prices as a hedge against the worldwide inflationary trend. Furthermore, there was an additional rise of 5 per cent per barrel to compensate for future increases in the prices of refined products. Another increase in government revenue equal to an average of 10 cents per barrel was then expected to be realized as a result of the Participation Agreement signed in December 1972. Moreover, as a result of the second devaluation of the US dollar in February 1973, there was a further increase of 11.9 per cent in posted prices as of June 1973 in accordance with the Geneva Agreement.

The most highly publicized and hard-felt price increase was the unilateral increase by OPEC members which resulted in the renegotiation of the Teheran Agreement concluded in September 1973.[23] Saudi Arabian light 'marker' crude price was adjusted from the December 1973 level of $5.04 per barrel to $11.65 in January 1974. By June 1976 prices had risen an average of 6 per cent, and after the Doha meeting in December of that year, Saudi Arabian light crude was posted at $13.00 per barrel. Table 2.7 traces the upward changes in the posted prices for Saudi crude in the decade.

Finally, Saudi Arabia's voice has been frequently that of price moderation within OPEC.[24] In December 1976 OPEC convened a price-fixing conference in Doha (Qatar), where the majority of members supported a 10 per cent price increase as of January 1977, to be followed by a further rise of 5 per cent in July of that year. Saudi Arabia, as well as the United Arab Emirates, chose instead to pursue an individual course of action. By raising crude petroleum prices only 5 per cent following that conference, Saudi Arabia effectively established a two-tier pricing system within OPEC.[25] This development should not have been unexpected, however, as two rather distinct schools of thought on pricing have existed within OPEC since 1974. Moreover, there has always been variation through *de facto* prices based upon differences in oil quality. The unanimity on price increases in the past was due overwhelmingly to the Saudi position enforceable by that country's massive petroleum reserves (now greater than 177.5 billion barrels) and its cushion of surplus funds which allow for a relatively wide range of output fluctuations.

The Saudi view of this pricing decision was conditioned by an evaluation of the international economy, which viewed the resultant imported inflation rate to be too high. Equally significant in Saudi decision-making seems to have been a belief that the world's economic recovery was insufficient to absorb or manage a 10 per cent oil-price rise. Furthermore, the Saudis saw their moderation in the price increase as an incentive to the industrialized consumer nations to deal with Third World problems in a constructive and affirmative manner.[26] Finally, the Saudis visualised the use of moderation in oil pricing as a method to secure an ongoing initiative and concern by the United States in

Table 2.7: Changes in the Posted Prices of Saudi Arabian Crude Oil (US $ per barrel)

	Light 34°		Index	Medium 31°		Heavy 27°		Berri 39°	
	Price	Per cent change	(1970=100)	Price	Per cent change	Price	Per cent change	Price	Per cent change
Sept. 1970	1.800	–	100	1.680	–	1.560	–	–	–
Feb. 1971	2.180	21.1	121	2.085	24.1	1.960	25.6	2.255	–
June 1971	2.285	4.8	127	2.187	4.8	2.059	5.0	–	–
Feb. 1972	2.479	8.4	138	2.373	8.5	2.239	8.5	2.554	–
Jan. 1973	2.591	4.5	144	2.482	4.6	2.345	4.9	2.666	4.4
June 1973	2.898	11.8	161	2.776	11.8	2.623	11.9	–	–
Oct. 1973	5.119	76.6	284	4.903	76.8	4.633	76.6	–	–
Jan. 1974	11.651	127.6	647	11.561	135.6	11.441	146.9	12.351	363.3
Nov. 1974	11.251	–3.4	625	11.161	–3.5	11.041	–3.5	11.951	–3.2
Oct. 1975	12.375	10.0	688	12.227	9.6	12.086	9.5	12.768	6.8
Jan. 1977	13.000	5.0	722	12.570	3.6	12.230	3.0	13.420	5.1
July 1977	13.660	5.1	759	13.250	5.4	12.920	5.6	14.220	6.0
Jan. 1979[a]	13.339	–2.4	741	12.886	–2.8	12.511	–3.3	14.060	–1.1
April 1979[a]	14.546	9.0	808	14.052	9.1	13.643	9.1	16.470	17.1
June 1979[a]	18.000	23.8	1,000	17.547	24.9	17.172	25.9	21.324	29.5
Nov. 1979[a]	24.000	33.3	1,333	23.547	34.2	23.172	34.9	24.721	15.9
Jan. 1980[a]	26.000	8.3	1,444	25.454	8.1	25.000	7.9	27.520	11.3
April 1980[a]	28.000	7.7	1,556	27.454	7.9	27.000	8.0	29.520	7.3
Sept. 1980[a]	30.000	7.1	1,667						
Dec. 1980[a]	32.000	6.7	1,778						

Note. a. Official selling prices.
Sources: SAMA, *Annual Reports* (1971/72), (1975), (1977); *Petroleum Intelligence Weekly*, 9 July 1979, p. 9, 26 May 1980, p. 9, 29 September 1980, p. 7; *Middle East Economic Survey*, 17 November 1980, p. 3.

resolving the Middle Eastern political conflict and in bringing peace to the region.

The second and illustrative case of the moderate Saudi stance in pricing policy occurred in December 1977 at the OPEC meeting in Caracas, Venezuela. The Kingdom, along with Iran, effectively led OPEC to hold prices at the July 1977 levels. The relative disarray in OPEC pricing in evidence through much of 1979 and 1980 had less to do with the moderate versus radical pricing groups in the Organization than with recurrent periods of consumer fear and jolts to the international petroleum market over real or imagined supply shortfalls due, first, to Iranian cutbacks and then to dislocations caused by the Iran-Iraq hostilities. More serious supply gyrations were avoided by the temporary raising of output by Gulf producers such as Saudi Arabia and the United Arab Emirates.

Government and the Oil Industry in Saudi Arabia

The Saudi government began developing its oil resources when the California Arabian Standard Oil Company (Casoc) was granted concessionary rights over an area exceeding 1 million square kilometres. The original concession agreement, concluded on 29 May 1933, was to last for a period of 60 years, during which time Casoc was to have exclusive rights over all phases of oil exploration and production. The agreement was subsequently revised three times, and now provides for a 66-year concession from the original date (see Table 2.8). In January 1944 the name of this company was changed to the Arabian American Oil Company (Aramco). By 1936 production levels of the operation required further marketing facilities which could be supplied through the Texas Company (now Texaco); as a result, the Texas Company acquired half-interest in the operation. By 1946 the magnitude of Saudi reserves had proved such that significantly greater market outlets and investment than these two companies could supply were required. Consequently, by 1948 arrangements were completed for the distribution of Aramco ownership between four major oil companies: Standard Oil Company of California, 30 per cent; Texaco, 30 per cent; Standard of New Jersey (now Exxon), 30 per cent; and Socony Mobil, 10 per cent.[27]

The original agreement established royalty payments as the government's basic compensation for the companies' development of oil resources. In the earliest dealings with the oil companies, the government seemingly lacked the necessary experience to establish more equitable privileges and obligations, and, although the agreement 'accurately reflected the relative bargaining positions of the two parties' at the time, subsequent contractual arrangements were subject to significant alterations.[28] The most notable change in the government-oil company relationship in the immediate postwar years was the 50-50 profit-sharing agreement signed on 30 December 1950. The new arrangement provided for an income tax that, when added to all other taxes, duties, rentals and royalties, would equal 50 per cent of the petroleum producers' net income.

Table 2.8: Oil Concession Areas at End of 1979[a] (thousand km^2)

Company	Original concession area	Retained area	Date of concession	Period of concession
Aramco			1933	66 years
Onshore	1,228	189		
Offshore	57	31		
Total	1,285	220		
Getty Oil			1949	60 years
Onshore	4	4	Concession does not call for periodical relinquishment	
Offshore	1	1		
Total	5	5		
Arabian Oil			1960	40 years
Offshore	6	3.4		
Exploring companies				
Tenneco Saudi Arabia	27	6	Concession starts on the date of discovery of oil in commercial quantities; expired on 21 February 1976	

Note: a. Total area of the Kingdom 2,240,000 km^2.
Source: Ministry of Petroleum and Mineral Resources, *Petroleum Statistical Bulletin, 1979*, p. 12.

The Kingdom now realized financial rewards from all aspects of domestic oil operations and was determined to further improve their position relative to the international oil 'majors'.[29] Posted prices were later established as the basis for government revenues derived from oil-company taxes. Subsequent agreements established between the Kingdom and the Getty Oil Company in 1949 and with the Arabian Oil Company in 1957 revealed the improvement of their relative bargaining position as well as the opportunity to have more control over an industry so vital to the country's economic well-being.

Government participation in the production activities of oil companies initiated a new era when, in December 1972, Saudi Arabia signed an agreement with its major oil concessionaires for an initial 25 per cent participation as of January 1973. The arrangement also made provision for the right of Saudi Arabia to acquire increasing shares of the ownership of the companies at an annual rate of 5 per cent between January 1978 and the end of 1982 and later at a rate of 6 per cent until a final 51 per cent participation in oil operations has been reached. However, within a year of the signing of the agreement the Saudi government obtained renegotiations and its participation in Aramco was raised to 60 per cent.

The relationship between the government of Saudi Arabia and Aramco has undergone several changes for the better since 1933. It was not until 1950 that, as noted earlier, a significant revision of the agreement which empowers Aramco to explore and extract crude oil enabled Saudi Arabia to have a 50 per cent share of the profit of the company. After this 50-50 profit-sharing arrangement, negotiations centred on what constituted profit. The post-1970 Aramco-Saudi relationship has been dominated by the role which OPEC has come to play in the oil industry. The nature of this role, its effect on crude oil prices and/or the extent of government participation in production facilities have been analysed previously in the chapter.

The relationship which has existed between Aramco and the Saudi government has been cordial relative to those which exist between the oil companies and the governments in some countries, such as Libya and Iraq.[30] The step-by-step increase in the extent of government participation has been achieved within a format which involves the government proposing new arrangements and Aramco agreeing, sometimes after long bargaining. A case in point is the 30 December 1950 agreement which provided for income-tax payment on the profit on the sales of crude oil, concluded only after prolonged and intensive negotiations between the Ministry of Petroleum and Aramco. The negotiations were so intense that government-company relations were strained for a period.

The sheer size of Aramco operations makes negotiations with the company a delicate matter. Aramco payments over the years have contributed more than 96 per cent of the Saudi governmental oil revenue. The largest oil-producing fields in Saudi Arabia continue to be (1) Ghawar, (2) Abqaiq, (3) Safaniyah, (4) Zuluf and (5) Berri (Figure 2.1). All exist within Aramco-concession territory and collectively account for 80 to 90 per cent of total Saudi crude output. In order to

Figure 2.1: Oil Fields Discovered in Saudi Arabia and the Saudi-Kuwaiti Divided (Neutral) Zone

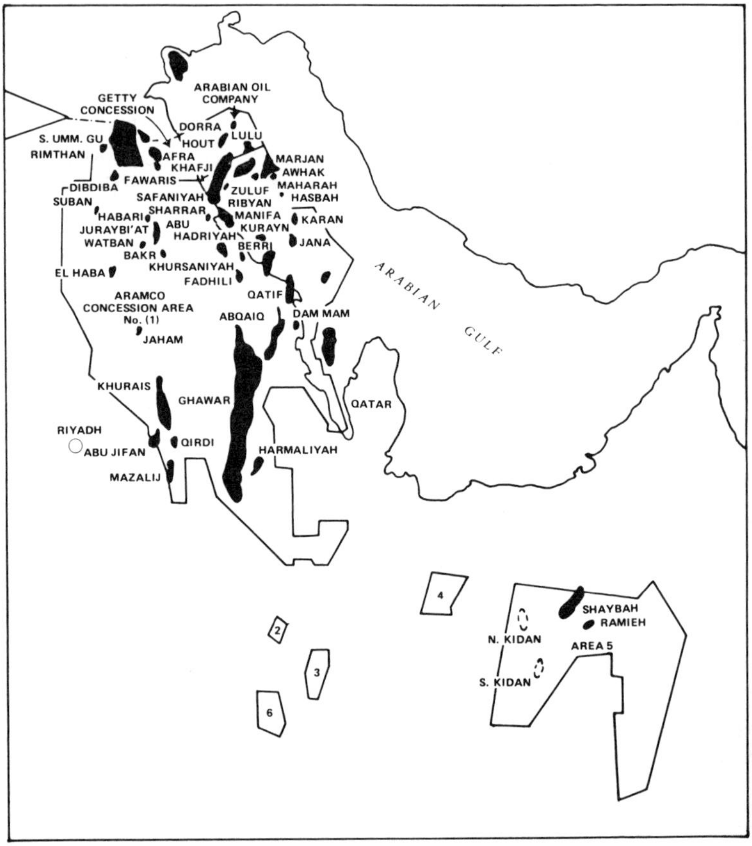

Source: Kingdom of Saudi Arabia, *Third Development Plan, 1400-1405 / 1980-1985,* Chapter 4, p.165

realize the practical problems which a take-over of even a small part of the ownership of a firm such as Aramco could generate, some details of the participation agreement ought to be outlined.[31]

The government of Saudi Arabia was expected to (and did) pay for the initial percentage of participation – an amount equal to 25 per cent of the updated book values of the crude-oil production facilities. The percentage increment of the take-over was also to be paid on the same basis. For these payments the government had rights to a percentage of each grade of oil available at a specified offtake point equal to its share of participation for each year. The government would then sell back to the operating companies 75 per cent, 50 per cent, and 25 per cent of its share for 1973, 1974 and 1975, respectively, to enable the oil companies to fulfil previous commitments. The amount of oil resold in this way was termed 'bridging' crude oil. In order to ensure a smooth entry into overseas markets, the government was given the right to sell back to the operating companies 15 per cent, 30 per cent, and 50 per cent of its share for 1973, 1974 and 1975, respectively. This amount of oil resale is called 'phase-in' crude oil.

Once the government's capability grew fast enough to execute the provisions of the participation agreement effectively, these developments provided the Kingdom of Saudi Arabia with an interest in the concessions' crude-oil production facilities which included exploration, development, production, pipelines, storage, delivery and export facilities. In addition, Saudi Arabia gained on the average about 40 cents per barrel above the cost for 'bridging' oil and about 30 cents a barrel for 'phase-in' oil on its share of 25 per cent. These gave rise to the average increase of about 10 cents per barrel in total revenues mentioned earlier.

A new kind of partnership is being forged between Aramco and the Saudi government, with the former becoming involved in the non-oil-related development programmes of the country. Thus, Aramco is responsible for directing the $14 billion gas-gathering project which will feed both Jubail and Yanbu industrial complexes. The company also has been entrusted with the planning and direction of the electrification project for the Eastern Province of the Kingdom. This new image of Aramco signifies the high regard in which Saudi Arabia still holds the company, and also the confidence which Aramco has in the country's future.

Petromin

On 2 November 1962 the General Petroleum and Mineral Organization was established under the auspices of the Ministry of Petroleum and Mineral Resources. Petromin (as it has come to be known) has, under the new government-industry relationship, become so important and has such potential that some details about it should be offered.[32]

Petromin is envisaged as a major contributor to the development of Saudi Arabia through its participation in various industrial and commercial activities related to the petroleum sector. Among its undertakings have been: (1) the implementation and administration of public petroleum and mineral products in Saudi Arabia; (2) the importation (directly or through agents) of the mineral needs of the Kingdom; (3) the preparation (on its own or through others) of both theoretical and practical oil research and studies as well as the actual operations entrusted to it by the government with regard to exploration, production, refining, transportation, distribution and marketing of petroleum and mineral resources in Saudi Arabia and abroad; and (4) the establishment of domestic and/or foreign oil-related companies or enterprises.

The power of Petromin is rather all-encompassing; it is not only authorized by the government to hold an interest or participate in companies or organizations engaged in activities similar to its own, but also has the authority to buy, annex or amalgamate such companies or organizations.

In May 1973 the Ministry of Petroleum and Mineral Resources outlined the Kingdom's policy toward its participation share of crude oil by authorizing Petromin to market that oil directly. This is merely a fraction of the organization's responsibilities, the expansion of which will form the base for the integration Petromin seeks to bring about in the oil sector. Among its most notable projects have been:

(1) in the area of oil exploitation concessions, agreements with Agip-Phillips, Sun Oil Natomas-Pakistan Group and Auxerap-Tenneco;
(2) in exploration and drilling, agreements with the French Compagnie Générale de Géophysique in the formation of the Arabian Geophysical and Surveying Company and with the Forex company to establish the Arabian Drilling Company;
(3) in refining, Petromin is negotiating for the construction of new refineries which would more than double Saudi Arabia's present refining capacity.[33] The importance of expanding existing refining capacity cannot be overstated as the Kingdom seeks to ensure its future economic

development by commanding a share in all aspects of the oil industry (see appendix for statistics on output of refined products). While possessing more than one-fourth of the world's proven reserves and over 14 per cent of world production capacity, at present Saudi Arabia manages less than 1 per cent of the world's capacity. Furthermore, as development in the Kingdom proceeds, domestic requirements of refined products will quickly rise. While Saudi Arabian consumption of refined products has been steadily increasing in real terms, it is interesting to note that the rate of growth in domestic demand for products has been accelerating even more rapidly. Comparatively, the increase in consumption in 1971 over 1970 was 10.8 per cent, while 1976 over 1975 consumption levels increased by an overwhelming 42.4 per cent.

The Oil Industry under the Second and Third Development Plans

The oil industry during the Second Development Plan (1975-80) maintained its dominant role in the economy of Saudi Arabia. The proportion of government revenue provided by the oil sector remained relatively level at the high figures of 90.9 per cent in 1976 and 89.6 per cent in 1979. Foreign-exchange receipts also remained quite steady at approximately 90 per cent of the Kingdom's total.

Achievements of the 1975-80 period include extensive exploration for new hydrocarbon reserves; 14 new fields were discovered and proved reserves increased by about 20 per cent to reach in the area of 167-169 billion barrels. Production averaged 8.54 million b/d over the plan period, with a peak output of 9.5 million b/d achieved in 1979. A major project to sustain oil-reservoir pressure was implemented in the world's largest field at Ghawar by the injection of 4.2 million b/d of seawater. Pricing of oil was increased from $10.46 in January of 1975 to $26 per barrel in January 1980 (to $32 per barrel at the Bali OPEC meeting in December 1980), thereby enabling real purchasing values of crude-oil exports to be maintained and oil revenues to be raised without production increases.

Major objectives and related policies for the oil sector as outlined in the Third Development Plan (1980-5) will continue to be administered by the Ministry of Petroleum and Mineral Resources. These goals include:

(1) the pursuit of a production policy which emphasizes the resources required for the implementation of the Third Plan, which takes into

consideration the ratio of the various hydrocarbon types contained in the national reserves, and which optimizes individual reservoir life;
(2) the support of the development of hydrocarbon-based industries within the Kingdom;
(3) the maintenance of the best methods, technologies and facilities in the Kingdom's hydrocarbon exploration, production and distribution;
(4) the encouragement of conservation, both domestically in terms of the onshore and offshore environment and groundwater resources, and abroad in terms of the efficient utilization of hydrocarbon resources;
(5) the continuation of Saudi Arabia's major role in OPEC. Co-operation will be maintained with member countries to protect the value of hydrocarbons and to achieve a fair petroleum income to support the welfare of OPEC citizens while, at the same time, taking into account the development of the world economy;
(6) the strengthening of the Organization of the Arab Petroleum Exporting Countries (OAPEC), with continuous co-operation and participation in petroleum projects with other nations maintained.[34]

Relation to Development

The significance of the oil sector, as noted earlier, extends far beyond its financial contribution. In addition to revenues, the oil sector's direct contributions are to foreign exchange earnings, the balance of payments, employment, GNP, not to mention energy supply and use of domestic inputs.[35] More important from the long-run point of view, however, is the indirect contribution of the sector to the economy's development and structural change.

Taking all the direct and indirect contributions of the oil sector into account, no one can argue with the conclusion that 'for nations with enormous oil deposits such as Venezuela, parts of the Middle East and North Africa, oil is the economic life'.[36] It is also true that '[oil] . . . represents the great asset which could potentially provide all the capital necessary for economic development'.[37] However, it is difficult to agree with the view that 'these countries represent prime candidates for testing the validity of the theory of economic development through unbalanced growth . . .'[38] An unbalanced growth pattern may be feasible, and it has certainly been historically practical, but what is economically or technically possible may not always be socially desirable. Rapid capital accumulation, especially in a single sector which is not fully integrated with the rest of the economy, may lead to socio-economic distress and to socially wasteful allocation and underutilization of resources.

Therefore, when a single commodity such as oil plays so vital a role in the economy and when that commodity is a wasting asset, it is then crucial that not only the asset itself be exploited by a very sound and rational production utilization programming policy, but also the actual and potential proceeds from it must be utilized in a way that contributes most to the objective of achieving a stage of self-sustaining economic growth.

Efforts, however, have been made increasingly by the Saudi government to strengthen the linkages between the oil sector and the rest of the economy. Available data also indicate somewhat greater spending by the oil companies in the domestic markets of the oil-producing countries. In Saudi Arabia, in addition to the reforms brought into the contractual agreements and the participation agreement mentioned earlier, the establishment of a number of petrochemical industries and other actions during the last decade have expanded linkages between the oil and other sectors. Yet it is widely recognized that in all the major petroleum-exporting developing countries, the oil sector is essentially isolated from the rest of the economy. The relationship between the oil and non-oil sectors at this point in time is fundamentally financial, with the former providing funding for the extensive development of the latter. This has (as often occurs in a developing country when efforts are made to exploit an export commodity) created a dualistic type of development in which a modern sector exists side by side with a traditional sector. Moreover, by its nature, the oil industry is capital-intensive rather than labour-intensive, employing only a relatively small portion of the labour force in light of its undeniable predominance in the economy as a whole. The vast majority of Saudis have no direct tie with the driving source of their nation's wealth.

The degree of isolation and/or dualism, of course, varies from country to country. This phenomenon may be due partly to the technological, political and economic structures of the oil industry and the specific nation. It is also traceable in part to the inability of the existing domestic industries and markets to supply the quantity and quality of required materials and services. This aspect of the oil sector – i.e. being weakly integrated with the rest of the economy – once again necessitates the diversification of the economy by rational and effective utilization of the oil proceeds.

Notes

1. An excellent study of this industry is that of Neil H. Jacoby, *Multinational Oil* (New York, Macmillan Publishers, 1974).

2. Ibid., pp. 16-19.

3. Ibid., p. 20.

4. For more information on this issue, refer to Jacoby, *Multinational Oil*, p. 93.

5. L. Donald Fixler and Robert L. Ferrar, 'An Application of Economic Theory to Middle Eastern Oil Pricing', in Naiem A. Sherbiny and Mark A. Tessler (eds), *Arab Oil: Impact on the Arab Countries and Global Implications* (New York, Praeger Publishers, 1976), p. 21.

6. J.S. Burrows and T.A. Domenish, *An Analysis of the United States Oil Import Quota* (Lexington, Mass., D.C. Heath & Co., 1970), p. 106.

7. British Petroleum Company, Ltd, *BP Statistical Review of the World Oil Industry* (London, 1977), p. 21. The world, as used here, includes the USSR, Eastern Europe and China.

8. Naiem A. Sherbiny, 'Arab Oil Production in the Context of International Conflicts,' in N. Sherbiny and M. Tessler (eds), *Arab Oil: Impact on the Arab Countries and Global Implications*, p. 44.

9. Peter Hallock Johnson, 'Saudi Arabia's Oil Production Level: Influences in the Decision-Making Process and Appropriate U.S. Policy,' Fletcher School of Law and Diplomacy, unpublished paper, January 1977, p. 5.

10. Actual production capacity in 1977 of 11,840 million b/d was expected to increase. *Petroleum Intelligence Weekly*, 17 October 1977, p. 7.

11. Ambassador Sheikh Ali A. Alireza, speech before the National Foreign Trade Council at the Waldorf Astoria Hotel, New York, 16 November 1976.

12. Walter J. Levy, in *Saudi Arabia's Approaching Choice* (London, July 1976), p. 9. At May 1980 prices for oil, Saudi Arabia could reduce output from the 9.5 million b/d level of 1979 to slightly under 5.3 million b/d and still earn sufficient revenue to finance development per the third plan.

13. Interview with Sheikh Ahmed Zaki Yamani in the *Los Angeles Times*, 9 January 1978. The ceiling was understood to be the preferred maximum level of output; however, this upper limit was not deemed immutable but could be exceeded under special circumstances as, for example, supply shortfalls as occurred in 1979 and 1980.

14. Abdul A. Kubbah, *OPEC: Past and Present* (Vienna, Austria, Petro-Economic Research Centre, 1974), p. 7. A brief historical evaluation of OPEC since its creation is that of Shukri Ghanem, 'OPEC: A Cartel or a Group of Competing Nations?' in Ragaei El Mallakh and Carl McGuire (eds), *Energy and Development* (Boulder, Colorado, International Research Center for Energy and Economic Development, 1974), pp. 175-84.

15. They are: Aramco, Arabian Oil Company, and Getty Oil Company. The Arabian American Oil Company (Aramco) was granted the major onshore and offshore concession for Saudi Arabia proper; its original parent firms were Standard Oil Company of California, Texaco, Exxon Corporation, and Mobil. Since the conclusion of the participation agreement between Aramco and the Saudi government, Saudi Arabia now has a participation interest in the company's producing operations. The majority Japanese-owned Arabian Oil Company (with local government equity) holds the offshore concessions of both the Saudi and Kuwaiti shares of the Neutral Zone, the territory between the two countries which is jointly administered by them. Getty Oil Company was granted the onshore concession for the Saudi share of the Neutral Zone.

16. The February 1971 Teheran Agreement included significant changes in previously existing arrangements, the most important of which are: an increase in the tax rate to 55 per cent; a uniform increase of posted prices by 33 per cent per barrel plus a 2 per cent per barrel increase 'in satisfaction of claims to freight disparities'; annual adjustment of prices as a guard against loss of purchasing power through inflation. (This agreement was later to be revised in September of 1973.) For a more detailed discussion of the provisions of these agreements, see R. Knauerhase, *The Saudi Arabian Economy* (New York: Praeger Publishers, 1975), Ch. 7.

17. SAMA, *Statistical Summary* (September 1972), p. 18.

18. Refer to Chapter 10 for a detailed analysis of the Saudi balance-of-payments position.

19. 'Saver' and 'spender' country dichotomization was introduced by Robert S. Pindyck, 'OPEC Oil Pricing, World Energy Markets, and U.S. Energy Policy', p. 4 (mimeographed).

20. Ibid.

21. A more detailed discussion of the relationship between the Saudi government and the operating companies appears later in this chapter.

22. Recently customs duties either have been reduced drastically or abolished completely. Consequently, the share of these revenues in total Saudi government revenue has further diminished. As of 1 January 1977, Aramco's income-tax payments to the Kingdom of Saudi Arabia were to be based upon the official selling prices of crude, and no more upon the long-standing posted price criterion. The official selling price may currently be calculated as 93 per cent of the posted price.

23. There were three upward revisions of royalties and oil-company tax rates in 1974 alone. Royalty rates rose from 12.5 to 14.5 per cent in July 1974, to 16.67 per cent as of October 1974, and 20 per cent the month after. Income-tax rate for oil companies increased from 55 per cent to 65.6 per cent in October 1974 and to 85 per cent in November the same year. The marker crude selected by OPEC is a standard by which to fix posted price, tax and royalty rates, that is, Arabian Light, refers to crude oil of 34° API gravity. Most Gulf crudes range from 25° to 40° API gravity. The higher gravity crudes in general demand a greater price.

24. This analysis was presented in a report to the Subcommittee on Energy Joint Economic Committee of the Congress, Dr. Ragaei El Mallakh, *Congressional Record*, 2 March 1977, pp. S3335-7.

25. The two-tier system effectively ended when, in July 1977, Saudi Arabia and Abu Dhabi raised prices by another 5 per cent to parity with the rest of OPEC members' prices, while at the same time persuading OPEC to maintain prices at existing levels, i.e. 10 per cent over pre-Doha prices.

26. For example, Saudi policy strongly supports the North-South dialogue and had expectations of some significant progress at the Conference on International Economic Cooperation (CIEC) in Paris. Although no major breakthrough was realized in 1978, the CIEC impetus remains alive.

27. For further analysis of the early concessions and explorations see Ray Labkicher *et al.*, *Aramco Handbook* (Dhahran, Saudi Arabia: Arabian American Oil Company, 1960), pp. 135-41.

28. R. Knauerhase, *Saudi Arabian Economy*, p. 1616.

29. The 'majors' are large American, Dutch, French and British oil firms having a high degree of vertical integration, i.e. activities in the many sectors of the petroleum industry ranging from exploration and production to transport, refining, marketing and distribution. The so-called 'seven sisters' include: Exxon, Standard Oil Company of California, Texaco, Mobil, Royal Dutch/Shell, British

Petroleum, and Compagnie Française des Pétroles.

30. David Hirst, *Oil and Public Opinion in the Middle East* (London, Faber and Faber, 1966), p. 30.

31. The full text of the participation agreement is published in a special supplement of the *Petroleum Intelligence Weekly*, 25 December 1972. See also SAMA, *Statistical Summary* (December 1972), p. 15.

32. Petromin's goals and evaluation of its performance appear in several studies, including Dr. Abdulhady H. Taher, 'The Middle East Oil and Gas Policy', *Journal of Energy and Development*, Spring 1978, and Jobarah E. Suraisry, 'Petromin: Its Activities and Role in the Development of the Economy of Saudi Arabia', University of Colorado, unpublished paper, 1977.

33. Existing refineries include Aramco's Ras Tanura, Petromin's Jeddah and Riyadh refineries, Getty Oil Company's Mina Saud refinery and Arabian Oil Company's Al-Khafji refinery.

34. Greater detail on the oil sector's role and performance in the three development plans is offered in Chapters 5, 6 and 7.

35. In 1978 the oil sector alone contributed more than 90 per cent of total export earnings and commanded 59 per cent of GDP calculated at current prices. SAMA, *Annual Report, 1979*, pp. 165-6.

36. Michael Tanzer, *The Political Economy of International Oil and the Underdeveloped Countries* (Boston, Beacon Press, 1969), p. 3.

37. Ibid.

38. Ibid.

3 AGRICULTURE AND DEVELOPMENT OF WATER RESOURCES

Introduction

Saudi Arabia's agricultural sector, while isolated somewhat from the direct effects of the oil boom, cannot be separated from the pervading influence of the oil-based prosperity. Agriculture has benefited from increased oil revenues in the form of improvements, including expanded markets, cost reductions in transportation, and increased supply of modern inputs such as fertilizers, improved seeds, machinery and more readily accessible sources of credit. In addition, the Kingdom's current vast revenues have spared it some of the problems frequently encountered in agricultural development. Poorer countries are often dependent on surplus production of the agricultural sector to provide capital for development of other sectors; as development proceeds and the demand for food increases, failure to raise agricultural productivity quickly enough to satisfy demand can actually draw physical and financial resources from other sectors. Saudi Arabia need not worry about such a capital constraint.

Another problem often faced by those developing nations without sufficient revenues, concerns the growth of the domestic markets necessary to absorb expanded output. To the extent that capital is transferred from the agricultural to the industrial sector, the purchasing power of the rural sector and the size of the market for industrial goods are decreased. Saudi Arabia's oil revenues provide an indirect but very important advantage in this respect as the domestic market is limited by size only. Income produced by the agricultural sector can be retained by the rural population, increasing purchasing power for the farmers which is reflected in stronger demand and larger markets for the output of the non-agricultural sector. Furthermore, as a result of the revenues received from oil sales, Saudi Arabia is not dependent on agriculture as a source generating the foreign exchange for imports of goods and services necessary for development.

This does not imply, however, that the agricultural sector is unimportant in the Saudi development process. Indeed, agricultural development is regarded as an integral part of economic diversification, reducing long-term dependence of the economy on the single commodity of oil, a wasting asset. Agricultural development remains a vital element in the overall Saudi development process for other reasons.

First, although financial and perhaps physical capital resources are no problem for the economy as a whole, managerial and manpower resources are scarce. Thus increased agricultural productivity is necessary to release labour to other sectors, especially to the industrial sector. Unless agricultural productivity is raised through higher technology, this sector will continue to compete with other sectors in the economy for the limited manpower resources of the Kingdom.

The second reason originates in the traditional role of agriculture in feeding the populace. As a result of the rapid growth of population and prosperity, food consumption has increased rapidly. Food consumption is expected to increase in the future as purchasing power increases, particularly in a shift from cereal consumption to higher protein intake. An obvious goal, therefore, is to achieve an acceptable level of self-sufficiency in food production. This is no doubt a difficult task considering that, over the years, the proportion of domestically produced food of the total consumed has been falling. While the Kingdom was self-sufficient in food in the 1930s, by 1975 about 66 per cent of its foodstuffs was supplied from external sources.[1] It is encouraging to note, however, that recent rises in production have enabled Saudi Arabia to produce half of its food requirements in 1976.[2] Nevertheless, during the Second Development Plan, the agricultural sector grew at approximately 5 per cent annually compounded – a rate only one-third as fast as the total non-oil sector.

But perhaps the most important contribution which increased agricultural production can make to the development efforts of Saudi Arabia, is in the area of providing the raw materials for agricultural-based industries. This aspect of agriculture has received relatively slight attention from commentators on Saudi economic development. To the extent that a true diversification of the economy could be achieved only if more industries utilizing non-oil inputs spring up in the Kingdom, the need for co-ordinating agricultural and industrial objectives of the development process is imperative.

The significance of water to the agricultural development of the mostly arid Kingdom cannot be overemphasized. Thus, these two sectors of water and agriculture are discussed in a single chapter in this study, and they come under the purview of the same Ministry in the Saudi governmental machinery. Of course, water is not used only for agricultural purposes; it is needed for drinking, for domestic or personal consumption and for industrialization. Desalination for the production of fresh water is discussed both in this sector and within the context of the industrial sector and the push toward industrialization.

Agriculture in Saudi Economic Development

The Contribution of Agriculture

Agricultural production in Saudi Arabia includes nomadic agriculture, settled farming, fishing, range resources and forestry. As the economy has expanded, the relative contribution of agriculture measured in terms of output has declined. In 1974/5 agriculture provided only 8.5 per cent of real GDP of the non-oil portion of the economy, or 3.6 per cent of total real GDP. In 1977/8, these figures had fallen to 6.6 per cent of real non-oil GDP and 3.2 per cent of total real GDP.

The percentage of the labour force engaged in agriculture is smaller in Saudi Arabia than in many developing countries. While agriculture has remained the primary occupation of the Kingdom's population, the number has been falling from 695,000 persons or 40 per cent of the civil labour force in 1975 to about 600,000 persons (approximately 25 per cent) of the urban labour force in 1980 (see Table 1.3).[3] The decline in both the number and the share of agriculture in the labour force has been motivated by the low incomes from that sector relative to incomes from alternative employment forms. As a result, part of the Kingdom's farm land has been abandoned, and some villages are becoming smaller. One method to halt this rural-urban migration would be to raise the incomes of rural dwellers through increased agricultural productivity; this is one of the cardinal objectives of the government's development policies.

Generally, development efforts in the agricultural sector have been less successful to date than those dealing with other parts of the economy. The value added by agriculture during the period 1973-8 increased only 3.5 per cent per annum at constant prices, in spite of fairly substantial investment by the Saudi government in irrigation and drainage projects in the preceding decade. During the five-year period covered by the Second Development Plan, agricultural output rose at an annual average rate of 5 per cent.[4]

A number of factors have contributed to the relative lack of success. Overall, agricultural development has been hampered by the very nature of Saudi agriculture. Elements such as small landholdings, inefficient farming operations, dispersion of farms over an extensive land area, inadequate water supply, and harsh climate have all tended to hinder growth in the sector. Existing institutions, including the systems of land tenure and water rights, have also slowed down growth by impeding adoption of improved technology. Given Saudi Arabia's vast oil revenues and the ability to finance a multi-front attack to stimulate economic development, agriculture has sometimes been forced to take a back seat to more immediate problems, such as providing a modern infrastructure. Finally, the major factor impeding Saudi agricultural development is the scarcity of water.

General Characteristics of Saudi Agriculture

Saudi agriculture is characterized by small farms operated by the owner or by tenant farmers.[5] Three-fourths of the cultivated land in Saudi Arabia is in the southwest, which receives sufficient rainfall to support farming operations. The remainder of the Kingdom's cultivated land is scattered over the country near oases, towns, and the wadis which drain mountain areas. Figure 3.1 delineates the main agricultural areas in the Kingdom. As the map indicates, only the Asir region in the southwest receives enough rainfall to support cultivation; the remainder is dependent on irrigation. It would appear that the future of farming in the Kingdom depends on the extent to which irrigation facilities can be extended. Almost all of the land in the Kingdom is too dry to support more than periodic livestock grazing, and true grasslands are almost non-existent. But while it is possible that the total area of the Kingdom's cropped land could be increased if water were available, less than 1 per cent of the nation presently has enough water to support crops. Table 3.1 summarizes the current data on agricultural land distribution in the Kingdom.

Contrary to popular opinion, the Kingdom has a large amount of land which can become cultivable, provided the right amount of water were available to it. Recent studies on this issue show that there are presently about 4.5 million hectares of arable land; thus, the approximate half million hectares which were under cultivation in 1970/1 constituted a small proportion of the cultivable area in Saudi Arabia. Clearly, there are reasons other than scarcity of arable land to explain the poor performance of agriculture in Saudi economic development; the most obvious constraint is the lack of sufficient water.

Another consideration which surfaces in the discussion of agricultural development in the Third World is the size of the landholdings.

Similarly, most of the holdings in Saudi Arabia are too small to be cultivated economically. And, as might be expected, agricultural machinery is rarely used on this size of farm. There are historical and institutional causes for such a system of land ownership in the Kingdom.

Figure 3.1: Main Agricultural Areas of Saudi Arabia

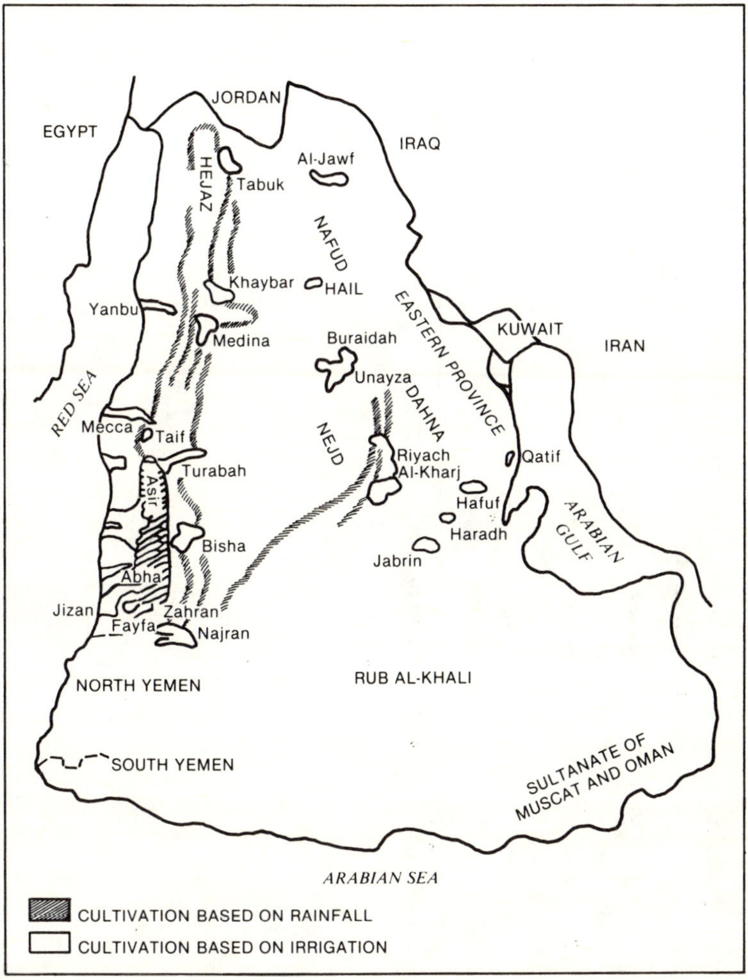

Source: Ramon Knauerhase, *The Saudi Arabian Economy* (New York, Praeger Publishers, 1975), p. 112.

Table 3.1: Comparison of Cultivated Area and Land Use, 1970/1 to 1975/6 (hectares)

Year	No. of holdings	Area in holdings	Dryland	Irrigated	Perennial and orchard	Total	Average holding land use		
							Cultivated	Uncultivated	Total
1970/1	180,789	1,391,274	403,654	78,362	42,709	524,725	2.90	4.79	7.69
1975/6	180,670	1,213,462	357,713	91,126	143,162	592,001	3.28	3.44	6.72
Changes									
Hectares	–119	–177,812	–45,941	+12,764	+100,453	+67,276	+0.38	–1.35	–0.97
Per cent	same	–12.8	–11.4	+16.3	+235.2	+12.8	+13.1	–28.2	–12.6

Source: Kingdom of Saudi Arabia, *Third Development Plan, 1400-1405/1980-1985*, Chapter 4.

Landholdings in the central region are often larger due to the past practice of granting farms in this area to soldiers as rewards, and to the prevalence of extended family farming in this region. These larger holdings make more use of machinery and hired labour than the smaller operations do, for obvious economic reasons. In some cases laws which provide for distribution of land among all heirs upon the death of the landowner have been responsible for these uneconomically small tracts. However, in the 1960s, less than one-third of the arable land in the Kingdom was subject to these inheritance laws.[6] Over the years, several kinds of ownership have evolved to combat this fragmentation. In some cases land might be owned by an extended family unit with family members sharing the farming and produce of their aggregated plots. A second method used to avoid splitting the land into uneconomically small units is to place it in a trust, possibly as an endowment for a charitable organization, with the owner or his agents continuing to farm the land and retain the produce.[7]

While most of the land, including the vast amounts not suitable for farming, belong to the government, any Saudi may own land. The government has a formal programme for distributing land to private citizens. Under the Barren Land Distribution Law, passed in 1968, provision was made for free grants of potentially productive land to any Saudi citizen willing and able to farm it. Participating citizens receive from 50 to 100 dunums each, while organizations are granted up to 400 dunums.[8] The new landholder has from two to three years to put the land to productive use. If he has not put the land to productive use by the end of the period, it reverts to the government to be granted to another potential farmer. In distributing land under this programme, the government gives priority to farmers with other land in close proximity, to individuals with proven ability in investment and farming, and to citizens who own no other property. As of 1980, some 98,950 hectares had been distributed to 14,554 recipients and 60 projects in poultry breeding, dairy farming, and sheep rearing under this policy. The programme has been unsuccessful in markedly increasing agricultural productivity, largely due to such constraints as water shortages, lack of credit, and the uneconomically small size of landholdings. At the end of the Second Plan, these problems were undergoing review.

As might be expected, there are few trees in Saudi Arabia, and those that do survive are often stunted, with soft, porous wood. Trees do grow in some mountain areas and in some instances are cultivated as windbreaks and as barriers against shifting sand dunes. Date palms are widely cultivated for their fruit. With these exceptions, however, trees are a scarce commodity in Saudi Arabia, and forestry is a negligible item in the agricultural sector.

Through the centuries Saudi farmers and herdsmen have developed a mutually dependent socio-economic relationship to survive in the country's harsh arid climate. Farmers cultivated the limited areas around oases which had enough water to grow some crops for human needs, but could not supply additional adequate forage for livestock production. The nomadic Bedouin developed special abilities in ekeing an existence from the extensive dry lands which support a limited number of animals. They became experts in locating areas which had recently received rainfall and in finding water and forage for their camels and a limited amount of livestock and horses. The nomads were forced to travel continually to find adequate feed for their animals and were dependent on the settled farmers for some of their food and supplies. The Bedouin, in addition to supplying the farmers with camels, also provided protection for the farmers and markets where they traded.[9]

Recent events in Saudi Arabia, including the substitution of trucks for camels and the unification of the country under a central government, have upset this balance, creating a special development problem in the agricultural sector. The impact of these events has been felt most keenly by the Bedouin, whose culture is based on their nomadic life-style. Kinship and tribal ties are extremely important. Over time, tribes had established control over territories, which they owned and vigorously defended. They supplemented their income from camel raising and caravans and by taxing the caravans of other tribes for safe passage through their territories. Wells and springs were developed and maintained by the tribes. In some cases, where water was adequate, parts of a tribe might settle down and raise sheep and goats or dates. With the passage of years, a very intricate social and economic framework evolved within and among the tribes.[10]

Agricultural Production and Marketing

Despite the fact that agriculture's share in the total GDP has been falling over the years, agricultural production has not experienced a circular decline. Consequently, the decreasing role of the agricultural sector is attributable to the faster rate of growth of other sectors in the economy of Saudi Arabia, especially that of oil. As Table 3.2 shows, real agricultural GDP has been rising since 1966/7, yet the share of this category of GDP to total or non-oil real domestic output fell consistently during the 1966/7-1977/8 span. While total real GDP has grown dramatically in recent years, the falling proportion attributable to agriculture reveals that the sector has not kept pace. The declining percentage of non-oil GDP represented by agriculture is an even more cogent indicator of the lag in food production.

If agricultural production has not been able to keep up with the general economic boom of the Kingdom, it is because this sector, more than any other, is faced with special climatic, socio-cultural, and human resource limitations. Given the climatic conditions, the problem of increasing agricultural output is essentially summarized in making available the necessary inputs of the right quality, in the right amounts, at the right time and place, and in the labour force having the correct attitude and aptitude to utilize these inputs.

Table 3.2: Share of Agriculture in Gross Domestic Product (GDP), 1966/7-1977/8

Year	Agriculture GDP (in 1969/80 SR millions)	Agriculture GDP as percentage of non-oil GDP	Agriculture GDP as percentage of GDP
1966/7	884.6	13.4	6.5
1967/8	924.8	12.9	6.3
1968/9	956.5	12.3	6.0
1969/70	984.1	12.2	5.7
1970/1	1,017.8	11.8	5.1
1971/2	1,050.1	11.4	4.6
1972/3	1,088.7	10.3	4.0
1973/4	1,129.6	9.4	3.6
1974/5[a]	1,174.1	9.1	3.7
1975/6[a]	1,221.0	7.5	3.5
1976/7[a]	1,282.0	7.0	3.2
1977/8[b]	1,359.0	5.8[c]	3.2

Notes: a. Revised. b. Preliminary. c. Estimated per the *Third Development Plan, 1400-1405/1980-1985*.
Sources: Computed from SAMA, *Statistical Summary*, 1st issue (1974/5), Table 29 and 2nd issue (1977), Table 29; SAMA, *Annual Reports, 1977*, Table 29 and *1979*, Table 29.

The question of marketing then becomes a secondary matter in a system in which output is not sufficient to meet the available demand. It is not surprising, then, that writings on Saudi agricultural development have skimmed over the marketing aspect of this sector.[11] Very soon, however, marketing (including transporting the product to the sources of consumption) will become a real problem. It is perhaps for this reason that the government has proposed to undertake economic analysis of marketing channels, incentive programmes, price support systems, and the like.

Water-resource Development

The primary consideration in Saudi Arabia's agriculture is the supply of water. While the presence of oil provides Saudi Arabia with advantages not enjoyed by many developing nations, the water shortage imposes constraints on agricultural development to a degree not often encountered by the poorer countries. The Kingdom has no lakes, rivers or streams. While some arable lands receive rain, such rainfall is relatively sparse in all areas. Too often, precipitation is in the form of downpours occurring in very short periods of time, which results in wasted runoff and damaging floods. Some water has a high salinity content which damages crops. Most of the Kingdom's water supply is groundwater, which must be regarded as a depletable resource, although it is estimated that fossil-water aquifers exist under as much as two-thirds of Saudi Arabia's territory.

Substantial progress in water development was made during the First and Second Development Plans, bringing increased water supply for consumption as well as additional information to guide future development. As of 1980, 41 dams were operational and five more were under construction. During the Second Plan 760 wells were dug or repaired to add to the 1,025 of the First Plan. A total of 237 new municipal water-supply projects were built in the Second Plan period and over 150 potable water systems were also expanded. Emphasis was on the distribution networks of Riyadh and Jeddah during both Plan periods because of the cities' high growth rates. The preparation of a much-needed national water plan was begun during the Second Plan.[12] Development must proceed more rapidly, however, if the water supply is to keep pace with the demand of a growing population, industrial development, and a more productive agricultural sector.

Saudi officials emphasize that because water is so scarce and so critical, development of water resources must proceed slowly and carefully; the Kingdom has a number of sources which have not been tapped as yet. The supply of seawater for desalination is virtually unlimited. Development of these resources will be costly, but the money is certainly available. The primary consideration in water-resource development is the maintenance of the water-resource base. At the same time, the rapid expansion of the Kingdom's population, urban centres, industrial operations, and agricultural activities require large and immediate increases in the water supply.

With these requirements in mind, the development of water resources has been formulated to meet two complementary objectives. First is the short-term programme in which a number of projects to improve water quality and increase availability are planned. Desalination plants providing both water and electricity are a major part of this scheme. Secondly, long-range water-resource development will proceed only after extensive studies assure Saudi officials that development policies are in accord with optimal long-term resource usage. With this latter objective in mind, the Third Development Plan provides for the preparation of the above-mentioned national water plan to provide for the country-wide use and reuse of the water resources available to the Kingdom.

Table 3.3: Supply of Water for Major Uses 1974, and Forecast of Production Requirement, 1980 (thousand m^3 per day)

	Supply 1974	Production requirement 1980	Quantity increase	Per cent increase
Urban centres	211	545	334	158
Industrial complexes	---	95	95	100
Oil-well injection	1,100	2,400	1,300	118
Irrigation-agriculture	5,370	7,060	1,690	31
Total	6,681	10,100	3,419	51

Source: Adapted from *Second Plan*, p. 105.

Table 3.3 summarizes present water usage and development requirements in the 1975-80 period. Figure 3.2 portrays exploitable water resources and projected water utilization for the 20-year span of 1980 to 2000. Principal demand sectors are urban/industrial uses, rural and livestock needs, and irrigated agriculture. Irrigated agriculture demands beyond 1985 are approximated and in need of further analysis of crop-production potential. Surplus water will remain in deep aquifer storage.

The required increase in water supply is expected to come from a number of sources, including desalination plants, groundwater development, construction and improvement of supply and distribution systems, and construction of small dams as well as reclamation of water from urban waste water. This latter source will add a valuable and economic source of water for agricultural and industrial uses. By the year 2000 it is projected that reclaimed water can add 15 per cent to

Figure 3.2: National Water Balance

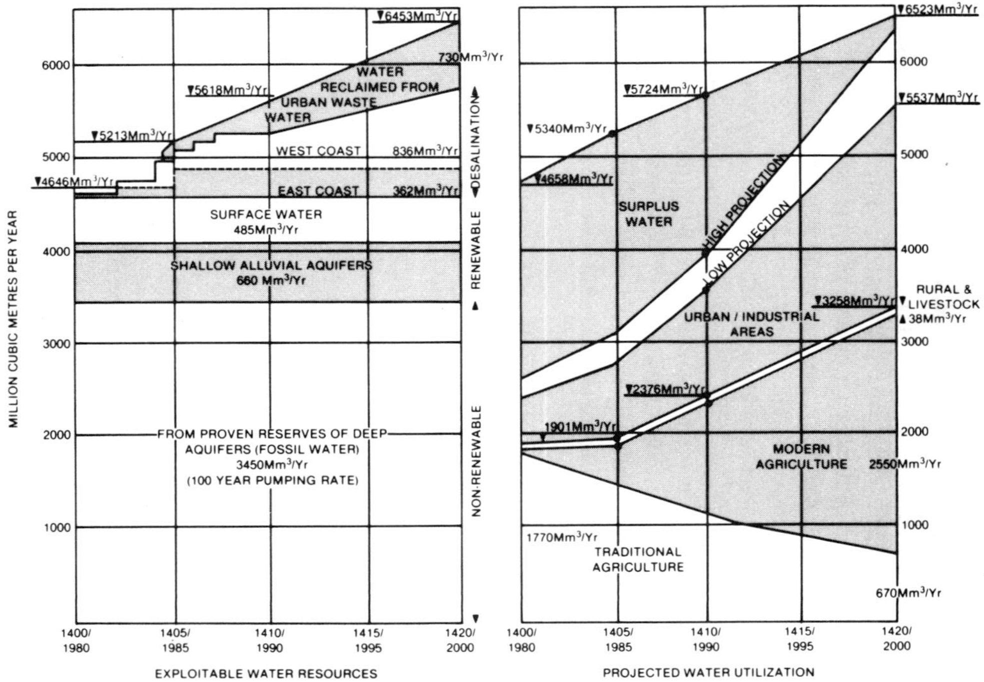

Source: Kingdom of Saudi Arabia, *Third Development Plan, 1400-1405/1980-1985*, Chapter 4.

the Kingdom's known conventional water sources, as compared to an anticipated 25 per cent from desalinated water. As of 1980, water desalination capacity from 14 operations plants was 65.4 million cubic metres per year. Six additional plants were under construction and scheduled for completion by 1983, bringing the total installed capacity to 523 million cubic metres per year. Intentions are for the interconnection of desalination plants in a network to provide maximum efficiency and flexibility in emergency situations. But this means concentration of large industrial areas; major users of water are likely, therefore, to be concentrated near the coast, where water will be readily available. And to cut cost, water will not usually be supplied to new industries located inland, away from the desalination plants.

Of all the non-conventional methods for supplying water, desalination has now attained wide usage in Kuwait, Oman, Saudi Arabia and even in Hong Kong. It remains, however, a very expensive source of water supply, estimated to cost about $1.00 per cubic metre based on an energy cost of $80 per ton. Three desalination plants are in operation in Jeddah supplementing groundwater sources. The third facility was completed in 1979, adding 5.2 million litres capacity to the 4 million litres prior capacity in existence. A fourth plant (Jeddah IV) is planned for 1983. Although this type of water is too expensive for irrigation, its availability will tend to free other sources of water for agricultural use.

As the process of industrialization progresses, the demand for water will intensify even if agricultural requirements could be adequately supplied from brackish sources. An estimated population in Jubail Industrial City in 1980 of 50,000 is projected to triple within seven years. To meet both domestic and industrial needs, large-scale desalination plants have been planned as part of both the Jubail and Yanbu industrial projects. The project at Jubail is expected to produce 35 million gallons of water a day when it is in full production. This capacity is expected to expand in the future.

Large-scale desalination plants are power consuming, but they also have electricity as a by-product. Since the primary power source of these plants is gas, which is currently in abundance in the Kingdom, cost of producing water is not yet a pressing economic problem. However, to the extent that a plausible consequence of the industrialization programmes at Jubail and Yanbu is the elimination of free gas supply, the cost of desalinated water will become real sooner or later. It is hoped that, by then, the antarctic iceberg scheme is no more a dream but a practical reality.

Groundwater and limited rainfall constitute the primary water supply for most inland areas at this time, and these sources will be developed as rapidly as possible to meet growing needs without jeopardizing the resource base. Major projects in this area include drilling of new wells, repair and replacement of old wells, expanded and upgraded distribution networks, and construction of dams.

The spectacular population growth in Riyadh has caused greatly increased demand for water supply. The 1980 estimated capacity of the system of 265 to 355 thousand cubic metres/day was to double by 1987. With existing groundwater sources near Riyadh nearing depletion, the largest water development project in the Kingdom's history was initiated to import 200,000 million cubic metres/day from the Wasia aquifer well field near Khurais and up to 660,000 million cubic metres/day from the desalination complex at Jubail. Rural area water supply during the Second Plan period was increased by the construction of 237 new municipal water-supply projects and the expansion of over 150 potable water systems. During 1975-80, 28 dams were added, bringing the total completed to 41. An additional five dams were still under construction at the end of the Second Plan.

Better water-resource management and conservation will also increase the available water supply. Increased public awareness of the importance of water is necessary for maximum effectiveness of this part of water resource development, and programmes will be developed on a community level to involve all citizens in the effort to use water efficiently. Simultaneously, studies and research programmes will be undertaken to provide the necessary information for further development of groundwater supplies. A national water plan is to be completed before 1985 in order to organize the activities of the various agencies of the government dealing with water supply as well as the water-consuming private sector. This water plan should increase the efficiency of decisions relating to water policy by co-ordinating the activities of the Ministry of Agriculture and Water, the Municipalities Department of the Ministry of Interior, and the Water Desalination Organization. The Ministry of Agriculture and Water (MOAW) has primary responsibility for management of the Kingdom's water resources. In addition to supervising the national water policy and development, the MOAW has been directly involved in supplying water to most of Saudi Arabia's urban areas and to many industrial users. In some localities the Municipalities Department of the Ministry of Interior has responsibility for supplying water, while in other towns water is supplied by both the MOAW and the Municipalities Department. The third agency involved in water-resource development is the Water Desalination Organization (WDO). Formerly a part of the MOAW, the WDO is now a public corporation responsible for supplying desalinated seawater to urban areas and industrial users in coastal regions.

Role of the Government

Regardless of political ideology, in any formalized national development strategy the central government necessarily assumes a critical role, setting goals and priorities, allocating resources, and co-ordinating economic activities. In an agricultural development programme such as Saudi Arabia's, the government is the only sectorwide entity able to perform certain vital functions. Improved inputs, such as better seed and fertilizers, modern machinery, and new techniques are frequently key elements in agricultural development. In an economy based on small landholdings and subsistence farming, the individual farmer is usually dependent on an outside entity to develop and produce those improved inputs, at least initially. Research programmes for the development of these inputs and the determination of their optimal relative proportions, as well as training and education programmes for farmers, require government participation in some form. Rapid development of sectorwide support systems, such as roads and distribution networks for seeds, fertilizer and fuel, also call for some centralized entity, usually the government.

Government Agricultural Policy and Incentives

The Saudi government has formalized its role in the development of agriculture by means of policies elucidated in the five-year Development Plans. Well-defined policies contained in the Second Plan[13] and maintained in the Third Plan are directed toward reducing the Kingdom's dependence on food imports and developing the rural areas. The policies provide for the government to: (1) encourage private enterprise in food production, processing and marketing while confining its own activities to those into which private enterpreneurs are unable or unwilling to enter; (2) aim at a reasonable balance between the economic and social rewards available from agricultural activities in the rural areas and the rewards available from other economic endeavours in the urban areas; and (3) recognize future as well as present needs and both consumer and producer requirements in implementing agricultural programmes. The government's strategy for effecting this national policy is based on the eight principles: (1) the best use of water resources, especially depletable resources; (2) maximum feasible self-sufficiency in the production of farm machinery, seed, fertilizer and other inputs; (3) development by the private sector, including co-operatives, of the facilities and services required for food processing and distribution; (4) the same guarantees for foreign investors in agriculture as for foreign investors in industry; (5) provision by the public sector of the physical infrastructure and the safety and animal-health services required by the private sector in agriculture; (6) expansion of the credit available from both government and private sources for the development of agriculture, including fisheries; (7) the provision, when studies show they are needed and feasible, of special economic incentives and programmes to stabilize prices or support farm incomes; and (8) protection of the environment from pollution associated with agricultural activities.[14]

In order that agricultural production increases at a rate consistent with national economic growth, the traditional smallholdings mode of farming ought to be changed. There are basically two methods, barring direct government participation, in which this can be done. First, the formation of co-operative farming societies could be intensified at both the production and marketing levels. The Saudi government is in a position to encourage such institutions which would serve to pool the resources of individual farmers and allow them easier accessibility to modern agricultural inputs. Provided that the problems commonly associated with co-operative organizations such as managerial bottlenecks are reduced, co-operative farming would enable traditional farmers to produce on economic-sized holdings, to buy agricultural inputs more cheaply, to use agricultural machinery more intensively and efficiently, and to acquire new techniques of production. In general, these institutions would stimulate the agricultural sector's adoption of more flexible and productive methods of production. Indeed, the potential which such institutions hold for effective use of water, the spread of new seeds, and acquisition of research results through agricultural extension services is enormous. Experience in most developing countries, however, tends to make one cautious when evaluating the impact of producer co-operative societies in the agricultural sector of Saudi Arabia. The land tenure system, the level of literacy of farmers, their traditional beliefs, and as already mentioned, the dedication of the management of the co-operative societies, all will determine how successful these organizations will be in practice.

An alternative method is to invite private firms or individual Saudis who have agricultural management training to enter into large-scale agricultural production. The success of this programme will initially depend on the availability of easy agricultural credits. As will be examined in the next section, this is not likely to pose much problem. More importantly, however, sufficient incentives must be available in terms of guaranteed prices, regular supply of agricultural inputs at subsidized prices, and improved agricultural infrastructure, so that private firms and individuals are assured of reasonable returns on their investments. It will probably be no easy task to attract Saudi agriculturalists into this sector of the economy considering the relatively high wages/incomes in alternative activities in the Kingdom which are open to them and the attractiveness of city life. Even with regard to private firms, the alternative to investment in the agricultural sector (for example, real estate) might be too lucrative to permit them to shift scarce manpower and managerial resources to agricultural production. Indeed, 'western agribusiness concerns are finding that Saudi Arabia is a difficult market to penetrate . . . [It does not lend] itself to the quick-in-quick-out approach'.[15] It is not surprising that the Ministry of Agriculture and Water has found disappointing the level of the response from firms to the opportunities which have been created by the government in this sector.

Nevertheless, the government continues to expand these opportunities to compensate for not only the high cost of agricultural production, but also for the initial cost of research into soil quality, water resources, and adaptability of crops and plants to climatic variations. In line with the objectives of its agricultural policy, the Saudi government has involved itself in several broad areas which directly or indirectly will tend to influence agricultural production in the country. These include: comprehensive water planning and irrigation; a programme to provide physical infrastructure to enhance agricultural production; subsidy of machinery, fertilizer, seeds and other agricultural inputs and price support; provision of soft credit through the Agricultural Credit Bank; and finally, research and agricultural education.

In the late 1970s, a reorganization of the Ministry of Agriculture and Water took place, considerably strengthening the organization.[16] New departments in animal resources, subsidies, statistical studies and agricultural development were created and top positions were filled by Saudi graduates in agriculture and economics. Additionally, activities of the Ministry have been decentralized; the Kingdom has been divided into 14 agricultural zones, each headed by a director with a substantial degree of autonomy over his area. Indeed, many agricultural economists no longer sit only behind the desk, but are doing field work. Although it is too early to evaluate the impact of this reorganization on the agricultural sector, it is hoped that the intended flexibility in the administrative machinery of agricultural production will be achieved so that the Ministry's incentives and direction for the private sector are not hampered by rigidities.

In terms of giving direction to the development of agriculture, the government, 'after considering the strategic importance of crops and livestock production, the need for water conservation, the relative value of crops in total agricultural production and potentials for rapid increase in yield',[17] has identified a number of farming activities which should receive special emphasis. The crops targeted for increased production over the 1980-5 period are wheat, potatoes, dairy products and vegetables, as well as animal forage.

With respect to physical infrastructure, apart from providing free water to Saudi farmers through several irrigation schemes, the government's investment in rural road construction, begun in the First Plan, expanded in the Second, and continued in the Third, will no doubt go a long way to reduce those infrastructure constraints which might be posed for agricultural production and marketing. For example, the new asphalt roads which have been constructed in the countryside have allowed farmers in the Kingdom to export to neighbouring Arab markets, such as Abu Dhabi, Dubai, Iraq, Jordan, Kuwait and Syria, and thus take advantage of facilities provided by the Arab common market, including exemption of agricultural exports from customs duties.[18]

While the use of fertilizers is increasing, much greater quantities are needed in order to increase agricultural production to meet its potential. In 1978 optimal use of fertilizers on lands irrigated would have required 25,000 to 30,000 tons of nitrogen and similar amounts of phosphates, while in 1974 the actual amount of these chemicals used was about 11,000 tons each.[19] Consequently, in terms of economic efficiency, there have been fertilizer shortages in the Kingdom despite the government subsidies on this important agricultural input. The shortages, on the other hand, have been due to the inability of distribution to respond effectively to needs. The expanded governmental efforts to establish petrochemical industries (including fertilizers) in the Kingdom, coupled with the reorganization of the Agriculture Ministry may serve to lessen the distribution bottlenecks. Moreover, the formation of effective co-operative societies could streamline distribution channels.

Government incentives are listed in Table 3.4. It is seen that apart from subsidies on inputs, there are substantial supports on major agricultural outputs. The latter tends to supplement the former by providing the necessary incentives for resources to shift from other sectors and abroad to the agricultural sector. The subsidy programme is regarded by Saudi policy-makers as essentially a short-term measure which should be discontinued in the future. However, there are plans to study the feasibility of additional subsidies on date production and marketing operations, fruit and vegetable processing and the like. Thus, agricultural subsidies appear to be fairly deeply entrenched. As with the criticism often levelled against the infant industry argument of tariffs, once the subsidies become a part of the system, it is difficult to remove them. It may be expected, therefore, that the short-run effects of price distortion and resource misallocation of subsidies will persist for a considerable period. Yet if the subsidies are perceived as a means of achieving the diversification objectives of the country, then these distortions may be an acceptable price to pay for a balanced growth.

Agricultural Credit[20]

Two government activities aimed at increasing agricultural output are so important that they deserve more extensive discussion: first is agricultural credit and secondly, research and agricultural education.

The Agricultural Development Bank (ADB), established to aid in the development of that sector, was founded in 1965; the institution is now well established with a respectable operating history. By 1980 it had branches in 11 cities, operating 52 local offices. The Bank extends three types of loans: (1) short-term loans for inputs on a seasonal basis, (2) medium-term credits for equipment, and (3) longer-term loans for the purchase and improvement of land. Starting from a modest first year operation of 714 loans totalling SR 4.4 million, ADB made 20,298 loans amounting to SR 585.688 million in 1978. Table 3.5 gives the details of the composition of loans given by the Agricultural Development Bank. It will be noted that the medium-term loans account for no less than 60 per cent of total credits extended in 1966/7 and as high as 93 per cent in 1977/8; the regional distribution has been relatively wide, although the northern agricultural sites Al-Jauf and Tabuk, and Al-Kharj in the east have only recently begun to participate in the lending.

The primary objective of the Bank is to encourage investment in the agricultural sector, with the intention of attaining an appropriate degree of self-sufficiency. Operations are to be decentralized and extended on a regional basis so that the availability of loans will be increased. The

Third Development Plan will place special emphasis on developing the productive sectors. Programmes in that Plan call for disbursing SR 5 billion in loans and SR 2.5 billion in subsidies to the private agricultural sector during the period 1980-5.[21] An effort will be made to improve the quality of the loans while, at the same time, reducing the complexity of borrowing money from the Bank. In the Third Development Plan, national economic and social benefits will be the criteria for loans as opposed to the previous policy of relying solely on financial evaluations.

Table 3.4: Incentives for Agricultural Production

Type	Amount	Source[a]
Production input		
Fertilizer	50% of cost	MOAW
Animal feed	50% of cost	SAAB
Potato seed	5 tons free, SR 1,000/ton thereafter up to 15 tons	MOAW
Machinery and equipment		
Poultry equipment	30% of cost	SAAB
Dairy equipment	30% of cost	SAAB
Engines and pumps	50% of cost	SAAB
Fish trawlers	variable	SAAB
Transportation		
Air transport of cows	100% of cost	SAAB
Output		
Wheat	SR 3.50/kg[b]	GSFMO
Rice	SR 0.30/kg	MOAW
Corn	SR 0.25/kg	MOAW
Millet/barley	SR 0.15/kg	MOAW
Dates	SR 0.25/kg	MOAW
Date palms planted	SR 50.00/tree	MOAW
Agricultural credit		
All types	variable conditions	SAAB
Agro-industrial credit		
All types	variable conditions	SIDF
Land acquisition		
Land distribution	free	MOAW

Notes: a. MOAW = Ministry of Agriculture and Water; SAAB = Saudi Arabian Agricultural Bank; GSFMO = Grain Silos and Flour Mills Organization; SIDF = Saudi Arabian Industrial Development Fund. b. Purchase price (1978/9).
Source: Kingdom of Saudi Arabia, *Third Development Plan, 1400-1405/1980-1985*, Chapter 4.

Individual farmers, agricultural co-operatives and nomadic herdsmen are all eligible for loans. Credit is also readily available for farmers

Table 3.5: New Loans Granted by the Agricultural Bank by Branch, Type and Average Value Per Loan in Selected Years, 1966-78 (value in SR thousands)

Branch	1966/7			1968/9			1970/1			1972/3		
Type	No.	Value	Average	No.	Value	Average	No.	Value	Average	No.	Value	Average
Total	3,149	13,220	4.2	3,674	13,877	3.8	4,381	16,628	3.8	4,477	19,593	4.4
Short-term	885	1,082	4.6	1,227	1,676	1.4	1,741	2,575	1.5	1,537	2,916	1.9
Medium-term	2,264	12,100	5.3	2,447	12,201	5.0	2,640	14,052	5.3	2,940	16,677	5.7
Abha	527	1,539	2.9	893	2,566	2.9	1,323	3,201	2.4	1,268	4,795	3.8
Short-term	2	20	10.0	118	84	0.7	580	580	1.0	300	514	1.7
Medium-term	525	1,519	2.9	775	2,482	3.2	743	2,621	3.5	968	4,281	4.4
Al-Jawf	–	–	–	–	–	–	–	–	–	–	–	–
Short-term	–	–	–	–	–	–	–	–	–	–	–	–
Medium-term	–	–	–	–	–	–	–	–	–	–	–	–
Buraidah	889	2,945	3.3	771	3,102	4.0	688	3,221	4.7	379	2,427	6.4
Short-term	347	246	0.7	370	444	1.2	345	575	1.7	189	659	3.5
Medium-term	542	2,699	5.0	401	2,658	6.6	343	2,646	7.7	190	1,768	9.3
Hail	–	–	–	–	–	–	–	–	–	266	904	3.4
Short-term	–	–	–	–	–	–	–	–	–	85	65	0.8
Medium-term	–	–	–	–	–	–	–	–	–	181	839	4.6
Hafuf	186	1,153	6.2	227	1,180	5.2	306	1,497	4.9	309	1,834	5.9
Short-term	68	327	4.8	114	269	2.3	164	433	2.6	154	451	2.9
Medium-term	118	826	7.0	113	911	8.1	142	1,064	7.5	155	1,383	8.9
Jeddah	657	2,845	4.3	960	3,222	3.4	914	2,623	2.9	1,080	2,733	2.5
Short-term	258	251	1.0	362	581	1.6	301	425	1.4	478	569	1.2
Medium-term	399	2,594	6.5	598	2,641	4.4	613	2,198	3.6	602	2,164	3.6

Table 3.5: (continued)

Branch	1966/7			1968/9			1970/1			1972/3		
Type	No.	Value	Average	No.	Value	Average	No.	Value	Average	No.	Value	Average
Jizan	–	–	–	–	–	–	–	–	–	–	–	–
Short-term	–	–	–	–	–	–	–	–	–	–	–	–
Medium-term	–	–	–	–	–	–	–	–	–	–	–	–
Medina	–	–	–	–	–	–	328	1,689	5.1	359	2,365	6.6
Short-term	–	–	–	–	–	–	39	96	2.5	48	207	4.3
Medium-term	–	–	–	–	–	–	289	1,593	5.5	311	2,158	6.9
Riyadh	890	4,811	5.4	823	3,807	4.6	822	4,395	5.3	816	4,534	5.9
Short-term	210	238	1.1	263	299	1.1	312	466	1.5	283	451	1.6
Medium-term	680	4,573[a]	6.7	560	3,508	6.3	510	3,929	7.7	533	4,083	7.7
Tabuk	–	–	–	–	–	–	–	–	–	–	–	–
Short-term	–	–	–	–	–	–	–	–	–	–	–	–
Medium-term	–	–	–	–	–	–	–	–	–	–	–	–
Al-Kharj	–	–	–	–	–	–	–	–	–	–	–	–
Short-term	–	–	–	–	–	–	–	–	–	–	–	–
Medium-term	–	–	–	–	–	–	–	–	–	–	–	–

Table 3.5: (continued)

Branch Type	1974/5 No.	1974/5 Value	1974/5 Average	1976/7 No.	1976/7 Value	1976/7 Average	1977/8 No.	1977/8 Value	1977/8 Average
Total	16,251	145,506	8.9	21,377	489,838	22.9	20,298	585,668	28.9
Short-term	3,835	7,182	1.9	3,633	17,288	4.8	3,572	43,713	12.2
Medium-term	12,416	138,324	11.1	17,744	472,550	26.6	16,726	541,955	32.4
Abha	2,881	10,332	3.6	2,647	26,025	9.8	2,865	42,329	14.8
Short-term	824	1,523	1.8	4	85	21.3	11	32	2.9
Medium-term	2,057	8,809	4.3	2,643	25,940	9.8	2,854	42,297	14.8
Al-Jawf	765	8,463	11.1	689	16,175	23.5	560	17,744	31.7
Short-term	30	36	1.2	5	8	1.6	10	17	1.7
Medium-term	735	8,427	11.5	684	16,167	23.6	550	17,727	32.2
Buraidah	2,623	37,120	14.2	2,775	85,388	30.8	2,126	85,735	40.3
Short-term	708	1,529	2.2	300	581	1.9	180	1,040	5.8
Medium-term	1,915	35,591	18.6	2,475	84,807	34.3	1,946	84,695	43.5
Hail	2,437	7,544	3.1	1,618	19,196	11.9	1,745	26,622	15.3
Short-term	757	520	0.7	296	355	1.2	352	777	18.2
Medium-term	1,680	7,024	4.2	1,322	18,841	14.3	1,393	25,845	18.6
Hafuf	1,857	18,750	10.1	1,613	57,679	35.8	1,135	50,093	44.1
Short-term	496	1,446	2.9	377	2,348	6.2	371	3,205	8.6
Medium-term	1,361	17,304	12.7	1,236	55,331	44.8	764	46,888	61.4
Jeddah	2,043	20,124	9.9	4,142	84,942	20.5	4,629	111,919	24.2
Short-term	652	1,275	2.0	1,075	8,406	7.8	778	32,252	41.5
Medium-term	1,391	18,849	13.6	3,067	76,536	25.0	3,851	79,667	20.7

Table 3.5: (continued)

Branch	1974/5			1976/7			1977/8		
Type	No.	Value	Average	No.	Value	Average	No.	Value	Average
Jizan	–	–	–	1,493	12,241	8.2	1,688	14,694	8.7
Short-term	–	–	–	1,076	2,152	2.0	1,287	2,574	2.0
Medium-term	–	–	–	417	10,089	24.2	401	12,120	30.2
Medina	1,118	9,986	8.9	1,865	43,341	23.2	2,011	57,684	28.7
Short-term	46	413	9.0	13	538	41.4	25	278	11.1
Medium-term	1,072	9,573	8.0	1,852	42,803	23.1	1,986	57,406	28.9
Riyadh	2,527	33,186	13.1	3,432	109,829	32.0	1,407	68,742	48.9
Short-term	322	440	1.4	359	2,285	6.4	195	910	4.7
Medium-term	2,205	32,746	14.9	3,073	107,544	35.0	1,212	67,832	56.0
Tabuk	–	–	–	492	8,691	17.7	375	12,553	33.5
Short-term	–	–	–	14	135	9.6	26	163	6.3
Medium-term	–	–	–	478	8,556	17.9	349	12,390	35.5
Al-Kharj	–	–	–	611	26,331	43.1	1,757	97,553	55.5
Short-term	–	–	–	114	396	3.5	337	2,465	7.3
Medium-term	–	–	–	497	25,935	52.2	1,420	95,088	67.0

Note: a. Includes long-term loans amounting to SR 109.7 thousand granted by Riyadh branch.
Sources: SAMA, *Statistical Summary*, 2nd issue (1977), pp. 38-9 and *Annual Report, 1979 (1399)*, pp. 155-6.

receiving land under the barren-land distribution programme, persons establishing dairy enterprises, and for expansion of Gulf and Red Sea fisheries. As Table 3.6 indicates, funds were also available for development of such agricultural marketing and processing enterprises as cold storage plants, processing plants for the dairy industry as well as numerous other products, leather tanning and preserving, and mixing of poultry feed. Finally, the Bank serves as the fiscal agent in the government's agricultural subsidy programme.[22]

Table 3.6: Planned Loan Finance of the Agricultural Bank (SR millions)

	1975/6	1976/7	1977/8	1978/9	1979/80	Plan total
(1) Agricultural production						
Agricultural production requirements	64.4	74.1	84.2	96.4	108.2	427.4
Development of virgin land	14.4	14.4	14.4	14.4	14.4	72.0
Development of apiary industry	0.3	0.3	0.3	0.3	0.3	1.3
Nomadic herdsmen	2.5	3.0	3.5	4.0	4.5	17.5
Development of fisheries	2.0	2.0	2.0	2.0	2.0	10.0
	83.6	93.8	104.4	117.1	129.4	528.2
(2) Marketing and Processing						
Cold-storage plants	5.0	5.0	5.0	5.0	5.0	25.0
Processing plants	5.0	5.0	5.0	5.0	5.0	25.0
Poultry and animal feed plants	3.0	3.0	3.0	3.0	3.0	15.0
Dairy farms, milk processing and collection centres	15.0	15.0	15.0	15.0	15.0	75.0
	28.0	28.0	28.0	28.0	28.0	140.0
Total (1) + (2)	111.6	121.8	132.4	145.1	157.4	668.2

Source: *Second Plan*, p. 137.

Research and Education

It has been noted already that technological transformation is a prerequisite for an agricultural revolution in the Kingdom. This will be possible only if intensive research is undertaken to gather knowledge of soil characteristics, water distribution, pests, and the feasibility of adapting modern technology to Saudi conditions. Additionally, more agricultural graduates are needed, and other levels of manpower require training to translate the targets of the Ministry of Agriculture and Water into reality. Hence the critical nature of research and agriculture education in the Saudi development programmes for this sector.

Table 3.7: Agricultural Research Centres and Subjects

Centre	Subjects
Research stations Hafuf	Dairy, cattle, sheep; irrigation, reuse of drainage water; forage, rice; agro-climatology
Qatif	Poultry, grapes, dates, melons, vegetables
Unayzah	Citrus, vegetables, cereals, dates, grapes, olives
Jizan (Hakmah)	Cereals, vegetables, cotton, papaya; irrigation
Dirab	Cereals; dairy, horse breeding, goats
Al-Kharj	Cereals, vegetables, grapes, melons, citrus; irrigation
Jeddah	Locust and insect control
Haddah Asham[a]	Tropical and citrus fruit, vegetables
Baljarshi[a]	Deciduous fruit; irrigation
Bishah[a]	Citrus, dates, grapes, cereals
Medina	Poultry, dairy, cattle
Marine development (Jeddah)	Fish movement and classification; fishing; training
Range development (Arar)	Water spreading; extension, training; fodder storing
Central Research Laboratory (Riyadh)	Soil and water analysis; plant protection; animal disease
Range and Forest station (Taif)	Water spreading; extension, training; fodder storing

Note: a. Functioning as nurseries and demonstration farms but no organized research as of 1974/5.
Source: *Second Plan*, Table IV-11, p. 133.

Training centres established by the Ministry to offer services to Saudi farmers are listed in Table 3.7. It is apparent that the activities of the agricultural research stations cover a wide range and go hand in hand with students returning from overseas with agriculture-related degrees and training. Together they will provide a human resource base and offer needed skills to implement domestic development efforts.

Conclusion

Although the problems facing rapid development in the agricultural sector of the Saudi economy are many, and in some cases formidable, the government of Saudi Arabia has taken measures to support a high degree of success in this sector. A primary objective has been to increase agricultural production so that real farm incomes would reverse their recent decline and to raise the availability of domestic foodstuffs; in turn, the Kingdom's dependence on imports of food could be diminished. Agricultural development is part of the diversification policy of the government and in line with a push toward balanced sectoral growth. Water remains the predominant constraint on both farm and livestock production. The shortage of skilled agricultural technicians and the small size of landholdings pose economic problems.

Measures which the government has taken to make agricultural activities attractive include provision of inputs at low prices, output subsidies, agricultural credit, extension services, and training and research programmes, the goal of which is to find solutions to the bottlenecks confronting the indigenous farmer and rancher and potential foreign entrepreneurs. With the reorganization of the Ministry of Agriculture and Water, coupled with adequate financial outlays and determination on the part of Saudi officials, agriculture should play an increasing role in Saudi economic development in the future.

Notes

1. Richard Nyrop *et al.*, *Area Handbook for Saudi Arabia*, 3rd edn (Washington, DC, American University, Foreign Area Studies, 1977), p. 287.

2. Chase World Information Corporation, *Mideast Markets*, 14 March 1977, p. 11. (Hereafter cited as *Mideast Markets*.)

3. The figures on labour-force participation in the agricultural sector are obtained and/or computed from the Kingdom of Saudi Arabia, Ministry of Planning, *Second Development Plan*, Table III-2, p. 68 (hereafter cited as *Second Plan*), and from the Kingdom of Saudi Arabia, *Third Development Plan, 1400-1405/1980-1985* (hereafter cited as *Third Plan*).

4. The evaluation of the contribution of the agricultural sector to Saudi economic development during this period is contained in Chapter 5. During the decade 1963-72, value added by agriculture increased only 1.6 per cent annually at constant prices. The 1970-5 span of the First Plan saw agricultural output rise at an annual average rate of 5 per cent, which was below the 4.6 per cent target stated in the plan.

5. Richard Nyrop, *Area Handbook*, points out that estimates of the existence of tenant farming vary widely, ranging from 10 per cent to more than two-thirds of all farmers. He concludes that the actual percentage is somewhere between those two extremes, with no reliable data on whether tenant farmers constituted a minority or majority of the farming population.

6. *Mideast Markets*, 11 April 1977, p. 3.

7. For further discussion of the Saudi land tenure system, see Richard Nyrop *et al.*, *Area Handbook*, Chapter 13.

8. A dunum = 1,000 m^2 (0.1 hectare).

9. R. Nyrop, *Area Handbook*, p. 287.

10. Ibid., pp. 287-8.

11. Even the publication by the Ministry of Information, *The Kingdom of Saudi Arabia: Facts and Figures – Agriculture and Water* does not make mention of marketing, but the *Second Plan* refers to it briefly, p. 134.

12. The figures on dams, wells and desalination plants used in the analysis in this section are obtained from *Second Plan*, Chapters IV-A and IV-B and *Third Plan*, Chapter 4.

13. *Second Plan*, p. 124.

14. Agricultural targets and water-resources development in the Third Plan will be outlined in Chapter 7.

15. *Mideast Markets*, 11 April 1977, p. 3.

16. Ibid.

17. *Second Plan*, pp. 130-1.

18. *Mideast Markets*, 14 March 1977, p. 11.

19. *Second Plan*, p. 121.

20. For further analysis of the Agricultural Development Bank, also known as the Saudi Arabian Agricultural Bank (SAAB), see Chapter 9.

21. See Table 9.3 for a listing of the composition of loans by purpose. In the Second Plan, the Bank projected 64 per cent of the value of its total lending for such agricultural production needs. *Third Plan*, Chapter 4.

22. *Second Plan*, p. 136.

4 INDUSTRIALIZATION: BRIGHT HOPES AND OBSTACLES

Rationale for Industrialization

While the industrial sector may be the most dynamic sector in the economy, the road to industrialization is very long indeed and involves a highly complex process.[1] This process essentially entails changing the existing economic structure into one of greater efficiency and diversified modes of output. The transformation covers a far wider scope than simply establishing more factories and plants, for industrialization remains an input in the development process rather than a goal in itself. Industrialization involves increased capital equipment and improved productivity per worker, as well as expansion in the variety of goods produced; it also includes the development of mining and electric power, because of their significant contribution in the early stages of industrial growth in developing countries such as Saudi Arabia. An overall economic-development strategy designed for the particular country in question should enable the industrial sector to innovate, not only as a means of increasing output or national income, but also as a means of introducing modern technology and changing attitudes towards development.[2] Saudi Arabia has been, and will continue to be, affected by (1) the availability of capital, (2) the availability of cheap energy,[3] (3) diversification as a means of offsetting a wasting asset, and (4) industrial ramifications of the participation agreements.[4] With respect to these conditions, oil and natural gas, so abundant in the Kingdom, will act as generators of capital today and simultaneously offer the physical base for viable industry in the future. Moreover, should petroleum lose its dominant place in energy consumption, as it inevitably will, the amassed wealth could allow continuation of large-scale financing of industrial development. It must be pointed out, however, that industrialization becomes critical in order to cushion the eventual end of governmental revenue derived from these wasting and non-renewable hydrocarbon assets.

Industrial Strategy and Policy in the Kingdom

The primary objective of the country's programme of industrialization is to lessen the overwhelming dependence of the economy upon the export of crude oil, in a word, diversification. Thus, the strategy plotted for the expansion of this sector as summarized briefly in the following pages underpins Saudi industrial policy and targets.

In its desire to achieve the maximum economic and social benefits for Saudi nationals from industrial development, and in order to familiarize the ministries, government departments and the business community within and outside the Kingdom with the basic policy of the government regarding industrial development, eleven main principles of the industrial development policy of the Kingdom were drawn up and announced in 1974.[5] They included:

(1) The government seeks to encourage and expand manufacturing industries, including agro-industries, which will contribute to an increase of national income, a raising of the standard of living, increased employment, and/or to diversification of the country's economy. Diversification should not only increase the national income, but should reduce the impact of external economic disturbances on the Kingdom. Moreover, widening employment opportunities will be needed as Saudi citizens acquire broader skills and specialities of training.

(2) The Saudi economy is based on an open and generally free enterprise system; competition between the private commercial and industrial enterprises is viewed positively. Hence, the government conclusion is that the objectives of industrial development may be more effectively attained if, in the long term, the business community bears the responsibility of implementing industrial projects. Following in this pattern, to those businessmen prepared to assume the risks of success or failure, the government is willing to extend full support during all stages of preparation, establishment and operation of industrial projects deemed beneficial for the country. The government is also ready to supplement the efforts of the private sector by establishing, financing and participating in the management of the large industrial projects requiring wide technical experience and which the private sector cannot undertake alone – in short, mixed ventures.

(3) As noted earlier, competition is a cornerstone of Saudi industrial policy; it is perceived as serving the interests of local consumers by influencing the business community in the industrial field towards beneficial manufacturing and market-oriented projects. Moreover,

competition is considered the most effective means for selecting the investment schemes which suit the market requirements, for encouraging low-cost production, and for fixing fair prices for both consumer and producer. However, the government will not allow excessive, harmful foreign competition, such as dumping.

(4) The government envisages an informational function for itself by ensuring that those businessmen prepared to launch or participate in industrial ventures be apprised of results of industrial and feasibility studies and other relevant data required for identification, implementation, and successful operation of such projects. Existing industrial establishments also have access to the services available in the management and technical fields as provided by the government.

(5) For those industrial projects having potential benefits for the country's economy and evidencing sound planning and management, the government has declared a policy of financial incentives. The same incentives are to be granted to all projects meeting the planning and management guidelines within the industrial sector, among them being: (a) the extension of loans and participation in equity capital under encouraging conditions; (b) aid to businessmen in the formation and organization of new industrial companies; (c) the provision of assistance in selecting of industrial projects, as well as in the preparation of economic feasibility studies and evaluation; (d) technical and financial, i.e. operational, assistance; (e) customs duties exemption on imported equipment and primary materials; (f) the exemption from taxes on the company's profit of the share of the foreign partners, as provided in the Foreign Capital Investment Statute; (g) preference to be given to local producers in government purchases; (h) protective customs tariffs may be imposed on competing imports; (i) the provision of space or siting in industrial areas; (j) subsidies for training Saudi employees;[6] and (k) assistance in exportation of the products.

(6) With the goal in mind of reducing the number of failures among industrial ventures and avoiding excessive duplication or redundancy in projects, the government has instituted a programme of licensing of industrial projects which exceed a specified size of invested capital, employment or production capacity. Refusal of an application for licence should be made only for practical considerations relating to the supreme national interest of the overall economy.

(7) Some industrial projects by the nature of their size and scope can only be undertaken by the public sector. In such instances and in those cases where there is government participation in the capital of private projects to supplement the investment of the private sector, it is

government policy eventually to sell the share it owns to the general public if this is determined to serve the nation's interest. This does not apply to those industries falling under the classification as relevant to the national security.

If such an industrial project exhibits signs of failure due to an inability of private businessmen to operate it, the government can assume management temporarily until the private sector can reassume the responsibility. Above all, the government sees itself as a partner, not a competitor, to the producers in the private sector.

(8) Further, official policy is to avoid imposition of quantitative restriction or price controls. Restrictions may be utilized in those cases where competition cannot have an effective role, as, for example, commodities which by their nature are characterized by monopoly.

(9) In the industrial field, the private sector can choose, use, and manage the economic resources, including industrial labour, unless prohibited by statutes in force. The objective is to raise the productive efficiency of industry to the maximum.

(10) Both foreign capital and know-how are welcome to participate in the industrial development projects in co-operation with Saudi businessmen. Among the benefits accruing to the industrial development of Saudi Arabia aside from the entry of foreign capital are the accompanying administrative, technical and international marketing capabilities. The Saudi government offers foreign investors assurances that there will be no restrictions imposed on the entry and exit of money to and from the Kingdom; this policy is based on the respect of private ownership in the Islamic Law (Shari'a).

(11) Finally, the government undertakes the provision of public utilities and other basic arrangements required for the establishment of economically feasible industries. Since industry is but one sector within the economy, its development will be part and parcel of the expansion of all the sectors. Thus, larger quantities of local resources will be available for inputs into industrial production while simultaneously diversifying the economy.

The Kingdom of Saudi Arabia has chosen to emphasize the development of those industries in which it has a long-run comparative advantage.[7] In other words, this emphasis will be directed towards the development of hydrocarbon-based industries due to the extensive supply of raw materials related to these industries, mainly natural gas and crude petroleum. Import substitution of certain goods for which there exists economic justification is a second desired goal of the

Kingdom's industrial policy. In some instances, the overall process of economic development as well as the growth in domestic markets have made it feasible to establish new industries on the basis of this increased demand.

'The rationale behind (the development of) hydrocarbon-based industries is to fully utilize the abundant reserves of petroleum and gas as feedstock and energy'.[8] These industries include the establishment of four ethylene equivalent petrochemical complexes, several fertilizer plants, a steel plant, as well as an aluminium smelter. Furthermore, a system of secondary and support facilities is planned, including refineries, and petroleum and gas-gathering and distribution systems. In this respect the Royal Commission for the Jubail and Yanbu Industrial Complexes was established for the sole purpose of implementing planned projects, and to expedite the establishment of the necessary infrastructural facilities.[9]

In the area of non-hydrocarbon industries, the principal goal is to widen the industrial base by producing 'an increasing range of food, chemical, metallic and non-metallic products for which the Kingdom is at present dependent mostly on imports. The main criteria are efficiency and economic viability'.[10] During the period defined by the Second Development Plan (1975-80), the growth rate of the non-hydrocarbon industries was 15.4 per cent – slightly higher than the 14 per cent figure that was projected. For the Third Plan (1980-5) a rate of 6.2 per cent growth is targeted.[11] This decline is a result of the low rate of employment growth that is anticipated for the 1980-5 span as well as an expected disappearance of favourable effects from employment shifts. As reflected in Table 4.1, the quite small contribution of non-oil manufacturing activity to the GDP minimizes the overall impact of the percentage attributable to the sector.

Further objectives for the non-oil manufacturing sector are: (1) increasing the economy's capacity to produce at competitive costs a wide range of products for domestic as well as for export markets; (2) exploiting industrially the substantial comparative advantages arising from low-cost energy, raw materials from hydrocarbon-related industry, minerals, and agricultural and fishing resources; (3) expanding the country's access to modern technology; (4) encouraging further utilization of capacity in the private manufacturing sector's capacity; (5) securing regional-balanced development of industry; (6) raising productivity through closer attention to the optimal size of plants; (7) reducing reliance on expatriate labour by national skill-creation through the development of general and technical education and on-the-job training of citizens; and (8) promoting linkages between and among industries.[12]

Table 4.1: The Share of Manufacturing in GDP, 1968/9-1977/8

Year	Oil sector as percentage of GDP	Manufacturing[a] as percentage of GDP	Non-oil manufacturing as percentage of GDP	Non-oil manufacturing as percentage of non-oil GDP
1968/9	50.9	8.8	2.4	4.9
1969/70	53.7	9.6	2.5	5.4
1970/1	56.6	9.2	2.4	5.5
1971/2	59.8	8.1	2.4	6.0
1972/3	56.6	7.2	2.2	5.7
1973/4	57.4	6.6	2.1	5.5
1974/5[b]	54.6	6.4	2.3	5.4
1975/6[b]	50.8	6.3	2.4	5.1
1976/7[b]	50.1	6.2	2.4	5.2
1977/8[c]	46.9	6.4	2.6	5.3

Notes: a. Includes petroleum refining. b. Revised. c. Preliminary.
Sources: Computed on the basis of GDP figures at constant 1970 prices in Central Department of Statistics, Ministry of Finance and National Economy, *National Accounts of Saudi Arabia, 1386/87 through 1393/94 AH (1966/67 through 1973/74)*, 10 March 1976; SAMA, *Statistical Summary*, 2nd issue (1977), Table 29, pp. 68-9 and *Annual Reports, 1977*, Table 29, p. 148 and *1979*, Table 30, p. 167.

All in all, the Saudi policy has been 'explicitly clear that private enterprise would be the main vehicle of industrial growth'.[13] In view of this position, the country has established a wide range of incentives and financial institutions, such as the Industrial Development Fund, for the purpose of securing private investment.[14] While the Ministry of Industry and Electricity is the principal agency for the general administration of industrial policies and licensing of new manufacturing utilities, the Industrial Studies and Development Centre (ISDC) acts as a special agency under the Ministry for the purpose of continuing studies of domestic industrial opportunities in non-hydrocarbon-based manufacturing. (Petromin is of course responsible for the major ventures in hydrocarbon-based manufacturing.) Private investment has been further encouraged by government subsidization of various factors of production and complementary resources. Through the provision of three major industrial estates in the nation[15] and the progressive development of the Jubail and Yanbu industrial projects, the necessary infrastructural facilities for rapid industrial development are being supplied.

Institutional Structure for the Promotion of Industrialization[16]

The cornerstones of the institutional structure for the encouragement of industrialization in Saudi Arabia are the Ministries of Planning and Industry. Within the framework of the various development plans, and more generally the overall development of the Kingdom, the Ministry of Planning determines the pace and direction of industrialization through budget allocations and development targets.

The implementation of industrial plans falls more under the supervision of the Ministry of Industry and Electricity. Its main functions are to ensure steady and balanced growth in the industrial sector as well as to secure the necessary climate for the promotion of domestic industries. Within the Ministry of Industry and Electricity the Deputy Minister for Industrial Affairs is in charge of the following departments.

(1) The Foreign Capital Investment Committee seeks to ensure that investments are intended for development projects and to prepare and administer investment regulations (see Chapter 12 for a detailed discussion of this Committee and the Foreign Capital Investment Code).
(2) The Industrial Protection and Encouragement Department administers the 'Regulations for Protection and Encouragement of National Industries', including franchise, subsidy and tariff privileges.
(3) The Industrial Estates Department supervises existing as well as future industrial estates in the country.
(4) The Industrial Licences Department reviews applications for industrial licences by potential investors.
(5) The Projects and Engineering Department provides technical and engineering services and supervision to the various departments and projects.

Another institution which has sought to promote industrialization in the Kingdom is the Industrial Studies and Development Centre (ISDC) mentioned earlier. Established by royal decree in 1967, the ISDC has since been engaged in industry-oriented research, policy formulation and planning. The Centre has been a major input into implementation of industrial projects through the provision of technical assistance. The work of this agency in providing feasibility studies and guidelines for the establishment of non-hydrocarbon-based industries in particular has proved invaluable to the encouragement of industrial development.

The Saudi Basic Industries Corporation (Sabic) is also a key organization that has been in existence since 1976. In contrast to the ministries and the ISDC, which are involved essentially in the planning stages of industrialization, Sabic is responsible for implementation of plans with respect to a wide range of undertakings. Included are: petrochemical, fertilizer, and other hydrocarbon-based industries; iron, steel, and aluminium production; and primary and secondary industrial activities necessary for the support of those industries. Furthermore, Sabic is responsible for domestic and foreign marketing of the products derived from these industries.

A discussion of institutional infrastructure would certainly be incomplete without mention of the General Petroleum and Minerals Organization (Petromin). Since 1962 this establishment has accepted wide-ranging responsibilities for nearly every aspect of petroleum and minerals projects in Saudi Arabia. From recovery to marketing, Petromin is involved in both planning and implementation; it also seeks to establish co-operative efforts with private firms to promote investment in the petroleum and minerals industry.[17]

With respect to food industries, the Grain Silos and Flour Mills Organization was established in 1972 for the purpose of forming an integrated system of mills and storage facilities to meet the nation's rapidly expanding food requirements. Grain silo and flour and feed mill projects at Riyadh, Dammam and Jeddah became fully operational in 1979 at costs of SR 219.4 million, SR 246.2 million and SR 373 million, respectively (Table 4.2). Two more projects consisting of metal silos and packing units for handling locally produced wheat are planned for Qasim and Khamis Mushayt at costs of SR 53 million and SR 64 million.[18]

The most notable financial institution for the promotion of industry is the Saudi Industrial Development Fund (SIDF). Established in Riyadh in 1974, the Fund has effectively assisted the expansion, replacement and modernization of new or existing industrial projects and firms through the extension of medium and long-term loans.[19] The SIDF will finance up to 50 per cent of a project's capital requirements if approved. By 1978/9 the Fund had committed more than SR 22.5 billion in loans for industrial and electricity projects (Table 4.3).

Other financial and administrative institutions which should at least be noted are:

The Electricity Corporation
Saudi Arabian Standards Organization (SASO)
Directorate General of Mineral Resources (DGMR)
Chambers of Commerce and Industry
Saudi Arabian Agricultural Bank

General Investment Fund
Real Estate Development Fund
Contractors' Financing Programme
Islamic Development Bank
Arab Investment Company
Saudi Investment Bank
Saudi International Bank

Table 4.2: Grain-silo, Flour-milling and Feed-milling Complexes at Riyadh, Jeddah and Dammam

	1976/7	1977/8	1978/9	1979/80
Cumulative capacity (all complexes)				
Silos (metric tons)	40,000	160,000	210,000	210,000[a]
Vessel discharging equipment (tons/hr)		400	800	800
Flour mills (tons/24 hr)	270	1,080	1,350	1,350
Feed mills (tons/8 hr)	100	200	300	300
Annual production of main products, fall complexes (thousands of metric tons)				
White flour				
85 per cent extraction	40.1	135.2	166.1	175.9
75 per cent extraction	24.5	63.0	94.7	100.6
Whole wheat flour	1.6	9.9	18.2	26.5
Bagged wheat	14.4	73.1	64.8	56.5
Pelletized mill feed (exports)	11.4	30.9	42.5	37.2
Poultry feed	3.6	16.4	31.5	48.4
Feed concentrates	8.8	29.7	32.3	35.2

Note: a. At end of 1979/80, grain silo capacity was 320,000 tons/year at plants located in Dammam, Riyadh, Qasim, and Jeddah as well as 20,000 tons/year capacity plant under construction at Khamis Mushayt.
Source: *Second Development Plan*, Table IV-20, p. 186.

The Problems of Industrialization in Saudi Arabia

The most obvious constraints to achieving rapid industrial development remain the paucity of (1) technological and management know-how, (2) technical and skilled manpower, and (3) adequate infrastructural facilities.

Saudi Arabia shares with many other developing countries not only a dearth of technological expertise but also of an entrepreneurial class capable of undertaking the desired industrial investment. Moreover, management capabilities within the nation are extremely limited, thus

Table 4.3: Saudi Industrial Development Fund Applications Given Loans for Industry and for Electricity, 1975/6-1978/9[a] (SR millions)

	1975/6		1976/7		1977/8		1978/9		Total		Applications Backlog[b]	
	No.	Amount	No.	Amount	No.	Amount	No.	Amount	No.	Amount	No.	Amount
Industry												
Food and beverages	8	101	3	31	18	218	26	159	55	509	26	434
Textiles and clothing	3	47	–	3	–	–	1	21	4	71	11	59
Wood and wood products	4	12	4	31	3	6	–	6	11	55	8	94
Paper and paper products	1	6	6	47	7	74	7	41	21	168	5	46
Chemical and chemical products	14	66	19	321	17	75	14	194	66	656	27	207
Ceramics, glass products	–	–	4	72	2	31	2	11	8	114	5	44
Cement	1	360	–	–	4	863	–	–	5	1,223	–	–
Other building materials	17	174	68	506	51	484	40	404	176	1,568	9	997
Basic metal products	9	202	16	88	20	183	16	124	61	597	14	165
Machinery and equipment	8	60	10	77	14	154	4	25	36	316	13	142
Other	–	–	4	73	–	1	1	2	5	76	–	–
Industry total	65	1,028	134	1,249	136	2,089	111	987	494	6,076	118	2,188
Electricity	na	2,076	na	2,221	na	6,388	na	5,827	na	16,512	na	na
Total		3,104		3,470		8,477		6,814		22,588		

Notes: a. Value figures include loans made for extensions, whereas number of loans are for new projects. b. As of first half of 1979/80.

creating the need for imported labour with necessary skills. This in turn provides the Kingdom with further incentive to promote foreign investment 'in the form of joint ventures whereby foreign technology and Saudi financial resources can be combined to produce significant mutual benefits'.[20]

While Saudi Arabia most certainly possesses the necessary financial resources for successful industrial development, the shortage of manpower is a constraint which will receive much attention during the Third Development Plan. Over the Second Plan period, actual employment increased by 725,000, at a 7.2 per cent per annum growth rate. Projected growth for the five-year Third Plan span (1980-5) is reduced to 155,000, a 1.2 per cent annual growth rate (Table 4.4a, 4.4b and 4.4c). The Saudi labour force is to grow by 1.9 per cent per year as compared to a 0.2 per cent per annum rate for expatriate workers. If the targets are achieved, the percentage of non-Saudi workers will drop from approximately 43 to 41 per cent over the five-year period. As discussed elsewhere, one of the main objectives of Saudi long-term strategy is to reduce the dependence upon foreign labour.

Table 4.4a: Projected Civilian Employment in Saudi Arabia, 1979/80-1984/5

Nationality/ Sex	Civilian employment (thousands) 1979/80	1984/5	Net change	Annual growth rate (in %) 1979/80-1984/5
Saudi men	1,308.4	1,437.4	129.0	1.9
Non-Saudi men	1,014.9	1,023.9	9.0	0.2
Subtotal	2,323.3	2,461.3	138.0	1.2
Saudi women	103.0	120.0	17.0	3.1
Non-Saudi women	44.9	44.9	0	–
Subtotal	147.9	164.9	17.0	2.2
Total Saudi	1,411.4	1,557.4	146.0	1.9
Total non-Saudi	1,059.8	1,068.8	9.0	0.2
Grand total	2,471.2	2,626.2	155.0	1.2

Source: Kingdom of Saudi Arabia, *Third Development Plan, 1400-1405/1980-1985*, Chapter 3.

The third major constraint to industrialization previously mentioned is the lack of adequate infrastructural facilities. This area received the highest priority in the Second Plan, with approximately 50 per cent of spending directed to the improvement and establishment of infrastructure.[21] Considerable progress was made in achieving infrastructure development objectives, so that targeted spending for infrastructure in the Third Plan was reduced to about 35 per cent of the total plan expenditures on development.

Table 4.4b: Estimated Saudi Manpower by Occupational Group 1975 and 1980 (thousands)

Occupational group	1975	1980	Increase 1975-80
Managers, officials	7.4	8.7	1.3
Professionals	48.4	52.9	4.5
Technicians and sub-professionals	25.0	33.4	8.4
Clerical workers	67.5	99.6	32.1
Sales workers	82.3	97.2	14.9
Service workers	105.2	134.5	29.3
Operatives	40.0	57.1	17.1
Skilled workers	70.1	93.5	23.4
Semi-skilled workers	170.0	265.0	95.0
Unskilled workers	244.0	296.4	52.4
Farmers	311.2	281.0	(30.2)
Bedouins	114.9	98.8	(16.2)
Total	1,286.0	1,518.0	232.0

Table 4.4c: Estimated Non-Saudi Manpower by Occupational Group 1975 and 1980 (thousands)

Occupational group	1975	1980	Increase 1975-80
Managers	6.3	12.4	6.1
Professionals	15.7	23.5	7.8
Technicians and sub-professionals	31.4	81.3	49.9
Clerical workers	31.4	121.8	90.4
Sales workers	47.1	112.6	65.5
Service workers	47.1	145.2	98.1
Operatives	25.1	51.4	26.3
Skilled workers	47.1	101.9	54.8
Semi-skilled workers	62.8	162.5	99.7
Total	314.0	812.6	498.6

Source: Ministry of Planning, *Second Development Plan, 1395-1400/1975-1980* (Riyadh, 1976), p. 217.

Additional constraints to the process of industrialization in Saudi Arabia in the past have included an insufficient industrial capital from the private sector. Although Saudi Arabia now commands an overwhelming position of dominance among the oil-rich nations, the government has had difficulty in mobilizing domestic investors. In the past those individuals possessing large amounts of capital were reluctant to invest in industry over other enterprises which yielded more immediate and higher returns, such as trading and real estate. The previous absence of an organized industrial capital market forced the entrepreneur to rely upon limited personal resources. However, the establishment of organizations such as SIDF may serve to spur greater private investment in this sector.

Policies directed at overcoming manpower and technological constraints are so vital to the development strategy of Saudi Arabia that they deserve further analysis. The solutions of the problems posed by these constraints require not only dynamic domestic policies on the part of the Saudi government, but also foreign policies capable of inducing favourable responses from foreign private investors, labour, and governments. Consequently, co-operation between Saudi Arabia and the rest of the world (especially the advanced Western countries), is a precondition to successful implementation of the country's industrialization programmes.

Whereas Western technology is needed in all aspects of the industrial development, the nature of hydrocarbon-based industries necessitates highly sophisticated technology, the source of supply of which is limited even in the Western world. A greater degree of scarcity has been created by the synchronization of petrochemical industries in the major oil-producing countries in the Middle East. Competition among these countries not only drives costs up, but also necessarily entails the tendency to make the attractiveness of industrial policies to foreign investors and consultants in excess of what would otherwise prevail.

In any event, if Saudi Arabia were the only oil-producing country in the Middle East, co-operation between the nation and foreign private investors and governments will constitute an important condition for a successful implementation of its industrialization programmes. The relationship which still exists between the country and the oil companies, especially Aramco, is sufficient evidence. This has become necessary because of the need to market the share of the crude oil obtained from the government's participation in the production facilities. The role of foreign firms in the marketing of petrochemical products is more vital, to the extent that at present the Middle East region produces only a small percentage of total world outputs of these products. Thus, if a foreign firm undertakes to market Saudi Arabian petrochemical products, it means creating competition for its own products manufactured in its home country and/or those of other firms. Thus, a condition for successful completion of all the hydrocarbon-based projects (and future expansion) in Saudi Arabia, Kuwait, United Arab Emirates, Qatar, etc., is at least the freezing of petrochemical industrial expansion in the Western world. However, this condition presupposes continued expansion of world demand for petrochemical products at a certain rate, otherwise a reduction in the production of these products in the plants in the advanced Western countries appears to be the only way the industrial development in the Middle East can continue.

Of course, this will be unacceptable to the governments of the advanced countries. A reasonable option is a slowdown in the rate of establishing hydrocarbon-based plants so that those in the Middle East could be developed. However, this will be acceptable only if there is a reciprocal commitment on the part of the Middle East countries to increase imports and moderate oil-pricing policies.

The policies of Saudi Arabia have not been limited to establishing good working relations with foreign private companies. Thus, in addition to instituting tax incentives, promising protection for infant industries, providing necessary social and physical infrastructure, and offering to participate in and to make financial capital available for industrial ventures, liberal trade policies (both economic and political) have been geared towards forging a workable co-operation between the Kingdom and the rest of the world. In particular, its oil policies have been supportive of the USA. The continued confidence which it has demonstrated in the dollar both as a unit in which crude oil is priced, and as a store of value for the Kingdom's vast foreign assets, is an ample manifestation of its desire to co-operate with the United States.

Saudi Arabia has had a moderating influence on OPEC pricing policies, as has been discussed earlier. However, events of the 16 December 1978 Abu Dhabi meeting of OPEC have underscored the fact that the Kingdom cannot hold off price increases forever. Indeed, the policy makers are acutely aware of the realities in the oil industry, and regard the eventual 14.5 per cent price increase for 1979 as reasonable given the losses OPEC members have suffered in the wake of the falling dollar and the rising prices of imports. It may, therefore, be concluded that there is a trade-off between the losses which the Kingdom sustains from the declining real price of oil and the deteriorating value of the US dollar on the one hand and the flow of foreign technology and investment and security which cordial relations with advanced Western nations give to the Kingdom, on the other. Needless to say, the country has not found it easy achieving an optimum balance; the trade-off curve has not been stable.

Established Industry and Infrastructure

As is the case in many developing countries, the industrial sector in Saudi Arabia experienced extremely modest rates of growth prior to its take-off in the early 1970s. The effect of small, self-sufficient firms as well as more traditional rural ties to agriculture, allowed manufacturing industry to expand only within the parameters of local market conditions. However, as revenues derived from the oil sector became more and more pervasive in the economy, new markets began to develop accompanied by a growing desire to invest in somewhat larger, more productive manufacturing establishments. A survey conducted by the Industrial Studies and Development Centre in 1973 indicates the continued importance of the small, light-manufacturing firm (Table 4.5). Approximately 96 per cent of all industrial establishments employed less than ten people. The importance of the larger firms is demonstrated however by the fact that 64 per cent of gross output from the private, non-oil manufacturing sector was contributed by firms employing more than ten people, and nearly 40 per cent from those firms employing more than 50 people. Moreover, as seen from Table 4.6, approximately 62 per cent of the labour force employed in industry was engaged in light manufacturing while the remaining 38 per cent were employed in heavy industries, such as petrochemicals, minerals and metal products.

By 1977 a somewhat different profile of industry had evolved (Table 4.7). Employment in manufacturing had grown at the rate of 8.4 per cent per year since the 1972 survey. However, the growth in GDP from manufacturing significantly outpaced the growth of employment during this period due to the capital-intensive nature of the industries being established.[22]

Industry in Saudi Arabia is concentrated mainly in a few cities: Jeddah, Mecca, and Medina in the Western Province; Riyadh in the Central Province; and Dammam and Al-Khobar in the Eastern Province. During the Second Plan, areas became available for the first time for industrialists in Hafuf and Qasim. Regional distribution of industry generally has followed the population pattern of the country. Other major factors that have influenced the concentration of industry in these areas are: (1) a relatively short history of industrialization in the nation; (2) the overwhelming physical size of Saudi Arabia and thus extremely long distances between cities; (3) lack of adequate transportation infrastructure; (4) the dependence of industry upon raw materials imports for non-oil manufacturing; and (5) a lack of water resources and extreme climate conditions.

Table 4.5: Non-oil Manufacturing in Private Sector: Classification by Employment Size, 1972

Employment size	Number of establishments	Fixed assets (SR 000)	Net value added (SR 000)	Gross value of output (SR 000)
1	3,835	3,514	21,015	33,969
2–4	4,386	106,271	112,453	230,759
5–9	766	27,818	52,199	138,704
Subtotal: 1–9	8,987	137,603	185,667	403,432
10–19	198	29,923	36,183	114,095
20–49	127	96,427	66,694	158,763
50 and over	48	451,644	210,278	431,381
Subtotal: 10 and over	373	577,994	313,155	704,239
Grand total	9,360	715,597	498,822	1,107,671

Sources: Central Department of Statistics, *Survey of Manufacturing Establishments*, 1973; ISDC, *Survey of Industrial Projects Established after 1390* (1970).

In spite of manpower and infant industry problems, in addition to other constraints previously mentioned, development progress in private-sector light industry moved steadily ahead during the Second Plan, with the establishment or planning of over 20 relatively small-scale plastic factories that used imported plastic resins. Heavy industry, however, progressed somewhat sluggishly. From the beginning of the Second Plan, the Ministry of Industry and Electricity assumed responsibility for practically the entire petrochemicals export industry. Process plant operations (excluding NGL and refining) have been controlled by the Ministry-established Saudi Basic Industries Corporation (Sabic). The only operating company for which Sabic presently assumes responsibility is the Saudi Arabian Fertilizer Company, which has been in operation since 1970.

The Jeddah Steel Rolling Mill was established in 1967 and was

Table 4.6: Principal Economic Characteristics of Non-oil Private-sector Manufacturing, 1972

ISIC[a]	Subsectors	No. of units	Employment	Net fixed assets (SR million)	Estimated working capital	Net value added (SR million)	Gross value of output (SR million)
31	Food, beverages and tobacco	2,526	10,601	91.0	18.2	119.1	320.3
32	Textile, wearing apparel, leather and leather products	3,563	5,959	14.3	2.8	41.6	88.6
33	Wood, wood products including furniture	1,474	4,429	18.8	3.8	35.7	76.2
34	Paper, paper products, printing and publishing	67	1,594	34.0	6.8	26.9	59.3
35	Chemicals, coal, rubber, plastic, products (excl. petroleum refining)	38	2,042	103.3	20.7	47.8	170.8
36	Non-metallic mineral products (except petroleum)	793	6,065	364.7	72.9	155.5	253.0
37	Basic metal industries	33	1,022	62.9	12.6	19.2	35.8
38	Fabricated metal products machinery and equipment	864	4,260	26.5	5.3	51.9	99.5
39	Other manufacturing	2	40	0.5	0.1	1.0	5.1
	Total	9,360	36,012	716.0	143.2	498.7	1,108.6

Note: a. For the purposes of analysis, ISIC nos 31-34 shall be considered light industry and nos 35-39 heavy industry. ISIC stands for International Standard Industry Classification.

Source: Central Department of Statistics, *Survey of Manufacturing Establishments*, 1973; Industrial Studies and Development Centre, *Survey of Industrial Projects Established After 1390* (1970).

Table 4.7: Characteristics and Distribution of Licensed Establishments Among the Various Subsectors up to the End of 1976

ISIC No.	Industrial grouping	Number of establishments No.	Number of establishments %	Licensed capital (SR million)	Licensed capital %	Number of workers No.	Number of workers %
31	Manufacture of food, beverages and tobacco	112	12.5	397	7.5	4,973	10.3
32	Textile, wearing apparel and leather industries	25	2.8	87	1.6	1,514	3.2
33	Manufacture of wood products including furniture	39	4.3	139	2.6	2,120	4.4
34	Manufacture of paper and paper products, printing, publishing	60	6.7	151	2.9	1,801	3.7
35	Manufacture of chemicals and chemical, petroleum, coal, rubber and plastic products	115	12.8	766	14.5	5,245	10.9
36	Manufacture of non-metallic mineral products	290	32.3	2,971	56.3	20,459	42.5
37	Basic metal industries	30	3.3	313	6.0	2,348	4.9
38	Manufacture of fabricated metal products, and machinery and equipment	219	24.4	436	8.3	9,359	19.5
39	Other manufacturing industries	8	0.9	16	0.3	304	0.6
	Total	898	100	5,276	100	48,123	100

Source: Industrial Studies and Development Centre, *Survey of Manufacturing Establishments*, Riyadh (1976).

initially designed to have a capacity of 45,000 tons per year of simple steel products.[23] While proposals have been made to expand existing capacity to 100,000 tons per year, it appears that the newly planned steel mill for Jubail will sufficiently supplement existing plant capacity. As of the end of the Second Development Plan, Sabic and its joint-development partner, Korf-Stahl of West Germany, had agreed to the construction of three steel projects: a basic direct reduction plant of 850,000 tons/year capacity at Jubail; a rolling mill at Jubail, linked to the basic steel plant; and the modernization and expansion of the existing Jeddah steel mill. The projects are all designed to serve the domestic market.

Existing plants in the oil refining and natural gas liquids (NGL) industries remain under the authority of Petromin. The Jeddah refinery, with a planned expansion from a capacity of 45,000 b/d to 210,000 b/d, and the Riyadh refinery, where capacity is to be upped from 15,000 b/d to 115,000 b/d, are both oriented to meet domestic-consumption requirements. The principal export refinery in Saudi Arabia, located at Ras Tanura, has a daily capacity of 415,000 barrels. During the Second Development Plan, three further export refineries were planned. Agreements to commence export refineries at Jubail and at Yanbu were signed between Petromin and its joint-venture partners. Agreement was also reached to proceed with a fuel export refinery to be located at Rabigh.

Other refineries, primarily owned by the private sector, include Getty Oil Company's Mina Saud facility and the Arabian Oil Company's refinery located at Al-Khafji. A gas-gathering system, owned and operated by Aramco, has been established in the southern area of the company's operations in the Eastern Province. The network collects and redistributes natural gas for reinjection into the oil fields; as fuel for the Saudi Cement Company plant at Hafuf for separation into natural gas liquids at Abqaiq and pumped to Ras Tanura; and as a feedstock for the Saudi Arabian Fertilizer Company (SAFCO).

With respect to the existing power-plant infrastructure in the Kingdom, the electricity generating industry is 'battling' to keep pace with 'the ever-increasing demand for power arising from the country's development boom and rising living standards'.[24] A half-dozen major power companies in the private sector presently provide electricity to the major cities of the country. In addition, government-owned desalination plants are providing increasing amounts of the Kingdom's electricity needs.

Finally, one of the largest heavy industries already existing in Saudi

Arabia is cement production (see Table 4.8). The three plants established at Hafuf, Riyadh and Jeddah together produced 1.8 million tons in 1978 as compared to 1 million tons in 1973. However, the rapid rise in demand for cement as a result of overwhelming construction requirements for development have placed the industry under considerable strain. Third Plan expansion of existing plants and construction of new facilities is to increase production to 36,000 tons/day (12 million tons/year).

Table 4.8: Planned Expansion of Cement Plant Capacity (tons per day)

	1974-5	1979-80
Existing plants		
Hafuf	1,300	4,300
Riyadh	1,100	4,100
Jeddah	2,000	5,000
Subtotal	4,400	13,400
New plants		
Jubail area	–	3,000
Buradah	–	3,000
Tabuk	–	3,000
Yanbu	–	3,000
Hafuf	–	3,000
Southwestern area	–	3,000
Subtotal	–	18,000
Total daily capacity	4,400	31,400
Annual capacity[a]	1,450,000	10,360,000

Note: a. Based on 330 operating days per year.
Source: *Second Development Plan*, Table IV-22, p. 187.

Manufacturing projects in light and medium industries presently under way or planned for the near future will be implemented through private investment or in conjunction with governmental assistance (Tables 4.9 - 4.14). These ventures reflect not only the demands placed upon industry by the public sector for development projects, but also the economic consequence of increasing demand for consumption goods by the individual Saudi citizen as well. While estimated investment for construction materials and products in 1976 approached $70 million, combined investment for manufacturing projects in consumer, agricultural and commercial products was estimated to be more than $300 million in that year.

Development of infrastructural facilities, as listed in Table 4.15, include the construction of industrial estates beyond those already established at Riyadh, Jeddah and Dammam. The expansion of existing estates, in addition to four more such complexes planned for Mecca, Al-Abha, Qasim and Hafuf, is under the administrative authority of the Ministry of Industry and Electricity. The facilities provided for industry through these estates include roads, water, electricity, sewage systems, communications and similar requirements. Once established, priority for the use of the estates will be given to those industries outlined in the Development Plan, subsidiaries of existing industries, and to industries financed by local capital. Moreover, those industries using new and advanced technologies receive favourable treatment.

Table 4.9: Number of Licensed Companies, 1974-8

	Kingdom	Central region	Western region	Eastern region	Northern region	Southwest region	Region not defined
In production							
1974	285	103	120	52	5	3	2
1978	687	275	239	129	11	24	9
Under construction							
1974	17	8	5	4	–	–	–
1978	282	110	84	65	5	12	6
Planned							
1974	18	6	7	4	–	–	1
1978	319	121	95	73	3	21	6

Source: *Third Development Plan, 1400-1405/1980-1985*, Chapter 4.

However, major industrial projects planned for the future in Saudi Arabia noticeably emphasize hydrocarbon bases. As noted earlier, the primary objective under this programme is to increase the uses of petroleum and gas as feedstocks and sources of energy. The major development programmes in this field, outlined in Table 4.16, should entail expenditures approaching $14.5 billion by 1985.

The gas-gathering and treatment system, soon to become the largest industrial project in the world, involves a network of crude petroleum and liquefied natural-gas pipelines that will run from production zones in the Eastern Province to points of export in the Western Province. Moreover, the system will link up with expanding hydrocarbon-based industries on the Red Sea coast. Initially this project was scheduled for completion in 1979 (see Table 4.17). It now appears that the

Table 4.10: Number of Licensed Product Lines, 1974-8

Product code/description	In production 1974	In production 1978	Under construction 1978	Planned 1978
In production				
31 Food and beverages	40	85	82	71
32 Textiles, clothing	25	37	13	16
33 Wood/wood products	54	80	26	17
34 Paper/paper products	47	79	10	16
35 Chemicals, plastic, rubber	69	145	51	48
36 Non-metallic mineral products	78	388	81	115
37 Basic metals	5	9	3	–
38 Fabricated metal products	152	262	133	108
39 Other manufacturing	4	7	4	3
All manufacturing	474	1,092	403	394

Source: *Third Development Plan, 1400-1405/1980-1985*, Chapter 4.

Table 4.11: New Manufacturing Projects for Consumer and Related Products (Licences Issued or Applied for)

Region/project	Annual capacity	Estimated investment (SR thousands)
Western		
Polyester fabrics	12,000 tons	5,000
Perfumes and cosmetics	2.8 million m^3	4,200
Plastic products	3,900 tons	16,000
Medical solutions	3,114 kilogrammes of glucose	14,000
Glass products from waste glass	950 tons	1,000
Cloths and tents	3,000 tents	840
Central		
Nylon bags and plates	525 tons	500
Plastic containers – 1	370 tons	1,400
Plastic containers – 2	310 tons	1,530
Cologne and perfumes	300 tons cologne 120 tons perfume	1,940
Cooking utensils	1,000 tons	40,000
Ready-made apparel	150,000 pieces	11,500
Eastern		
Household utensils	30,000 units	3,230
Medicines	180 million tablets	3,800
Southwestern		
Perfumes	6,000 grammes of rose oil 100,000 litres of cologne	1,950
Total investment		106,180

Source: *Second Development Plan*, Table IV-25, p. 190.

project will be only partially finished by 1981, while completion of the remaining facilities will be staggered through to the mid-1980s; this readjustment of the schedule is apparently in direct response to the rapid inflation of construction costs in recent years.[25]

Table 4.12: New Manufacturing Projects in Agriculture and Food Processing (Licences Issued or Applied for)

Region/project	Annual capacity	Estimated investment (SR thousands)
Western		
Dairy products	5,490 tons	8,000
Rice milling	20,000 tons	13,000
Oil and soap	200,000 tons	45,000
Sugar refining	100,000 tons	93,000
Mineral water	4.5 million bottles	7,000
Date packing	150 tons	70
Central		
Dairy products 1	6,088 tons	10,000
Dairy products 2	4,680 tons	14,600
Poultry feed & broilers	12,000 tons feed 3 million broilers	17,000
Livestock & poultry feed	4,800 tons	2,000
Yoghurt and milk 1	345 tons	640
Yoghurt and milk 2	1.2 million litres	3,780
Halawa and tahina	300 tons	390
Glass bottles plant	3,000 tons	24,000
Tomato paste and juice	3,000 tons paste 600 tons juice	6,000
Agricultural pumps assembly	300 pumps	590
Eastern		
Leather tanning	139,350 square metres	1,680
Sugar refining	100,000 tons	93,000
Phosphate fertilizers	500,000 tons	200,000
Northern		
Bottling plant	7 million bottles	4,600
Strawboard plant	2,400 tons	2,600
Skin pickling	175,000-350,000 skins	1,300
Total investment		548,250

Source: *Second Development Plan*, Table IV-20, p. 186.

Table 4.13: New Manufacturing Projects for Household and Commercial Products (Licences Issued or Applied for)

Region/project	Annual capacity	Estimated investment (SR thousands)
Western		
Machine-made carpets	7,100 tons	12,000
Metal furniture	460 tons	4,000
Wood furniture 1	3,000 square metres	8,000
Wood furniture 2	2,200 square metres	6,000
Printed paper bags	600 tons	460
Sensitive and carbon paper	187 tons	30
Paper sheets from rolls	8,000 tons	1,000
Envelopes	227 tons	1,500
Paper bags	900 tons	950
Paper bags and envelopes	1,110 tons	1,750
Metal car bodies	6,000 bodies	7,200
Truck bodies	1,000 tons	7,200
Bicycle assembly	3,600 bicycles	1,150
Lube oil tins and barrels	–	12,290
Barrels	240,000 barrels	5,440
Tyre retreading	13,200 units	1,000
Tyre manufacturing	3,000,000 units	60,000
Truck assembly	4,040 units	140,800
Dump-truck assembly	400 units	9,000
Mattresses	30,000 units	1,150
Floor carpets	684,000 square metres	12,000
Metal products (furniture and garbage containers)	350 tons	4,000
Safes	6,600 units	260
Paper and school copybooks	17 million units	5,070
Central		
Fibreglass products	200 sitting room sets 220 false ceilings	1,100
Bus bodies	200 units	1,200
Ceramics	2,700 tons	16,500
Sanitary fixtures	1,200 tons	460
Lighting equipment	12,000 units	1,270
Arc welding electrodes	1,200 tons	2,900
Construction barrows and equipment	10,000 barrows 40,000 buckets	1,720
Fluorescent appliances assembly	40,000 units	1,150
Prayer carpets	400,000 square metres	4,350
School desks	100,000 units	6,390
Oxygen	30,000 cylinders	1,100
Fluorescent lamps assembly	50,000 lamps	460
Floor carpets	600,000 square metres	13,690

Table 4.13: (continued)

Region/project	Annual capacity	Estimated investment (SR thousands)
Central (continued)		
Tin cans	–	10,000
Dry batteries	10 million units	15,000
Eastern		
Wood furniture	2,000 tons	6,200
Wood mobile platforms	110,880 units	2,000
Computer paper forms 1	45 million forms	900
Computer paper forms 2	40 million forms	1,800
Polypropylene bags	12 million bags	4,000
Air conditioners assembly	10,000 units	2,900
Copper wire and generator refurbishing	172,000 HP of engines	6,060
Total estimated investment		403,400

Source: *Second Development Plan*, p. 189.

Industrialization in the Future: Jubail and Yanbu[26]

To implement the objective of increasing the export value of the Kingdom's hydrocarbon resources, the Royal Commission for Jubail and Yanbu was established; its purpose is to plan and supervise the establishment of primary industries for the conversion and refining of Saudi crude and natural gas as well as associated hydrocarbon-based industries. This goal is to be realized through the construction of two large industrial complexes: one on the Red Sea coast at Yanbu, the other located on the Gulf coast near Jubail. The primary industries, to be established through joint ventures with the private sector, are to be the responsibility of Sabic and Petromin. The secondary and support industries are the responsibility of the Ministry of Industry and Electricity.

Both complexes are characterized by the following major aspects: (1) primary industries; (2) secondary and support industries; (3) construction support facilities; (4) infrastructure systems; and (5) a community (i.e. housing and other systems for the new workers employed within the complexes).

By far the larger of the two complexes, Jubail was originally estimated to entail an expenditure of more than $2.5 billion; the cost for

Table 4.14: New Manufacturing Projects for Construction Materials and Products (Licences Issued or Applied for)

Region/project	Annual capacity	Estimated investment (SR thousands)
Western		
Aluminium doors and windows 1	1,500 doors 6,000 windows	3,000
Aluminium doors and windows 2	40 tons	370
Electrical wire and cable	6,000 tons	30,000
Central		
Paints 1	1,500 tons	1,000
Paints 2	3,000 tons	1,360
Slurry seal (emulsion)	60,000 tons	2,260
Cement blocks	21 million blocks 15 million bricks	3,890
Red bricks	81,000 square metres	12,000
Prefabricated structures	800 units	10,300
Insulating materials	507,000 square metres	3,090
Electric power poles	10,000 poles	1,000
Pre-cast concrete	247,000 square metres	12,000
Tile and ornamental stone	200,000 square metres gypsum 25,000 square metres tiles	7,220
Insulating paper	1.8 million square metres	1,890
Insulated concrete walls & ceilings	133,750 square metres	16,000
Metal doors	30,000 units	9,100
Eastern		
Aluminium doors and windows 1	3,900 square metres	400
Aluminium doors and windows 2	50 tons	800
Pipes and manholes	2,400 tons	1,980
Wire netting	14,000 rolls	420
Pipe and joints	1,800 tons	510
Oil piplines	1,525 pipe units	1,790
Spiral-welded pipes	84,000 tons	77,000
Metal mesh and net	6,000 tons	1,500
Bricks and blocks	10 million blocks	1,500
	15 million bricks	15,000
Oil-well drilling mud	85,000 tons	12,500
Nails	1,000 tons	3,000
Steel pipes	3,400 tons	9,950
Northern		
Iron pipes	470 tons	590
Total estimated investment		241,420

Source: *Second Development Plan*, Table IV-23, p. 188.

this complex has since risen substantially to perhaps as high as $45 billion.[27] The primary industries planned for this overwhelming project include: (1) two export refineries; (2) one lubricating oil and low-sulphur refinery; (3) four petrochemical plants (of which three are to be initiated under the Second Plan); (4) one aluminium smelter; and (5) one steel mill (see Table 4.18).

Table 4.15: Industrial Estates (millions of square metres)

Location	Area in 1974/5	Area in 1980/1
Riyadh	0.45	4.95
Jeddah	1.04	4.04
Dammam	1.00	3.60
Mecca	–	0.42[a]
Qasim	–	0.50
Hafuf	–	0.50
Total	2.49	14.01

Note: a. Not fully developed.
Source: *Third Development Plan, 1400-1405/1980-1985*, Chapter 4.

Of these industries, Petromin is to be responsible for the refineries, and Sabic for the remaining primary industries. These projects are only now emerging from the design and engineering stages; the international corporation most involved with Jubail, particularly with refining and petrochemicals, is the Royal Dutch Shell Company. Other companies involved in the development of petrochemical plants at Jubail include Dow Chemical and Exxon.

Secondary industries are to be established for the utilization of materials produced by these primary industries. It appears that these industries emphasize the manufacture of consumer-related products for both domestic consumption and export. Support industries are also needed for the provision of goods and services to these industry groups and to the general public. Included in this category are such industries as steel, aluminium, plastic and chemical manufacturers and plants.

Construction support facilities at Jubail cover 'all works that are required to accomplish the procurement and construction of the permanent facilities'.[28] This programme includes such items as site surveys and preparations; construction camps, ports, and materials; transportation access; power; water; communication; and other public facilities.

The provision of an extensive infrastructure system at Jubail is a must for the primary industries previously mentioned. Basic infrastructural components include power, potable and process-cooling water, waste disposal and other utilities, as well as an adequate transportation system. The transport network involves everything from railroads to airports, and the harbour facilities will eventually be capable of handling more than 26 million tons of liquid cargo, 5 million tons of general cargo and 5 million tons of bulk cargo.

Table 4.16: Major Development Programmes for Hydrocarbon-based Industries, 1975-80

Programmes and projects	Investment (SR millions)	Capacity	Peak employment
Eastern Region			
Gas gathering and treatment	16,000	43.3 million m^3	2,300
Petrochemical complexes (4, of which 3 to be initiated, 1395-1400)	9,000	2.0 million tons/year	6,800
Export refineries (2)	4,600	500 thousand b/d	1,700
Lube oil refinery	2,040	107 thousand b/d[a]	550
Fertilizer plants (4, of which 2 to be initiated, 1395-1400)	1,400	2 million tons/year	2,000
Aluminium plant	1,300	210 thousand tons/year	1,900
Steel plant	5,500	3.5 million tons/year	8,600
Subtotal	39,840		23,850
Western Region			
Crude line to West	5,300	2.4 million b/d	550
NGL line to West	1,200	356 thousand b/d	
Export refinery	2,100	250 thousand b/d	850
Petrochemical complex	2,250	500 thousand tons/year equivalent ethylene	1,700
Subtotal	10,850		3,100
Total	50,690		26,950

Note: a. 12,000 b/d of lube stock; 95,000 b/d of low-sulphur oil.
Source: Ministry of Planning, *Second Development Plan*, Table IV-18, p. 182.

Finally, a new community will be needed to house the personnel required for the successful development and operation of a project of such magnitude. At Jubail this community will be of substantial size sufficient for an expected population of some 170,000 people. One should keep in mind that Jubail's pre-industrial complex size was about 4,000 inhabitants to understand the impact of this massive industrialization programme.

Table 4.17: Schedule for Design and Construction of Major Projects in Hydrocarbon-based Industries[a]

	1975	1976	1977	1978	1979	1980	1981	1982	1983
Eastern Region									
Gas gathering									
South	—	—	—	—	—				
North		—	—	—	—	—			
Central			—	—	—	—	—		
Petrochemical									
I	—	—	—	—	—	—	—		
II		—	—	—	—	—	—	—	
III				—	—	—	—	—	—
Refinery									
I	—	—	—	—	—	—			
II				—	—	—	—	—	—
Lube oil refinery				—	—	—	—	—	—
Fertilizer									
I	—	—	—	—	—				
II		—	—	—	—	—	—		
Aluminium	—	—	—	—	—	—	—		
Steel									
Metal pellets	—	—	—	—	—				
Liquid steel	—	—	—	—	—	—	—		
Continuous casting		—	—	—	—	—	—		
Finished products		—	—	—	—	—	—	—	
Pipeline to West									
Crude		—	—	—	—	—	—	—	
NGL		—	—	—	—	—	—	—	
Western Region									
Refinery	—	—	—	—	—	—	—	—	
Petrochemical	—	—	—	—	—	—	—	—	

Note: a. Projects to be initiated in period 1975-80. All projects' schedules are subject to continuous review based on implementation progress.
Source: Petromin.

The Yanbu complex in the western region of the country will ultimately include an industrial zone with harbour facilities in addition to an airport and urban area (see Table 4.19). According to the Royal Commission:[29]

> This site was selected . . . after a preliminary investigation by Petromin and [the] Mobil Oil Company and a decision by the

Government of Saudi Arabia, to bring a crude oil pipeline to Yanbu from the Khurais Oil Fields on the East coast. In addition Aramco made a decision to bring a natural-gas liquids pipeline to Yanbu and to build a fractionation plant to provide ethane for feedstock and fuel for the refinery and petrochemical complex.

The primary industries at Yanbu are structured upon these pipelines from the Eastern Province to the west, including (1) an export refinery, (2) a crude-oil terminal, (3) a natural-gas liquids fractionation plant, and (4) an ethylene-based petrochemical complex. Mobil Oil Company is presently the principal foreign investor in this complex.

Table 4.18: Jubail Facilities and Progress

Area/Project type	Activity/Status[a]
Site survey/Preparation	comprehensive surveys under way; industrial sites 50% completed
Materials handling systems	design 40% completed; work under way in 5 packages
Self-supporting camps	9 construction camps completed; 1 under construction
Transport	
Airport	4,000-metre runway completed; other facilities under construction
Roads	129 km of roads and modular pathways designed; 63 kilometres of roads completed
Industrial parks	
Support industries	development plan completed; one development contract let
Secondary industry	master plan completed
Electric power	power system design completed
Water	
Potable	15,650 m^3/day treatment capacity, 37,000 m^3/day of storage tankage; 66 kilometres of conveyance lines; 19,000 m^3/day of desalination capacity
Cooling	seawater system design completed; some contracts let
Waste treatment	initial phases in operation with capacity of 6,200 m^3/day
Public/Community facilities Mosque, warehouses; other service, community, recreation facilities	design under way; mosques with an area of 2,450 square metres completed; 4 warehouses of 8,000 square metres completed
Training	design completed for 74,000 square metre facility.

Note: a. At end of 1979/80.
Source: *Third Development Plan, 1400-1405/1980-1985*, Chapter 4.

The secondary and support industries at Yanbu could eventually develop into three additional areas involving the production of (1) terepthalic acid or TPA, (2) hydrocarbons and chlorine, and (3) sulphur and phosphates necessary for fertilizers.

Table 4.19: Yanbu Facilities and Progress

Area/Projects	Activity/Status[a]
Site survey/Preparation	comprehensive surveys under way
Housing	prefabricated temporary housing completed
Offices	12,600 square metre complex completed
Water	2,040 m^3/day mounted desalination plant operating; 2,850 m^3/day groundwater supply
Electric power	initial generation capacity/distribution installed
Transport	
Airport	airport facilities with B-707/DC-8 capability completed
Roads	20 km completed
Port	2 berths completed
Telecommunications	2,000 telephone lines and other facilities installed

Note: a. At end of 1979/80.
Source: *Third Development Plan, 1400-1405/1980-1985*, Chapter 4.

Construction and infrastructural facilities required at Yanbu are similar in nature to Jubail, although not nearly as demanding in size. Harbour and port facilities at Yanbu, however, are rather significant in scope. The crude and NGL shipping terminal will have approximately 16 berths, while the general cargo port will have about 12 berths.

Reflections and Prospects

The scheme of future industrialization in Saudi Arabia is a programme of immense and awe-inspiring proportions. Planned projects in the industrial sector are perhaps indicative of the overall strategy of the Kingdom under the development plans: a rush for development, engaging every resource available to accomplish the required task.[30]

Although diversification is a major objective of the country's industrial policy, it is clear that Saudi Arabia fully intends to utilize her abundant reserves of petroleum and natural gas to develop those hydrocarbon-based industries in which she has a long-run comparative advantage.

Through the system of incentives and financial and administrative institutions such as the Saudi Industrial Development Fund, it appears that industrialization will be effectively encouraged through private and public-sector co-operation. If at all possible, private enterprise is intended to be the major vehicle of economic growth.

Moreover, as import substitution is also an important objective, particularly for the non-oil manufacturing sector, the desire to expand the domestic economy's capacity to produce those products in which competitive markets exist will present attractive opportunities for foreign and Saudi businessmen alike.

The particular obstacles to this programme of development in Saudi Arabia remain technology, manpower, and inadequate infrastructural facilities. Once these barriers are overcome the only limits to the industrial development potential of the country lie in international marketing efforts by Saudi Arabia and the general working of supply and demand for specific industrial commodities – the same limitations facing industry in the advanced Western economies.

Notes

1. Ragaei El Mallakh, 'Industrialization in the Arab World: Obstacles and Prospects', in Naiem A. Sherbiny and Mark A. Tessler (eds), *Arab Oil* (New York, Praeger, 1976), p. 58.

2. United Nations Industrial Development Organization (UNIDO), *Industrial Development Survey* (New York, United Nations, 1970).

3. In heavy industry the share of energy is approximately 25 per cent of total cost.

4. Participation, as detailed in Chapter 2, is advantageous to industrialization, as it creates an element of continuity and certainty about the future for foreign investment in Saudi Arabia, as opposed to the fear of abrupt cutbacks of unilateral nationalization.

5. Industrial Studies and Development Centre (ISDC), *Guide to Industrial Investment in Saudi Arabia*, 4th edn (Riyadh, 1974), pp. 29-33.

6. To be expanded and emphasized in the Third Development Plan.

7. H.E. Dr. Ghazi Algosaibi (Minister of Industry and Finance), 'The Strategy of Industrialization in Saudi Arabia', *The Journal of Energy and Development*, Spring 1977, p. 219.

8. *Industrialization of Saudi Arabia – Strategy and Policy* (Washington, DC: Office of the Commercial Attache, Royal Embassy of Saudi Arabia, November 1976), p. 3.

9. A special section later in this chapter details this Commission and the Jubail and Yanbu industrial complexes.

10. *Industrialization of Saudi Arabia*, p. 2.

11. Kingdom of Saudi Arabia, *Third Development Plan, 1400-1405/1980-1985*, Chapter 3.

12. ISDC, *Guide to Industrial Investment in Saudi Arabia*, 4th edn, p. 29.

13. *Industrialization of Saudi Arabia*, p. 3.
14. For a detailed discussion of the programme of incentives and subsidies, refer to Chapter 12.
15. Established industrial estates include Jeddah, Riyadh and Dammam, all of which are being greatly expanded. Work was under way in 1980 on smaller estates in Mecca, Qasim and Hafuf; consideration is being given to establishing new centres in Medina and Abha.
16. For a detailed discussion of these institutions, refer to ISDC, *Guide to Industrial Investment in Saudi Arabia*, 5th edn (Riyadh, 1977).
17. Petromin was detailed in Chapter 2.
18. SAMA, *Annual Report, 1979*, p. 72.
19. Although these loans are specified as interest-free, there is presently a service charge of 2 per cent on outstanding credits.
20. *Industrialization of Saudi Arabia*, p. 5.
21. Of total outlays under the Second Plan, social infrastructural development commands 6.7 per cent, while physical infrastructural development accounts for 22.7 per cent. For the development sector alone, infrastructure is accorded approximately 48 per cent of project outlays. See Table 6.1, or Ministry of Planning, *Second Development Plan 1395-1400/1975-1980* (Riyadh, 1976), Table VIII-1, p. 529. (Hereafter cited as *Second Plan*.)
22. GDP by manufacturing increased at more than 12 per cent per annum over the period 1972-6.
23. The Jeddah steel mill remains the direct responsibility of the Ministry of Industry and Electricity instead of Sabic.
24. *Financial Times* (London), 26 March 1977, p. 19.
25. Ibid.
26. The most detailed statement of these plans are contained in the report of the Royal Commission for Jubail and Yanbu, *Jubail and Yanbu Industrial Complexes (A Conspectus)* (February 1977). (Hereafter cited as *Royal Commission 1977 Conspectus*).
27. See Table 4.17 for the projected investment in each of the industries. The newer estimate for Jubail was given in the *New York Times*, 13 February 1978, and reflects industry projections on costs as contrasted to Saudi press estimates in the area of $20 billion to $30 billion. Contracts already completed or in progress through June 1980 amounted to SR 1,706.9 million in Jubail ($513 million) and SR 864.4 million ($260 million) in Yanbu.
28. *Royal Commission 1977 Conspectus*, p. 5.
29. *Royal Commission 1977 Conspectus*, p. 12.
30. The scope of industrialization and more specifically of selected undertakings will be treated in Chapter 7.

5 PLANNING FOR ECONOMIC DEVELOPMENT: THE FIRST EXPERIENCE

Introduction

'Making development plans has been the most popular activity of the governments of underdeveloped countries since the war [World War II]'.[1] Considering that there has been very little success in development planning in most of these countries, one may like to know what do countries which decide to have development plans hope to achieve by undertaking this approach to development? A development plan must promote growth if it is to be a worthwhile enterprise. But more importantly, development within the framework of a plan must generate a higher rate of growth than one based only on government budgetary allocations which are undertaken without the overall guidance of a comprehensive plan. The crucial issue therefore, is what function a development plan performs which cannot be performed by ordinary government annual budgetary policies. This is an important question which a country contemplating the initiation of an economic development plan will have to face considering that there has been found to be little correlation between development planning and economic growth among developing countries.[2]

A realistic comprehensive plan must create a better environment for growth by providing 'a sense of direction and consistency'.[3] The purpose of annual budgets then, is to translate the overall objectives of a plan into annual projects and expenditures. A plan does not replace government budgetary and other policies, but instead provides an overall framework within which government expenditures and policies could be geared towards long-term development of the country concerned. In other words, a plan gives a sense of direction to both the government and other public organizations on the one hand, and to the private sector on the other, in order that consistency is achieved between government policies and the private sector's reactions to them.

Several conflicts are likely to develop between specific plan objectives and their translation into reality by annual budgetary directives. The resolution of such conflicts is not easy, since a comprehensive plan must necessarily be flexible enough to take into account changing conditions, but at the same time, should not be too flexible to be subjected to the whims and caprices of politicians. This is, of course, not to say that political considerations need necessarily be subordinated to economic considerations envisaged in the plan. In fact, if during the plan formulation process a sufficiently wide base of involvement is achieved it will be possible to take the political considerations into account from the very beginning. What should be guarded against is the tendency for government departments to manipulate annual budgets in such a way that maximization of overall welfare through successful implementation of a plan, is constrained.

If a development plan is able to inject consistency into the public sector and in the economy as a whole, ensure feasibility and permit rational assessment of priorities, it would have provided the framework within which the government, through its policies, and the private sector, through its response, would co-operate in order to achieve a reasonable rate of growth. This will be an improvement if the rate is higher than the one which could be realized in a situation in which a plan does not exist.

The fact that plan failures have been rampant in developing countries is an indication that development plans have not been successful in performing the above three functions. Several factors have been blamed for these failures. Financial constraint, physical bottlenecks, political instability, bias towards macro plans, bias towards urban development at the expense of rural development, bias towards plan formulation *vis-à-vis* plan implementation, excessive industrialization to the neglect of agriculture, unrealistic targets often based on either political expediency, inadequate data base or inadequate basic surveys, inadequate specification of major targets and programmes designed to achieve them, lack of and shortage of qualified manpower and administrative capacity; these and many others are regarded as the causes of failures of development planning in developing countries.[4]

Resource-poor countries try to expand and maximize the range of their limited resources. However, nations with abundant but narrow base of resources (particularly those with extractive and wasting assets such as oil) attempt to diversify their economic base and convert their temporary wealth into renewable forms. Also, the latter countries ought to reduce the waste which frequently accompanies early stages of demonstration of wealth. There are other reasons why Saudi Arabia may benefit from a comprehensive development plan. One of the principal constraints on successful implementation of a plan, financial or capital constraint, is eliminated in the Saudi case and the Kingdom therefore stands a better chance than most developing countries of carrying out projects which are envisaged in a plan. Secondly, although financial aid and capital constraints may not exist for Saudi Arabia, other constraints do: human, administrative and physical constraints. On the other hand, the main purpose of a plan is to ensure 'the efficient use of a country's resources in accordance with certain rationally determined priorities for the attainment of nationally cherished goals'.[5] The non-existence of financial constraint could generate extravagance in an environment devoid of guidelines in the form of a development plan. This is especially important with reference to the long-term development needs of the people of Saudi Arabia. In a surplus-funds country the input constraint simply shifts from capital to other inputs as will be observed in the Appendix to this volume when the relevance of the Harrod-Domar model of growth is discussed. Further, as will be seen from discussions in the next section, the history of planning in Saudi Arabia shows that a greater effort at development planning was made when the Kingdom found itself with surplus funds in the 1970s. But the history also indicates that the need for a development plan was motivated by the economic and financial crisis which afflicted the country in the middle of the 1950s.

In a country in which most of the revenue accruing from oil goes to the government, there is the need for rational allocation or disbursement of this wealth throughout the Kingdom. It is not sufficient to carry out such allocation through physical and social infrastructural expenditures. The Saudi government sees in a development plan a mechanism through which a more efficient allocation of the country's abundant financial resources could be made. It must be stressed once again that such a rational allocative mechanism is necessary from the point of view of the constraints which the non-existence or inadequacy of co-operating factors imposes on meaningful government spending activities. The utilization of limited physical capital and administrative capacity requires as much attention to efficiency as is required for the utilization of financial capital when the latter is scarce in the case of non-surplus-funds countries. The government of Saudi Arabia thus hopes that a comprehensive development plan, like the one for 1975-80 would provide the necessary central direction for development in order to reduce waste, diversify the economy, and ensure internal consistencies in government finances and in the overall development process of the Kingdom.

The History of Economic Planning in Saudi Arabia

Ideas about planning in Saudi Arabia date back to 1958 when it was found necessary to inject rationality into the economy after the crisis which occurred in 1955-7. The need for some sort of economic management, particularly in government financial matters, was prompted by the desire to establish stability in the Saudi Arabian economy.[6]

The 1955-7 economic crisis took the form of government budgetary deficits, which necessitated large government borrowing from SAMA, inflation, balance of payments deficits resulting from the small production-base of the economy which could not, therefore, expand fast enough to meet the increased effective demand, and the concomitant fall in the rate of exchange of the riyal. The crisis was primarily caused by the inability of oil revenues and foreign exchange derived from oil to increase at a rate consistent with the rate at which the level of spending was growing. Indeed, in this period both government revenue and export earnings from oil reached a plateau level. These underlying causes reiterate the extent to which the Saudi economy is vulnerable to the vagaries of the single product, oil. The significance of the crisis from the point of view of planning can be found in two developments which were generated; these developments were to give rise to the formulation of a development plan for the Kingdom.

The first was the appointment of an able economist, the late Anwar Ali, to head the Saudi Arabian Monetary Agency (SAMA). Shortly after his appointment, he submitted several proposals to the government aimed at achieving economic stability. One of his recommendations was the preparation of a plan for future development of the country after stability had been achieved. In the light of the recommendations a committee of financial and economic advisors, which may be regarded as the nucleus of a planning body in Saudi Arabia, was formed in 1958.

The economic development committee in mid-1959 was made up of the Deputy Minister of Commerce and the Director Generals of the Ministries of Agriculture, Education, Health, Oil and Mineral Affairs, and Communications. Instead of setting up the basis for economic development in Saudi Arabia, the committee occupied most of its time with specific cases, most of which concerned applications for customs duty exemptions and other tariff matters. Ironically, the committee appeared to be aware of the deviation of its deliberations from its basic functions related to planning and research. The most meaningful task which it accomplished was the drafting of regulations for an Economic Development Board at its last meeting. The recommendations were very similar to those later to be submitted by the International Bank for Reconstruction and Development (IBRD) mission to Saudi Arabia, in 1960.

The second development was the decision of the King in 1960 to ask IBRD for a mission to Saudi Arabia to study her economic problems and make recommendations as to the best ways of developing the Kingdom's resources and for providing a sound foundation for future economic development.[7]

Based upon the recommendations of the World Bank Mission, and also noting that the then Governor of SAMA, Anwar Ali, had made similar recommendations, the first Planning Board was created in Saudi Arabia by a Royal Decree on 4 January 1961. The Supreme Planning Board consisted of the following members: The Prime Minister or his deputy as the Chairman, the Ministers of Finance and National Economy (as Deputy Chairman), Communications, Petroleum and Mineral Resources, Commerce, Agriculture and Health. Although it was the World Bank's recommendation that the executive secretary of the Planning Board have a ministerial rank (i.e. that the Board be administered by a Minister for Planning), the Secretary General was given limited powers – powers inconsistent with the responsibilities bestowed upon his secretariat.

With regard to the functions of the Planning Board, it was responsible for recommending 'to the Council of Ministers the annual budgets necessary for the execution of economic development programs and to approve from time to time . . . defined appropriations from allocated funds in the budget to Ministry or Ministries concerned in the execution of such projects'.[8]

Also the Board was responsible for 'planning and drawing up the economic development policy'.[9] In its anxiety to study and approve projects of various ministries, the Board gave little time to the function of planning and policy recommendation. Thus the Supreme Planning Board failed to achieve the primary goal, for the purpose of which it was established, that is to set up an implementable development plan based on sound studies of the economy of the Kingdom. In fact the Board did not begin the establishment of the institutional framework for the formulation of a comprehensive plan, and remained only as a 'holding company' of the various ministries of the government. For example, the recommendation for the establishment of planning units within various ministries was not implemented.

Apart from the fact that there were inconsistencies among the functions which it was supposed to perform, several other factors accounted for the poor performance of the Planning Board. These include inadequate supply of qualified technical staff, lack of and unreliability of statistics needed for planning, and the low status given to its Secretary General.

Despite its failures, reorganization of the planning body had to wait for two other reports (one by the Ford Foundation group and the other by a United Nations team for Social and Economic Planning) to be submitted in 1964. The recommendations submitted by the Ford Foundation team about the reorganization of the planning body gave rise to a Royal Decree which established the Central Planning Organization (CPO) on 19 January 1965. Whether the reorganization would pay off depended at the time on the future activities of the Central Planning Organization. It is these activities and the declared functions to which we now turn our attention.

The status of the planning organization was raised by making it accountable to the King, and its functions were more clearly specified. Article 4 of the Royal Decree states the following six functions:[10]

(1) preparing a periodic economic report about the Kingdom;
(2) preparing the first Economic Development Plan for a five-year period;
(3) projection of the total capital needed for the carrying out of development plans which are approved by the Council of Ministers. These projections would form the basis for preparing the national budget, supplementary budgets and the budgets of independent departments;
(4) preparing economic studies on special subjects;
(5) assisting the Ministries and related departments in planning affairs;
(6) submitting technical advice on matters referred to it by the King.

Thus, what the Decree did was to transfer the functions of the Supreme Planning Board which were related to non-economic matters to other ministries. For example, project preparation was distributed between the Ministry of Finance and National Economy and the ministries and departments which were directly related to the projects. Also matters pertaining to technical assistance and co-operation were transferred to the office of the President of the Council of Ministers. It will be seen that the first transfer tended to circumscribe the power of the Central Planning Organization (CPO). Further limitation of the power of the CPO can be seen in its heavy reliance on SAMA for data on banking and balance of payments, and for other forms of statistical information. In addition the establishment of planning units in the various ministries could be looked upon as the creation of independent and competitive planning bodies *vis à vis* the CPO. But apart from the financial control which the Ministry of Finance and National Economy had over projects, the relationship between the CPO and SAMA on one hand and the planning units in the ministries, on the other, need not be of conflicting nature. Indeed, close co-operation between the latter organizations and the planning body is the most effective way to achieve co-ordination among the activities of various government departments.

In order to carry out the functions ascribed to it effectively, the CPO adopted four practical steps of plan formulation:[11] step one consisted of examining the state of the economy at a given period, and making its findings known through a report which it published. This first step is consistent with the first of the functions enumerated above. Secondly, in the light of the findings in this report, the CPO co-operated with the various ministries to develop a broad outline of measures which could be undertaken to achieve economic progress. The outline was then to be submitted to the Council of Ministers for approval. The third step was to co-ordinate the activities of the ministries in transforming the broad strategies for economic development contained in the final outline into specific targets, projects, etc. and then to combine them into a comprehensive development plan, which would then be submitted to the King for approval. The final step involved a follow-up which CPO would undertake during the implementation process by reviewing past and current events and future direction of the economy for each year of the plan.

In the spirit of these planning procedures the CPO, in co-operation with Ford Foundation economic advisors, submitted a report entitled *Planning for Growth* which aimed at giving broad direction for the entire economy. However, the guidelines contained in this report could not be translated into practical budgetary proposals due to (1) the degree of generalization, (2) the weak leadership of the CPO, (3) the little support which was given to the report by policy-makers and other executive officials in the ministries, and (4) inadequately trained manpower in the ministries and other government departments and in the CPO to carry out the tenets of the report.

Among the four reasons for the failure of the CPO to have its report put into practice, perhaps the most crucial one was the lack of strong and dynamic leadership of the planning organization. This is evidenced by the active role which the CPO came to play in the Saudi Arabian development process after Hisham Nazer was appointed to head the planning organization. Nazer's management was helped by earlier achievements which had been recorded in the programme of streamlining the governmental machinery. A case in point was the establishment of a Central Department of Organization and Management in the Ministry of Finance and National Economy.

The CPO in August 1970 submitted to the King the now-famous First Development Plan, 1970/1-1974/5. The content of the Plan, the problems connected with its implementation, and the lessons to be learned for future plan formulation are what this chapter is all about. This introductory section has been directed primarily at providing a historical foundation upon which the discussion of the First Development Plan is built.[12]

The First Development Plan

Overall Objectives, Strategy, and Targets

The outline of the Development Plan for the five years 1390/91-1394/95 (1970/1-1974/5), prepared by the Central Planning Organization was approved in September 1969.[13] The general objectives of the development policy implicit in the Plan were to increase the productive capacity of the economy and to raise the standard of living and the wealth and welfare of the people of Saudi Arabia. At the same time the Plan intended to provide for national security and to maintain economic and social stability along the path of development. Specific objectives of this Plan were:

(1) to raise the rate of growth of the gross domestic product (GDP);
(2) to diversify the economy and to reduce the country's dependence on oil by increasing the contribution of the other productive sectors to the national product;
(3) to lay the foundation for sustained economic growth; and
(4) to develop human resources so as to enable different elements of society to contribute more effectively to the growth of the economy and to participate more fully in the process of development.

The Plan projected an increase in the GDP from about SR 16 billion to SR 26 billion during the Plan period, indicating an average annual growth rate of about 9.8 per cent.

To achieve the above target and other objectives, the Plan projected an outlay of SR 41.3 billion in the public sector for the five years. Of this, project outlay received SR 18.4 billion (44.6 per cent) and current expenditure the remaining SR 22.9 billion or 55.4 per cent. In addition, emphasis was given to the private sector to increase its ability to participate in the process of development.

Among the items listed in Table 5.1, defence received the largest share of the total planned outlay, accounting for SR 9,555 million or 23.1 per cent. The share of this sector in project outlay is even higher, accounting for SR 5,575 million or 30.0 per cent of the total project outlay for the five years.

Table 5.1: Plan Outlay, 1970/1-1974/5 (SR million)

Sectors	Current expendi- tures	Percentage of total	Project expendi- tures	Percentage of total	Total expendi- tures	Percentage of total
Public administration	6,794.6	29.6	922.8	5.0	7,717.4	18.6
Defence	3,980.0	17.4	5,575.0	30.0	9,555.0	23.1
Social services (education, health, labour and social affairs)	7,763.1	33.9	1,535.7	8.4	9,298.8	22.5
Urban development and public utilities	1,246.9	5.4	3,325.4	18.1	4,572.3	11.1
Transport and communica- tions	1,767.3	7.7	5,709.2	31.1	7,476.5	18.1
Industry	321.8	1.4	776.7	4.2	1,098.5	2.7
Agriculture	973.8	4.2	493.9	2.7	1,467.7	3.6
Trade and services	83.5	0.4	43.8	0.2	127.3	0.3
Total	22,931.0	100.0	18,382.5	100.0	41,313.5	100.0

Source: M.A. Asiel, 'Public Finance and Economic Development in Saudi Arabia, 1960/61-1973/74' (paper, University of Colorado, Boulder, August 1974), Table 20.

Among the development sectors, the Plan assigns major emphasis to social services subsector with an allocation of SR 9,298.8 million or 22.5 per cent of total plan outlay, followed by transport and communications sector with SR 7,476 million or 18.1 per cent, and urban development and public utilities with SR 4,572.3 million or 11.1 per cent.

Sectoral allocation pattern of project outlay differs from that of total development expenditures. Defence accounts for 30.3 per cent of the project outlay, while two closely related sectors between them share almost half of the total allocation. These are transport and communications with allocation of SR 5,709.2 million or 31.1 per cent, and urban development and public utilities with SR 3,325.4 million or 18.1 per cent, respectively. The social services sectors (including education, health, labour and social affairs) as a whole share only 8.4 per cent of the total project allocation, or SR 1,535.7 million.

In order to diversify the economy and to reduce its dependence on oil, the Plan aimed at increasing the contribution of other productive sectors, specifically agriculture and industry, to the national product. However, the amount allocated to these sectors was relatively very small, accounting for only 6.3 per cent of the total planned outlay and 6.9 per cent of the project outlay. Industry (including mining and power) received only 2.7 per cent and 4.2 per cent of the total and project outlays, respectively. The agricultural sector accounted for only 3.6 per cent of the total and 2.7 per cent of the project outlay.

It seems that with regard to the development of agriculture and industry, the Plan relied heavily upon the private sector. Given the crucial importance of these sectors and the objective of diversifying the economy, and the fact that the development of traditional sectors in developing countries is a most difficult task, it would appear the government put too much faith in the private sector's ability to contribute to investment and in this sector's overall participation in the economy.

Specific Sectoral Targets of the Plan

In the industrial sector the Plan recommended the issuance of a general industrial policy for the Kingdom, the completion of the construction operations at the industrial estates in Jeddah, Riyadh and Dammam, and the initiation of feasibility studies for establishing further estates in other parts of the Kingdom. Execution of the grain-silos project, a sulphur plant, the Riyadh refinery and the bulk plants (for petroleum products) in Qasim and Khamis Mishayt was recommended. The Plan also provided guidelines to the private sector for various fresh investment opportunities, among which were the establishment of plants for cotton textiles, plumbing tools, batteries, canning vegetables, packing and shipment of fish, a plant for the production of medical tablets, and paper-product industry in the Western Province. From the public sector's point of view, the Plan allocated a total outlay of SR 1,098.5

million to this sector, while from the total project outlay, industry accounted for SR 776.7 million. As a result of the projected investments, the contribution of manufacturing industries was estimated to increase from about SR 335 million at the beginning of the Plan to SR 562 million at the end of the Plan, implying an average annual growth rate of 13.5 per cent.

In the agricultural sector the Plan aimed at achieving a growth rate of 27 per cent in production. An amount of SR 1,467.7 million was allocated for this sector, SR 493.9 million for projects and the rest for the current expenditure outlay. The Plan, however, recommended expansion in services and programmes that would encourage private investment in agriculture and allied industries with emphasis on research programmes, studies and statistics, and the provision of agricultural loans and credits.

With a view to creating the necessary physical infrastructure for sustained economic growth, the Plan, in general, followed the policies pursued prior to the period. A total of 4,312 km of main roads was earmarked for construction during the five-year period. In addition, 2,000 km of rural roads were planned to be built. The expansion schemes for the Jeddah and Dammam ports would be implemented, and expansion of the ports of Yanbu, Jubail and Jizan was given consideration under the infrastructural budget. Seven airports were to be developed to a level capable of accommodating jet planes. Further, the number of graduates from civil aviation training centres per year was expected to double in five years. Provision was also made for the expansion of the automatic telephone network. This would involve an extension to cater for 137,200 lines and the establishment of satellite stations for telegraph services. Another communication development envisaged in the Plan was the building of additional post offices to increase the number from 210 to 479 by the end of the Plan period. Financial allocation made to achieve these targets amounted to SR 7,476.5 million for the transport and communications subsector.

The Plan also recommended the setting up of a department for electricity services to be responsible for initiating and carrying out necessary changes in the electricity sector to enable it to meet growing demands, execute programmes for supplying electricity to cities and large rural centres, and to initiate studies on the electricity tariff so as to find ways and means of reducing it to increase private and industrial consumption. In addition, the construction of sewerage networks in Riyadh, Mecca and Medina was expected to be completed during the Plan period along with networks for another six cities. A number of slaughter houses and meat, vegetable and fish markets was envisaged for various cities of the Kingdom. For the purpose of achieving these targets, the financial allocation of SR 4,572.3 million, or 11.1 per cent of the total outlay was made for urban development. Project expenditure outlay for this sector accounted for SR 3,325.4 million, or 18.1 per cent of total project expenditures in the Plan.

With regard to human capital and social development, appreciable targets were set in the Plan. In an attempt to develop a manpower programme which would reduce the shortage of both skilled and semi-skilled labour, an expansion in educational and vocational training facilities was given priority. The objective was to raise the number of students at all levels of education substantially during the period of implementation of the Plan. Especially concerned with the traditional attitude towards female education, the Plan provided for increases in female enrolment in primary schools from 114,800 to 224,500, in intermediate schools from 4,400 to 23,500, and in secondary schools from 350 to 4,900. The anti-illiteracy programme was to be intensified, the number of evening schools for this purpose was scheduled to rise from 592 to 792 by the end of the Plan period. Higher levels of education were, of course, not de-emphasized, despite the provisions made for the lower educational levels in the Plan. Expansion of educational programmes at Riyadh University, King Abdulaziz University (Jeddah), and the College of Petroleum and Minerals in Dhahran (later on to become a university) were to be undertaken as part of the Plan's objectives.

The Plan also aimed at opening six vocational training centres in different parts of the Kingdom, expanding the training facilities available at the existing centres, and the opening of new sections in response to the needs of the economy. These, it was hoped, would supply about 1,600 skilled and semi-skilled workers domestically as compared to an estimated demand of more than 61,000.

In the public sector's health services – public health – the Plan aimed to increase the number of doctors from 775 in 1970 to 1,200 in 1974/5. In 1970 Saudi doctors and medical technicians constituted 15 and 23 per cent respectively of the total number of doctors and technicians, while it was planned that by 1975 the number would have risen to 35 and 50 per cent, respectively.

Finally, the Plan envisaged the completion of the population census for the Kingdom; recommended co-operation between various ministries and departments for improving the collection of data needed for better estimation of the GNP, and for improvement in the availability and reliability of statistical information for a better appraisal of the development taking place in the economy.

In summary, it can be argued that the broad outline of the Plan, despite its alleged emphasis on social development, was a continuation of the general pattern indicated by the decade prior to the Plan. Physical development (urban development and transport and communication) received a place of prime importance as indicated by the allocation of almost one-third of the total outlay, or about half of the project (development) outlay. Despite its strong emphasis on diversification of the economy, the Plan allocated a relatively very small proportion (6.6 per cent) of the total outlay, and only 7.1 per cent of project outlay to industry, agriculture and allied activities. Given the prospect of the oil sector and the overall performance of the economy in the late 1960s, the targeted outlays and the projected growth rates could be considered moderate and conservative except for human-resource development which can take place only slowly. One may even argue that the targets could have been achieved even without the Plan, assuming the budgetary policies of the earlier decade were to continue. None the less, an important aspect of the Plan was its allocative mechanism and budgetary process in the sense that it involved decisions beyond a single year. It also gave the government a central direction for development purposes.

Plan Implementation

One of the reasons why planning in developing countries has not been successful as a weapon for rapid economic development, is the tendency for the governments of these countries to overemphasize plan formulation at the expense of its implementation. If a development plan for a given period does not envisage expenditures greater than what the government will normally spend over the period through ordinary budget appropriation (i.e. without a comprehensive plan), then one may be tempted to conclude that such a plan may not call for much extra effort for its implementation. However, to the extent that the objective of the plan might be to ensure co-ordination of all expenditures so as not only to achieve internal consistency, but also to give an overall direction for development, even such a small plan will require institutional changes in the governmental machinery to realize the objectives of the plan. Especially, the task of the planning body of co-ordination will become an important determinant of how successfully the plan is implemented.

In practice, development plans tend to have outlay proposals which by far outstrip the total expenditures for the plan period which would ordinarily be appropriated by annual budgets if there were no plan for the period.[14] One reason is that the preparation of a development plan has become one of the preconditions for external assistance by international financial bodies. Also, during the process of plan formulation, the country's authorities and their advisors are more able to identify the needs of the country, and also to realize the size and composition of the resource base, which may give rise to increased (and often exaggerated) aspirations of the country. There is, of course, the additional tendency for governments to undertake ambitious development plans in an attempt to create an impression of a high development capacity of the country. Consequently, most development plans tend to be more ambitious than what could be efficiently implemented by the government's administrative machinery, and also than is consistent with the supply of the projected rate of growth of some essential ingredients in development, namely capital, manpower, management, physical infrastructure, attitude of the citizens towards modernization, and so forth.

Whether a development plan is too big, too small, or is of the right size, it is not uncommon for annual budgets and for budget allocations over a plan period to deviate from the size and composition contained in allocations under the development plan. There is a problem of interpretation in connection with such inconsistencies between corresponding figures for the plan and the budgets. In the case of Saudi Arabia, the issue is whether to interpret the inconsistencies between the 1970-5 Plan figures and the budget projections for the 1970-5 period as elements of flexibility built into the Plan-implementation process, or as an indication of the inability of the government to follow the Plan allocations because they were too unrealistic, or because of any other reason which indicates that the Plan was doomed to be unsuccessful. A way out of this dilemma is to examine the specific reasons for the deviations for the 1970-5 Plan. An attempt is made to do this in the next subsection.

Another way to analyse the implementation of a development plan is to examine its performance, by comparing the performance of the economy during and in the last year of the plan period with the projected performance. This will be the subject of discussion in following pages.

Budget Estimates and Plan Allocation

The First Development Plan of the Kingdom of Saudi Arabia was prepared under a financial constraint, which faced the country after the Middle East war of 1967. The Plan budgeted for a deficit ranging between SR 3.9 billion to SR 7.5 billion, depending on whether estimated revenue of SR 33.8 billion or SR 37.4 billion is respectively used. However, increased oil revenues changed the outlook of government revenue during the Plan period.[15] As a result, actual revenue which accrued to the government of Saudi Arabia during the 1971-5 period was in the neighbourhood of SR 180 billion compared to the projected and much lower revenue mentioned earlier. Consequently, both budget estimates and actual expenditures during the five-year period 1970/1-1974/5 increased and were by far greater than outlays proposed under the Plan. Whereas it was projected to spend SR 41.3 billion during the Plan period, budget estimates for the five financial years 1970/1-1974/5 allocated SR 98.9 billion.[16] On the other hand, actual expenditures for the Plan period were SR 78.2 billion.[17]

It can be provisionally concluded, therefore, that the unexpected increase in government revenues, especially from oil, generated the divergence between the size of the budgetary allocation for the 1971-5 period and the figures envisaged under the Plan. From the point of view of overall expenditures, it appears the increased revenue from oil enabled the government, at least, to make an attempt to fulfil (or overfulfil) the Plan's expenditure objectives. Indeed, in actuality, overfulfillment of the objectives of the budgetary proposals was achieved since the actual expenditures during the 1971/5 period was 89.2 per cent more than the outlay proposed in the Plan. However, the crucial consideration is the composition of the expenditures actually undertaken and not the total size. For example, if it is found that most of the expenditure was in the form of foreign aid, then despite the oil revenue, the objective of the Plan might not be realized although the total actual expenditures may give the impression that fulfilment was inevitable.

Unfortunately, the composition of actual expenditures for various years of the Plan is not available. Therefore, sectoral analysis is done in terms of budget estimates, in order to give a clue as to the actual sectoral allocation of expenditures. However, as we will see in Chapter 8, it is recognized that budget estimates are poor proxies for actual sectoral expenditures. It must also be warned that even with respect to the expenditure appropriations in the annual budgets, the categorization in the budgets are different from that found in the Plan, and as a result the analysis is put on a slightly shaky ground. On the other hand, since a breakdown of actual expenditures into recurrent and project is available, it is at least possible to look at broad structural changes in expenditure patterns which the increased revenue generated.

Table 5.2 indicates that the amount appropriated for project expenditures in various budgets during 1971-5 amounted to 299 per cent of total project outlay envisaged in the Plan. This substantial increase in total project allocation which was due to the change in revenue prospects of the government after the inception of the Plan, was not shared equally by all sectors, as the last column of Table 5.2 indicates. Agriculture and water sector was by far the biggest gainer. The proposed budgetary allocation for projects in this sector increased by more than six times over the amount earmarked for it under the Plan. The amorphous sector, miscellaneous, followed as the next big gainer, with a 309 per cent increase over the Plan allocation. It is within this sector that substantial allocating might have been made for foreign aid, essentially to Arab nations directly involved in the Arab-Israeli conflict. Generally speaking, transport and communications, social services, urban development and administration all gained from the unexpectedly large government revenue. The exception was industry and commerce. However, all of these sectors gained at a rate lower than the overall increase of budgetary allocation compared with allocations in the Plan; agriculture and water and miscellaneous were the only two sectors which had more than average gain in budgetary expenditures.

One phenomenon which stands out from Table 5.2, and which is surprising in view of the pronounced objective of the First Plan (and, indeed, in the subsequent two development plans) of diversifying the economy by industrialization, is the fact that the project appropriation for industry and commerce for the 1971-5 period was only 27.8 per cent of what the Plan proposed for this subsector during the same period. As a result, the share of this sector in total project expenditures fell from 4.4 per cent for Plan allocation to 0.4 per cent according to budget allocations.

If Table 5.2 is reliable, then one would make the following generalizations. It appears that what the improved prospects for government revenue did to the government's priorities was to shift emphasis to agriculture and water and to defence and finance. Defence and finance, incidentally, are the most important components of 'miscellaneous' sector. This is because all sectors except these two sectors (agriculture and miscellaneous) lost their shares of total project allocation when it came to yearly allocation of budgetary expenditures. Therefore, even

Table 5.2: Comparison Between Plan Outlay and Budget Project Estimates, 1970/1-1974/5

Sectors	Plan outlay, 1970/1-1974/5						Estimated project expenditures, 1970-5		Budget project appropriations as a percentage of first plan allocations
	Total		Recurrent		Project				
	SR million	%	SR million	%	SR million	%	SR million	%	
Transport and communications	7,476.5	18.1	1,767.3	7.7	5,709.2	31.1	11,415.4	20.8	199.9
Agriculture and water	1,467.7	3.6	973.8	4.2	493.9	2.7	3,167.1	5.8	641.2
Industry and commerce	1,225.8	3.0	405.3	1.8	820.5	4.4	228.4	0.4	27.8
Social services	9,298.8	22.5	7,763.1	33.9	1,535.7	8.4	3,425.6	6.2	223.1
Urban development (municipalities)	4,572.3	11.1	1,246.9	5.4	3,325.4	18.1	8,349.6	15.2	251.1
Administration	7,717.4	18.6	6,794.6	29.6	922.8	5.0	2,023.4	3.7	219.3
Miscellaneous[a]	9,555.0	23.1	3,980.0	17.4	5,575.0	30.0	26,399.4	48.0	409.3
Total	41,313.5	100.0	22,931.0	100.0	18,382.5	100.0	55,008.9	100.0	299.1

Note: a. Plan outlay figures for 'miscellaneous' appear to coincide with defence expenditures in Table 5.1. On the other hand, 'miscellaneous' figures of the budget estimates for project expenditures for the fiscal years 1970/1-1974/5 include expenditures in the following categories: petroleum and minerals, finance, mosque and Hajj affairs, and 'others'.
Source: Computed from Table 5.1 and from Table 3 (3) of the Plan chapter on public finance.

from the analysis of budgetary project allocations alone, and despite recognizing that the private sector's involvement in the development of Saudi Arabia is mainly seen in activities which directly or indirectly contribute to industrial growth, one cannot help but conclude that the budgetary allocation of the government for the 1970/1-1974/5 financial years did not give sufficient emphasis to industry.[18] There was thus no reason to expect success in achieving the growth targets envisaged in the Plan for this sector. Consequently, some of the failures of the First Plan should be expected, considering the expenditure pattern found in the annual budgets for the Plan period.

It is interesting to note some qualitative evaluations of the composition of actual expenditures undertaken under the Plan which may be worthwhile in lieu of non-availability of data on composition of actual budgetary expenditures during this period. Research findings of the US Department of State on the absorptive capacity of oil-producing countries indicate that 'the actual expenditures were even more divergent from the goals of the Plan. Defense, foreign aid, administration and infrastructure dominated the development program. The productive sectors, except petroleum-based industries, received little attention . . . On the whole, the First Plan's objectives were completely ignored.'[19]

Actual budget expenditure for the period 1971/5 was 89.3 per cent more than the amount envisaged under the Plan. However, budgetary allocation for this period was 107 per cent more than Plan allocation. Of the total actual budget expenditures, 51.3 per cent (or SR 40,138 million) was actually spent on projects. On the other hand, according to financial allocations under the Plan, only 44.5 per cent of total expenditures was to be spent on projects. Consequently, in actuality, the increased government revenue shifted resources from recurrent to project expenditures. To the extent that project expenditures could roughly be regarded as capital formation, then the government's priorities shifted from current consumption to future consumption – i.e. to capital accumulation. This is a healthy sign for a country which faces physical bottlenecks in the development process.

Plan Performance

As discussion in the previous section indicates, it is possible to make at least a qualitative evaluation of the First Plan of Saudi Arabia. In this section, an attempt will be made to present a more detailed analysis of the performance of the Plan. And although the First Plan is now history, an attempt at analysing the successes and/or failures of the Plan is inherently beneficial to setting the stage for subsequent development planning efforts.

In any case, government sources in Saudi Arabia consider the implementation of the First Plan a success. Several indicators are used to support this assertion:[20]

(1) actual government expenditures, both recurrent and project for the 1971-5 period by far exceeded the five-year projections made under the Plan (see Table 5.3);
(2) annual growth rate of GDP of 13.2 per cent exceeded the projected growth rate of 9.8 per cent.

However, these sources are careful to point out that 'because of the non-financial constraints to the country's development potential, the growth of some crucial sectors fell below plan expectations, inspite of efforts in this direction'.[21] Such a statement is an honest admission that the 13.2 per cent growth rate of GDP might not reflect the rate of growth of the non-oil sector, which is a better measure than the rate of growth of GDP of how the economy is performing, or to put it in a different context, it is a better measure of the rate at which the economy is absorbing the Kingdom's surplus funds. The actual rate of growth of 3 and 11 per cent for agriculture and manufacturing, respectively, as against projected 4.6 and 14 per cent, respectively, is a further indication of the poor production base of the Saudi economy so far as consumer goods (food and manufactured goods) are concerned.

Although the qualification to the admission of failures in agriculture and industry, namely, that efforts were made by the government to achieve a rapid rate of growth in these sectors, may apply to the agricultural sector, it does not appear to apply to industry when budget estimates for projects in this sector are considered. It will be recalled that the budget allocation for projects in the industry and commerce sector was only 27.8 per cent of what the Plan had envisaged, and was only 0.4 per cent of total project appropriations. The budget proposals for the plan period did not give any indication that sufficient efforts were made by the government to achieve industrial growth. Indeed, given this low emphasis on industrial development by the government, it is to the credit of the private sector that such a substantial rate of growth of 11 per cent was achieved, although this rate fell short of the Plan target. Ironically, therefore, it appears industrial growth during the Plan period, considering the meagre support given by the Saudi government,

Table 5.3: Government Revenues and Government Expenditures in the First Plan (SR billions)

	1970/1	1971/2	1972/3	1973/4	1974/5	Total	Five-year projection
Government revenue	7.9	11.1	15.4	44.8	101.4	180.6	33.8-37.4
Government expenditure	6.4	8.3	10.1	19.5	42.2	86.5	41.3
Recurrent	4.1	4.9	5.9	9.2	27.2	51.3	22.9
Projects	2.3	3.4	4.2	10.3	15.0	35.2	18.4

Source: SAMA, *Annual Report, 1975*, Table 5, p. 52.

was commendable. Yet it fell short of Plan projections and therefore the Plan had only a partial success in this area; this occurred in large part because of the limited role the government played in the industrialization process. The above analysis confirms our earlier contention that the government of Saudi Arabia has tended to rely too much on the private sector in its attempts to diversify the economy through industrial growth.

Table 5.4: First Plan Growth Rates (per cent)

	First plan projection	First plan actuals	Actuals minus projections
Total GDP	9.8	13.5	3.7
Oil sector	9.1	14.9	5.8
Non-oil private sector	12.0	11.0	–1.0
Agriculture	4.6	3.6	–1.0
Manufacturing	14.0	11.6	–2.6
Construction	10.4	18.6	8.2
Transport, communications and storage	12.9	17.0	4.1
Government sector	7.0	7.8	0.8

Source: SAMA, *Annual Report, 1977*, Table 5, p. 47.

Table 5.4 allows a further sectoral comparison between the plan projections and actual rate of growth achieved. Generally speaking, non-oil sectors grew at rates less than the projected growth rates envisaged in the Plan. Despite the physical bottlenecks, which still exist in the Saudi economy, however, the target for construction was exceeded. The actual growth rate in this sector was in fact almost double the targeted rate of growth, while transportation and communications were next according to the extent of performance which is measured by the amount by which actual rate of growth exceeded projected growth rate – the final column of Table 5.4. But for the poor performance of agriculture and manufacturing, the Plan could be said to have been successful so far as growth rates are concerned.

However, two reasons prevent the making of such a statement. First, the projected expenditures (both recurrent and project) were far smaller than actual expenditures. It follows that, had the government spent exactly an amount equal to the one proposed under the Plan, the actual rates of growth would have been lower than Table 5.4 shows. Two implications can be drawn from the above: (1) perhaps the growth targets were too optimistic in relation to the expenditures allocated under the Plan; (2) in terms of the amount actually spent, the productivity of expenditures was very low compared with the output-expenditure ratio assumed under the Plan. These implications, it can be seen, are two sides of the same coin.

The second reason is that agriculture and manufacturing happen to be crucial sectors of the Saudi economy. And in terms of the goal of diversification, these sectors become even more vital. Therefore, for the Plan to have performed poorly in these sectors is something which takes a lot of points from the overall success of the Plan. It is not, however, uncommon for development plans to fail in the agricultural sector. But manufacturing is an area which might be considered as having the greatest hope for the diversification aspirations of the Kingdom. The failure in this sector is especially unfortunate, considering the attitude of the Saudi government towards this sector as expressed in the budget appropriations in the 1971-5 five-year period.

Table 5.5: Gross Capital Formation (GCF) by Sector, 1970/1-1975/6 (SR millions)

	1970/1	1971/2	1972/3	1973/4	1974/5	1975/6
Government	1,204	1,443	1,985	3,416	7,348	23,421
Non-oil private	1,151	1,290	1,669	2,351	3,853	5,926
Oil	577	671	2,040	2,633	3,659	4,396
Total (GCF)	2,932	3,403	5,694	8,400	14,866	33,743
Inventories	–205	95	–113	335	2,402	2,091
Total (GCF)	2,727	3,498	5,581	8,735	17,268	35,834

Source: SAMA, *Annual Report, 1977*, Table 3, p. 45.

To conclude the evaluation of the First Development Plan of the Kingdom of Saudi Arabia, and consequently to conclude this chapter, several observations can be made. There is no doubt that both the Saudi government and the planning authority have learned many lessons from the implementation aspect of the Plan. If the Plan did not achieve anything at all, one can point to the high rate of capital formation (see Tables 5.5 and 5.6) which it generated during the five-year period, to say nothing of the planning experience which all departments of the government have had. The question which remained at the end of the First Plan period was whether the lessons learned would be translated into successful formulation and implementation of

Table 5.6: Gross Fixed Capital Formation (GFCF) by Type of Capital Goods, 1969/70-1975/6 (SR millions)

	1969/70	1970/1	1971/2	1972/3	1973/4	1974/5	Five-year compound annual growth rate	1975/6
Construction	1,969	2,196	2,596	4,706	6,214	11,505		27,050
% Growth rate		11.5	18.2	81.4	32.0	85.2	45.7	135.0
Transport equipment	309	313	335	468	757	1,331		1,966
% Growth rate		1.3	7.0	39.7	61.8	75.8	37.1	47.0
Machinery and equipment	319	423	473	520	1,429	2,030		4,717
% Growth rate		32.6	11.8	9.9	174.8	42.1	54.2	132.0
Total (GFCF)	2,597	2,931	3,403	5,694	8,400	14,866		33,743
% Growth rate		12.9	16.1	67.3	47.5	77.0	44.2	127.0

Source: SAMA, *Annual Report, 1977*, Table 4, p. 46.

subsequent development plans. As it turned out, and as we will see in Chapter 6, one lesson was surely put into practice: that there is a positive correlation between oil revenue and plan size. But plan size does not depend solely on the capacity to finance the plan. In the case of a country like Saudi Arabia where finance is no constraint, the relevant factors which should collectively determine the size of a plan are those other than finance. But to the extent that manpower, administrative capacity and physical capital did not sufficiently determine the size of the Second Plan, it can be said that the absorptive capacity of the Kingdom was not given a more careful consideration during the Plan-formulation process. As will be seen in Chapter 6, these factors were later to provide serious constraints on the successful implementation of the Second Development Plan of Saudi Arabia.

Notes

1. Arthur W. Lewis, *Some Aspects of Economic Development* (Accra, Ghana Publishing Corporation, 1969), p. 37.

2. The observation about the relationship between development planning and economic growth has been made by Arthur W. Lewis, ibid. However, like most cross-country analysis, this conclusion suffers from the criticism that the relevant comparison is perhaps not among growth rates of different countries, but between the growth rates of a single country in periods with a plan and in periods without a plan.

3. W.F. Stolpher, 'Comprehensive Development Planning', *East African Economics Review*, I, New Series, December 1964, reprinted in G.M. Meier, *Leading Issues in Economic Development* (New York, Oxford University Press, 1976), p. 819.

4. For a more comprehensive discussion of failures of development plans in developing countries, vide G.M. Meier, *Leading Issues*, Chapter 13.

5. Kingdom of Saudi Arabia, Ministry of Planning, *The Second Development Plan, 1975-80*, p. 3. (Hereafter cited as *Second Development Plan*.)

6. Most of the discussion of the early years of planning history is based on the work of Said M.A. Adam, *A Report on the Development of Planning Organization in Saudi Arabia* (Saudi Arabia, June 1965).

7. Said M.A. Adam, *Report on Development of Planning Organization*, p. 10.

8. Said M.A. Adam, *Report on Development of Planning Organization*, pp. 14-15.

9. Article VI of Royal Decree No. 50, 4 January 1961.

10. Said M.A. Adam, *Report on Development of Planning Organization*, pp. 36-7.

11. R. Knauerhase, *The Saudi Arabian Economy* (New York, Praeger, 1975), p. 318.

12. After the inception of the Second Development Plan (1975-80) in July 1975, the Central Planning Organization was elevated to ministerial status. It is now the Ministry of Planning. *Second Development Plan*, p. viii.

13. A complete translation of the document in English was available at the

time of writing. The description here is based on the work of Saiel, who used the original outline in Arabic and secondary sources. Murad A. Asiel, 'Public Finance and Economic Development in Saudi Arabia, 1960/61-1973/74' (paper, University of Colorado, Boulder, August 1974), Chapter 6. The First Development Plan is referred to as the Plan in the subsequent discussion in this chapter.

14. Except in circumstances such as the case of the Saudi First Development Plan, when increases in oil revenues during the Plan period made the initial plan outlays underestimated.

15. See Chapter 2 for factors which have contributed to substantial increase in government revenues from oil royalties and income taxes. Also see Chapter 8 for discussion of budgetary estimates.

16. Computed from Table 8.5, below. The discrepancy between this amount and the total one would obtain from adding figures from Table 8.5 is due to the fact that the latter figures contain project expenditures earmarked under the Second Development Plan which were included in the 1974/5 project allocation.

17. Computed from same source as note 16 above. However, in 1975 SAMA, *Annual Report*, p. 6, estimated that 'actual expenditures, including substantial amounts of foreign aid' was SR 86.5 billion for the period 1971-5.

18. It is interesting to note in the discussion of the Second Plan in the following chapter that actual expenditure for industry and commerce was far below planned expenditures for the 1975-1980 period as well. Despite inability to achieve sectoral objectives in the First Plan with low expenditures on industry and commerce, expenditures did not reflect a change in policy from apparent reliance on the private sector in the Second Plan.

19. United States, Department of State, Policy Sciences Division, *Medium-Term Ability of Oil-Producing Countries to Absorb Real Goods and Services*, vol. 2 of Research Findings, May 1976, pp. 14-15.

20. SAMA, *Annual Report, 1975*, pp. 51-2.

21. Ibid., p. 52.

6 PLANNING FOR ECONOMIC DEVELOPMENT: THE SECOND EXPERIENCE

Introduction

Unlike the First Development Plan, the Second Development Plan for the period 1975-80 embodies efforts by Saudi Arabia to develop in a manner unconstrained by finance, specifically foreign exchange.[1] Since the increase in oil prices in 1973 raised the foreign exchange resources of Saudi Arabia, the major economic problem has been that of finding domestic avenues for absorbing the so called 'surplus funds'. Even when compared with other wealthy OPEC countries, Saudi Arabia is considered to be the one with the lowest absorptive capacity.[2]

If the proposition that the principal objective of a development plan is to facilitate efficient utilization of a country's scarce resources in an attempt to accelerate economic and social development is valid, then one wonders whether a plan as comprehensive as the Second Plan is necessary for a country which is currently not faced with the problem of scarce financial resources. But the scepticism about the need for such a plan erodes as one reads it. The rationale for planning on such a scale in Saudi Arabia can be found in the fundamental principles which guide the Kingdom's development objectives. The principles, on the other hand, are expressed by the goals contained in the Second Development Plan.[3]

Some important questions, however, still remain: How large must a Saudi development plan be since there is no financial constraint? What are the chances of its successful implementation? What role has been given to the private sector (both domestic and foreign) in the planning process? What is the future of oil in Saudi Arabia, as envisaged in the Plan? In the analysis of planning in Saudi Arabia which follows, attempts will be made to discuss what the Second Development Plan has to say on these and other equally relevant questions.

The goals of the plan are to:[4]

(1) maintain the religious and moral values of Islam;
(2) assure the defence and internal security of the Kingdom;
(3) maintain a high rate of economic growth by developing economic resources, maximizing earnings from oil over the long term, and conserving depletable resources;

(4) reduce economic dependence on export of crude oil;
(5) develop human resources by education, training, and raising standards of health;
(6) increase the well-being of all groups within the society and foster social stability under circumstances of rapid social change;
(7) develop physical infrastructure to support achievement of the above goals.

Plan Goals

An inference could be made from above that the Saudi Arabian government recognizes the difference between development and growth. Thus non-economic conveniences to good life – religion and moral stability – are to be maintained; also, the existence of law and order and protection from attack which are necessary for the creation of a conducive climate within which the fruits of economic growth are enjoyed, are considered important. Like most economic plans, however, the detailed emphasis is on economic well-being, although 'advance towards the social and economic goals *would be provided for* while maintaining the religious and moral values of Islam'.[5] Rapid development entails the utilization of physical, financial and human resources; this becomes the cardinal goal of the plan. It is through such development efforts that the social and economic well-being of the peoples of Saudi Arabia could be improved in the shortest possible time.

No doubt these seven goals are not mutually exclusive. More importantly, however, there are bound to arise conflicts among specific policies which could be followed to fulfil the goals. For example, it will not be easy to 'foster social stability under circumstances of social change'. Further, it is well known that education tends to change a person's attitude toward traditional beliefs, social values, authority and the like. However, one thing which often works to the advantage of resolving conflicts between social and economic goals is that the social changes need not keep pace with economic development. This is because social change, as an institutional phenomenon, occurs only slowly. This is, of course, not to say that all socio-cultural changes are growth-promoting; changes which create unfavourable social upheavals do not help growth.

It must be emphasized that conflicts among goals of development plans (and for that matter of all forms of development strategies) are the rule rather than the exception whenever a serious and systematic attempt at planning is made in a country as diversified and as traditionally based as Saudi Arabia. In any case, resolutions of conflicts among programmes which seek to attain different goals of a plan are themselves a crucial aspect of the development planning process.

In order that the details of a plan and the policies which effect their implementation could be understood correctly, it is imperative that the context within which the goals of the plan is discussed should be made clear. The goals of the plan under consideration are placed within the framework of the Saudi Arabian domestic policies.

A long-term policy of Saudi Arabia is to diversify the economy so as to reduce the dependence of the economy on the primary exhaustible resource, oil. In this regard, an important goal of the Plan is diversification of the Saudi economy based on the efficient utilization of human and natural resources of the Kingdom. This involves the shifting of resources into agriculture, industry and mining to expand these important sectors of the economy. There is no doubt that it is in the expansion of these sectors that the participation of private entrepreneurs would be most needed and welcomed by the Saudi government.

In spite of the fact that the goal of diversification of the Saudi economy is an indication of good foresight on the part of the planners, one wonders whether the emphasis which the planned industrialization programme places on the petrochemical industry will not only serve to sustain the dependence of the economy on oil. If this happens, then the economy may be in trouble when crude oil in the Kingdom has been exhausted, unless the oil-based manufacturing industry has been established so strongly that it continues to reap other locational advantages to make it profitable even after the comparative advantage which Saudi Arabia currently enjoys in this field ceases to exist. It is perhaps in the recognition of this potential problem which resource-exhaustion might bring that conservation is emphasized in the Plan. Effective conservation policies will no doubt contribute considerably to an extension of the life-span of oil in Saudi Arabia, especially if they are undertaken within a regional or especially global framework. Also, the discovery of alternative energy sources will enhance the ability of Saudi Arabia to stretch the life of oil and consequently improve the long-term health of the petrochemical industry.

The planners appear to be aware of the tendency for development in a surplus-funds country to encounter bottlenecks in the area of manpower supply.[6] The Plan puts the 'development of human resources' in a broader context to include not only the provision of education and training, but also the provision of health and medical services to the people of Saudi Arabia.[7] The government hopes that the free education proposed will eliminate illiteracy and in addition, not only produce the needed efficient labour force, but also inculcate correct attitudes towards work into the labour force.

It cannot be denied that these two factors – a trained and educated labour force, and the right attitude towards work – are indispensable to successful implementation of development programmes. It is important to note that all these goals affecting human capital development are expected to be achieved within an environment which allows individuals to enhance their capabilities while contributing to the overall welfare of the country.

Apart from social services which contribute directly towards the development of an effective labour force, the government of Saudi Arabia is also committed to raising the average standard of living of the people. The objective of the income-distribution policies is to ensure a 'dignified minimum standard of living',[8] by making necessities available at low prices, providing low-cost housing, extending the welfare system, and making credits readily available to poor people in need of financial help.

The Plan also sees the indispensable role which infrastructure plays as the basis upon which any meaningful development should be executed. This role is especially important in a surplus-funds country in which abundance of foreign exchange resources is likely to create port congestion, problems of storage and transportation bottlenecks.[9] It is, therefore, envisaged to expand and improve port facilities, transportation, communication and housing, and to develop existing municipalities and establish new ones.

The government of Saudi Arabia believes that the objectives of the Plan could be achieved without sacrificing the freedom of the individual to perform and improve his well-being. The principle of freedom is entrenched in the Plan. The government, therefore, supports the free-enterprise system, although it would not look on unconcerned if the market system were behaving in a way inconsistent with the social interests of the population.

The rest of the Plan, after outlining the goals, consists essentially of specification of policies, and allocations which would achieve the stated broad goals. The specifics of the goals are expressed in terms of projections or forecasts of output in the various sectors of the economy: water and agriculture, infrastructure, manufacturing, mining, human resources, etc.

Before we go into the detailed discussion of the Plan, it must be noted that, like most comprehensive plans, it conforms to the criterion enunciated by Professor Arthur Lewis, who writes,

> 'A Development Plan may contain any or all of the following parts:
> (i) a survey of current economic conditions;
> (ii) a list of proposed public expenditures;
> (iii) a discussion of likely developments in the private sector;
> (iv) a macroeconomic projection of the economy;
> (v) a review of government policies.'[10]

The Saudi Plan contains all of the above, but in addition, it devotes space to plan implementation and management, aspects of a plan which are as important as any of the above five portions.

It is hoped that the discussion which follows would show the extent to which these parts of the Plan interact, aside from elucidating the details of each aspect of the planning process.

Development Strategies and Pattern of Development

The Second Development Plan is certainly ambitious. It is, however, not oversized within the context of the financing of it. On the other hand, from the point of view of physical and manpower constraints which exist in Saudi Arabia, the 1975-80 Plan could be seen as too big.

The planners seem to recognize the problems posed by the size of the Plan in connection with its implementation. It is noted, for example, that 'inherent in this opportunity and challenge is the risk that achievement will fall far short of expectation'.[11] Further, the Plan suggests that the capabilities of the planning agency be developed to enable it to define manpower and infrastructural priorities – lower priority projects and programmes would then be rescheduled according to the revealed manpower and physical constraints.[12]

The Second Plan proposes to spend a total of SR 498 billion on programmes. This is about nine times the total expenditures proposed under the First Plan (at 1974-5 constant prices). The size of the Second Development Plan is only one of the features that distinguish it from the First Plan. From Table 6.1, which gives expenditure breakdown for the two plans, some very interesting shifts of emphasis can be observed.

Although all sectors experienced multiple increases in planned expenditures as indicated by the ratio of the Second Plan to the First Plan expenditures in the last column, the relative shares did not remain the same. At an aggregate level it can be seen that, whereas the First Plan allocated 58.3 per cent of the total expenditures to be expended on development sectors, the current plan has made provision for 63.9 per cent of the total expenditures for development purposes. Upon this basis alone one may conclude that the Second Plan is more development-oriented. This characteristic is important because it is a measure of the emphasis the government of Saudi Arabia places on the development of natural and human resources, and the extent of the diversification programmes which altogether summarize the principal goal of the development effort; namely, successful transformation of the country 'into a modern nation capable of sustaining a high standard of living for all its people'.[13]

Table 6.1: Comparison of Estimated Financial Requirements of First and Second Plans[a] (SR millions)

	First Plan		Second Plan		Ratio: Second Plan to First Plan
	Amount	Per cent	Amount	Per cent	
Economic-resource development	6,033.3	10.7	92,135.0	18.5	15.3
Human-resource development	10,198.7	18.1	80,123.9	16.1	7.9
Social development	2,443.0	4.4	33,212.8	6.7	13.6
Physical-infrastructure development	14,086.8	25.1	112,944.6	22.7	8.0
Subtotal (Development)	32,761.8	58.3	318,416.3	63.9	9.7
Administration	10,466.5	18.6	38,179.2	7.7	3.7
Defence	12,994.7	23.1	78,156.5	15.7	6.0
External assistance, emergency funds, food subsidies, and general reserve	–	–	63,478.2	12.7	–
Subtotal (Other)	23,461.2	41.7	179,813.9	36.1	7.7
Total Plan	56,223.0	100.0	498,230.2	100.0	8.9

Note: a. First Plan values have been adjusted to 1974/5 prices (used uniformly for the Second Plan except for certain long-term projections that included inflation factors).
Source: *The Plan*, Table VIII-1, p. 529.

If there is any single innovation in the expenditure pattern of the Second Plan, it is the inclusion of expenditures on the last item in Table

6.1. This item is an amorphous package which gives the authorities charged with the implementation of the Plan some flexibility. It consists principally of unallocated provisions for both developmental and non-developmental sectors of the Saudi economy. Also, since the feasibility studies of some of the programmes which come under this expenditure item had not yet been completed at the time the Plan was launched, the inclusion of such an item enabled the government to get the Plan under-way while the financial needs of those programmes were still being determined; in this way, those few programmes would not hold back the implementation of substantial parts of the Plan.

Table 6.2: Development Expenditures under the First and Second Plans (SR millions)

	First Plan		Second Plan, 1975-80 Total		Project	
	Amount	Per cent	Amount	Per cent	Amount	Per cent
Economic resource development	6,033.3	18.4	92,135.0	28.9	87,616.5	36.6
Human resource development	10,198.7	31.1	80,123.9	25.2	36,216.6	15.1
Social development	2,443.0	7.5	33,212.8	10.4	15,064.0	6.3
Physical infrastructure development	14,086.8	43.0	112,944.6	35.5	100,413.8	42.0
Total development expenditure	32,761.8	100.0	318,416.3	100.0	239,310.9	100.0

Source: *The Plan*, Tables VIII-1 and VIII-2.

From the point of view of diversification of the economy, and human and physical constraints which often emerge in the development process, it is perhaps more fruitful to analyse the relative growth of the sectors of planned expenditure by concentrating on development expenditures. Table 6.2 indicates that whereas economic resources and social development increased their shares, the percentage of total expenditures envisaged for manpower and infrastructural development fell from the First Plan figures of 31.1 per cent and 43 per cent to 25.2 per cent and 35.5 per cent, respectively, under the Second Plan. These developments are despite the fact that there were increases in the amounts of expenditures for all sectors.

Another way of analysing changes in the relative importance which has been placed on the development sectors is to discuss the relative changes in terms of project expenditure breakdown. When this is done, physical infrastructure recovers some of the grounds it lost to social development and economic resources. But although infrastructure commands 42 per cent of the project expenditures allocated for development purposes, economic resources development is by far the biggest gainer: 36.6 per cent of expenditures envisaged for projects in the developmental subsector will take place in the economic resource development sector.

Considering that there is always the danger of overextension of infrastructural facilities during the development planning process, it is possible to argue that such a relative shift of emphasis to development which directly contributes to the well-being of the society merits commendation rather than condemnation. It must especially be pointed out that, despite the decline of the share of its allocated expenditures, physical infrastructure still constitutes the largest sector in terms of both project and total developmental expenditures of the Plan.[14]

The development strategy under the Second Plan consists of three substrategies. First, the Plan gives priority to agricultural and industrial expansion as avenues for diversification of the Saudi Arabian economy. The second substrategy is to expand both the quantity and the quality of manpower resources. Lastly, the Plan makes provision for a fair and efficient regional distribution of economic and social programmes.

The principal objective of the diversification strategy is, as indicated in the broad goals of the Plan, to reduce the overdependence of the Saudi economy on oil. This is the kind of economic self-sufficiency which the planners hope to achieve, in the long run, through the expansion of investment in petrochemical and other mineral-based industries. In this area of the plan implementation, the Saudi government expects a great deal of co-operation from the private sector. This may take the form either of direct private (foreign or domestic) participation in the industrialization effort, or partnership with the Saudi Arabian government to establish joint ventures. Since finance is no problem to Saudi Arabia, the most important contribution which foreign capital could make to development programmes of the country should necessarily be in the area of managerial and technical know-how. In this connection, foreign firms must be prepared to pass on this knowledge to Saudi nationals at the appropriate time.

Several policies have been proposed with the objective of providing incentives needed to generate an adequate amount of private-capital and entrepreneurial involvement in the implementation process. The Plan proposes the institution of credits and other special incentives for the benefit of the private sector. With respect to agriculture, the government's involvement includes spreading the results of research which the institutions it would establish will undertake, providing credit facilities to farmers and instituting a programme to subsidize agricultural inputs.[15]

The planners are acutely aware of the special place which labour has in the Saudi's planning process. Thus, the importance of a large supply of efficient manpower is given practical recognition by the Plan. Not only is it planned to increase the size of the labour force, but also provision has been made to improve its quality through education and training programmes, and the creation of an industrial climate conducive for the attainment of increased productivity. The labour force is expected to grow at an annual rate of 3.4 per cent over the five-year period, 1975-80, with the non-Saudi component taking the lion's share of the increases.[16]

The gross domestic product of Saudi Arabia is projected to grow in real terms at 10 per cent annually, the oil sector at 9.7 per cent, while the non-oil private-plus-government contribution is expected to achieve a combined growth of 13.3 per cent. The growth differential between oil and non-oil sectors of the economy reflects the goal of the government of reducing the overdependence of the Saudi economy on oil. However, the composition of projected GDP at the end of the current plan period is not significantly different from that estimated for the First Plan. Oil will remain the major component of GDP, accounting for almost 75 per cent at the end of the current plan,[17] and will continue to be the principal foreign-exchange earner.

Projected sectoral growth is uneven. Non-oil mining and quarrying, utilities, construction and services which belong to the private sector, are expected to grow annually at 15 per cent. This can be contrasted with an estimated growth rate of crude-oil and natural-gas production, and petroleum refining of 10 per cent and 5 per cent, respectively, which gives an average oil-sector growth rate of 9.7 per cent. On the other hand, manufacturing and petrochemical industries are projected to grow at 17 per cent.

One interesting trend which a careful examination of Table III-5 of the Plan reveals is that despite the size of the budget, the share of the government in projected total non-oil output falls from 18 per cent in 1974-5 to a projected 17.7 per cent in 1979-80.[18] Again, this is consistent with the goals of the Plan – the promise to give the market system a free hand.

With financial constraint removed in the Saudi Arabian case, the crucial problem remaining is that of optimum utilization of depletable oil revenues, in order to meet both the short and long-term objectives of development. As a result, monetary and fiscal policies receive different emphasis; from policies which seek to increase financial resources to those which tend to allocate the necessary finance for various development projects, at the time they are needed and in the right quantities.

The problem of maintaining both domestic and external stability is, however, not eliminated by the abundance of finance. Monetary and fiscal policies are expected to be combined in such a manner that inflation is controlled while maintaining the openness of the economy. Considering that one of the monetary objectives is to prevent the use of Saudi Arabian currency for speculative purposes, it would be very difficult for the banking system to achieve external equilibrium since the exchange rate must be prevented from fluctuating in order to abate speculative activities in the riyal. There is, of course, an alternative: the establishment of exchange controls; a device more consistent with the behaviour of policy-makers in countries with balance-of-payments problems. But this will be contrary to the desire to maintain an open economy, so it must be discounted.

Other specific policies upon which fiscal and monetary management in Saudi Arabia plans to concentrate are as follows:[19]

(1) ensure optimum productivity of both physical and financial capital in the long-run;
(2) make the banking system responsive to exporter demand for banking services;
(3) ensure that all citizens of Saudi Arabia enjoy the fruits of development through the spreading of property widely;
(4) promote international co-operation and live up to the international obligations of the Kingdom.

In its attempt to encourage the private sector to utilize resources efficiently, the government plans to do two things. First, it plans to develop physical and commercial infrastructure, such as the building of industrial estates which would directly encourage the private sector in its industrial efforts. Secondly, the government of Saudi Arabia is committed to ensuring that adequate financial resources are channelled to the private entrepreneurs through the provision of special funds, equity capital, and encouragement of investment consortia involving banks, other Saudi investors and foreign capital. It is important to note that the formation of investment ventures in which Saudi and foreign investors jointly participate will go a long way to remove the fear of possible nationalization which might prevail in the minds of foreign entrepreneurs.

Sectoral Analysis of Development Programmes under the Second Development Plan

In the previous analysis we have discussed the importance which the planners attach to development programmes. The reason for this emphasis, it must be reiterated, is to reduce the excessive dependence of the Saudi economy on crude-oil production. To this end it is planned to diversify the economy by expanding the non-oil sectors of the economy – increasing the quantity and the variety of food, mineral and manufactured products, and to expand the range of options in the service sector.

In this section we seek to examine detailed strategies which are envisaged in the Second Plan in order to achieve the desired diversification objective.

Economic Resource Development[20]

The Second Plan provides SR 92,135 million for the development of economic resources. The composition of the broad sector and financing is given in Table 6.3, and as the table indicates, the country is assigning primary importance to the development of manufacturing and to water resources, although, as will be realized later, much of the investment in water resources development could be more correctly regarded as investment in agriculture.

Water. The development of Saudi Arabia's limited water resources is vital to support the agricultural production, industrial development, and urbanization which usually accompanies population growth and diversified programmes of economic development. Between 1974 and 1980 the Kingdom's water requirements were expected to increase by 51 per cent, from 6,681 to 10,000 cubic metres per day. According to the Plan, three-fourths of the funds committed to water resources development, SR 25,374 million, will be spent on providing desalination facilities, which, it is hoped, will increase the production capacity of this source of water supply by 1,341.3 thousand cubic metres per day. In addition to water, the desalination plants will supply 3,525 MW of electricity.

Table 6.3: Expenditures on Economic Resource Development (SR millions)

	Recurrent	Project	Total	Percentage
Water	101.8	33,963.0	34,064.8	37.0
Manufacturing[a]	341.4	43,939.2	44,280.6	48.1
Agriculture	2,205.7	2,479.2	4,684.9	5.1
Electricity	880.0	5,360.0	6,240.0	6.7
Others[b]	989.6	1,875.1	2,864.7	3.1
Total	4,518.5	87,616.5	92,135.0	100.0

Notes: a. Aggregation of financial requirements of the agencies concerned with the development of manufacturing (namely, Industry Department of the Ministry of Commerce and Industry, Industrial Studies and Development Centre and Petromin Headquarters) gives an amount of SR 1,605.6 million, which when added to proposed additional investment of SR 46,150 million in hydrocarbon-based industries, Jubail complex and other manufacturing industries, gives a total financial requirement of the manufacturing sector of SR 47,755.6 million. Assuming, therefore, that the figures for the other sectors are correct, there is a discrepancy between the total economic resources figure as shown in Table VIII-1 of *The Plan* (SR 92,135 million) and the total which our computation originally showed (SR 95,610.0 million). In order to bring our total projected expenditure on Economic Resource Development into consistency with the figure in Table VIII-1 we simply subtracted the amount of the discrepancy (SR 3,475.0 million) from SR 47,755.6 million to obtain SR 44,280.6 million which is the financial requirement for the manufacturing sector shown in this table. b. Includes expenditures earmarked for petroleum, minerals, public works of the construction sector, and Commerce Department of the Ministry of Commerce and Industry.
Source: Compiled from budget figures of institutions responsible for the various sectors. These figures are contained in Chapter 4 of *The Plan*.

At the beginning of the Plan period, desalination plants which were either in operation or under construction had production capacity of 868.7 thousand cubic metres of water per day, and 140 MW of electricity.[21] With respect to water, therefore, the Plan provides for an increase in capacity of desalination plants of 54.4 per cent by the end of the Plan period. Since these plants are the principal sources of water supply for both the urban centres of the east and west coasts of the country, as well as for irrigation, the planned increase in the capacity of desalination plants is vital to the economic health of the Kingdom. One could also interpret the projected increase in desalinated water supply as an attempt to achieve the goal of reducing the overdependence of any sector of the economy on a single source of supply of a vital resource. In the case under consideration, water, the increased capacity of desalination plants will tend to redress the overdependence of the country on ground water – an overdependence which has evolved out of scarcity of fresh surface water due to the climatic conditions of the Kingdom.

A greater effort at diversification can be seen in the expansion of electric power from non-oil sources, i.e. water power. Utilization of water as a significant source of energy in Saudi Arabia is certainly reflected in the increase in the power capacity of the desalination plants from a meagre figure of 140 MW in 1974 to a projected capacity of 3,525 MW – an increase of 3,385 MW or by more than 25 times.

Table 6.4: Major Uses of Water 1974 and Production Requirement Forecasts 1980 (thousand m^3/day)

Uses of water	Supply 1974	Production requirement 1980
Main cities		
Riyadh	57.5	163
Jeddah	57	142
Mecca	18.5	74
Taif	6	41
Medina	22	35
Dammam and others[a]	50	90
Subtotal	211	545
Industrial complexes		
Jubail	–	76[b]
Yanbu	–	19[b]
Subtotal	–	95
Oil-well injection	1,100	2,400
Irrigation agriculture	5,370	7,060
Total	6,681	10,100

Notes: a. Subject to rescheduling of implementation of industrial projects.
b. Dhahran, Al-Khobar, Safwa, and Qatif.
Source: *The Plan*, Table IV-1, p. 105.

Further analysis of the development of water resources can be done by the aid of Table 6.4 which shows the planned water requirements by major uses, *vis-à-vis* the supply in 1974 (i.e. just before the Second Plan began). The table indicates that the bulk of water supply is utilized for irrigation purposes, although the proportion of total water resources devoted to this usage is expected to fall from 80.4 per cent in 1974 to 70 per cent in 1980. One may infer, therefore, that the success of the agricultural programmes in the Plan is closely linked with the successful implementation of the water development programmes. It is because of the substantial use of water for irrigation that we implied earlier that investment in agricultural development as expressed in Table 6.3, rather underestimates the importance which the government attaches to the agricultural sector of the Saudi Arabian economy or the new concern about the use of water for urban and industrial purposes.

A brief analysis of overall water policy envisaged in the Second Plan is in order before we shift our attention to the discussion of other development expenditure sectors. Water policy consists of several subpolicies most of which are embodied in the water programmes already discussed. In summary, however, it can be said that the overall objective is to provide adequate water supply for urban, industrial (including oil-well injection) and agricultural needs, in both quantitative and qualitative terms and from both the short-run and long-run points of view.

In furtherance of this broad goal, the Plan gives priority to urban, industrial and agricultural requirements. Water for mining operations is to be provided 'after taking into account urban industrial and agricultural needs'.[22] From an optimization point of view, we may interpret this as 'after the social marginal benefits for water utilization in the three priority sectors is low enough to warrant the provision of water for other purposes'. However, even among the three priority sectors emphasis differs. Water for agriculture is to increase only if it is in the long-term interest of the public. This explains the planned reduction of the proportion of total water supply which is to be used for irrigation. Whereas there are several interpretations one can place on this, an obvious explanation is that the government of Saudi Arabia is aware of the need to apply a long-term efficiency criterion whenever it becomes necessary to allocate additional water resources to the agricultural sector. This is a rational behaviour, to the extent that water for irrigation has opportunity costs in the form of industrial and municipal development constraints which may not be able to take place because of insufficient supply of water for these purposes.

Perhaps the most important policy on water-resource development and utilization is the establishment of an information system on the Kingdom's sources of water supply and the projected national water plan. These are obviously mechanisms through which a genuine effort could be made towards a more comprehensive and efficient development and utilization of one of the scarcest resources in the Kingdom of Saudi Arabia, i.e. water.

Agriculture. To reiterate the close relationship between the development of agricultural and water resources, it will not be overemphasis to restate that because much of the land in Saudi Arabia is too dry for crop production or for extensive livestock grazing, achievement in agricultural development is dependent on the success in the development of water resources.

Saudi Arabia's rapid development and population growth have increased her demand for food and to a lesser extent agricultural raw materials for industrial purposes. At the same time, rural-urban migration has persisted and intensified due to the increasing attractiveness of the cities. Consequently, the already low agriculture manpower has been decreasing and there is no reason to believe that this trend will change in the near future. With these trends in mind, it is not surprising that agricultural development efforts during the Plan period are projected to be concentrated on increasing agricultural productivity in order to raise the *per capita* income and welfare of the rural population and reduce Saudi Arabia's dependence on imported food; and on increased agricultural productivity so as to release farmers for other non-traditional economic activities without sacrificing agricultural output.[23]

The government is relying heavily on the private sector to undertake development activities in this area. The Second Plan includes a relatively small amount, SR 3,858.7 million, for agricultural development to be spent on recurrent expenditure and projects in areas of agriculture 'into which private entrepreneurs are unable or unwilling to enter'.[24]

In addition, the Saudi Arabian Agricultural Bank is expected to give out SR 427.7 million in agricultural loans. Also, an additional amount of SR 60.0 million has been earmarked for financing agricultural projects, while SR 338.0 million is for recurrent expenditures of the Bank. The credit facilities are directed mainly to more than 15 per cent of the farmers to enable them to obtain seeds, fertilizers, machinery, irrigation equipment, and other inputs necessary for increased agricultural production. These loans may also be used to purchase and improve agricultural land, marketing, transporting and processing of agricultural products. More vital to the success of the agricultural-credit programme is the establishment of a system which seeks to cut down red tape in the processing of loan requests or applications. This system, which the Plan provides for, will attempt to ensure that farmers obtain the loans at the right time; since proper timing is an indispensable element in agricultural production, the importance of speed in the processing of agricultural loans cannot be ignored.

As the country's area is large, studies and programmes will be carried out on a regional basis. Based on the results of previous studies, the

Second Plan emphasizes production of wheat, barley, sorghum, sheep, poultry, dairy products, beef, fruit and vegetables as the most beneficial areas for expansion. In agriculture, as in other sectors, the Second Plan also calls for further feasibility studies and programme development to provide a base for further expansion in the future.

Manufacturing. To meet the targets envisaged for industry, policies have been devised to generate an expansion in this sector which is the strongest alternative to crude-oil exports if overdependence is to be reduced.[25] In an economy which has such an overwhelming dependence on a single product for its foreign financial resources and thus for development, diversification cannot be completed overnight. Indeed, initial industrialization efforts are bound to begin and/or to be concentrated on oil-related manufacturing industries; after all, this is the area in which Saudi Arabia has a comparative advantage. Several important plants are thus envisaged in order to gather and treat gas, most of which is flared during the process of crude-oil production. Also petrochemical plants, refineries, fertilizer, steel and aluminium plants are to be constructed to produce exports. Most of these plants will be situated in the oil-rich eastern region of the Kingdom. However, a refinery and a petrochemical manufacturing complex are planned in the western region because of its proximity to European markets.

Thus, whereas the government expects the private sector to contribute significantly to the industrialization process of the country, provision has been made for direct government involvement. Further, attention is given to the government's encouragement to the private sector in the form of supporting services, including proposed numerous feasibility studies, and studies of long-range manpower needs and new industrial possibilities.

About half of the financial resources budgeted for economic-resource development, SR 44,280.6 million, has been allocated to the expansion of the manufacturing sector. Apart from those areas related to petrochemicals, the Second Plan proposes also to expand the country's industrialization effort to cover industries which are important from the point of view of national security and overall welfare of the people. Regional imbalance would be corrected by investing in regional industries so as to expand local employment and incomes.

Other manufacturing industries would also be expanded. These include increasing the annual capacity of cement production from 1.5 million tons to 10 million tons. There are also provisions for the construction of other non-hydrocarbon-based plants such as three big integrated grain-silos, flour and feed mills, and plants for food processing, automobiles and parts, construction materials, fabrics, carpets and other consumer products.[26]

There is an element of division of labour in the implementation process of the various programmes under the industrialization plan. The Industrial Development Corporation (IDC) will be responsible for major non-hydrocarbon-based industries. The development of petrochemical industries is under the control of Petromin, which is the agency of the government in charge of petroleum, and mineral affairs. It can be seen here that even with respect to administrative arrangements, these industries are not completely independent of oil. This can, however, be explained on the grounds that there is the need for co-ordination between crude-oil-production activities and processing of crude oil, if for no other reason because of the linkages which exist between crude oil and petrochemical products. Also, such an administrative arrangement will enable the government to utilize the expertise of Petromin personnel, to the extent that petrochemical production is technically sophisticated.

The Ministry of Commerce and Industry is responsible for developing commercial policies and for providing services to encourage foreign, private-capital participation in the industrialization programmes. The various departments in the Ministry are expected to work in close co-operation so that industrial expansion is facilitated through improved assistance to businessmen (both domestic and foreign) and provision of efficient financial arrangements. With respect to the latter, the Saudi Industrial Development Fund and the Saudi Arabian Monetary Agency are the institutions through which funds are channelled to both new and existing private enterprises.

Some practical steps which will be undertaken to ensure the implementation of the industrial programmes in the Plan are as follows:[27]

(i) Review of current incentives to foreign private enterprises will be continued for the purpose of making it comparable to incentives in other parts of the world. Policies to be reviewed include those on tax incentives, tariffs, subsidies, performance stipulation, capital transfer, investment risk insurance, tendering and contracting positions.

(ii) Expedite the completion of the planning studies of the Jubail hydrocarbon industrial complex, and construct petrochemical plants in the Eastern region and one in the Western Region.

(iii) Review tender laws so as to reflect the problems of

manufacturers; problems such as inflation in cost of production and uncertainty about production shutdowns.

(iv) Finally, implement other major programmes such as the utilization of gas and petroleum for both energy and feed purposes, construction of an aluminium plant in the Eastern region of the Kingdom and complete feasibility studies of other projects, including rolling mill in the Western Region.

Electricity. The Second Plan provides for an expenditure of SR 6,240 million for the improvement and expansion of electrical power to meet the industrial and domestic requirements of the country. Projects include an integrated electricity system which is expected to increase the generating capacity by 3,282 MW. Also the programme for the integrated system provides for the construction of an additional 3,540 kilometres of transmission lines to effect efficient distribution of the electricity generated. It will be recalled that the proposed desalination plants would supply 3,525 MW during the Plan period. (In actuality, power generation capacity during the Second Plan was increased to some 3,500 MW, with six additional plants still under construction in 1980 which are to add 2,795 MW when completed.)

One observation which must be pointed out here is that apart from financial resources, it is in the supply of electricity that the Kingdom may not experience serious supply bottlenecks during the period of plan-implementation, in view of the present capacity and planned expansion. Estimates for 1974 indicate that out of total generating capacity of electrical plants in the Kingdom of 1,256 MW, only 828 MW were being utilized. It will be wrong, however, to use this 34 per cent undercapacity utilization of electricity resources in the country as a case for making judgement about the rationale for expansion of electricity capacity as envisaged in the Plan. Industrialization tends to generate rapid increase in the demand for electricity. It is, therefore, within this framework that the projected electricity-generating-capacity expansion should be evaluated.

The Second Plan also calls for the initiation of a fifteen-year electricity plan and a management-training programme, as well as a number of feasibility and system-design studies. These are long-term oriented proposals. In the short run, owing to a worldwide shortage of skilled manpower in this area, the technical personnel already employed in the existing electrical centres will have an important role to play in the implementation of the new electricity programmes.

Petroleum, Minerals and Construction. The balance of the funds for economic-resource development, SR 2,864.7 million, has been earmarked for financing the development of petroleum and mineral resources and general costs related to construction and commercial developments which have not been included in other specific sectors. While the monetary resources allocated to some of these costs are small, the importance of these projects in the development process should not be underestimated. The importance should be analysed within the context of the fact that they are basically supplementary to the larger expenditures allocated to the specific sectors.

In spite of the fact that Saudi Arabia has the largest proven petroleum reserves in the world, and in spite of the stated policy of reducing the dependence of the economy on crude oil, the Second Plan calls for accelerated exploration efforts and seismic studies of the entire area to locate future exploration sites. Also emphasized are effective management of proven reserves, including long-range studies of world energy consumption and demand patterns, international marketing policies affecting future demand for Saudi oil, and the co-ordination of future development with use of the oil resources.

Why should Saudi Arabia still explore for oil? The answer is simple: oil is a depletable resource, therefore further exploration is necessary to extend the life-span of the Kingdom's oil resources. Further, it will be an unsound economic judgement to propose that because the country wants to diversify her production capacity she must neglect further exploration for oil, since, despite efforts to shift from oil to alternative sources of energy, the day when such a shift will be significant enough to make oil plentiful relative to demand is not well in sight. In any case, to the extent that most of the industrialization programmes are based on oil, a case is certainly made for any effort aimed at ensuring continuous supply of raw-material inputs into petrochemical industries.

Consequently, a management training programme for personnel to administer the country's natural resources has been proposed. The planned development in mineral resources is intended to provide additional framework for future development. The extensive programme of geological mapping and studies which were begun under the First Development Plan is to be continued with emphasis on the Pre-Cambrian Shield. Specific exploration of possible uranium deposits, compilation and interpretation of a gravity anomaly map of the country, and the establishment of a laboratory for rock analysis are to be undertaken.

Human-resources Development

The Plan defines the concept 'human resources development' from a broad perspective to include manpower development, training programmes, other factors affecting labour, education and cultural development. If one is to mention a constraint which may single-handedly prevent the implementation of all aspects of the Second Plan, it will be the constraint which might be posed by inadequate supply of manpower. Manpower development, or from a broader point of view, human resource development, is a vital aspect of the Plan. We discuss what the Plan says on human resources development under three headings: *Manpower Development*, here defined to include training and other factors affecting the labour force; *Education*; and *Cultural Affairs and Information Services*.

Manpower Development

An important lesson which the planners in Saudi Arabia have learned from the First Development Plan is that labour-force developments affect the rate at which projects in a plan are implemented. Also, the implementation of the First Plan demonstrated the dependence of the Saudi economy on non-Saudi workers. This dependence should be expected to continue in the Second Plan period, given the size of the Plan and the current age composition of the Saudi population, not to mention traditional factors affecting the female labour-force participation rate in the Kingdom. In the short run, therefore, it appears the country has no choice but to depend on an imported labour force.

The Plan details the expected demand for manpower resources by various economic activities. The projected demand figures are then compared with the present level of employment. As Table 6.5 indicates the greatest pressure on the Saudi Arabian labour market originate from services, a sector which, though it consists of activities that are traditionally labour-intensive, are known to increase very fast as a country grows. Also this is the sector which employs many professionals, who are in very short supply. The pressures which the services sector will put on the market for lawyers, doctors, nurses, teachers bankers, management consultants, etc. will continue to grow with time.

Restricting ourselves for a moment to the broad aspects of the manpower development programme in the Plan, we can see that by the end of the planning period the labour force would have increased by 53 per cent. This gives an annual rate of growth of 10.6 per cent. Since the population growth of Saudi Arabia is estimated at 4.0 per cent pe annum, there is no doubt that the labour market will continue to be tight. From Table 1.3, it looks as if services and construction will become the largest employers of labour, while the agricultural sector will lose its dominant place.[28] However, this behaviour of the agricultural sector is consistent with the observed circular decline of the labour force engaged in agriculture as development gets underway in developing countries. During the development process agriculture is expected to provide manpower resources to the other sectors of the economy, especially to the manufacturing sector.

Table 6.5: Present Employment Compared with Projected Labour Demand by Economic Activity

Economic activity	Present employment (1975) Quantity (thousands)	Present employment (1975) Per cent of total	1980 projected labour demand Quantity (thousands)	1980 projected labour demand Per cent of total
Agriculture and fishing	426.1	28.0	395.1	16.9
Mining and quarrying	45.6	3.0	62.1	2.7
Manufacturing	46.5	3.1	77.5	3.3
Utilities	18.3	1.2	29.5	1.3
Construction	314.2	20.6	591.9	25.4
Commerce	211.0	13.8	361.4	15.5
Transportation and communications	103.2	6.8	162.5	7.0
Services	357.2	23.5	650.6	27.9
Total	1,522.1	100.0	2,330.6	100.0

Source: Compiled from Figure III-3 of *The Plan*, p. 71.

It is not the mere size of the labour force that matters, it is the quality that counts. To raise the effectiveness of the labour force there is the need to train a high percentage of workers to acquire improved or new skills. Since the labour market is tight, in-service training programmes are the most practical schemes through which skills could be improved. Unfortunately, these programmes are at developing stages in most areas of the private sector. One way to encourage private firms to institute in-service training is to give them incentives. If there is a way of doing this, then much of the problem posed by the influx of unskilled rural labour to the modern sector will be reduced, especially if workers are trained while on the job, the intensity of the training declining as more and more skill is acquired.

Apart from on-the-job-training programmes, the Plan makes provision for other ways to increase the productivity of the Saudi Arabian labour force. The objectives of manpower development programmes in the Plan are to raise labour productivity and in doing so enable more and more Saudis to acquire managerial and technical skills to fill in for imported labour in the future, and generally to increase the participation of Saudis in the labour force while at the same time supplementing with non-Saudis, especially in the highly skilled and top levels of employment.

The above objectives will be carried out by policies which will involve the creation of better educational and training opportunities through both formal and informal programmes, introduction of wage policy based on productivity, provision of better working conditions and lastly measures necessary to ensure adequate supply of skilled foreign labour. For the purpose of implementing the manpower programmes, a new manpower training organization will be established. This organization when established will also be responsible for the overall manpower policy of the Kingdom and also supervise the special manpower planning department within the Central Planning Organization which will be responsible for projections of manpower needs of the country.[29]

As in most developing countries, a government-funded institution is responsible for the training of government employees. The Saudi Institute for Public Administration (IPA) is expected to reach a capacity of 3,340 trained per year by 1980, almost twice as much as it presently trains each year. IPA training emphasizes both intermediate and high administrative levels of manpower, English language training, and training in industrial management for new university graduates who want to join the public and civil services.

From the point of view of manpower resources for the private sector, it is planned to increase the effort in expanding vocational training centres at which training in technical and other vocational skills could be given. The expansion will take the form of enlarging existing facilities and the establishment of new centres. It is, of course, expected that the private sector would supplement the government efforts by instituting more in-service training programmes for their existing and new workers.

It is natural during the industrialization process of a developing country for conflicts between labour and management to emerge. In order to ensure cordial labour relations between employers and employees in Saudi Arabia, the Ministry of Labour and Social Affairs (MLSA) is planning to establish several labour offices in addition to the 25 which existed at the beginning of the Plan period. Even more important for the well-being of the worker, MLSA is going to establish labour health laboratories in the two industrial centres, Jeddah and Dammam, and expand and improve the services of the one at Riyadh. MLSA, which is also responsible for the vocational training programmes, intends to create a congenial labour atmosphere so that both workers and management can go about their respective businesses in harmony for the common goal of both parties.

Education

Eighty-three per cent of the total financial resources allocated to the development of human capital will be spent on the expansion of facilities at all four levels of the Saudi Arabian educational system: elementary, intermediate, secondary, and the post-secondary and graduate levels.[30] The importance which the Saudi Government attaches to education is thus demonstrated. Enrolment of boys and girls in elementary schools is expected to go up substantially during the Plan period. The projected increase in enrolment certainly calls for increased expenditure in the training and salaries of teachers, expansion of classrooms, laboratory facilities and other educational infrastructure.

Perhaps from the point of view of top-level manpower, it may be more relevant to analyse what provisions have been made for the expansion of higher education in the Kingdom. This, of course, is not to imply that other levels are unimportant: they are important because they are part of an interrelated process through which technical and managerial manpower is created. Also lower and intermediate-level manpower is crucial to any development effort, and to this extent the role which secondary and technical levels of education play in meeting the manpower requirements of the Plan is real. To ensure that top-level manpower is available to take over from their foreign counterparts when it becomes feasible in the future, the Plan seeks to expand the facilities at the universities in the Kingdom. The expansion programme includes completion of new campuses for the University of Riyadh, the King Abdulaziz University, the Women's Colleges system, Imam Mohammed Ibn Saud Islamic University, and a new College of Medicine in Jeddah. Whereas university enrolment is expected to increase, it is also envisaged that programmes within each university will be expanded and diversified to reflect the manpower needs of the country's development.

Successful implementation of the educational segment of the Plan will mean that by 1980 all boys, and at least 50 per cent of all girls, will receive elementary school education; and all elementary school students will have an opportunity for secondary school education, while higher education will be available for all qualified graduates of secondary schools. More importantly, continuing education for adults will also be expanded throughout the Kingdom.

It may be noted that although efforts to educate a large segment of the population are noteworthy, mere production of graduates from the various levels of education does not necessarily solve the manpower needs of the country. It is in this connection that there could be a co-ordination between the manpower-planning aspect and the educational aspect of the human resource development sector. From an institutional angle, co-operation will have to take the form of a close and sustained interaction and exchange of information among the following three bodies which influence education and manpower development in the Kingdom: the Ministry of Labour and Social Affairs, the Ministry of Education, and the special manpower planning department within the Central Planning Organization. If such a close co-operation among the education/manpower-related institutions is effected within a comprehensive manpower plan, the educational system, and the content of education and training programmes, could be tailored in such a way that they reflect the manpower needs of the country. To reiterate, therefore, there is a need for a comprehensive manpower plan for the Kingdom. For effectiveness, such a plan must come under a single authority, possibly the Special Manpower Planning Department, with its board membership to include representatives from the Ministries of Labour and Social Affairs and Education.

Cultural Affairs and Information

The bulk of the budget earmarked for cultural affairs will be used to supplement efforts which will be made in the provision of education. It is planned to expand the library system in Saudi Arabia, to expand the facilities at King Abdul Aziz Research and Cultural Institute, and to expand the country's museums.

In order that the people of Saudi Arabia become aware of government policies and to encourage increased input of all people into the development efforts, the Plan intends to extend the coverage of the Kingdom's television system and also to expand her telecommunication network so that a substantial proportion of the population will be reached. One other benefit from improved and expanded information systems will be their function as a medium through which informal education could be extended. Especially the use of the radio in rural and agricultural development – in transmitting information about cultivation methods, the weather, and the other research results of the extension division of the Ministry of Agriculture and Water Resources – will be invaluable.

Social Development

'Economic advances and social development are interdependent and mutually reinforcing.'[31] The Second Plan, in recognition of this principle, has allocated SR 33,212.8 million for social development. Development in this sector comprises the following: health (SR 17,301.6 million), social security and social affairs (SR 11,896.9 million) and miscellaneous expenditures of SR 4,014.9 million.

Health programmes would emphasize both curative and preventive services. Planned expansion of curative services includes increasing hospital facilities to a level capable of providing 2.5 beds per 1,000 persons, and upgrading existing dispensaries and establishing new ones. Despite the fact that 2.5 per 1,000 persons (or 400 persons per hospital bed) is a lower level of hospital facilities than the levels existing in advanced countries (for example, in the USA there were only 155 persons per hospital bed in 1978), the figure projected for Saudi Arabia in 1980 is a very big improvement. Five years ago, there were as many as 897 persons per a hospital bed in the Kingdom, or 1.1 beds per 1,000 persons. If the number of persons per hospital bed is a good index of the level of health facilities in a country (the population-hospital bed ratio being inversely related to the level of health facilities), then, perhaps a comparison of figures for Saudi Arabia and an advanced country is not appropriate. A more realistic comparison might be the one between Saudi Arabia and a developing country, preferably another surplus-funds country, Kuwait. But even in this case, Saudi Arabia falls very much behind Kuwait in the provision of health facilities as indicated by the population-hospital bed ratio. In 1978 Kuwait hospitals could provide a bed for every 240 persons.[32]

However, the number of hospital beds per population, or its inverse, the number of population per hospital bed, is an imperfect social index of the level of health facilities provided by a country. This is because there are many health services other than accommodating patients in the hospital, although an inadequate supply of hospital beds does provide constraints on the provision of the curative health services. The Plan, therefore, makes provision for an expansion of preventive medical/health-care programmes. If these programmes are successful, then the Kingdom will be in a better position to meet the curative health needs of her people with the limited hospital facilities. It is, consequently, proposed to establish mother-and-child care and other types of clinics to provide medical services for children and expectant mothers. It is projected that these clinical facilities would help reduce the infant mortality rate to a minimum of 110 deaths per 1,000 births, and reduce the overall death rate over time. Although both curative and preventive health services will help improve the quality of the potential and existing labour forces, another aspect of their impact will be to reduce the death rate, and thus increase the size of the labour force.[33] The Plan makes provision for supplementing health services with programmes aimed at providing the population with better nutrition. The effect of the nutrition programmes is of course obvious: to improve labour productivity and the general health of the population.

The second major expenditure category in the social development sector is social security and social affairs. At present, Saudi Arabia has a non-contributory social security system which provides pensions for persons over 60, disabled people, orphans and women who are without support. Victims of various calamities are also provided for through aid from the social security system. Social affairs programmes include aid for the handicapped and community development services. Expenditures allocated to social security and social affairs under the Second Plan will be used, therefore, primarily to expand existing programmes to meet the needs of a rapidly growing and urbanizing population which is undergoing social and structural changes.

The miscellaneous expenditure category includes expansion of the judicial system and youth welfare programmes; the latter involves religious studies, art festivals, science-programme work camps and other social activities such as athletic contests.

Although the economist often has little to say on social matters, it is interesting to note here that the existence of the right attitude towards development, and a conducive social environment within which individuals could identify their needs with that of the society as a whole, is an important precondition for the successful implementation of development programmes. This is especially crucial for Saudi Arabia, a country which is more traditionally oriented than most developing countries. Attempts to reorientate the youth, to prepare them for increased responsibility in the future, to imbue them with positive values like hard work in relationship to reward and initiative, and to keep them fit and healthy, will go a long way to making the tasks of future planners of the Saudi economy less difficult – even after the oil money is gone. These appear to be the objectives of the social programmes envisaged in the Plan.

Physical Infrastructure Development

In discussing the priorities of the Second Development Plan, Dr Farouk Akhdar, advisor to the Planning Minister, emphasized that, 'What is vital is infrastructure. We must build that before we can industrialize'.[34] The largest fund committed to an individual sector in the Second Plan is allocated to the development of physical infrastructure, which it is thought is necessary to support a large diversified economy. Expenditure projections for this sector are as shown in Table 6.6.

Table 6.6: Infrastructural Expenditures (SR millions)

	Recurrent	Project	Total
Roads	3,229.9	10,852.1	14,082.0
Ports	88.0	6,837.0	6,925.0
Airports	1,336.4	12,476.3	13,812.7
Communications	686.5[a]	3,538.9	4,225.4
Municipalities	7,190.0	46,137.8	53,327.8
Housing		14,263.0	14,263.0
Other[b]			6,308.7
Total			112,944.6

Notes: a. Made up of (1) net telecommunication recurrent expenditure of SR 22.3 million (total recurrent expenditure of SR 1,162.6 million *less* expected revenue of SR 1,140.3 million) and (2) Posts Department recurrent expenditure of SR 664.2 million. b. Includes railroads, SAUDIA (the national airline), and projected physical infrastructure and services to be provided for the holy cities by various government agencies (the latter to cost SR 5,000.0 million).
Source: *The Plan*, pp. 437, 450, 457, 466, 470, 483, 488, 507, 518 and 524.

The estimated increase in traffic of 15 per cent or more per year during the Plan period makes road construction one of the major projects in the development of infrastructure. The number of vehicles during the period is expected to more than double from 200,000 in 1975 to 500,000 in 1980.[35]

The main objectives for the roads sector are to provide a linkage of all major population concentrations, and to provide more than one route between areas which are most frequently travelled. Out of the SR 14,082 million allocated to road construction, therefore, nearly SR 10,000 million is to be spent on completing the road network shown in Figure 6.1. This will involve the construction of 13,066 km of main, secondary and paved feeder roads, as well as 10,250 km of unpaved rural roads. Funds are also provided for the maintenance of existing roads, purchase of equipment, studies and design of more than 20,000 additional kilometres of roads, and a training programme

Figure 6.1: Main-road Network at End of Second Plan, 1980

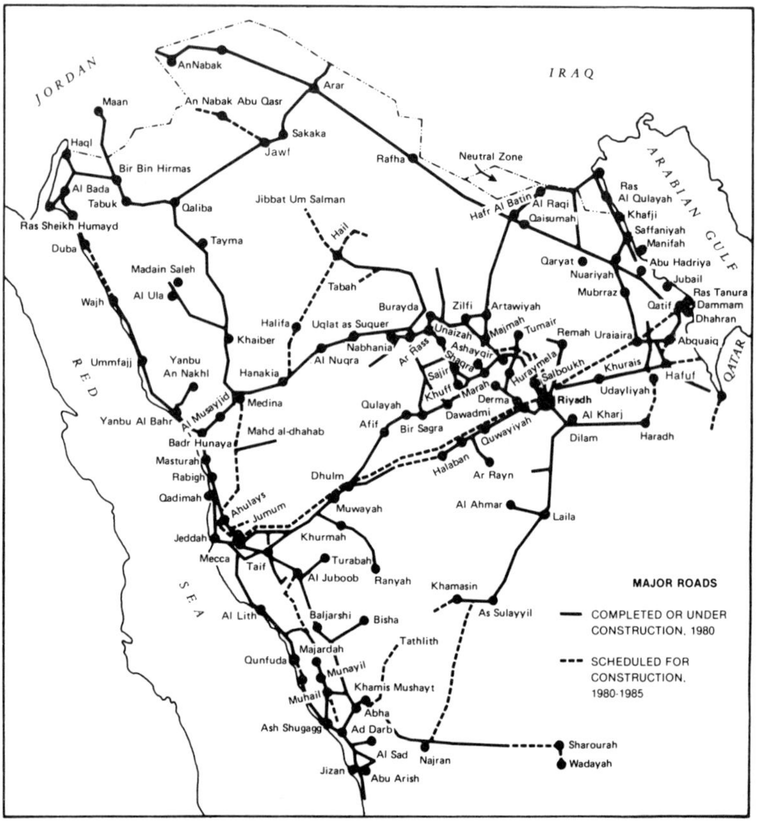

Source: *Third Development Plan*, Chapter 7, p. 401.

for personnel who will administer and implement the net work projects.

Almost half the funds earmarked for infrastructure improvement will go to municipal development, which has the following goals:[36]

(1) to improve the social and economic well-being of the cities, towns, and villages – to make them 'healthier, more comfortable, more enjoyable, but less costly places in which to live, work and travel';
(2) the expansion and improvement of amenities in these locations will also create a basis for efficient trade, manufacturing and provision of economic services.

Specific programmes include improving 77 communities which are expected to achieve municipality status during the Plan period, the construction of drainage and sewerage systems, institution of efficient garbage collection and disposal systems, and the construction of sidewalks, street lights and bridges. Several municipal buildings and facilities have been proposed. These include markets, cultural centres, municipal offices and warehouses. Also other projects envisaged in the Plan are aimed at improvement and expansion of public transportation systems and recreation areas. It is also planned to resettle six communities plagued by flooding problems, and establish 33 model communities. As is the case with all expenditure sectors, the Plan also makes provision for feasibility studies, and training of manpower resources for municipal development.

Housing in a rapidly growing population has been a major problem for Saudi Arabia in recent years, due to supply bottlenecks and inflation, as well as to the rapid urbanization. Although 75,000 dwellings were built during the First Plan period, estimated demand was 154,000 units. During the Second Plan, demand for new units is projected to be 338,000 units. The plan cautiously notes that, 'because of technical constraints and long lead-times between program initiation and housing occupancy',[37] it will be impossible to provide proper housing for the entire population by the end of the Second Plan period. Major advances towards the housing goal are planned, however. The Plan includes SR 14,263 million to construct enough housing to accommodate the additional labour force necessary for planned development, as well as to improve the housing situation for the balance of the population, and to build the proper institutional framework for continuing housing development.

An extensive programme aimed at improving and expanding the airport facilities of the Kingdom which was begun in the First

Development Plan will continue under the Second Plan. Introduction of wide-bodied jets, coupled with the expansion of routes to include North America and the Far East, will make SAUDIA one of the major airlines in the Middle East. In order to ensure safer aviation, it is planned to provide the airways with the highest-quality navigation and control equipment that is available.

Apart from air and road, the other important means of transportation in the Kingdom is by rail. Thus, maintenance and improvement of the rail systems are considered as worthwhile at least from the point of view of the role which railways play in accommodating the increasing number of pilgrims who visit the holy cities each year.

Inadequate port facilities have been responsible for some of the worst supply bottlenecks hampering development efforts to date. In 1973 Saudi Arabia's two major ports, Jeddah on the west coast and Dammam on the east, handled over two-thirds of the Kingdom's 3 million tons of cargo. Volume is expected to quadruple by 1980. Adequate development of port facilities is imperative for the success of the Plan as a whole. Handling the increased volume of cargo will require the construction of additional berths as well as increasing the volume of cargo per berth with additional mechanization. The Plan emphasizes expansion of the facilities at Jeddah and Dammam, and construction of specialized port facilities to serve the new industrial operations around Jubail. Specifically, the port expansion at Jeddah will include the construction of 20 additional berths, dry-dock facilities and improvement of the entry-exit channel in order to enable full utilization throughout both night and day. Similar improvement is envisaged for Dammam, where an additional 16 berths are planned. As in Jeddah, automatic, self-rotating cranes will be installed to make loading and unloading of cargo more efficient. Other port facilities have been planned at selected sea towns, Yanbu, Jubail, and other Red Sea and Arabian Gulf ports.

Other telecommunication programmes planned are aimed at upgrading local telephone networks, improving international and intra-Kingdom telecommunications, and to achieving an efficient administration and co-ordination of telecommunications systems in the country. Since the demand for telecommunication services usually grows more rapidly than the rest of the economy during the process of development, it appears that targets for the telecommunications sector must be met at a faster rate if the overall social and economic goals of the Plan are to be achieved. To this end, in the communications sector, the emphasis has been to complete the telecommunications network begun during the

First Plan, and expansion of these services to meet projected growth in the long run.

The role of physical infrastructure in the implementation of the Plan cannot be overemphasized. Indeed, the importance of this sector can more readily be seen in the form of potential constraints which it may place on the overall success of the Plan. This issue is analysed further in the next section.

Plan Implementation and Achievements

In an assessment of the Second Plan it is important to keep in mind one of the primary reasons why planning has been undertaken in Saudi Arabia. A basic purpose of the planning is to introduce fundamental structural changes into an expanding economy rather than to simply enlarge the entity in existence. Planning decisions must pay close attention to the need for maintaining social stability in a traditional society, while providing for the often conflicting objectives of development.

The Second Plan was compiled at a time when the income flow from oil revenues had increased dramatically so that the financial constraints to development were very few. Nevertheless, constraints did exist in the form of rapidly increasing inflation, a narrow base of domestic resources, an underdeveloped physical infrastructure, an inadequate manpower supply, and an overburdened administrative system. To deal with these limiting factors, it was determined that the real effectiveness of the Second Plan would depend on successful completion of four high-priority areas of development.[38]

(1) Previous experience had revealed that a main constraint of growth was inadequate physical infrastructure. Exceptionally heavy investment was to be channelled to this area.
(2) Steps were to be taken in medium and long-term programmes to preserve hydrocarbon resources and at the same time to promote energy-intensive industries with their high export value.
(3) A growing economy and society obviously begets a more complex economy and society to manage. An improvement of administration and a substantial expansion of the network of government institutions was in order.
(4) Encouragement of the private sector and development and diversification of the non-oil sector was to be a main thrust of the Second Plan

and was to be accomplished through four main policies: (a) additions to the foreign labour force to assist in development during the five-year plan, (b) encouragement of rural-urban internal migration, thereby moving surplus manpower to areas of industrial employment opportunity; (c) all possible government assistance to the development of the productive sectors of private enterprise; and (d) technological advancement through prudent utilization of international co-operation agreements whereby access could be had to technical and managerial expertise as well as to skilled labour.

An evaluation of the Second Plan should determine how well growth projections were met, whether plan objectives were satisfied, and what was done to provide for the maintenance of social stability.

One economic phenomenon threatened the feasibility of the Second Plan even before it got off the ground. Table 6.7 indicates that by the two available measures of inflation, the cost of living index and the GDP deflator, prices were increasing rapidly at the end of the First Plan and early in the Second Plan. Besides being a considerable economic threat to a developing country, inflation in general plays considerable havoc with social justice, striking harder at certain groups of citizens than it does at others. That inflation was brought down to more manageable levels is a tribute to the government's being able to identify the real causes and to introduce appropriate measures of control.

Primary causes for the high inflation in Saudi Arabia were the increased purchasing power which generated a high level of demand for goods and services that could not be satisfied by an economy beset with supply problems, an inflationary monetary policy that provided for large amounts of government funds to be channelled into the private sector, excessively high fixed prices written into contracts, and imported inflation that came from trading partners in the West.

Government strategy that proved effective in dealing with the above causes featured elimination of a number of the supply constraints by allowing market forces to prevail. While increased competition had a significant effect on reducing inflation, other specific measures helped to reduce supply bottlenecks: port capacity and efficiency were improved; the volume of available domestic assets was increased (for example, freehold land titles were distributed to low-income families); and internal transportation and distribution systems were improved.[39]

Another effective government action involved monetary policy. The annual expenditure budgets were consolidated at exactly their 1976/7 nominal level of increase for the following two years, with only a

Table 6.7: Price Trends during the First and Second Plans

	First Plan (1970-5) Per cent changes on previous years in:			Second Plan (1975-80) Per cent changes on previous years in:		
Price changes	1st Year	5th Year	5-year period	1st Year	4th Year[a]	4-year period[a]
Cost of living index	4.9	34.5	15.8	31.5	3.5	10.5
Transaction prices (= GDP deflators)	2.7	25.6	11.6	40.4	9.2	21.1

Note: a. Estimated values.
Source: Kingdom of Saudi Arabia, *Third Development Plan, 1400-1405/1980-1985*, Chapter 2, p. 45.

minimal increase in 1978/9.[40] The unchanged cash totals meant that inflation was absorbed at the expense of some economic growth. In actuality, however, the timing was good in that there was a relatively low rate of plan implementation at the time of constraint, and the budgets still offered scope for future volume growth. An important overall contribution of this monetary policy was that it reduced the widespread expectation of sustained expansion at all costs.

Gross Domestic Product

Growth targets for the Second Plan were drawn up, as mentioned earlier, in an atmosphere not only of rapidly increasing oil revenues, but also of strong inflationary pressures. The government's main aim was to secure a high rate of growth in the GDP, primarily in the non-oil economy, while keeping inflation at a tolerable rate of around 10 per cent. Whereas GDP had been increasing at an overall rate of 13.4 per cent per year (in constant 1969/70 prices) during the second half of the First Plan, projected growth for the Second Plan was to be about 10 per cent per year.[41] As a component of this figure, non-oil GDP was planned to grow at an average of 13.3 per cent per year, the producing sectors at 13.0 per cent, and the service sectors at 13.3 per cent.

As indicated in Table 6.8, actual GDP growth was 8 per cent annually, less than was planned for. The reason for this was that the expected growth in absorptive capacity and activity in general could not be achieved without inflationary pressures and consequent fluctuations in the growth rate. Accordingly, the first year of the Second Plan was the peak year for growth, with deceleration in both growth as well as inflation in subsequent years. Government monetary policy of reduced expenditures was a primary cause of this deceleration in growth of GDP. While overall GDP growth was less than projected, the Second Plan was successful in attaining a higher rate of growth in the non-oil sector than had been targeted. Overall non-oil-sector growth was 15.1 per cent per annum (16.6 per cent for the producing sectors and 14.1 per cent in the service sectors) against a projected rate of growth of 13.3 per cent. These figures compare with the First Plan's results of 11 per cent annual actual growth falling short of the targeted 12.0 per cent. At the same time, the oil sector's contribution to GDP fell to one-half of the projected growth, recording a 4.8 per cent annual increase.[42] Causes for this decrease were exogenous factors of imbalance and fluctuation in world oil markets, particularly during 1978.

These GDP growth figures, broken down into oil and non-oil-sector components, are particularly significant in light of one of the primary objectives of the Second Plan – to encourage the diversification of the economy by the growth of the non-oil sectors. As Table 6.9 indicates, the share of GDP accruing from the non-oil sector rose during the Second Plan, regardless of the price base used. This statistic is relevant, based as it is on the tendency world oil prices have had to rise, thereby altering the value proportions between the oil sector and the rest of the economy.

Table 6.8: Gross Domestic Product (GDP), 1975-80 (SR millions)

	1975	1980	Second Plan annual growth rates Constant price (per cent)	
	(1980 constant prices)		Planned	Actual
Non-oil economy producing sectors				
Agriculture	2,505.8	3,259.4	4.0	5.4
Mining	679.1	1,497.5	15.0	17.1
Manufacturing	3,303.4	6,753.3	14.0	15.4
Utilities	117.5	350.1	15.0	24.4
Construction	20,291.9	45,994.3	15.0	17.2
Subtotal producing sectors	26,897.7	57,854.6	13.0	16.6
Service sectors				
Trade	6,439.1	17,447.1	15.0	22.1
Transport	7,756.1	20,227.5	15.0	21.1
Finance[a]	7,137.8	13,144.2	9.7	13.0
Other services	2,741.3	5,257.3	14.0	13.9
Government[b]	15,751.1	21,036.4	12.9	6.0
Subtotal services sectors	39,825.4	77,112.5	13.3	14.1
Total				
Non-oil Economy	66,723.1	134,967.1	13.3	15.1
Oil Sectors	176,076.3	222,374.4	9.7	4.8
GDP[c]	242,799.4	357,341.5	10.0	8.0

Notes: a. Includes GDP from ownership of property. b. Excludes contribution to GDP of non-civilian employment. c. Excludes import duties.
Source: Kingdom of Saudi Arabia, *Third Development Plan, 1400-1405/1980-1985*, Chapter 2, p. 28.

Productivity

An examination of productivity figures tempers somewhat any undue optimism for the non-oil sector. The figures in Table 6.10 reveal that growth in the services sector is primarily the result of employment increase; growth in the producing sector is due to productivity increases: 4.1 per cent from favourable cost/price changes and 9.6 per cent from employment shifts.[43] It is evident that the GDP growth in the non-oil sector was dependent upon sizable employment shifts, primarily from agriculture, that are unlikely to continue to the same extent in the future. Hence, the growth of the non-oil sector will continue to be an area in need of attention in the Third Plan.

Table 6.9: The Changing Weight of the Oil Sector in the Kingdom's Economy

	Gross Domestic Product (value in SR billions) 1974-5	1979-80	Annual growth rate (per cent)	Percentage shares in GDP 1974-5	1979-80
At current prices of year concerned					
Oil	110.5	222.4		79.3	62.2
Non-oil	28.8	135.0		20.7	37.8
Total	139.3	357.4	20.7	100.0	100.0
At constant 1979/80 prices					
Oil	176.1	222.4		72.5	62.2
Non-oil	66.7	135.0		27.5	37.8
Total	242.8	357.4	8.0	100.0	100.0
At constant 1969/70 prices					
Oil	18.6	23.4		59.1	47.2
Non-oil	12.9	26.2		40.9	52.8
Total	31.5	49.6	9.5	100.0	100.0

Source: Kingdom of Saudi Arabia, *Third Development Plan, 1400-1405/1980-1985*, Chapter 2, p. 29.

Employment

The scope and size of the Second Plan required a substantial increase in manpower. The civilian labour force grew at an estimated average of 7.2 per cent per year during the five-year period, well above the 3.8 per cent annual growth recorded during the First Plan (Table 6.11). While this growth of the labour force was taking place, the proportion of Saudis in the working population was declining from 72 per cent in 1975 to 57 per cent in 1980. Accounting for this significant change was the presence of substantially more foreign workers in the labour force

Table 6.10: Output, Employment and Productivity Growth in the Non-oil Economy Annual Compound Growth Rates: Per Cent (1979/80 prices)

	Producing sectors			Services sectors		Total Non-oil economy	
	Plan	Actual		Plan	Actual	Plan	Actual
		a	b				
GDP	13.03	16.55	17.48	13.43	14.13	13.29	15.13
Employment	6.41	2.20	12.19	11.83	12.46	8.96	7.21
Productivity[c]	6.22	14.04	4.72	1.43	1.48	3.97	7.39
from:							
Cost/price changes	2.25	4.09	3.85	1.59	1.17	1.82	2.36
Employment shifts	3.88	9.56	0.84	–0.15	0.31	2.11	4.91

Notes: a. Including agriculture. b. Excluding agriculture. c. Measured by ratio of GDP employment.
Source: Kingdom of Saudi Arabia, *Third Development Plan, 1400-1405/1980-1985*, Chapter 2, p. 33.

and less availability of Saudis as the participation rate for Saudi males 12 years of age and over fell from 69 per cent to 65 per cent over the Plan period (that of females remained stable at 6 per cent). The decline in the male participation rate is readily explained by observing that two categories accounted for the drop: 12 to 19-year-olds were in education and training programmes introduced by the government to improve the work force, and those 60 years and over were retiring earlier as a result of improved financial and social conditions.

Table 6.11: Growth of the Civilian Labour Force, 1975-80

	1975	1980	Average growth 1975-80
	(thousands)		(%)
Male	1,651	2,323	7.1
Female	96	148	9.0
Total	1,747	2,471	7.2
of which:			
Saudi	1,253	1,411	2.4
Non-Saudi	494	1,060	16.5

Source: Kingdom of Saudi Arabia, *Third Development Plan, 1400-1405/1980-1985*, Chapter 2, p. 35.

The implications of the above figures regarding foreign-worker employment are significant in regard to future planning. Social problems can possibly increase with the expanded foreign population; as a result, economic strategy for the Third Plan calls for more selective growth objectives with the aim of consolidating the size of the foreign labour force while more effectively utilizing Saudi manpower.

Sizable shifts took place in the structure of employment as well (see Table 1.3). As noted there, agriculture was the big loser of workers, declining by 96,000 persons over the period. Its share of total employment almost halved between 1975 and the end of the Plan (1980), falling from 40 per cent to 24 per cent of total employment. Primary gainers were the more attractive urban job opportunities, reflecting the continuing rural-to-urban population shift. Service sectors averaged 15.3 per cent employment growth per year. Producing sectors grew more slowly, averaging only 2.2 per cent annually, and government employment grew at approximately 5.4 per cent per year. As will be very evident in Chapter 7, where the objectives of the Third Plan are discussed, manpower development is a critical area and one of the biggest national priorities.[44] Indeed, the effective utilization of available manpower is the key element in the whole strategy of the Third Plan and will emphasize solving some of the problems which became apparent during the Second Plan. Available manpower must be increased and made more productive, while the dependence on foreign workers has to be reduced as much as possible.

Expenditure

With the tremendous amount of oil revenues available, the government budget plays a very dominant role. Expenditure appropriations for the five years before the First Plan were SR 25,424 million. During the First Plan this figure increased to SR 98,915 million, but the real jump was during the Second Plan when appropriations increased more than six times to SR 623,270 million.[45] More meaningful as an economic indicator, however, is the actual expenditure figure for each of these years, a measure of the absorptive capacity of the economy. In the pre-Plan period, actuals tended to be close to appropriations, but during the latter part of the First Plan, actuals began to lag behind the rapidly rising appropriations. For the Second Plan, the gap in absorptive capacity was not only filled, but actuals exceeded the original appropriations because of supplementary allocations. For the first four years of the Second Plan, actual government expenditures were SR 495,484 million as compared to the appropriated SR 463,270 million (see Tables 6.12 and 6.13). For the last year of the Second Plan (1979/80) estimated expenditures were SR 160 billion as compared to 130 billion for the year earlier. These figures would seem to indicate that Saudi Arabia has made important steps in improving its absorptive capacity during the Second Plan period.

Foreign Trade

This improvement in absorptive capacity is reflected in Saudi foreign trade. The value of imports increased almost four times in current-value terms from SR 27.3 billion at the beginning of the Second Plan, (1974/5) to over SR 104.4 billion in 1978/9.[46] As a percentage of exports, imports rose from 23.8 to 69.7 over the same span. This increased ability to absorb imports was a main factor in all-round growth in consumption, production and investment.

Both consumption and investment were able to increase without any interference from each other (as occurs in most other economies) or to the balance of payments. Consumption, a principal indicator of economic welfare, increased substantially during the Second Plan. Increased

Table 6.12: Plan versus Budget Expenditure Allocations, 1975/6-1979/80 (SR millions)

Sector			Plan allocations			5-year
	1975/6	1976/7	1977/8	1978/9	1979/80	total
(1) Municipalities and rural affairs	8,064.0	9,797.4	10,743.1	11,948.2	12,775.1	53,327.8
(2) Public works and housing	391.5	714.8	1,776.7	4,096.0	7,664.0	14,263.0
(3) Information	531.8	701.8	723.7	490.0	486.9	2,934.0
(4) Labour and social affairs	2,527.0	2,912.4	4,470.1	4,005.6	3,878.1	15,955.0
(5) Health	6,599.0	3,925.2	3,346.3	2,004.8	1,536.3	17,301.6
(6) Education	11,497.1	12,053.3	13,532.3	7,069.7	7,739.6	51,892.0
(7) Transport and communications	5,647.0	5,510.9	9,220.4	7,374.9	5,771.0	40,353.8
(8) Petroleum and minerals	244.5	302.2	11,775.7	397.7	461.9	1,778.3
(9) Industry, commerce and electricity	2,929.8	7,257.6	11,775.7	15,555.3	17,023.9	54,542.3
(10) Agriculture and water resources	11,620.5	2,988.2	4,053.9	9,058.1	9,029.0	38,749.7
Total	51,568.8	51,381.3	59,781.5	62,000.3	66,365.6	291,097.5
Subsector A (1+2+7)	14,102.5	16,023.1	21,740.2	23,419.1	26,210.1	107,944.6
Subsector B (1+10)	19,684.5	14,785.6	14,740.2	21,006.3	21,804.1	92,077.5
Subsector C (3+4+5+6)	20,911.4	19,374.2	22,072.4	13,580.1	13,640.7	88,082.6
Subsector D (9+10)	14,550.3	12,246.0	15,829.6	24,613.4	26,052.9	93,292.0

Table 6.12: continued

Sector	1975/6	1976/7	Budget allocations 1977/8	1978/9	1979/80	5-year total
(1) Municipalities and rural affairs	14,396.3	16,077.6	13,384.0	10,266.9	12,224.5	66,349.3
(2) Public works and housing	222.1	9,130.9	7,947.9	5,810.2	3,190.8	26,301.9
(3) Information	802.6	1,164.7	1,356.7	1,136.3	1,054.8	5,515.1
(4) Labour and social affairs	3,891.9	3,693.1	4,421.6	3,289.9	4,182.2	19,478.7
(5) Health	3,197.4	2,972.7	3,384.1	4,040.5	4,177.0	17,771.7
(6) Education	12,973.9	14,029.8	15,167.2	15,221.7	16,410.6	73,803.2
(7) Transport and communications	11,564.6	16,567.8	8,541.9	8,346.2	10,778.7	55,799.2
(8) Petroleum and minerals	401.4	429.1	587.0	622.5	999.5	3,039.5
(9) Industry, commerce and electricity	841.8	1,430.9	856.1	1,379.9	4,506.4[a]	9,015.1
(10) Agriculture and water resources	2,178.4	2,336.0	2,187.9	2,940.0	4,169.2	13,811.5
Total	50,470.4	67,832.6	57,834.4	53,054.1	61,693.7	190,885.2
Subsector A (1+2+7)	26,183.0	41,776.3	29,873.8	23,713.3	26,194.0	147,740.4
Subsector B (1+10)	16,574.7	18,413.6	15,571.9	13,206.9	16,393.7	80,160.8
Subsector C (3+4+5+6)	20,865.8	21,860.3	24,329.6	23,688.4	25,824.6	78,115.2
Subsector D (9+10)	3,020.9	3,766.9	3,044.0	4,319.9	8,675.6	22,826.6

Note: a. Including gathering and liquefaction of gas.
Source: SAMA, *Annual Report, 1979*, p. 160.

employment, higher prices and higher incomes resulted in private consumption expenditure rising from SR 17.9 billion in 1974/5 to over SR 63 billion in 1978/9. Investment likewise grew in volume as gross fixed capital formation increased at an average annual rate of 19.4 per cent (at constant 1974/5 prices), from SR 17.84 billion in 1974/5 to SR 78.01 billion in 1978/9.[47]

Table 6.13: Ratio of Budgetary Estimates to Plan Allocations, 1975/6-1979/80

	1975/6	1976/7	1977/8	1978/9	1979/80	5-year total
(1) Municipalities and rural affairs	1.78	1.64	1.25	0.86	0.96	1.24
(2) Public works and housing	1.32	14.4	4.67	1.42	0.42	1.84
(3) Information	1.5	1.7	1.87	2.32	2.17	1.88
(4) Labour and social affairs	1.95	1.77	1.11	0.82	1.08	1.22
(5) Health	0.49	0.77	1.02	2.02	2.72	1.03
(6) Education	1.12	1.2	1.12	2.15	2.12	1.42
(7) Transport and communications	1.45	1.71	0.89	1.13	1.87	1.38
(8) Petroleum and minerals	1.6	1.4	1.58	1.57	2.16	1.71
(9) Industry, commerce and electricity	0.3	0.2	0.07	0.09	0.26	0.17
(10) Agriculture and water	0.2	0.5	0.54	0.32	0.46	0.36
Subsector A (1+2+7)	1.6	2.1	1.4	1.0	1.0	1.37
Subsector B (1+10)	0.8	1.2	1.05	0.63	0.75	0.87
Subsector C (3+4+5+6)	1.0	1.2	1.1	1.7	1.9	0.89
Subsector D (9+10)	0.2	0.3	0.19	0.18	0.33	0.24

Source: Compiled from Table 6.12.

This high rate of growth in investment was significant in easing several problems that exist in Saudi Arabia. As Table 6.14 indicates, expenditures on 'other construction' were substantial throughout the Second Plan, reflecting the heavy commitment to infrastructure development, a high priority of that plan. 'Transport' and 'machinery and equipment' likewise received considerable investment, giving credence to the idea that greater emphasis was being placed on more 'productive' types of investment than at the beginning of the Second Plan. 'Non-residential buildings' received substantial investment as a result of increased private-sector investment in offices and other commercial developments. The percentage for 'residential buildings', while less than that of five years earlier, reflects the continuing need for housing.[48]

Table 6.14: Composition of Gross Fixed Capital Formation, 1974/5-1978/9

	Growth in per cent per year		Percentage share[a]	
	Value[a]	Volume[b]	1974/5	1978/9
Residential buildings	17.7	(2.8)[c]	19.6	8.6
Non-residential buildings	63.9	35.3	19.1	31.4
Other construction	47.8	22.0	36.4	39.7
Transport	35.4	11.8	12.4	19.6
Machinery and equipment	40.2	15.8	11.3	10.0
Other	26.6	4.4	1.2	0.7
Average/Total	44.6	19.4	100.0	100.0

Notes: a. Based on nominal (current price) values. b. Based on constant 1974/5 prices. c. Negative growth rate.
Source: Kingdom of Saudi Arabia, *Third Development Plan, 1400-1405/1980-1985*, Chapter 2, p. 42.

Sectoral Analysis

A sectoral analysis of development programmes undertaken during the Second Plan reveals more information on its achievements. In this analysis, economic-resource development is viewed along with human-resource and social development.

Economic-resource Development

Water

Water-development programmes are very closely tied to the agricultural sector and, as Table 6.8 shows, more than 40 per cent of total economic-resource-development funds were allocated to these two areas. Much headway was made during the Second Plan in this high priority area as much additional water-supply capacity was developed. Numerous groundwater studies were completed in keeping with the ongoing preparation of a National Water Plan; 760 production wells were drilled or improved; 237 municipal water-supply systems were constructed; 150 potable-water systems were expanded; 28 dams were completed; the water-supply works for Riyadh and Jeddah were expanded; and considerable increase was made in water desalination and power-generation capacities.[49]

Agriculture

Agriculture remains a problem area in the Kingdom's objective of diversifying the economy and reducing dependence on imported agricultural products. While employment in this area fell considerably during the Plan, productivity gains were responsible for an annual average growth rate of about 4 per cent, insufficient in light of the increasing food demands as the standard of living has improved in Saudi Arabia.[50] Capital-intensive areas of commercial agriculture showed the most progress, while many producers employing traditional methods fell to new lows of output and real income-earning capacity.[51]

Manufacturing

In the manufacturing sector considerable emphasis was given to diversification during the Second Plan in recognition of the finite nature of hydrocarbon resources. Table 6.8 shows that almost half the total economic resource development funds were allocated to manufacturing. Non-hydrocarbon manufacturing recorded a 15.4 per cent per annum growth rate during the Second Plan as compared to an 11.4 per cent per year rate for the First Plan.[52] Progress was such that a reasonable, secondary manufacturing base was successfully established. While all product areas showed expansion, this was particularly true in those areas serving the construction sector, such as non-metallic mineral products, fabricated metal products, chemicals, plastic and rubber. While progress was considerable in diversification, emphasis will continue during the Third Plan in this area, which is considered to be of national interest.

The establishment of a heavy-industry base is considered to be vital in the Kingdom's industrial and economic development strategy, in which the government's role is a direct one despite the key role assigned to private sector investors. The Saudi Arabian Basic Industry Corporation (Sabic) was established in 1976 as a government corporate entity for the implementation of a basic-industry programme in conjunction with suitable overseas joint venture partners or unilaterally, if required.

The government gas-gathering scheme, the largest in the world, the creation of the serviced heavy-industry centres of Jubail and Yanbu by the Royal Commission, and the substantial improvement in national infrastructure, all of which commenced during the Second Plan, have provided the foundation for the construction and operational stages for several major industrial projects during the Third Plan.[53]

Electricity

Related to industrial and economic development is the generation and demand for electric power. During the Second Plan substantial expansion programmes were undertaken, mostly by private power companies financed by loans from the Saudi Industrial Development Fund (SIDF).[54] By 1979 electric power was available to 4.2 million persons, 11 per cent above the target. Consumption per consumer rose from approximately 4,100 kilowatt-hours (kWh) in 1975 to over 7,000 kWh in 1979. Installed generator capacity increased from 2,235 kilowatts (KW) in 1975/6 to 5,207 KW by 1979/80. The rural electrification programme implemented by the General Electricity Corporation had provided 41,000 new rural households in 143 villages with electricity by 1980.[55]

Petroleum, Minerals, Construction

The balance of economic-resource-development funds was allocated to financing the development of petroleum and mineral resources and general costs related to construction. Crude-oil production averaged 8.5 million b/d throughout the period, reaching 9.5 million b/d in 1979. The exploration programme was increased and the number of drilling rigs in operation went from three in 1975 to ten in 1979. Other highlights of the period were the acquisition of stock by the government in 1976 from Aramco shareholders, and the beginning of construction in 1978 of the cross-country pipeline and export terminal at Yanbu.[56]

Mineral-resource development was rather limited; none the less, advancements were made. The number of operating stone quarries increased to 76 in 1980, an eightfold increase over 1975. Eight major exploration licences for metallic minerals were held actively in 1980, of which five were issued during the Second Plan. In 1975 the Saudi/Sudanese joint Red Sea Commission was established to exploit the Red Sea's mineral-rich sediments.[57] Infrastructural development enabled the construction industry to increase its GDP contribution by an average annual rate of 17 per cent in constant prices during the Second Plan. Besides substantial infrastructure progress at the two major industrial complexes of Jubail and Yanbu, improvements in infrastructure occurred in commercial sectors, where the number of hotels increased from 73 in 1975 to 115 in 1979; in telecommunications, where telephone exchange line capacity was considerably increased and a major microwave network programme was completed; in transport, where, most importantly, port capacity was increased from 24 commercial berths in 1975 to 130 in 1980, thereby reducing an obvious bottleneck; and in housing, where, although Plan targets were not met, considerable progress was made.[58]

Housing

During the Second Plan progress was made in increasing the number of dwellings and improving the quality of housing in Saudi Arabia. During the First Plan 17,500 units per year were constructed; during the Second Plan this number jumped to 40,000 units annually. Such progress has been a result of government involvement since 1977 in large-scale housing programmes and also by active private-sector construction aided through SR 31.5 billion in residential credit dispersed over the five-year period by the Real Estate Development Fund.[59] Continuing urbanization of Saudi Arabia makes this sector an area of continuing concern.

Human-resource Development

The importance of the human element in overall economic development is readily accepted in Saudi Arabia. Manpower needs, as has been discussed, are very significant in the Kingdom, but so is the need for bringing about a healthy transformation in the life-patterns and attitudes of the society. While the labour force was growing from 1.75 million in 1975 to 2.47 million in 1980, some progress was made in the institutions which shape that labour force. Budgetary allocation for education rose five times during the Second Plan, resulting in dramatic increases in enrolment at all levels. By 1980 almost 20 per cent of the Saudi population was participating in some form of organized education. However, while progress during the period in quantitative terms was generally good, qualitative improvement was less than had been hoped for. Instruction quality, responsiveness to the economy, and administration are all areas open to betterment. Labour affairs, in dealing with the administration and employment services of a rapidly growing labour force, are beset by administrative and organizational problems as well as inadequate statistical procedures for effective manpower research and planning. Cultural affairs saw the vast majority of Second Plan targets completed – museum construction progressed, including plans for the ready-for-construction new national museum in Riyadh; important archaeological work was done; publications were started.[60]

Social Development

A major objective of Saudi Arabian social development is to increase the well-being of all groups within the society, while at the same time maintaining the religious and moral values of Islam and social stability under circumstances of rapid economic change. While *per capita* income has been increasing and many people are sharing in the increasing wealth of the nation, many others have been left behind by economic development. Significant regional imbalances exist that were just beginning to be realized by the government as the Second Plan drew to a close. For example, the northern and southwestern regions are characterized by low-productivity occupations and above-average outward migration. Poverty is still a social problem, and there continues to be a large number of people with low incomes, especially uneducated and untrained residents of isolated rural villages. Another segment of the population not sharing fully in economic development includes citizens who have come to rely on government aid for improvement instead of channelling their own efforts into realistic opportunities. Problems such as this dependency on government welfare, and the social issues mentioned above, will continue to be areas of emphasis in the Third Plan.[61]

One of the main objectives of the Saudi Government is to provide adequate medical facilities free of charge or at nominal rates for all sections of the population. The implementation of the greater part of the Second Plan's programmes and projects led to substantial progress in all fields of health care. The numbers of medical manpower, hospital beds, dispensaries, health centres, preventive medical and educational health facilities, as well as educational and training institutes were increased and it became possible to integrate the preventive, curative, educational, and training components of the health services offered in hospitals and dispensaries. Despite all gains, the health conditions of the nation are not yet satisfactory, with high rates of infant mortality, malnutrition and serious diseases confronting a health service that is neither extensive enough, nor comprehensive enough, to fulfil health-care needs. The Third Plan will see particular attention being given to this area.[62]

Social care, social security and social insurance schemes make up a comprehensive system of social support to those in need of assistance. While the schemes are not yet extensive enough, the overall structure is sound and well developed enough from the Second Plan period to provide a good foundation for future social-support programmes. Social care has been extended to the population through Community Development

Centres, which grew from 17 to 24 during the Second Plan. Whereas the fundamental purpose of these centres is to 'help people help themselves', they had primarily operated as a means for the government to provide integrated services to a community from a fixed common-service centre. In this function, the centres have been successful in the past. Significantly, in the later years of the Second Plan, the activities of these centres increasingly emphasized self-help. Social insurance, a compulsory comprehensive occupational insurance scheme for employees in the private sector and state-owned corporations, increased enrolment from under 200,000 to almost 700,000 workers during the Second Plan. Social security provided regular income to persons unable to work because of special economic and social circumstances, and amounted to SR 930 million in 1977/8, a substantial increase over earlier years.[63]

Administration

An area that encompasses all that has been discussed is government administration. A fast-growing and increasingly complex society like that of Saudi Arabia puts tremendous strain on the administrative framework. Another of the primary objectives of the Second Plan was to improve the administration, and although results are difficult to quantify, administration was greatly expanded during the Second Plan. Twenty ministries incorporating 66 administrative agencies at the end of the Second Plan replaced the 14 ministries in existence in 1975. Besides reorganizations, training was increased for civil servants, administrative authority was dispersed, and salary levels were raised. Despite these achievements, however, many administrative problems still exist to be dealt with in the Third Development Plan.[64]

Summary

All in all, the Second Plan period was one of considerable progress in Saudi Arabia. Favourable growth rates were attained, inflation was reduced, absorptive capacity was increased, and infrastructure was improved – all in a period of relative social stability. The diminution of particularly glaring problem areas, however, brings to the fore new areas of concern. The Third Plan will have to deal primarily with the areas of manpower, efficiency and participation.

Notes

1. The First Development Plan covered the period 1970-5. The Second Development Plan (1975-1980), which was officially launched on 9 July 1975, will be referred to in this chapter as the Plan or Second Plan; the First Development Plan will be cited as the First Plan. Gregorian calendar years have been used throughout the discussion.

Saudi Fiscal and Hijra Year Dates and Gregorian Equivalents
(Source: *The Plan*, p. xii.)

Saudi Fiscal Year (1 Rajab to 30 Jumad II)	Starts on*	Hijra Year	Starts on*	Hijra months†
1385-86	25 Oct 1965	1385	1 May 1965	Muharram
86-87	16 Oct 66	86	21 Apr 66	Safar
87-88	4 Oct 67	87	11 Apr 67	Rabi I
88-89	23 Sep 68	88	30 Mar 68	Rabi II
89-90	12 Sep 69	89	19 Mar 69	Jumad I
				Jumad II
1390-91	2 Sep 70	1390	9 Mar 1970	Rajab
91-92	22 Aug 71	91	26 Feb 71	Shaban
92-93	10 Aug 72	92	15 Feb 72	Ramadhan
93-94	30 Jul 73	93	4 Feb 73	Shawwal
94-95	19 Jul 74	94	23 Jan 74	Dhul-Qi'dah
				Dhul-Hijjah
1395-96	9 Jul 1975	1395	13 Jan 1975	
96-97	28 Jun 76	96	2 Jan 76	
97-98	16 Jun 77	97	22 Dec 76	
98-99	6 Jun 78	98	11 Dec 77	*Gregorian*
99-1400	26 May 79	99	30 Nov 78	*months†*
				January
1400-01	15 May 1980	1400	19 Nov 1979	February
01-02	4 May 81	01	9 Nov 80	March
02-03	23 Apr 82	02	28 Oct 81	April
03-04	12 Apr 83	03	17 Oct 82	May
04-05	2 Apr 84	04	7 Oct 83	June
				July
1405-06	22 Mar 1985	1405	27 Sep 1984	August
06-07	11 Mar 86	06	27 Sep 85	September
07-08	28 Feb 87	07	4 Sep 86	October
08-09	17 Feb 88	08	24 Aug 87	November
09-10	7 Feb 89	09	14 Aug 88	December

2. See Chapter 13. For further detailed and informative discussions of surplus funds and absorptive capacity, see, for example, Y.A. Al-Awadi, 'OPEC Surplus Funds and the Investment Strategy of Kuwait' (PhD dissertation, University of Colorado, Boulder, 1975); J. Bridge, 'Financial Constraints on Absorptive Capacity and Investment Policies in the Arab World', in R. El Mallakh and C. McGuire (eds), *Energy and Development* (Boulder, Colorado: International Research Center for Energy and Economic Development, 1974); and T.

El-Jehaimi, 'Absorptive Capacity and Alternative Investment Policies: A Case Study of Libya' (PhD dissertation, University of Colorado, Boulder, 1975).

3. It will be noted that arguments in favour of planning in Saudi Arabia have already been offered in the introduction to Chapter 5.

4. *The Plan*, p. 4.

5. Ibid.

6. For a discussion of this problem in the case of Kuwait, within the context of 'economic requirements in the process of industrialization', see R. El Mallakh, *Economic Development and Regional Cooperation: Kuwait* (Chicago, University of Chicago Press, 1968), pp. 105-6.

7. This is in line with the new approach of national-income accounting proposed by W. Nordhaus and James Tobin, *Economic Growth* (New York, MBER Fiftieth Anniversary Colloquium V, 1972).

8. *The Plan*, p. 5.

9. Jeddah and Dammam ports, especially, have come under heavy pressure since implementation of the Plan was begun. See *Middle East Economic Digest*, Special report, December 1976, for analysis of this incident.

10. Arthur Lewis, *Development Planning: The Essentials of Economic Policy* (New York, Harper and Row, 1966), p. 15.

11. *The Plan*, p. 528.

12. Ibid., p. 532.

13. Ibid., p. 528.

14. See Table 6.2. As has been pointed out earlier and will be continually stressed, the most serious impediment to the implementation of the Second Plan has been manpower and infrastructural bottlenecks.

15. A more detailed examination of the role of the Saudi government in the development of agriculture can be found in Chapter 3. Also see pp. 102-6 of the Plan for further discussions of agriculture and water programmes.

16. *The Plan*, p. 217; see pp. 225-42 for more detailed discussion of manpower training.

17. Vide Table III-5, p. 75 of *The Plan* for detailed breakdown for sectors of economic activities.

18. *The Plan*, p. 75.

19. *The Plan*, p. 88. See Chapter 9 in this volume for a discussion of how these policies have been implemented.

20. Chapter IV of *The Plan* discusses this subsector under eight headings: water, agriculture, electricity, manufacturing, construction and commerce, petroleum, and minerals.

21. *The Plan*, p. 104.

22. Ibid., p. 106.

23. Ibid., p. 123.

24. Ibid., p. 124. But as has been noted in Chapter 3, the government also provides supporting services, for example, water for irrigation.

25. See Chapter 4 for the stated industrial policies.

26. Detailed schedules of industries included in the manufacturing sector can be found in Chapter 4. Also see *The Plan*, Tables IV-18 and IV.20-25.

27. *The Plan*, pp. 177-81.

28. See Chapter 1, section on population and labour force, for further analysis and population growth. In fact, agriculture retained its dominant position, although it did decline by an estimated 96,000 persons during the Second Plan. Its total employment declined 24 per cent by the end of the Plan.

29. *The Plan*, p. 229, Table V-7.

30. Chapter 5 of *The Plan* details the general education system envisaged for the 1975-80 span.

31. *The Plan*, p. 369.

32. The population-hospital bed ratios for 1978 used in this section have been computed from the United Nations, *Statistical Year Book, 1978*, Table 207, pp. 894-5.

33. For a discussion of the relationship between labour force and population, and other demographic factors, refer to Chapter 1.

34. John K. Cooley, 'Saudi Arabia Planning Its Future', *Christian Science Monitor*, 22 March 1976.

35. *The Plan*, p. 432.

36. Ibid., p. 493. The amount envisaged for municipal development is SR 53,327.8 million.

37. Ibid., pp. 510-11.

38. Kingdom of Saudi Arabia, Ministry of Planning, *Third Development Plan, 1400-1405/1980-1985*, Chapter 1, section 1.3.4.1, pp. 12-13. (Hereafter this source will be cited as *Third Development Plan*.)

39. *Third Development Plan*, Chapter 2, section 2.4.3, pp. 44-7.

40. Ibid.

41. Ibid., Chapter 2, section 2.2.1, pp. 26-7.

42. SAMA, *Annual Report, 1979 (1439)*, p. 2.

43. *Third Development Plan*, Chapter 2, section 2.2.2.5, pp. 32-4.

44. Ibid., Chapter 3, section 3.1.3.2, pp. 83-4.

45. SAMA, *Annual Report, 1979*, pp. 11-12.

46. *Third Development Plan*, Chapter 2, section 2.5.2, pp. 49-52.

47. Ibid., Chapter 2, section 2.3.2.2, pp. 41-3.

48. Ibid.

49. Ibid., Chapter 2, section 2.9.1, pp. 63-4, and Chapter 4, section 4.2.2.5, pp. 115-18.

50. SAMA, *Annual Report, 1979*, p. 65.

51. *Third Development Plan*, Chapter 4, section 4.3.1.5, pp. 138-40, and SAMA, *Annual Report, 1979*, p. 68.

52. Ibid., Chapter 4. section 4.6.3.1, pp. 226-8 and Chapter 2, section 2.9.1.12, p. 65.

53. Ibid., Chapter 4, sections 4.4.3.3, pp. 173-9; 4.4.5, pp. 186-91; 4.6.2.3, pp. 221-4, and Chapter 2, sections 2.9.1.6, p. 64; 2.9.1.15, p. 66; 2.9.4, pp. 69-71.

54. SAMA, *Annual Report, 1979*, p. 81.

55. *Third Development Plan*, Chapter 2, section 2.9.1.8, pp. 64-5.

56. Ibid., Chapter 2, section 2.9.1.15, p. 66.

57. Ibid., Chapter 2, section 2.9.1.10, p. 65.

58. Ibid., Chapter 2, section 2.9.4, pp. 69-71.

59. Ibid., Chapter 2, section 2.9.4.9, pp. 70-1.

60. SAMA, *Annual Report, 1979*, p. 84 and *Third Development Plan*, Chapter 2, sections 2.9.2, pp. 66-7; 2.9.3.7, p. 69; Chapter 5, sections 5.2.1, pp. 289-92; 5.2.2, pp. 293-307; 5.3.2.1, pp. 327-8; 5.5.1, p. 338; 5.5.2, p. 338.

61. *Third Development Plan*, Chapter 2, sections 2.7.1, p. 59; 2.7.2, pp. 59-61; Tables 2-21 and 2-22, p. 60.

62. SAMA, *Annual Report, 1979*, p. 92 and *Third Development Plan*, Chapter 2, section 2.9.3, pp. 67-8; and Chapter 6, section 6.2.1, pp. 344-6.

63. *Third Development Plan*, Chapter 6, sections 6.3.1 to 6.3.1.4, pp. 352-6.

64. Ibid., Chapter 2, section 2.8, pp. 61-3.

7 PLANNING FOR ECONOMIC DEVELOPMENT: THE THIRD EXPERIENCE

Introduction

The Second Development Plan ending in 1980 entailed five successful years of development for Saudi Arabia. As discussed in the preceding chapter, substantial progress was achieved in attaining planned targets. Gross domestic product grew at an average annual rate of 8.04 per cent with the non-oil sector increasing at an average rate of 15.13 per cent annually. These figures alone do not reveal all the significant economic advancements that were made and that provide the framework within which the Third Development Plan (1980-85) was conceived.

At the beginning of the Third Plan period, Saudi Arabia ranked as one of the world's foremost financial powers, with great international strength arising from monetary wealth and an economic role as the major oil exporter to the free world. Of course, with this status there are added responsibilities and duties, not only in global finance but in the political areas as well.

Major physical constraints to development, while not completely eliminated, had been reduced in significance at the start of the Third Plan. While not yet fully sufficient for the demands of planned development, the infrastructural framework in 1980 was adequate. Special emphasis in the Second Plan, particularly in the first two years of the period, produced considerable improvement with the help of an influx of labour both from abroad and from the rural areas of Saudi Arabia. Absorptive capacity was also much improved at the beginning of the Third Plan compared to five years earlier as imports rose dramatically during the span, and government actual expenditures exceeded allocated amounts by the end of the Second Plan.

The Third Plan was to begin in a much more favourable situation than the previous plan relative to the rate of price increase. Inflation which was particularly severe at the end of the First Plan and during the first two years of the Second, was reduced to an average rate of increase of 10.5 per cent in 1979. Appropriate government monetary policy as well as increases in supply capability were crucial in alleviating this threat to the living standards of Saudis and to the price structure of the Kingdom.

With controlled inflation, most, but not all, of the population was able to have a much higher standard of living at the beginning of the Third Plan than at the comparable period of the Second. Average annual income from employment *per capita* increased from approximately SR 4,800 in 1975 to about SR 8,200 in 1980 (in constant 1979 prices). Moreover, government social-welfare programmes added an estimated extra 29 per cent to personal income levels during the period.[1] While distribution figures were not available, the 'average' Saudi was much better off in 1980 than in 1975.

While development accomplishments are evident from the Second Plan, so is the realization of constraints toward continued development. Shortfalls in the achievement of manpower goals indicate that this critical area will likely be very central to economic decisions in the Third Plan period. The problem consists of a continuing imbalance between the economy's growing manpower needs and the number of new Saudi entrants into the labour force. Also, a trend has developed which cannot continue indefinitely, that depends on an outmigration from agriculture to supply Saudi labour for new (non-agricultural) employment. As an employer the government has contributed to the problem by making great demands for Saudi labour, thereby reducing the supply of manpower available to other sectors. Another manpower-related problem evolving out of the Second Plan was that the concentration of demand for labour, particularly non-Saudi, occurred in the development of infrastructure in areas such as construction, transportation, distribution – all 'through-put' sectors which are vital but contribute in a supportive sense only to the growth of GDP. Viewed from this perspective, the use of manpower has not been in new productive enterprises in agriculture and industry, and these cannot yet be considered as a long-term potential alternative to the oil sector.

Plan Goals

While the long-term goals for development remain unchanged (see Chapter 6), the strategy for the Third Plan will be noteworthy in the selection of new focal points, some of which considerably modify the trends and modes of operation of the first two plans. The period 1970-80 emphasized high growth rates in all sectors and, by implication, the relatively free import of foreign labour to satisfy the demand created. The Third Plan stresses a more selective approach: high growth in certain areas with proven potential. The primary aim of this selectivity is to consolidate rather than continue the expansion of the foreign labour force – a significant shift of policy in so far as it signals a reduction in the emphasis upon all-around growth.[2] Where the Second Plan was a concentrated effort to expand infrastructure and increase absorptive capacity by elimination of physical constraints, the Third Plan will more efficiently utilize domestic and foreign skilled manpower in capital-intensive hydrocarbon and other manufacturing industries, in agriculture, and in mining with the objective of furthering diversification of the economy.

The above-mentioned strategy targets three important medium-term objectives and includes a set of policy measures to aid in accomplishing them. These objectives are: (1) structural change of the economy; (2) attainment of participation and social welfare in development; and (3) an increased economic and administrative efficiency.

Structural Change in the Economy

Structural change in the economy will occur through policies directed at three main areas of economic activity – oil and gas production; the development of productive sectors of agriculture, industry and mining; and the development of infrastructure. Oil and gas production is the most important of the three areas for it is the sector which bankrolls, so to speak, and consequently determines the policies of all other sectors. In the Third Plan, Saudi Arabia will produce oil and gas at a rate so as to conserve its reserves for the longest possible time, while at the same time generating enough revenue to cover the financial requirements of the Third Plan. Natural-gas production will continue to be developed, and crude-oil production will be optimized by balancing between heavy and light crudes and among the various oil fields.

Development of the agricultural, industrial and mining sectors is vital in terms of the government's long-term objective of diversifying the economy. Government policy continues to be one of support to the private sector, which is seen as undertaking the development in these areas. This support in the Third Plan will be to provide information and results of research, to provide an appropriate financial framework and incentives for investment, to take care of infrastructure needs, and to establish priority areas for investment.[3]

Structural change in the economy will also be facilitated by policies directed at infrastructure development. Significant in the Third Plan is that there will be a reduction in the volume of investment in infrastructure relative to other sectors so that development can be accelerated in the productive sectors and thus induce structural changes in the economy. Specific objectives for the Plan are to complete projects begun during the Second Plan and to provide needed physical infrastructure in areas which can be identified as having potential to become growth centres for productive economic activities in the future. Some 73 such areas have been designated to date. Development of municipalities in an integrated and organized manner will continue as will the development of infrastructure for the support of the two hydrocarbon-based industrial areas on the coasts at Jubail and Yanbu.[4]

Human-resource Development

A second objective of the Third Plan deals with the human aspect of development. The intent is to distribute the benefits of the accruing wealth in the society to more of the population while maintaining stability in the society and the strength of the Islamic faith. Particular goals are (1) to encourage and assist all Saudis to make an effective contribution to development; (2) to ensure that all regions of the Kingdom develop to their full potential with the entire range of government services available; (3) to assist the society in dealing with the problems of rapid changes; (4) to control inflation and reduce subsidies without affecting low-income groups; and (5) to expand and improve the social services.[5]

A broadening of the base of contributors to, and sharers in, the development of the country is a vital part of the Third Plan. To date, various segments of the population have not shared in the benefits of burgeoning national wealth as fully as they could, while many foreign labourers have benefited quite extensively from Saudi development. The government will urge citizens to participate through a broad programme of information dissemination that advises people of the role they can play in development. High priority will be given to the education system's role in preparing citizens for a place in the development process. The Islamic faith will not be neglected as a positive source of guidance concerning a citizen's role in development. Direct government involvement will take place in adult and vocational education and in the community development schemes which are designed to encourage self-help principles, especially in the rural areas. The manpower strategy will be instrumental in encouraging participation in that the Plan calls for the number of foreign workers employed in Saudi Arabia to diminish considerably, thus enhancing the job opportunities for Saudis.[6]

Recognition by the government at the end of the Second Plan of the great disparities in regional development has given rise to a provision in the Third Plan dealing with this issue.[7] With more co-ordinated and explicit approach it is hoped to avoid an overconcentration of resources in a few urban enclaves. The policy approach will be to introduce a system of national, regional and district centres throughout the Kingdom for the provision and co-ordination of development services. These services will not be the normal municipal services (electricity, roads, schools and the like, which will continue to be provided as before, but they will be the administrative and technical back-up services – for example, agricultural extension services – that support local activities and are not needed daily or continually. It is hoped that those development service centres will enable necessary institutional elements for development to be distributed more evenly and efficiently than earlier.

A society that undergoes rapid economic and social transformation such as has taken place in Saudi Arabia is bound to have problems of adjustment. Strains between the methods of maintaining social stability and those to stimulate economic growth exist and must be dealt with in some fashion. The strategy of the Third Plan calls for the impact of development to be softened by the provision of services by government social development agencies. Particular attention will be given to maintaining balance while not infringing upon the earlier-mentioned Plan objective of participation by citizens (i.e. 'self-help').[8]

A fourth area of the planners' concern for the welfare of the Saudi citizens pertains to inflation. Development in the Kingdom was severely threatened late in the First Plan period and early in the Second by very high inflation. Uncontrolled, the inflation could have resulted in serious structural changes that would have adversely affected the economic and social well-being of Saudis, especially members of the lower-income classes. The battle against the rapidly rising prices in the Second Plan included the introduction of subsidies on various items such as housing and essential foods. In the Third Plan all these government subsidies will be reviewed with the objective of abolishing or reducing them. At the same time the government will attempt to keep a lid on expenditures so that inflation is kept at a tolerable rate, considered to be 7-10 per cent.[9]

The expansion of social-development services, such as health, welfare and cultural needs, will be another major process in the Third Plan. While the functions begun in the Second Plan will be continued and made more efficient during the new period, there will be a subtle shift in emphasis to more health education, preventive medicine and primary care. As in all facets of social assistance in Saudi Arabia, the services will be applied selectively so as to help the truly underprivileged, while not curbing incentives to those who are able to improve their condition by working.[10]

Increased Economic and Administrative Efficiency

A nation growing as rapidly as Saudi Arabia puts tremendous strain on its administrative apparatus. The third medium-term objective concerns an improvement in the efficiency of the operation and management of the economy as well of the government's administrative system. Four areas are focused upon relative to this efficiency improvement: (1) administrative development; (2) manpower development; (3) preservation of national fixed capital; and (4) fiscal management.

(1) The intention in administrative development is to introduce basic changes in government administration while optimizing manpower usage, particularly in that Saudis are to occupy all managerial and senior administrative positions. In order to put these goals into practice, a comprehensive study of government administration will be completed during 1982 that should reveal where basic changes are needed in the administrative structure. Improvements in statistical-data collection and a greater emphasis on training will go hand in hand with any resulting reorganization.

Budgetary policies will also be directed toward administrative development as there will be restrictions on the recruitment of additional manpower for the Third Plan period. These requests run counter to the policy of reducing dependence on foreign manpower by increasing overall demand for labour, and have resulted in the decision that no additional government positions will be budgeted beyond those vacant at the beginning of the Plan and those required for entirely new programmes.[11] This decision will limit government hiring except in certain cases where an agency can verify that its current level of vacant positions is so low as to merit additional manpower. The above-mentioned government reorganization study to be completed in 1982 will decide the future of this 'freeze'.

(2) Manpower development has the highest priority during the Third Plan for it represents the area of greatest reward and greatest risk. If Saudi Arabia develops with optimal participation of its own population, stability will be greatly enhanced. If, on the other hand, large numbers of foreign workers continue to be employed when significant segments of the Saudi population are underemployed, dissatisfaction with the economy could result. It is with this reasoning that the Third Plan will seek to reduce dependence on foreign manpower while increasing the number of Saudi workers, improving their productivity, and deploying them into sectors with the greatest growth potential.

The Interministerial Committee of Manpower, which was established in 1979, will preside over manpower developments in a far-reaching programme that covers numerous areas. These areas, including education, training, research and administrative systems are worthy of further note.

Education will be encouraged at the primary level with adequate numbers of schools and teachers for all primary-age pupils. Beyond the intermediate level, steps will be taken to ensure that formal education is in line with national manpower needs. Students will be 'streamed' so that the more able students continue to university, with grants available for subject areas that are deemed in need of extra incentive. Students with aptitude for technical schools will be encouraged toward specialized technical-training institutes. It is hoped that the new policies will produce a system of education that is more efficient in supplying manpower for national economic needs.[12]

The private sector will be encouraged to provide training programmes by making the availability of government loans conditional upon a training programme being provided for Saudis. Further incentives will be employed where necessary to entice citizens to train for and seek employment in technical and skilled jobs.

A redeployment of manpower is a part of the efficient utilization of labour in the Kingdom. Workers in areas of limited economic potential will be encouraged to relocate in geographical areas and sectors with opportunities for productive activities. Young government workers in unskilled positions will be transferred gradually into training programmes or productive activities. Another redeployment of manpower will come from the introduction, where appropriate, of labour-saving technology.[13]

The government will undertake as well a comprehensive survey of its own manpower resources in light of the priorities and needs of the various agencies and of the private sector. More efficient manpower planning and management will emerge from this assessment, and from an expansion of research and a greater degree of co-operation between the universities and government ministries involved with manpower development. Implementation of measures resulting from the survey will be effected under the auspices of the Interministerial Committee for Manpower (established in 1979).

(3) The preservation of national fixed capital is a part of the economic efficiency that is an important impetus in the Third Plan. The high investment in infrastructure, such as buildings, roads, and machinery during the First and Second Plans means that proper maintenance is

vital to get full value from the emphasis that has been placed on infrastructure. Maintenance procedures will be encouraged and standardized; training will be emphasized in maintenance skills so that minor repairs are not overlooked until they develop into major overhauls; new projects will be designed and production technology selected that will minimize maintenance requirements as much as possible.[14]
(4) Administrative efficiency will be sought in terms of fiscal management. The goal will be to attain the planned growth rate in the various sectors in consideration of both the absorptive capacity of the economy and the rate of inflation. To accomplish this growth rate government expenditure will be tightly monitored in terms of the priorities established for the Third Plan. A new system of imposing ceiling on the allocations for expenditure by each government agency is being introduced; it is intended to give more control over expenditures in terms of Plan priorities. During 1982 a special review is to be completed that will reassess all planned programmes and allocations for expenditure for the remaining three years of the Plan. Fiscal policies will be devised so as to attain appropriate levels of expenditure relative to allocations, absorptive capacity and inflation.

Development Strategies and Pattern of Development

Like its immediate predecessor, the Third Plan is an ambitious undertaking. Expenditure will be vast – $235 billion compared with the Second Plan's $149 billion at current prices. The figure for the Third Plan includes a built-in allowance for inflation at 7 per cent per year but does not include defence spending and foreign aid, which could push the total to about $391 billion (compared to the Second Plan's total of $210 billion). While, as previously discussed, there will be no dramatic shifts in keeping with the Saudi desire for carefully orchestrated change, fundamental shifts in development policy are evident. As Table 7.1 shows, spending on infrastructure will drop from 50 per cent in the Second Plan to 35 per cent, while expenditure on productive activities such as industry and mining will increase from 25 per cent in the Second Plan to 37 per cent in the Third.[15] This trend is in line with the emphasis upon diversification. Human-resource development shows a modest increase in line with the Plan's stress on manpower development.

The Third Plan will be a period of consolidation with a more selective approach to growth in GDP and a constraint in the form of manpower (see Table 7.2). Projected growth for the oil sector is 1.34 per cent per annum with most of that growth arising from refined products, including the varying output of the new gas-gathering project. Estimated growth in the value of refined products alone is close to 15 per cent annually, while growth in crude-oil production is determined by government policy in keeping with its long-term policy to conserve oil resources while generating sufficient revenues for financing development. Some $79 billion was earned in 1979 on production of 9.5 million b/d and could be pushed still higher, depending on international as well as domestic considerations.[16]

Table 7.1: Government Expenditure on Development[a]

	Amount in SR billions (current prices)	Change in the direction of development expenditure Second Plan[b] (estimated %)	Third Plan (%)
Function of expenditure			
Economic-resource development	261.8	25.1	37.3
Human-resource development	129.6	15.9	18.5
Social development	61.2	9.4	8.7
Physical infrastructure	249.1	49.6	35.5
Subtotal: Development	701.7	100.0	100.0
Administration[c]	31.4	6.7	4.5
Emergency reserves, subsidies	49.6	15.9	7.1
Total civilian expenditure	782.7	122.6	111.6

Notes: a. The total excludes: (i) transfer payments; (ii) non-civilian sectors; (iii) foreign aid. b. Based on actual and estimated values converted into 1979/80 prices. c. Administration includes: (i) ministries and agencies with primarily administrative functions; (ii) judicial and religious agencies.
Source: Kingdom of Saudi Arabia, *Third Development Plan, 1400-1405/1980-1985*, Chapter 3, p. 88.

The projected growth rate for the non-oil economy in the Third Plan is down to 6.2 per cent from the Second Plan's average rate of over 15 per cent per year.[17] This projection is based on the low rate of employment growth as a result of the new Plan's constraining manpower policy and on the anticipated disappearance of the favourable effects of shifts in employment, primarily from agriculture. As Tables 7.3 and 7.4 show, the service sectors should out-perform the producing sectors as in the Second Plan. Much of the reason for this is that the producing sectors are affected significantly by decreases in the highly productive construction sector, part of the process whereby the emphasis in development is moving towards the creation of production capabilities, like manufacturing, and away from construction of infrastructure.

Table 7.2: The Growth of GDP in the Period 1966/7 to 1979/80 (annual compound growth in per cent per annum, in 1969/70 prices)

	1966/7-1969/70	First Plan 1969/70-1974/5	Second Plan[a] 1974/5-1979/80	Third Plan 1980/1-1984/5
Producing sectors				
Agriculture	3.62	3.59	5.40	5.35
Other mining	5.56	21.07	17.14	9.78
Other manufacturing	11.76	11.39	15.37	18.83
Utilities	11.31	10.93	24.41	29.46
Construction	3.32	18.57	17.78	(2.48)[b]
Service sectors				
Trade	10.09	13.94	22.06	8.42
Transport	10.58	16.97	21.13	12.93
Finance	7.94	8.16	12.99	7.29
Other services	9.76	7.09	13.91	2.95
Government	4.39	7.75	5.96	7.16
Non-oil economy	6.96	11.66	15.13	6.19
Oil sector	10.34	14.80	4.78	1.34
Total economy	8.75	13.41	8.04	3.28

Notes: a. Sectoral data for the First Plan period shown above include the old price system for 1974/5; the Second and the Third Plan figures, however, use the revised price system for each sector. Tables for the non-oil economy, the oil sector and the total economy for the Second and Third Plans are in 1979/80 prices, partly because the 1984/5 composition of the oil sector's output has no equivalent in 1969/70. b. Negative growth rate.
Source: *Third Development Plan*, Chapter 1, p. 20.

The first two years of the Third Plan will see a slight increase in construction activity due to government expenditure already committed, followed in the last three years of the Plan by a possible decline in that sector as a result of the shift in planning emphasis. The construction sector has traditionally been the leading sector in the non-oil economy averaging about 20 per cent of non-oil GDP throughout the Second Plan.[18] However, the effect of the government's policy changes leaves the overall prospects for construction in the Third Plan as mixed, with steady growth expected only from the private and non-civilian sectors.

The policy area with the most far-reaching changes in the Third Plan is the one dealing with manpower and employment. With significant reductions to be made in the foreign worker component of the labour

Table 7.3: Projections for Growth of the Non-oil Economy (per cent per year)

Growth rates for:	Producing sectors		Services sectors		Total non-oil economy	
	Second Plan	Third Plan	Second Plan	Third Plan	Second Plan	Third Plan
GDP	16.5	2.2	14.1	8.8	15.1	6.2
Employment	2.2	(1.5)[a]	12.5	3.1	7.2	1.2
Productivity	14.0	3.7	1.5	5.6	7.4	5.0
of which						
Cost/price effects[b]	4.1	5.1	1.2	4.4	2.4	4.6
Employment shift effects	9.6	(1.3)[a]	0.3	1.2	4.9	0.3

Notes: a. The rates in parentheses represent annual rates of decline relative to 1979/80. b. These represent lower unit costs and/or higher-value products.
Source: *Third Development Plan*, Chapter 3, p. 91.

Table 7.4: The Structural Composition of GDP in the Period 1966/7 to 1979/80 (per cent of non-oil GDP based on 1969/70 prices)

	1966/7	1969/70	1974/5[a]	1974/5[b]	1979/80	1984/5
			(A)	(B)		
Producing sectors						
Agriculture	13.9	12.6	8.7	9.1	5.8	5.1
Other mining	0.6	0.6	0.7	0.6	0.7	0.7
Other manufacturing	4.8	5.5	5.5	5.6	5.6	8.9
Utilities	3.1	3.5	3.4	2.5	3.8	8.9
Construction	13.3	12.0	16.2	19.1	21.3	12.6
Subtotal	35.7	34.2	34.5	36.9	37.2	36.2
Services sectors						
Trade	11.8	12.9	14.3	14.9	19.9	19.9
Transport	14.5	15.9	20.1	10.0	12.8	15.8
Finance	12.1	12.4	10.6	16.8	15.3	14.5
Other services	2.8	3.1	2.5	2.5	2.3	1.8
Government	23.1	21.5	18.0	18.9	12.5	11.8
Subtotal	64.3	65.8	65.5	63.1	62.8	63.8
Non-oil economy	100.0	100.0	100.0	100.0	100.0	100.0
Oil sector	109.1	119.8	137.6	144.5	89.5	64.1

Notes: a. New data have been incorporated by CDS in the revised estimates for the years from 1974/5 onwards (except for Agriculture). For this reason, figures from 1974/5 onwards are not strictly comparable with figures for earlier years. Column (A) shown above for 1974/5 is based on the old system of prices; column (B) is based on the revised data. b. Ministry of Planning estimate.
Source: *Third Development Plan*, Chapter 1, p. 20.

force and with a much slower average annual growth projected for the 1980-5 period (1.16 per cent as compared to 7.19 per cent for the Second Plan), government will continually monitor economic performance with the idea of re-evaluating policies where necessary.[19] This intent by government to review carefully and change policy where necessary indicates the potential constraining effect of this manpower policy on the growth of the economy.

Table 7.5: Changes in Civilian Employment in the Second and Third Plan Periods (comparison by economic activity)

	Employment increase (thousands)		Annual growth rate (%)	
Economic activity	Second Plan	Third Plan	Second Plan	Third Plan
Producing sectors				
Agriculture	(96.2)	(70.0)	(2.94)	(2.46)
Other mining	3.9	2.5	16.51	6.07
Other manufacturing	29.8	60.0	6.97	9.52
Utilities	15.4	15.5	14.37	8.33
Construction	157.8	(85.0)	13.89	(5.78)
Total: producing sectors	110.7	(77.0)	2.20	(1.48)
Services sectors				
Trade	157.0	29.0	15.12	1.80
Transport	100.1	60.0	13.39	5.05
Finance	21.7	10.0	21.58	5.18
Other services	252.3	23.0	15.96	0.94
Government[a]	74.3	100.0	5.41	5.57
Total: services sectors	605.4	222.0	12.46	3.06
Non-oil economy subtotal	716.1	145.0	7.21	1.16
Oil sector	8.6	10.0	5.61	5.02
Total Economy	724.7	155.0	7.19	1.22

Note: a. Excludes non-civilian employment.
Source: *Third Development Plan*, Chapter 3, p. 101.

As Table 7.5 indicates, agriculture and construction will be the sectors surrendering the most jobs, the former because of the already-mentioned change in government priority. Most other sectors will show large declines in annual employment growth in light of the more selective GDP growth projections, as well as from planned increases in productivity. 'Other manufacturing' is an exception and reinforces the emphasis in the Third Plan on the productive industries. Government itself is projected for a slight increase in annual employment growth, but, as referred to earlier, is subject to an efficiency review in 1982.

With the objective of sustained expansion of the non-oil economy and a policy of constraint with regard to labour-force growth, it is imperative that productivity increase. Without the achieved productivity improvement of the Second Plan, labour-force requirements would have been more than twice what they were. Likewise, the envisaged productivity increase of the Third Plan will mean 550,000 fewer workers needed, a significant figure when viewed in comparison to the 155,000 that are projected as required for the period. As the participation rate for Saudis has been slightly declining – a direct result of the expansion of educational and training programmes – the bulk of the workers that would have to be hired in the absence of productivity gains would be foreign, in direct opposition to government strategy.

The productivity growth is to come from capital and skill-intensive improvements and developments within individual sectors. Agriculture is to contribute as a result of a projected modest GDP growth against a background of outmigration of labour. Manufacturing is to contribute on the basis of high-productivity projects, financed with the aid of the Saudi Industrial Development Fund. Energy, water, transport, communications and storage are all to make contributions to productivity increase because of capital-intensive developments.

Contrasting this productivity growth to that of the Second Plan when gains were primarily a result of labour movements – away from low-productivity agriculture and towards high-productivity construction – causes some concern as to whether projected productivity can be attained and if not, what the effect will be on manpower policy and GDP-growth estimates.[20]

The role to be played by inflation during the Third Plan is open to question. As noted in Chapter 6, the high inflation of the middle 1970s threatened the implementation of Second Plan objectives. The same situation could arise once more if inflation is not kept close to the 10 per cent figure, a rate considered 'tolerable' to the planners. One potential source of inflation is the level of government expenditure. If not controlled, expansionary pressures could be ignited that would create a demand for skilled manpower beyond the economy's ability to supply. The resultant 'demand-pull' on wages might generate a 'cost-push' pressure which would aggravate the inflationary spiral. The private sector, too, could generate the same 'demand-pull' situation because at present investment outlays represent less than 50 per cent of gross profits, resulting in substantial funds for potential use.[21] Another potential source of inflation is trading partners in Europe and North

America, where the current rate of inflation is high. All evidence would suggest, then, that the danger of inflation remains and could seriously alter the Third Plan's implementation unless existing mechanisms for monitoring and controlling are continued and even extended.

Foreign trade in the Third Plan will continue to be dominated by exports from the oil sector. While crude-oil exports will still provide the financial cover for development and the strengthening of international financial reserves, refined products and gas also will become available to enter the international markets. Although the daily level of crude-oil exports (at May 1980 prices) needed to finance development during the Third Plan is slightly under 5.3 million b/d – far less than the 9.5 million b/d production level of 1979 – the government policy will be to maintain stability in the world economy and in the supply of energy, as it has been in the past.[22]

Imports of goods and services had close to a one-to-one relationship with non-oil GDP during the Second Plan, reflecting the use of many imported components in Saudi manufacturing industries. This high propensity to import is expected to continue in the Third Plan, as that sector is projected at a 7 per cent annual growth rate in relation to the 6.2 per cent for non-oil GDP annual growth. The slightly higher figure for imports is a result of an expected rise in components that substitute for labour.

Sectoral Analysis

So far in the analysis it has been reiterated that the Third Plan places a greater weight on the development of productive activities (see Table 7.1) such as agriculture, minerals, hydrocarbons (particularly natural gas) and manufacturing. While infrastructure has received less emphasis than in the Second Plan, it will be developed in so far as needed to support the productive sectors. The private sector will play an important role alongside the public sector in expanding the productive activities and will have the assistance of various government funds.

In this section the detailed strategies of different sectors are examined to determine how they accord with overall objectives.

Economic-resource Development

The Third Plan provides SR 261,209.8 million for the development of economic resources. The composition of this broad sector is given in Table 7.6.

Table 7.6: Third Development Plan Financial Requirements from Government Sources for Economic Resources Development (current prices in SR millions)

Sector components	Recurrent	Project	Total
Agriculture and water[a]	12,767.2	59,318.2	72,085.4
Energy and mineral resources	14,013.7	79,508.9	93,522.6
Manufacturing and commerce[b]	3,643.4	91,958.4	95,601.8
Total	30,424.3	230,785.5	261,209.8

Notes: a. Excludes expenditures by Ministry of Municipal and Rural Affairs (MOMRA). b. Includes SABIC capital contributions.
Source: *Third Development Plan*, Chapter 4, p. 284.

Water

The development of Saudi Arabia's limited water resources continues to be vital in order to support the total requirement of the population at large, of industry, and of agriculture. An *ad hoc* approach prior to the First Development Plan in 1970 was followed by 10 years of considerable accomplishment in the first two periods of planning, including the beginning of preparation of a national water plan to direct the rational use and reuse of the water resources available to the Kingdom.[23]

In the Third Plan the intention is to complete as soon as possible the national water programme in order to provide a firm data, regulatory and policy base. It is hoped that by 1983 a time schedule for enforcement of the water plan's stipulations will be in force. Within the water plan's framework, then, the objectives will be to provide sufficient quantities of good quality water to meet the urban and rural populations' needs, to secure water supplies to cope with industrial development and to increase agricultural expansion in the Kingdom, to develop efficiently the present known water resources, and to seek new water resources.

As the Ministry of Agriculture and Water's (MOAW) responsibility has diminished in recent years because of increasing complexities of water development and government reorganization, the role of the Saline Water Conversion Corporation (SWCC) has increased. The use of seawater and saline inland water deposits through desalination has become imperative as conventional water supply sources have become insufficient. Six new plants are scheduled for completion by the third year of the Third Plan, bringing to 20 the total of combined water desalination and power-generating plants. The production capacity of desalinated water will be significantly increased from 65.4 million m^3 per year in 1979 to 523 million m^3 per year in 1983 as will power generation, which will increase from 350 MW to 3,145 MW over the same period.[24]

Table 7.7: Third Plan Water Sector Targets

Urban water supply (towns over 5,000 inhabitants):	
From conventional sources:	600,000 m^3/day
By desalination:	1,640 thousand m^3/day[a]
Rural water supply (centres under 5,000 inhabitants): 50 per cent of the population and their livestock within easy access to safe water for drinking purposes.	
Industrial water supply (major industrial complexes):	
Jubail	114 thousand m^3/day
Yanbu (and Medinah)	95 thousand m^3/day
Other industrial areas at major cities	100 per cent service
Agricultural water supply	
New areas brought under irrigation by modern methods:	19,000 hectares (5,000 in the Al-Hassa Oasis and 14,000 included in Agricultural Plan Section)
Traditional, irrigated areas converted to modern method irrigation:	22,500 hectares (included in Agricultural Plan Section)

Note: a. 90 per cent provided by SWCC.
Source: *Third Development Plan*, Chapter 4, p. 131.

Of note is the water development project to provide the rapidly growing capital city of Riyadh with its water needs. The water system capacity will have to be twice its 1980 capacity of approximately 300 thousand m^3/day by 1987. To complicate the situation, the present groundwater sources near the city are quickly being depleted so that water will have to be imported from the Wasia aquifer well field near Khurais (200 thousand m^3/day) and from the desalination complex at Jubail (660 thousand m^3/day). The magnitude of the project makes it the largest water development project in Saudi history. Specific targets for the Third Plan are listed in Table 7.7.

Agriculture

Although the need for a sound agricultural sector has long been recognized and supported by the government, progress in agriculture to date has not been particularly good. In the Second Plan, agriculture's real value-added grew at approximately 5 per cent per annum compounded, one-third as fast as the non-oil sector, and its share of non-oil GDP fell from 12.1 per cent in 1970 to 2.4 per cent in 1978.[25] While the government's aspiration is to attain a prudent level of self-sufficiency in food production and provide opportunities for reasonable agricultural incomes, this self-sufficiency has so far been elusive; about 90 per cent of Saudi food is imported and producers employing traditional farming methods have fallen to new lows of output and real income-earning capacity.[26]

Nevertheless, continued striving for progress in the agricultural sector is important as demand for food has increased rapidly in response to an expanding and more affluent population. Just over 1 per cent of total Third Plan expenditure (excluding defence and foreign aid), $2,372 million, is allocated to agriculture. The close relationship between the agricultural sector and water development mentioned before means that the $4,017 million to be spent on development of water resources (excluding desalination) will benefit farmers as well.

Balanced against increasing demands for agricultural products has been the continued outmigration of labour from agriculture to the opportunities of urban life. Although still the primary occupation of the Kingdom's population, employment in the sector fell from about 40 per cent of the civilian labour force in 1975 to about 25 per cent in 1980. The $20,240 million set aside for municipal development in the Third Plan will contribute to ending the rural drift to the cities by stimulation of regional development and perhaps agro-business.

Productivity, which grew at about 8 per cent per annum in the Second Plan, will not surprisingly be stressed in the Third Plan to compensate for the loss of workers and to continue to free marginal farmers for employment in more productive sectors. To do this, emphasis will be on increasing efficiency all around, on promoting research, information dispersal, and training, and on encouraging the private sector to develop more productive large-scale projects ranging from major integrated agricultural projects to individual crop, dairy and livestock projects.

Agricultural credit, administered by the Saudi Arabian Agricultural Bank, will play an important role in the development of the sector and the improvement of productivity by encouraging investment in agriculture. In the 1980-5 period SR 5 billion in loans and SR 2.5 billion in subsidies are scheduled for the private agricultural sector, well above the amounts that were made available during the Second Plan. Also, as with the preceding plan, attention is being given to reducing the complexity of borrowing and to decreasing the time between applications and receipt of cash, thus optimizing the funds available to the sector.

While substantial progress is targeted for production of wheat, potatoes, dairy products, vegetables and forage in the Third Plan, the crucial ingredient to Saudi Arabia's future agricultural development remains water. Because of the Kingdom's southern latitude and abundant sunshine, crop production and forage can be five times higher than its European equivalent per acre if sufficient water is available. Accordingly, the linkage between water development and agricultural success is a close one, and one that will have considerable impact on the future successes of the agricultural sector in Saudi Arabia.

Manufacturing

Based on the clear understanding of the finite nature of hydrocarbon resources, Saudi Arabian policy will continue in the Third Plan to be one of diversification, of achieving a more balanced and self-sufficient non-oil-sector growth. The Second Plan provided a good basis from which to build, as progress was considerable in developing infrastructure needed for industrial development, in encouraging the private sector to invest in industry, in luring foreign capital and expertise to participate in projects with Saudi entrepreneurs, in creating government entities such as Sabic (Saudi Arabian Basic Industries Corporation) to facilitate industrialization, and in moving steadily ahead in the development of the industrial complexes at Jubail and Yanbu.[27]

In the Third Plan the establishment of a heavy-industry base will receive priority in the industrial development of Saudi Arabia. Direct government involvement through Sabic is required because of the nature of developing a heavy-industry base. The large amounts of capital required and the long time lag between planning stage and profitable operation of basic industry schemes make government participation important. Moreover, government's close tie to hydrocarbon policies and projects make its involvement in heavy-industry development logical and unexceptional.

Within this sector considerable emphasis will be placed in the 1980-5 period upon the natural-gas production that was begun during the Second Plan. While Saudi Arabia does not have the dominant position in world natural-gas reserves that it has in crude-oil reserves, considerable gas exists that in the past has been flared or used to maintain oil-reservoir pressure. This will now be utilized as feedstock and fuels for petrochemical and energy-intensive industries. In addition, linked, downstream industrial projects will be created which can be implemented both by Sabic and private investors. One potential problem which exists at the time of writing is the slow rate of growth in demand for most petrochemicals in the international marketplace, coupled with underutilization of chemical plants, particularly in Western Europe; this could create a less-than-receptive market for Saudi exports. Further, the European Economic Community, Japan and the USA impose tariffs on petrochemical imports that could be increased if Saudi Arabia's new projects were seen as a threat to jobs and domestic markets. Besides hydrocarbon-based manufacturing, Sabic's main programmes in the Third Plan are concerned with the construction and operation of steel projects as well as other basic-metal projects.

The private sector, per government strategy, will continue to be encouraged to play a significant role in industrial development. The 15.5 per cent compounded annual growth contribution to GDP by non-oil hydrocarbon manufacturing in the Second Plan buoys expectations in this area for the Third Plan. With the aid of up to 50 per cent financing available from SIDF for viable projects, areas where Third Plan expansion is anticipated are cement production, industrial-gas production, and intermediate petrochemical production, as well as production of glass products, metal products, automotive parts, animal-feed concentrates, building materials, and agro-industry products.

The industrial complexes at Jubail and Yanbu, administered by a Royal Commission established in 1975, are essential parts of the Saudi industrialization programme with the primary function of converting the Kingdom's petroleum resources into high-value processed products. Significant progress was made in the Second Plan on the construction of infrastructure for the two complexes, but considerably more investment and effort will be required during the 1980-5 Plan to provide the sites, utilities, and other infrastructure for the new basic and secondary industry projects that will be established at these locations.

The Saudi Industrial Development Fund (SIDF), which has played a very significant role in the development of Saudi industry since its creation in 1974, will continue to finance manufacturing and electric companies in the Third Plan, but with decided changes in emphasis. Early stress on the construction sector, with 54 per cent of loans going to related projects, shifted late in the Second Plan to more consumer-oriented developments such as dairies, bakeries, meat-packing and processing operations, and soft drink and healthy-water plants. In the Third Plan, SIDF will continue to favour consumer-oriented projects, particularly in the food and food-processing sector, but it will also give special encouragement to industries based on local raw materials, those introducing new technology and labour-saving techniques, and those projects which support manufacturing activity, such as maintenance, service and repair operations. Attention will be directed as well to promoting the development of agro-industry, mineral-based projects, and higher technology industries, such as those linked with downstream development of the petroleum industry and the secondary industry planned at Jubail and Yanbu.

Of significance in the operation of SIDF in the Third Plan is the fact that the projected lending is to increase to SR 10 billion as compared to SR 6 billion in the Second Plan; the projected absolute number of loan applications will continue to fall. The fewer, but larger and more sophisticated, loans will necessitate the creation of a new department to provide loans for viable and competitive small businesses. Also to be provided through this new department will be an industrial extension service to small businesses.

The trend will continue for SIDF to assume the role of a development agency in addition to its historic narrower role as a lending institution. Besides traditional loan-support services and market, financial, and economic feasibility studies, greater consideration in the Third Plan will be given to the social aspects of projects. The location of projects will be of importance, with more emphasis to be given to industries in rural areas. An increase in consultancy and advisory functions is also expected.

Electricity

Considerable growth in the demand for electric power during the Second Plan, coupled with the vital role of electric power in the development of Saudi Arabia, have added up to an ambitious programme in that sector in the Third Plan. With the aid of higher living standards and government-controlled low prices, electricity consumers grew in number at an average annual rate of 16 per cent while their consumption was expanding by 37 per cent annually between 1975 and 1980. The continued improvement in the welfare of the population and the diversification of the economy away from dependency on oil necessitates that this vital sector of electric power which interrelates with so many other sectors of the economy be adequately planned for.[28]

Confronting planners is the fact that demand, which has been limited, is projected to continue its growth. Estimates show that if each potential consumer in the Kingdom in 1978 had been supplied with all the electricity he actually needed, at the location he chose, then the total peak load would have been nearly twice the 2,150 MW actually provided. Additionally, the continuing emphasis on industrialization in the country will increase the need for electric power.

In order to provide a reliable electric service to all the population, and to industrial and agricultural centres in the Kingdom during the 1980-5 span, while allowing for a system capable of meeting future demands, the Third Plan will expand the infrastructure in terms of generation, transmission and subtransmission, distribution, and administrative and resource development. A generation-expansion programme to include 34 projects will increase capacity from 4,877 MW in 1980 to 12,445 MW in 1985, not including the Saline Water Conversion Corporation-associated power generation. A total of 35 projects will add 6,309 kilometres of transmission lines for interconnecting generation and load centres in the five regions of the Kingdom. Some 600,000 new consumers, or a total of over 4 million people, will be connected to the transmission network, and a development programme that includes manpower training, information systems and developmental studies will be initiated.

Further significant trends in the electric power sector are the continued expansion into areas that until now have either no, or an inadequate service, the installation of large efficient steam electric generating plants in coastal areas to form the backbone of a national grid, and the consolidation of the Western Region's utilities early in the Plan period to reduce the total number of operating companies from 74 to 11. By 1980 it is anticipated that the electricity sector will have made great strides with most of the national power system in operation or undergoing development. Administratively, the consolidated companies will have developed into independent and efficient organizations. The future development of the Kingdom depends heavily upon such progress in the provision of adequate electric power.

Energy

The energy sector, comprised of the three primary resources of crude oil, natural gas and solar energy, is a key factor in the future economic progress of Saudi Arabia. Approximately 90 per cent of the Kingdom's revenue as well as foreign exchange receipts come from the oil and gas sector. Moreover, in 1979 crude-oil and petroleum products provided almost three-fourths of the domestic primary energy requirements with natural gas making up most of the balance and solar energy less than half a per cent. The significance of the energy sector is apparent in the continued development of the Kingdom.[29]

It is anticipated that during the Third Plan energy demand, which had grown 27.5 per cent per annum between 1975 and 1980, will continue to experience rapid growth particularly in the utilities, industry, and transportation sectors. Natural gas, the 'associated gas' produced in conjunction with crude oil, is expected to satisfy much of this new demand; this energy source can provide high value hydrocarbon exports without an increase in crude-oil production.

The gas-gathering programme that commenced early in 1975 is expected to make considerable headway in the Third Plan in taking advantage of Saudi Arabia's 3.4 per cent of the world's estimated natural-gas reserves. Plants at Shedgum (fuel gas) and Ju'aymah (LPG) are expected to be on stream by 1981 and facilities at Uthmaniyah and Yanbu producing products such as sulphur, fuel gas, ethane and LPG for use domestically or for export by 1983.

Meanwhile, crude oil will continue its significant role in the Kingdom's economy, subject to close observation. Production, which has been about 15 per cent of world output since 1975, will be maintained at a level to provide adequate revenue for the implementation of the development plan while taking into consideration the ratio of the various hydrocarbon types in maximizing national reserves. Improved oil-reservoir practices and maintenance of plant and equipment will be stressed in line with Third Plan emphasis on efficiency. Exploration programmes consisting of geological studies, seismic surveys and exploratory drilling will attempt to improve Saudi Arabia's falling production/reserve ratio (see Table 7.8).

Table 7.8: Production/Reserve Ratio, 1968-79

Year	Production : Reserves
1968	1.0 : 124.0
1972	1.0 : 62.0
1974	1.0 : 45.0
1975	1.0 : 56.0
1976	1.0 : 49.0
1977	1.0 : 50.0
1978	1.0 : 56.0
1979	1.0 : 52.0[a]

Note: a. Estimated.
Source: *Third Development Plan*, Chapter 4, p. 167.

Of strategic significance in the Third Plan will be the completion in late 1981 of the 1,200 kilometre pipeline connecting the eastern oil fields to the newly constructed storage and shipping terminal at Yanbu on the Red Sea. This 1.85 million b/d pipeline will provide the Kingdom with an alternative and shorter crude-oil export route for northern destinations as well as furnishing a supply of crude oil for domestic and export refineries at Yanbu, scheduled for completion during the Third Plan.

Refinery capacity, which has been insufficient to meet domestic demand and has been declining in relation to the volume of crude-oil exports since 1970, will be expanded in the Third Plan. Domestic refinery capacity will be raised from 120,000 b/d in 1980 to 640,000 b/d in 1985. Subject to feasibility, 750,000 b/d will be added to existing export refinery capacity in new plants at Jubail, Yanbu and Rabigh by the end of the plan period (1985).

Considering the large amounts of solar energy received each day – estimated at the maximum to be the equivalent of 10 billion barrels of crude oil – Saudi Arabia has a significant potential energy source as the value of energy continues to rise and as oil reserves are gradually diminished. A five-year co-operative research programme was signed between the Saudi Arabian and the US governments (the Solar Energy Research Institute) in 1977. While various projects hold much promise, they are in the early stages of research and development at this time.

A major trend in the energy sector in the Third Plan will be the movement towards greater integration with the Kingdom's domestic economy. As more Saudis are employed, as more industrial linkages (such as refineries) are created, as the gas-gathering programme comes into operation, and as the petrochemical and metal industries are more fully developed, the interrelation of the energy sector with the Saudi economy as a whole will become closer.

Mineral Resources

During the Third Plan the mineral sector will be characterized by continuing efforts to lay the groundwork for future development. Besides more research into the basic geology of the Kingdom, mineral exploration at two levels will be undertaken. The first will be concerned with all aspects of general prospecting within a broad geologic division including volcanic, sedimentary, mafic and felsic plutonic, and Phanerozoic rocks. The second will centre on investigations for specialized mineral commodities (such as phosphorite, evaporite, uranium, bauxite, gold, copper and phosphate). In line with the Third Plan's overall strategy, development of a sound mineral sector will take place with particular reference to the industrialization of the Kingdom.[30]

Construction

The construction sector grew at an annual rate of 21 per cent and 18 per cent during the First and Second Plans, respectively, in meeting the backlog of projects representing infrastructure, government buildings and private-sector construction. However, with this backlog largely eliminated by 1980 and a shift in government emphasis away from infrastructure development, it is unlikely that the construction sector will increase in the Third Plan at anything approaching the rates of the decade of the 1970s. Nevertheless, SR 440 billion (in constant 1979 prices) is budgeted for construction in the Third Plan including defence, other government, and private-sector programmes. The sector will continue to be an important one as the industrialization plan will require a major construction effort.[31]

Perhaps the most significant trend in the construction field will be the continuing shift towards the use of Saudi contractors. The important role of foreign contractors to date makes this shift a possible source of bottlenecks in meeting construction objectives and Plan goals. Division of large contracts into smaller parcels will make projects feasible for the generally smaller Saudi construction firms. Efficiency will be imperative for the recipients of contracts, and hopefully will be attained by small Saudi firms merging where advantageous and operating with foreign firms in joint-venture schemes.

Another projection for the Third Plan will be for the labour force employed in construction to fall to 245,000 by 1985 from approximately 330,100 in 1980. This decrease represents a drop from 13 per cent of the total labour force in 1980 to 9 per cent at the end of the Plan. Increased productivity will make this decrease in employment possible. Whether the Kingdom can accommodate the reduced manpower levels as well as the shift away from the use of foreign contractors, and still meet construction objectives for the Plan, remains to be seen.

Human-resource Development

One of the main features to emerge from the Second Plan that affects the developmental planning at both the national and sectoral levels, is the problem of manpower supply and demand. Manpower has replaced to a large extent the earlier serious issues of absorptive capacity and inflation as an issue to be solved before development of the Kingdom can continue to progress. The significance of the various options available to planners is accentuated by the impact manpower policy decisions have not only on the economic well-being of the country, but on the structure of society as well.

The Second Plan indicated that an imbalance existed between the economy's growing requirements for manpower and the number of new Saudis entering the labour force. The plan also revealed that government demand for Saudi labour was restricting the availability of manpower for other sectors, and that the private services sector – including construction, transportation and distribution – was relying on non-Saudi labour for its needs. Further, the Second Plan indicated that much of Saudi labour needed for new employment was originating from an outmigration from agriculture that could not be counted on to continue indefinitely in the future. It is for these reasons that manpower development, or from a wider point of view, human-resource development, stands at the heart of the development process and has been allocated SR 130,013.5 million in the Third Plan. The policies for human-resource development are discussed with regard to the areas of education and training and labour affairs.[32]

Education and Training

Realization of an imbalance in manpower needed for development and the labour supply available in Saudi society is not new to planners in the Kingdom. In the First Plan the indigenous work force could supply only 72 per cent of the needed labour supply. When in the Second Plan rapid development resulted in the percentage of indigenous Saudis in the labour force dropping to 57 per cent of the total working population, the problem achieved a sense of immediacy.[33] Education and training of Saudis, which had been progressing well in meeting the social needs of the Kingdom, was upgraded in the Third Plan to satisfy what was clearly a very critical economic need.

In order to meet this demand the strategic goals for the sector were determined to be: (1) to improve the quality of education and training; (2) to make the education and training system more responsive to the needs of the economy; (3) to increase the efficiency of the system by improved administration and management; and (4) to facilitate a balanced quantitative growth of the system.[34]

(1) Fundamental to the improvement in quality of education and training will be the creation of an Education Development Centre (EDC) within the Ministry of Education, empowered to consolidate functions now within the Ministry but emphasizing the development of new curricula based on identified needs. Other major actions will be the

establishment of Regional Institutes of Education, in recognition of the special needs in education and training in different regions of the Kingdom, and the development of a capacity for qualitative planning in light of the demands to be placed on the education and training sector in the future. Further measures to improve the quality of education and training in the Kingdom include upgrading of teaching faculty, a continued Saudization of the teaching force, improved facility designs and improved performance assessment.

Technical and vocational education will be upgraded as well. A critical skills inventory will be instituted to reveal those vital occupations which need improved training programmes. Improvement of both teaching staff and programmes along with the provision of training also will take place. Of particular importance is the attention to be given to the flow of potential trainees from the literacy programmes.

(2) In general, education of the populace has been steadily improving with about 20 per cent of the Saudi population participating in some form of organized education programmes in 1979 and increasing numbers of students enrolled in higher-education programmes. Nevertheless, the education and training system has not been satisfactorily responsive to the economic needs of the society. Higher education has frequently stressed the arts at the expense of the sciences; the still-limited scope of the literacy programme has caused a large pool of illiterates to be excluded from skill training; and on-the-job training has been embryonic except for the largest public-sector firms and for civil servants in the Institute for Public Administration.

The single most important step in the Third Plan to counteract this insufficient responsiveness is envisaged to be the formation of an Interministerial Committee on Manpower. It is anticipated that this powerful regulatory body would be supported by a well-staffed permanent secretariat and would improve the co-ordination and internal and external efficiency of manpower-development programmes in both the private and public sectors. Other key elements aimed at making the system more responsive to the economy include a master plan for higher education that would provide for a balanced distribution of students by discipline and an appropriate concentration in specializations critical to economic development. A prototype polytechnic institute to deal with high-priority technician-training needs will be created, and vocational training will be made more responsive to employers' requirements through the already-mentioned critical skills inventory.

(3) Improvement of the system's efficiency is in keeping with the Third

Plan's intention to streamline and reorganize departments that have grown too rapidly and haphazardly due to the heavy demands upon them over the years. Review of the management and organization of the various sectoral agencies is paramount in any reorganization and will take place in addition to training and upgrading of the administrative staffs. The introduction of computer-based information systems and other high-efficiency techniques will further improve the operation of the system.

(4) A balance of quantitative growth of the education and training system will be furthered by the construction of numerous educational institutions and administrative structures. Construction plans for 1980-5 call for 848 primary schools, 270 intermediate schools and 105 secondary schools as well as a post-secondary polytechnic institute with 1,100 places, 10 new vocational centres, two prevocational centres, three on-the-job training centres, and a vocational-instructor training centre in Riyadh. Enrolments are projected to increase concomitant with the construction programme (see Table 7.9). Administrative facilities to be built during the Third Plan include the Ministry of Education's Education Development Centre and Regional Institutes of Education in addition to a new office for the National Centre for Adult Literacy. Overall plan expenditures for the 1980-5 span for both general and higher education and training were put at SR 128,337 billion (98.7 per cent of the financial requirements for human-resource development).

Table 7.9: Projected School Enrolments, 1979/80-1984/5

Category	Enrolments 1979/80	1984/5	Increase (%)
Elementary[a]	527,769	696,335	31.9
Intermediate[a]	126,215	188,844	49.0
Secondary[a]	50,489	79,625	57.7
Teacher training	9,594	17,335	80.7
Adult education	75,500	137,650	81.8
Other[b]	8,624	17,275	100.3

Notes: a. Data include Islamic education. b. Includes special education and technical education.
Source: *Third Development Plan*, Chapter 5, p. 309.

Labour Affairs

Workers actually employed in the labour market are administered and served by two separate government branches. Civilian employment in the public sector is under the jurisdiction of the Civil Service Bureau; employees in the private sector fall under the auspices of the Deputy Ministry of Labour Affairs. Third Plan programmes for both of these agencies will focus on more efficient organization and management of operations through more complete and up-to-date information and statistics. The Civil Service Bureau will be attentive to more effective utilization and motivation of government employees, while an important task of the Deputy Ministry of Labour Affairs will be to work through the Interministerial Committee on Manpower to reduce the dependence on foreign manpower and to concentrate on Saudization in all economic activities. Financial requirements for labour affairs in the Third Plan have been put at SR 1.677 billion.[35]

Social Development

> The concept of social development has always been comprehensive in Saudi Arabian development planning, aimed at bringing about sustained improvement in the well-being of the individual, at bestowing the benefits of economic growth on all, and at stimulating the participation in and contribution of citizens to development.[36]

Thus, the importance attached by the Third Plan to social development as a device to correct the imbalances which almost inevitably result from rapid economic growth and unchecked market forces. The rationale in the opening statement also helps to justify the near-doubling of funds allocated to social development: SR 33,212.8 million (in 1974 prices) in the Second Plan to SR 70,045.8 million (in current 1980 prices) in the Third Plan. The policies for social development are discussed here primarily with regard to health services and social and youth services.

Health Services

Saudi Arabia, which has a long-standing policy of providing the finest possible health care free to all inhabitants, has experienced considerable improvement in the services available; however, there remains much to be done. During the Second Plan the ratio of all doctors to population increased from 3.8 per 10,000 in 1975 to 6.7 per 10,000 in 1980, significantly above the target of 5 per 10,000. The ratio of hospital beds per 1,000 of the population increased from 1.4 to 1.9 in the same period. Both of these indicators reveal substantial progress, yet are still well below the statistics for developed nations.

Whereas in the past there has been a concentration on curative medical services and on secondary care through hospitals, in the Third Plan the emphasis will shift to preventive measures such as vaccination programmes, environmental health and hygiene, health education, early screening, and mother and child care along with primary care.

In order to institute the changes planned for the health services, a National Health Council will be created in the first year of the Plan (1980). The Council will have the responsibility of determining overall health policies of the Kingdom, guiding the development and improvement of services, establishing the responsibilities of the 14 government agencies that offer health care, as well as the responsibilities of the private sector, and generally co-ordinating all health care activities. The construction of health facilities will continue unabated. Priority will be on completing construction that commenced during the Second Plan. This will provide an additional 1,150 hospital beds. The Third Plan projects provide for 36 new hospitals to be built with a total capacity of 7,550 beds. Of these beds, some 2,388 will come into service during the 1980-5 period and the remainder completed under the Fourth Plan. Existing hospitals will be expanded and upgraded to provide 2,000 additional beds. The result of this construction programme will be 5,538 new hospital beds by 1985 and 5,162 more available early in the period of the Fourth Plan. Other construction during the Third Plan includes 300 new primary health-care centres, 8 malaria-control stations, new medical-supply stores for each health region, and expansion or improvement of various centres and clinics throughout the Kingdom.[37]

In order to ensure efficient use of all the new facilities, administration will be upgraded, training of health manpower will be emphasized, record-keeping will be strengthened and computerized, and various research programmes related to health care will be implemented. Health care should be more widely available and of higher quality by the middle of the 1980s.

Social and Youth Services

The various services included in this section of the Third Plan are social affairs, social care, social security, social insurance and youth welfare.[38] These programmes' importance in the overall development of Saudi Arabia cannot be overstated, for they determine how well the increasing wealth of the Kingdom is shared by all segments of the population. The services not only improve the quality of life of the populace but also serve to encourage citizens to participate in the development process. Another function of the services is that those citizens who are disabled or deprived are provided with remedial care and assistance.

Social affairs functions through Community Development Centres in seeking to improve living conditions by smoothing the process of social change that so often occurs because of rapid economic growth. The centres serve as a base for a community-development social worker to assist groups of local citizens in mobilizing their own resources and skills to provide for their own needs rather than relying wholly on government programmes. The Third Plan provides for the expansion to 41 from the 24 centres in existence in 1980, 6 in urban areas and 18 in rural locations. An estimated 3,160 local projects will be organized through these centres during the Plan period, including youth activities, health services, literacy training, agricultural extension assistance, local co-operative encouragement, and small-scale productive enterprise support.

Social care provides for those persons in distress due to physical disabilities or negative social circumstances. During the 1980-5 span, construction will take place of orphanages and residential nurseries, reform schools and probation institutes, and rehabilitation centres for the handicapped. Emphasis will be on providing vocational training and employment assistance to those who are able to learn so that they can become contributing members of society. While no construction of facilities will take place for the care of the elderly, support will be given to programmes for the aged to remain in their own homes and with families. The role of privately operated benevolent societies will be more clearly defined within the context of social development, and these societies will receive government assistance because of the expanded role planned for them. Consequently, they are expected to increase in number from 24 to approximately 64 by 1985.

Saudi Arabia's non-contributory social security system, which provides income support for the disabled and deprived and for poverty relief of the temporarily disadvantaged, will continue its previous services via 67 offices located throughout the Kingdom but with some shifts in emphasis. New in the Third Plan is the proviso that persons living in areas which have limited economic growth potential will receive particular attention. Private benevolent societies will be encouraged to play a larger part in assisting the temporarily disadvantaged in urban areas, while the social security system is to concentrate on rural inhabitants. Sixteen new offices and 10 mobile teams will be added during 1980-5, with the intent of improving coverage in regions of the country which have been neglected to date.

A final category of social support is the social insurance programme which is a compulsory comprehensive occupational insurance plan for employees in the private sector and in government-owned corporations. Pension coverage will be expanded during the Third Plan to cover 1,249,000 workers by 1985 compared with 718,000 in 1980. Occupational-hazards coverage will be implemented in all public corporations and private firms employing 500 or more workers, with 400,000 employees to be covered by this scheme by 1985. Further study during the Third Plan will prepare for Fourth Plan pension and occupational-hazard coverage of workers in sectors not presently covered by social insurance.

In the development of Saudi Arabia's human resources, perhaps no function is more important than that providing for the welfare of the Kingdom's youth. Preparing youth for the increased responsibilities of a dynamic economy and a society facing some change, seeks to smooth the path of Saudi Arabian development. Several institutions are viewed as providing for the interests of youth: the family, the schools and the ulema (religious leadership) of each community. The government's role is intended as one of support to these various institutions. Activities available are varied and include sports, arts and culture, public service and social affairs.

The Third Plan will feature an expansion and improvement of general youth clubs and societies to increase involvement in the various activities available throughout the Kingdom. Girls' clubs will be established as will special interest groups for such pursuits as literature, engineering, mechanics, science and outdoor survival. Studies will be undertaken to determine the future needs of the Kingdom's youth, and a strategy will be determined as to how best to meet these needs.

Physical Infrastructure

The development of physical infrastructure, which received top priority in the Second Plan, will be given less emphasis in the Third. As seen in Table 7.10, SR 247,344.3 million budgeted for physical infrastructure development in the Third Plan is roughly 35 per cent of total funds allocated for development in the Plan; approximately one-half of all development funds during the Second Plan were budgeted to the sector.[39] The sizable sum which is available to infrastructure development should assist in the continued diversification of the economy and support the industrialization that is planned for the 1980-5 period. The specific areas receiving attention in this are transportation, post and telecommunications, and municipal and residential development.

Table 7.10: Physical Infrastructure Expenditures (current prices – SR millions)

Sector components	Recurrent	Project	Total
Transportation and communications	27,725.8	115,292.3	143,018.1
Municipal and residential development	18,836.9	85,489.3	104,326.2
Total	46,562.7	200,781.6	247,344.3

Source: *Third Development Plan*, Chapter 7, p. 453.

Transportation

Roads are a vital component of the transportation infrastructure of Saudi Arabia, as more than 67 per cent of domestic intercity passenger trips are by highway, and even greater is the percentage of freight traffic that goes by road. At the end of the Second Plan the road system consisted of 11,394 km of main roads, 10,053 km of secondary roads, and 23,180 km of rural roads. During the Third Plan the main and secondary roads combined will be augmented by 32 per cent and the unpaved, rural roads by 75 per cent. More than simply the additions to the length, the road network will be improved by a shift of emphasis toward preventive maintenance, safety and traffic-flow improvements.

Saudi Arabia's port system, offering high freight capacity at low per unit cost, is the Kingdom's heavy trade link with the rest of the world. The importance of the port system to the economic development of the country was felt very acutely during the early and middle 1970s when bottlenecks in supply were caused by insufficient port capacity. Rapid expansion of capacity late in the 1970s alleviated the problems; the construction of an additional 15 berths is scheduled during the Third Plan. This additional construction will bring the total number of berths to 145 and should serve to accommodate the 50 per cent increase in imports anticipated by 1985. Particular attention in the Plan will also go to improving efficiency and safety in the ports following the rapid expansion of recent years.

Air transport is highly developed in the Kingdom compared to other modes of transportation, and serves as the primary means of travel for long-distance voyagers. Growth was early for this sector as a result of the restrained pace at which new roads were built. Construction and upgrading of facilities, highlighted by the new Riyadh International Airport that will be fully operational by 1985, will continue in the Third Plan. Receiving special attention in the air transport sector during the next five years will be the Kingdom's air traffic control and ancillary support facilities, including fire and rescue equipment and maintenance programmes.

The railroad network in Saudi Arabia is limited, consisting of only a 562 km line between the port of Dammam and Riyadh, and branches from the main line. Most traffic consists of imports bound from the port to the rapidly growing capital city, although by the end of the Second Plan there were two passenger trains on the route. Upgrading of track and the purchase of new equipment during the Second Plan will be continued in the Third with 345 km of track to be replaced, 150 km of a second track to be laid, and substantial new rolling stock acquired. In addition, 320 km of track are scheduled to be constructed between Riyadh and Hafuf, thus reducing the distance of the existing line by 100 km.

Posts and Telecommunications

With the emphasis on development of the regions through the growth of the productive sectors, adequate communication becomes more vital. The strategy of the Ministry of Posts, Telephone, and Telegraph has been to attempt to anticipate growth so that communications are available when required. In adhering to this policy, considerable progress was made in providing the Kingdom with basic postal and telecommunications services in the Second Plan. Major emphasis in the Third Plan will be upon augmenting these services to meet the demands of a developing country, with particular attention to be given to manpower development programmes so that productivity can be increased through greater mechanization.

Municipal and Residential Development

The migration to the cities and towns has put considerable strain on the infrastructure such as roads, water supply, sewage treatment, public buildings, and housing of the various municipalities. Tremendous progress has already been made in providing infrastructure, but the Kingdom's requirements are large and the process should be considered long term and ongoing. As an indication of the importance attached to this sector, more than 40 per cent of the total budget for infrastructure development in the Third Plan is allocated to municipal and residential development. This large expenditure reflects one of the major objectives, which is to extend the increasing wealth of the Kingdom to the various regions.

Through the Ministry of Municipal and Rural Affairs (MOMRA), whose responsibility it is to plan, design, construct, operate and maintain most of the urban public utilities, it is anticipated that nearly all the municipalities and villages will have water and sewer systems as well as many paved roads by 1985. The majority of the projects planned – more than 1,160 – will be administered by the 117 municipalities and towns, while approximately another 700 projects will be undertaken at the village level.

Housing remains a critical area in need of attention in Saudi Arabia. Despite the construction of over 200,000 new dwellings during the Second Plan, almost half the total population continues to live in substandard housing. Table 7.11 indicates the housing construction anticipated during the Third Plan for both the public and private sectors. Approximately 267,153 dwellings are scheduled for construction, an increase over the preceding plan. In addition, 14,800 serviced plots for lower-income families are to be provided. Emphasis in the public sector will shift to making residential accommodation available to lower-income families. The private sector will be dependent upon the Real Estate Development Fund which will finance more than 50 per cent of private-sector houses in the Third Plan. Control of construction location will be exercised as loans will be made only for residences in those places approved as national, regional or district centres and on sites which either have or will have public utilities.

Table 7.11: Housing Construction, 1980-5

	Dwellings	Serviced plots
Public sector		
Ongoing villas and apartments	12,601	
Riyadh rush housing apartments	1,152	
Special villa project	2,100	
New housing programme	10,000	
Special housing project	7,000	
Government agencies' employees housing	53,300	
Serviced plots scheme		14,800
Subtotal	86,153	14,800
Private sector		
REDF personal loans[a]	98,000	
REDF investment loans[a]	5,000	
Other investment	5,000	
Non-REDF construction[a]	73,000	
Subtotal	181,000	
Total	267,153	14,800

Note: a. Real Estate Development Fund (REDF).
Source: *Third Development Plan*, Chapter 7, p. 451.

Plan Implementation

A relevant inquiry about the Third Development Plan concerns whether it can be implemented as proposed. The Plan is an ambitious undertaking, not so much due to projected high growth rates; in fact the growth objectives are quite modest and attainable, particularly viewed in terms of the rates of increase of GDP for the various sectors in recent years. Rather, the Plan's goals that may prove difficult to attain involve certain structural changes that are to take place in the economy in light of the constraining manpower policy that has been adopted.

Many potential limitations to implementation have been controlled to the point they can be eliminated from consideration. Adequate revenue to fund the development plan should be available despite the slackening in worldwide oil demand as the 1980s open. Using the May 1980 oil prices, it has been noted that Saudi Arabia could reduce production from the 1979 level of 9.5 million b/d to slightly under 5.3 million b/d in the Third Plan and still earn enough revenue to finance development.[40] Such a reduction in oil output is not likely because of government policy to maintain stability in world oil markets; it is likely that the Kingdom will decrease production slightly and raise the price per barrel to the OPEC level which would still leave more than enough revenue for implementation of the Third Plan as drafted. The 9.5 million b/d production, it will be recalled, is considered a temporary situation above the 8.5 million b/d ceiling due to supply cutbacks in 1979 and 1980 from Iran and Iraq.

Inflation was a threat to the implementation of the Second Plan early in that period, but was brought under control by various measures. Although the possibility exists that inflation could once again rage and threaten implementation of the Third Plan, this event is unlikely. Supply capability has been greatly improved in the Kingdom; contracts are being written with consideration to their inflationary impact, and government expenditure fiscal policy is geared to keeping inflation under control and in the vicinity of 10 per cent annually.

Absorptive capacity which was such an obstacle to the development of Saudi Arabia in the later years of the First Plan seems to be adequate for the implementation of the Third. The accelerated rise in absorptive capacity during the Second Plan (1975-80) not only allowed for actual expenditures to meet the appropriated amounts, but in fact exceeded the original appropriations because of supplementary allocations during the fiscal years.[41] The Third Plan's budget, like its immediate predecessor, is considerably higher than the prior plan; nevertheless, the absorptive capacity of the economy is improved enough that it should not be a constraint to the implementation of the Plan.

Physical infrastructure development continues in the Kingdom as indicated by the 35.5 per cent of total development funds allocated to that function in the Third Plan. Planners are satisfied with the progress that has been made in the development of physical infrastructure during the first two development plans so that emphasis in this area has been decreased in the Third Plan from the 50 per cent of total development funds that were allocated during the Second.

Physical infrastructure construction in the 1980-5 period will concentrate on that development necessary to facilitate the continuing industrialization of the Kingdom, such as transportation systems and telecommunications and postal services. Also stressed will be that infrastructure which distributes the benefit of increased national wealth to the general population, such as municipal and rural area development and housing. The basic physical infrastructure of the Kingdom, however, is well enough developed as a result of emphasis in the First and Second Plans that no significant deficiencies should impede the implementation of the Third.

Having considered several of the potential constraints and pointed out their relatively low potential for obstruction of implementation of the Third Plan, it is appropriate to mention two measures that have been adopted by Saudi planners to enhance the promise of successful implementation. One deals with the follow-up procedures that are to be employed; the other concerns the flexibility that is built into this particular plan.

In 1976 the Council of Ministers' Resolution No. 1368 was passed. This resolution provided for an improvement of follow-up activities to the planning process with the objective of making annual budgeting – the most effective means in controlling plan implementation – more effective. In order to accomplish the improved follow-up procedures, the planning, budgeting and follow-up departments in all Ministries and government agencies have been integrated. It is hoped this step will go a long way to making annual budgeting more responsive to the objectives of the Plan.

The second measure which will help to ensure successful implementation, is the flexibility that is woven into the Third Plan. By the end of the second year of the Plan period, an assessment of government expenditure programmes and manpower policies for the remainder of the 1980-5 span will be effected by the Ministry of Planning. Strategy may be changed from that of the first two years based on the results of this review. This step towards 'roll-over' planning is deemed desirable as it enables a rapidly growing economy such as that of Saudi Arabia to adjust to changed conditions.

It is within the manpower sector that the greatest potential for difficulties in implementation exists. Shortfalls in achieving manpower goals in previous plans generally lead to this conclusion. For the Third Plan, expenditures will continue to increase dramatically – up more than 55 per cent over the Second Plan. Employment, on the other hand, is to increase by the average annual rate of only 1.2 per cent during the Third Plan, leaving a tremendous gap to be filled by increased productivity.

The strategy of 'Saudization' and reducing the growth of expatriate workers from 7 per cent a year to 1.2 per cent, leaves room for some doubt as well. The attention that is to be given to the operation, maintenance, and repair of buildings and equipment in the Third Plan is precisely the type of work which to date has required expatriate know-how. Trimming the foreign work force in the area of manual and semi-skilled labour will be difficult as well.

While 'Saudization' has worked for some of the best-established foreign institutions in the Kingdom – the foreign banks – given the objectives to be attained in the Third Plan, the policy may turn out to try to achieve too much too quickly. As Saudi Planning Minister Hisham Nazer has acknowledged, Saudization may actually require a generation – 20 to 30 years.

Notes

1. Kingdom of Saudi Arabia, Ministry of Planning, *Third Development Plan, 1400-1405/1980-1985*, Tables 2-7 and 2-8, Chapter 2, pp. 37, 38. (Hereafter this source will be cited as the *Third Development Plan*.)
2. *Third Development Plan*, Chapter 1, section 1.4.2, p. 16.
3. Ibid., Chapter 3, section 3.1.1.2-3.1.1.3, pp. 75-8.
4. Ibid., Chapter 3, section 3.1.1.3, pp. 77-8.
5. Ibid., Chapter 3, section 3.1.2, p. 79.
6. Ibid., section 3.1.2.1, pp. 78-80.
7. Ibid., Chapter 3, section 3.7.1, pp. 107-10.
8. Ibid., section 3.1.2.3, pp. 80-1.
9. Ibid., Chapter 3, section 3.1.2.4, p. 81.
10. Ibid., 3.1.2.5, p. 81.
11. Ibid., Chapter 3, section 3.1.3.1, pp. 82-3; the reorganization study is detailed in Chapter 9.
12. Ibid., greater detail on education and training is given on human-resource development in Chapter 5.

13. Ibid.
14. Ibid., Chapter 3, section 3.1.3.3, pp. 84-5.
15. Ibid., Chapter 3, section 3.2.2, p. 88.
16. *Middle East Economic Digest*, July 1980, p. 16.
17. *Third Development Plan*, Chapter 3, section 3.2.3.2, p. 90.
18. Ibid., Chapter 1, section 1.4.4.2, pp. 18-19.
19. Ibid., Chapter 3, sections 3.4.1, pp. 97-9, and 3.4.2, pp. 99-102.
20. Ibid., Chapter 3, section 3.4.3, pp. 102-4.
21. Ibid., Chapter 3, section 3.5, pp. 104-6. Further discussion of inflation control measures is given in Chapter 9 of *Third Development Plan*.
22. *Middle East Economic Digest*, July 1980, p. 6.
23. The national water plan and balance were discussed in Chapter 3.
24. *Third Development Plan*, Chapter 4, section 4.2.2.6, pp. 117-18.
25. *Middle East Economic Digest*, August 1980, p. 59.
26. *Third Development Plan*, Chapter 4, section 4.3.3, pp. 149-50.
27. Ibid., Chapter 4, section 4.6, pp. 216-19. Details on the industrial base of Saudi Arabia and the major industrial complexes at Jubail and Yanbu were offered in Chapter 4 of this volume.
28. Ibid., section 4.4.8, pp. 198-203.
29. Ibid., section 4.4, pp. 158-9.
30. Ibid., Chapter 4, section 4.5.4, pp. 214-16.
31. Ibid., section 4.7.4, pp. 258-61, which includes estimates for imports of construction materials and domestic production of such materials as well as labour projections for this activity.
32. Ibid., Chapter 1, sections 1.4.1.2-1.4.2, pp. 15-16; Chapter 5, section 5.6.1, p. 340.
33. Ibid., Chapter 2, section 2.2.2.6, pp. 34-6.
34. Ibid., Chapter 5, sections 5.2.1.1-5.2.1.4, pp. 289-92.
35. Ibid., sections 5.6.1, p. 340; 5.3.1-5.3.3, pp. 330-1.
36. Ibid., Chapter 6, section 6.1, p. 343.
37. Ibid., sections 6.2.3-6.2.3.9, pp. 350-1.
38. Ibid., Chapter 6, sections 6.3.1-6.3.5, pp. 352-7; 6.3.4, pp. 360-1; 6.3.5.3, pp. 362-5; 6.3.6.3, pp. 366-8; 6.3.7.3, pp. 370-1; 6.3.8.3, pp. 372-3; 6.3.9.3, pp. 374-8.
39. Ibid., Chapter 7, section 7.5, p. 453. Chapter 7 of the Plan covers physical infrastructure development.
40. *Middle East Economic Digest*, July 1980, p. 16.
41. Saudi Arabian Monetary Agency, *Annual Report, 1979*, pp. 11-12.

8 PUBLIC FINANCE AND BUDGETARY POLICY

Introduction

In Western economic literature, the need for government involvement in economic activities is often rationalized by reference to some generally recognized imperfections of the market mechanism. Thus, income inequality, the existence of public goods and externalities connected with both production and consumption, and other forms of market failure, are said to make the market inadequate for allocating economic resources and distributing economic benefits. The question about the role of the government has, therefore, shifted from whether the government must involve itself in economic activities at all, to how much should such an involvement be – how much government participation *vis-à-vis* the private sector.

Whereas the answer to the second question will differ from country to country depending on the historical, socio-cultural, political and economic factors which shape the aspirations of the people in each country, it is not an overstatement to say that discussions of the role of the government in non-developmental economic literature of market-oriented economies have not given sufficient attention to (and may even be said to have neglected) the role of the government in initiating, promoting and sustaining social and economic development, although the role of the government in stabilization is often recognized.

With respect to developing countries, it is generally recognized that, not only is the market system inadequate for most of the problems of development, and therefore the governments of developing countries have a duty to ensure that the effectiveness of the market mechanism is raised, its reliability is increased and its relevance to developing countries' problems is enhanced, but it is also realized that governments have the task of playing a positive role in the developing process in order to ensure a continuous, sustainable and decent standard of living for the average member of the communities which they govern.[1]

The government has several options open to it in the performance of the numerous tasks which are often ascribed to it by the structural features of the economy and by the hopes and aspirations of the people of the country. It has become fashionable in these countries for development plans (or some form of development programmes) to be advocated and undertaken. These plans are often regarded as the most effective means through which economic development could be achieved in the shortest possible time given the constraints (both physical, mental, financial and human) which invariably come to bear on such development efforts. But even where an implementable comprehensive plan is introduced, other policies – fiscal, monetary, direct controls and regulations – are indispensable complements to the plan. It is these policies which tend to ensure implementation of the programmes envisaged in the plan, and in addition not only sustain the 'rules of the game' at their optimal level, but also provide the desired incentives (or disincentives) to the private sector to respond positively to the general objectives of the plan.

Governments in developing countries may, therefore, find themselves performing important roles in areas which form crucial elements in the development process – elements such as promoting and increasing national self-reliance and awareness for development, manpower development within an overall framework of manpower planning, rural development aimed at increasing the standard of living of the rural population who are in majority, redistributing incomes, undertaking the slow process of structural transformation from both social and economic points of view, diversification of the economy and external economic ties, regulation and control, direct public-sector participation in production and distribution and provision of services, national mobilization of both human and natural resources for development, and protection of the resources of the country from unwarranted foreign exploitation.[2]

In Saudi Arabia the government has an even greater role to play, in view of the tradition-oriented nature of the country, the climatic conditions, and, above all, the role of Saudi Arabia in the world today, due incidentally to oil. This world position has been strengthened and elevated by the government of Saudi Arabia in its attempt to ensure that the people derive equitable benefits from the country's most important resource – oil – which is depletable.

Above all, governments in developing countries are mostly seen in the role of mobilizing both domestic and external savings and translating them into productive investment, either directly, or indirectly through the execution of appropriate policies. Although in Saudi Arabia this is not currently a priority role so far as mobilization of savings is concerned, the second part of the role is very relevant to the Saudi case. It is, therefore, crucial that the problems of mobilizing financial resources are recognized. Such an analysis will also serve to show how different surplus-funds countries are: a recognition of their special position will fortify them in their efforts to utilize their funds from oil as efficiently as possible. Therefore, although this chapter seeks primarily to analyse Saudi Arabia's government finance – sources and appropriations, their trends and structural changes and their implications for development – the next section will concentrate on problems of mobilizing financial resources in general terms within a developing framework.

Mobilization of Financial Resources

The process of capital formation, whether financed from internal or external sources, requires on the one hand generation of a growing surplus above current consumption for investment purposes, and on the other hand, it requires the actual mobilization, direction and allocation of the surplus generated into productive investment.

Historically, voluntary savings and reinvestment of entrepreneurs' surpluses have been major sources of capital formation in advanced economies. But in developing countries the process is more complicated. With regard to private savings, in general it has been recognized that the process at least, takes three essential steps:

(1) an increase in the volume of real savings, so that resources can be released for investment purposes;
(2) the channelling to savings through an efficient and effective finance and credit mechanism so that investible funds can be claimed by investors; and
(3) the act of investment itself by which resources are used for capital stock.[3]

The first step – an increase in the volume of real savings – is considered to be of fundamental importance, especially in capital-deficit economies, if a higher rate of investment is to be achieved without generating inflation. But an increase in voluntary savings would mean a cut in current consumption in the absence of growth in current income. Even with the growth of real income, more savings involves a sacrifice of consumption, which has to be weighed against the expected future increase in income and consumption to be brought about by the new investments.

Thus, more savings depend, to a large extent, on peoples' attitudes and expectations for the future (that is, their time preference) and the present level of income and consumption. It can be expected, however, that when real income rises, the marginal rate of saving will also rise, given that appropriate incentives and opportunities are forthcoming.

Sufficient data are, unfortunately, not available to indicate the level and pattern of private savings in the Kingdom of Saudi Arabia. However, there are indications that private savings have been increasing in recent years – e.g. rapid increase in incomes, increasing time and demand deposits with the commercial banks, purchases of new inputs and machinery, establishment of industries, construction of social and capital overheads, etc. Moreover, large investments by the government on infrastructure, construction, industry, agriculture and other financial institutions might have provided further incentives and attracted more private savings and investment.

Given the nature and availability of financial resources, the next crucial step is to direct, allocate and execute investment programmes so as to achieve the maximum net national benefits from the investment resources available.

In the case of Saudi Arabia, given the availability of funds and with the oil income increasing over time, the policy decision to be made by the Government of Saudi Arabia is to determine the optimal allocation of oil (and other) revenues among three broad uses:

(1) immediate consumption by the private and public sectors;
(2) capital formation, particularly within the non-oil sectors in the domestic economy; and
(3) net increase in foreign assets and in foreign aid, in the light of domestic constraints posed by co-operating factors such as skilled manpower.

The problem, thus, involves not only the issue of availability versus efficiency in utilization of resources, but also the issues relevant to immediate as well as long-run policies concerned with major goals (both economic and non-economic) of the country.

Some of the indicators will be discussed below and the data available will be presented whenever appropriate. It should be mentioned here that gross capital formation (GCF) in the Saudi economy expanded from SR 17.84 billion in 1974/5 to SR 78.01 billion (at current prices) in 1978/9. This increase of 44.6 per cent per annum was largely a result of heavy government expenditure made possible by the substantially increased oil revenues. The government's share in GCF spending over the period rose from 41 per cent to 62 per cent, with much of the expenditure going to gas-gathering programmes and to domestic refinery expansion. Despite these oil-sector expenditures, however, total fixed capital formation of the sector dropped from 21 per cent of the total in 1974/5 to 12 per cent in 1978/9. As the Second Development Plan drew to a close, greater emphasis was being placed on investment in productive activities.

In earlier years there had been continuous growth of capital formation relative to national income. However, it would appear that Saudi Arabia, until very recent times, has not been accumulating capital fast enough. For example, investment-GDP ratio fell from 16.13 per cent in 1970 to 12.87 per cent in 1975, once again emphasizing inadequate absorption of oil wealth.[4] Consequently, whatever the level of private savings, it is important to mobilize them and channel them into productive investment through rational investment policies within a framework of an efficient financial system.

Sources of Government Revenue

The pressing need for large government outlays for social and economic development in a majority of developing countries arise from:

(1) the need to increase the standard of living of the peoples of these countries, which requires adequate flow of investible resources;
(2) insufficient private voluntary saving to generate the needed capital formation;
(3) the desire to shift economic resources from foreign firms to endogenous entrepreneurs.

In order to perform these increased functions the government may find it necessary to resort to forced savings through taxation, compulsory lending, control and tax of foreign trade, or undertake deficit financing. The need for large government outlays and the financial position of the government strongly influence the overall approach to the level and methods of taxation in a developing country.

The taxation potential, or in general, the government's financial-resource potential, will differ from country to country and over time, depending on various socio-economic and political factors. In a very broad classification, however, the following can be listed to affect this potentiality: (1) real *per capita* income per head, at each given time period and over time, including the growth rate of *per capita* income, over time; (2) the distribution of current and future incomes;

Table 8.1: Government Budget: Estimated Revenues, 1960/1-1979/80 (SR millions)

	1960/1	1961/2	1962/3	1963/4	1964/5	1965/6	1966/7	1967/8	1968/9	1969/70	1970/1
Oil royalties	540.3	564.3	674.5	721.4	813.4	954.4	1,160.7	1,126.6	1,177.0	1,738.5	1,573.0
Income tax from oil companies	835.6	1,084.5	1,243.3	1,528.0	1,756.6	2,186.5	2,783.4	2,388.8	3,018.8	3,459.3	3,863.5
Tax on oil products	–	–	–	12.0	15.0	16.0	20.0	21.0	23.5	27.0	89.0
Subtotal	1,375.9	1,648.8	1,917.8	2,261.4	2,585.0	3,156.9	3,964.1	3,536.4	4,219.3	5,224.8	5,525.5
Income tax from companies and individuals	34.5	33.0	33.0	35.0	36.5	38.0	42.7	44.0	46.7	62.6	99.5
Tapline fees	–	–	–	18.5	1.8	3.3	–	–	2.5	–	3.5
Customs duties	146.4	140.7	128.0	128.0	135.0	165.0	175.0	192.0	242.5	242.5	292.0
Subtotal	180.9	173.7	161.0	181.5	173.3	206.3	217.7	236.0	291.7	305.1	395.0
Railways and ports	32.9	36.2	24.4	16.0	14.0	14.0	–	–	–	–	–
Car plates	2.6	3.6	3.4	3.4	5.0	6.0	10.0	10.0	10.0	12.5	16.0
Road tax	17.0	30.0	30.0	23.0	23.0	24.0	29.0	31.0	35.4	41.3	41.5
Subtotal	52.5	69.8	57.8	42.4	42.0	44.0	39.0	41.0	45.4	53.8	57.5
Gov't services fees and sales of properties	83.6	103.5	117.7	68.2	77.0	87.6	102.8	110.3	115.6	157.6	232.0
Miscellaneous income	15.5	11.2	11.7	72.5	84.7	118.8	126.5	141.7	228.0	224.7	166.0
Total revenue	1,708.4	1,907.0	2,266.0	2,626.0	2,962.0	3,613.6	4,450.0	4,065.4	4,899.5	5,966.0	6,380.0
Drawn from Reserve and Development Fund	77.6	159.0	186.2	60.0	150.0	347.4	575.0	871.6	635.5	–	–
Grand total	1,786.0	2,166.0	2,452.2	2,686.0	3,112.0	3,961.0	5,025.0	4,937.0	5,535.0	5,966.0	6,380.0

Table 8.1: (continued)

	1971/2	1972/3	1973/4	1974/5	1975/6	1976/7	1977/8	1978/9	1979/80
Oil royalties	2,226.7	2,528.9	5,336.0	37,561.0	21,458.0	23,002.0	31,817.0	27,042.0	37,403.0
Income tax from oil companies	7,628.2	9,568.8	15,930.0[a]	56,871.0[a]	65,702.0[a]	76,954.0[a]	99,337.0[a]	89,492.0[a]	119,003.0[a]
Tax on oil products	49.0	52.0	–	–	–	–	–	–	–
Subtotal	9,903.9	12,149.7	21,266.0	94,432.0	87,160.0	99,856.0	131,154.0	116,534.0	156,406.0
Income tax from companies and individuals	100.5	105.0	–	–	–	–	–	–	–
Tapline fees	4.5	8.3	–	–	–	–	–	–	–
Customs duties	313.5	315.0	330.0	400.0	375.0	500.0	1,000.0	1,400.0	1,512.0
Subtotal	418.5	428.3	330.0	400.0	375.0	500.0	1,000.0	1,400.0	1,512.0
Railways and ports	–	–	–	–	–	–	–	–	–
Car plates	16.0	16.0	–	–	–	–	–	–	–
Road tax	41.5	41.5	–	–	–	–	–	–	–
Subtotal	57.5	57.5	–	–	–	–	–	–	–
Gov't services fees and sales of properties	177.1	254.7	–	–	–	–	–	–	–
Miscellaneous income	225.0	310.8	1,214.0	3,415.0	8,312.0	10,579.0	14,339.0	12,066.0	2,082.0
Total revenue	10,782.0	13,200.0	22,810.0	98,247.0	95,847.0	110,935.0	146,493.0	130,000.0	160,000.0
Drawn from Reserve and Development Fund	–	–	–	–	15,088.0	–	–	–	–
Grand total	10,782.0	13,200.0	22,810.0	98,247.0	110,935.0	110,935.0	146,493.0	130,000.0	160,000.0

Note: a. Income tax from oil companies for 1973/4-1979/80 includes other income taxes. Taxes on oil products for the same period are included in Miscellaneous income, and so are transport taxes, fees for government services, and proceeds from government sale of goods.
Sources: Compiled from SAMA, *Annual Reports*, various issues; Ministry of Finance, *Statistical Yearbooks*, various issues.

(3) the composition of economic activities in the national product; (4) the social and institutional framework within which current and future incomes are earned, and (5) the socio cultural and economic maturity of the country.

In Saudi Arabia government revenues have increased very rapidly during the last 15 years – e.g. they rose from SR 1,638 million in 1960 to SR 5,966 million in 1970 and to SR 13,200 million in 1973, reaching SR 110,935 million in 1977. Revenues were estimated to be SR 160,000 million in 1980. The rapid growth in government revenue as well as in the absolute level of national income is dominated by a single source – oil.[5]

The relative share of various sources of government revenue other than oil remains not only relatively insignificant but in general has been declining. Non-oil incomes contributed about 23 per cent of estimated total government revenue in 1961, fell to 8 per cent of revenue in 1973 before recovering during the Second Development Plan to 10.4 per cent (1979). The government policy of diversification that has been in effect during both the Second and Third Plans should continue to increase the share of non-oil sector revenue in the future within Saudi Arabia.

In the past, however, non-oil income has had a relatively slow growth as compared to oil income because of: (1) rapid growth in oil income and overdependence on it as a source of government revenue; (2) the government's liberal foreign-trade policy; (3) encouragement of domestic private investment by giving tax exemptions or levying very low tax rates; (4) government subsidies, especially for consumer goods not produced domestically; (5) the refusal of the government to tax the incomes of Saudis and nationals from neighbouring Arab countries; and (6) weaknesses in the government's administrative machinery with regard to tax gathering and tax legislations.

In summary, the discussions in the above sections indicate that government revenue (from all sources) grew very rapidly during the decade 1960-70, increasing from $364 million in 1959/60 to $3,538.87 million in 1972/3. Revenue has grown even faster in the 1970s. The level as well as the growth of the total revenue is dominated by the rapid growth of government income from oil revenues. Although in general, non-oil sources have shown a rising trend, they have experienced growth that lagged far behind growth in oil revenue; consequently, their relative share in total revenue has declined from about 22 per cent in the early 1960s to 10.4 per cent in 1978/9. It should be mentioned here that actual revenues from oil, as will be seen later, exceeded in many years the amount projected in the annual budgets.

We will return to the implications of the discrepancies between estimated and actual revenue figures (and also expenditure figures) in our discussion of overall budgetary policy of the Kingdom of Saudi Arabia.[6]

Tax Policy[7]

Before we focus our attention on that source of government revenue which has made up about 90 per cent of the total revenues estimated in recent financial years, we will make some remarks about the tax policies in the Kingdom.

Currently, only foreign companies, foreign interests in joint Saudi-foreign companies, and certain foreign individuals meeting specific criteria, pay income tax in Saudi Arabia. An exception is the 2.5 per cent tax on current net assets (including annual profit) – or zakat – paid by Saudi companies and Saudi interests in joint Saudi-foreign ventures. The profit-tax paid by non-Saudi interests in companies is relatively low, ranging from 25 per cent on net profits of SR 100,000 or less to 45 per cent on net profits which are above SR 1 million.

Also, whereas foreign workers pay tax ranging from 5 to 30 per cent on wages and salaries of SR 16,000 and above, Saudi workers pay no income tax. Perhaps in order to improve relations with neighbouring Arab States in the Gulf area (and maybe for the sake of regional co-operation), Kuwaiti, Bahrain and Qatari interests in companies and nationals are given the same treatment as Saudis.

The tax system in Saudi Arabia could be described as nationalistic (or regionalistic, considering the preferential treatment given to the nationals and business interests of neighbouring states). However, as will be stressed later, the tax policy is also 'soft' on foreign nationals and interests when compared with profits tax and other forms of income tax in the United States and in other industrialized countries. There is, of course, nothing wrong with a tax system which seeks to encourage indigenous businesses, especially in a country like Saudi Arabia. Indeed, it is customary at the beginning of industrialization in developing countries for the policies of the government to be geared towards transferring business know-how to indigenous entrepreneurs, or at least to give them the necessary encouragement or incentives. In other words, there is the need to encourage the emergence of a Schumpeterian entrepreneurial class in Saudi Arabia. Also, to the extent that Saudi Arabia is in dire need of skilled indigenous manpower, both from the long-term and short-term perspective, there may be no need to complain about the tax holiday enjoyed by Saudi workers. The tax structure in Saudi Arabia, which also permits the majority of both imported and domestically produced goods to be free of tax, has an important shortcoming which we will discuss later. Before then, it is important to examine why the government of Saudi Arabia has been able to institute such a liberal tax system.

The obvious reason for such a tax system is that the government can do without revenues originating from sources other than oil, because of the large increases in oil revenues which have taken place in Saudi Arabia in recent years. Consequently, with the increased oil revenues came the abolition of some custom duties, sales tax, etc. There is no sales tax in the Kingdom at present. Also, apart from the low income taxes paid by foreign concerns and nationals, incentives exist for foreign investors under the foreign investment code, which allows certain approved projects to have a five-year tax holiday. Such a liberal tax system was made possible because of increased oil revenues which have made other sources of revenue insignificant and easy to eliminate.

However, although the growing revenue from oil sources might have been the immediate cause of these liberalization exercises, the principal motives probably belong elsewhere. For example, the policy on indirect taxes and taxes on the salaries and wages of Saudi nationals was no doubt conditioned by the desire of the government to assure an improved standard of living for the people of Saudi Arabia, by making goods and services available at reasonable prices while maintaining take-home pay. Thus, in the Second Development Plan, 1975-80, it has been the goal of the government to subsidize food and other necessary items – thus reinforcing the tax policy with respect to consumer goods and wages and salaries in the Kingdom.[8]

The shortcoming hinted at above is in connection with the effects which the absence of tax-experience may have on future development efforts. It will not be an easy task convincing members of one, or two, generations which have known little or no tax burdens, to pay income and other indirect taxes when the need arises. Also the tax system tends to underestimate both the costs of production (and consequently development) and cost of living in the country. Thus like oil, pegging the costs of resource utilization in the Kingdom at an artificially low level through subsidies and no-tax policies tends to generate distortions which invariably encourage overutilization of the country's resources. When this happens, the present and immediate future generations are likely to short-change more-distant future generations, although it is the latter who will be called upon to pay taxes unless the resources of the Kingdom are used efficiently in the near future.

Resource Allocation and Budgetary Policy

So far, we have been concerned with the quantitative aspects and availability of financial resources in Saudi Arabia. One must also consider the decisions on how to allocate the available resources among various uses as efficiently as possible. A general discussion of availability versus allocative efficiency will serve as a prelude to detailed discussion of budget appropriations in Saudi Arabia.

In developing countries the problem of allocating investment resources involves, in general, several choices among alternatives: among the various sectors in the economy; among various projects within a sector; and among techniques which might be applied to a given project.

Various hypotheses have been developed and suggestions have been made regarding these choices. But in a developing country the choice is very complex, partly because of inadequate working of the market system and partly because of the structure of developing economies. For example, as previously acknowledged, developing countries share with advanced market-oriented economies problems posed by imperfections in the market mechanism, externalities and other rigidities which tend to distort prices. Consequently, prices cease to provide sufficient signals for actions by economic agents. But peculiar to developing countries is the fact that factors which influence investment decisions and policies are uncertain. And this makes a choice for an appropriate investment criterion very difficult.[9] Also, the existence of multiple objectives which face policy-makers in developing countries, especially at the beginning of the development process, creates problems for choice. This is especially so when, because of the conflicting socio-economic and political factors generating the objectives, the set of objectives themselves acquire the character of internal inconsistencies.

In Saudi Arabia, the problem of allocation, as it confronts public finance, lies within four categories:

(1) The financing of social overhead investment which must be undertaken by the government, regardless of political or ideological factors.
(2) The second deals with public investment in industries and other establishments which private investment is either unable to undertake because of size, or because investment by the private sector in these

activities is not economically rewarding without substantial subsidies by the government.
(3) The third deals with an intermediate zone, in which the actual investment projects are in private hands but the funds are made available through government finance.
(4) These are reinforced by a fourth, which deals with necessary incentives to, and protection or promotion of, private investment both domestic and foreign, as they are influenced by taxation and other fiscal and monetary measures.

In all four categories, the efforts of the government are directed towards mobilization of resources for investment so as to serve the purposes of economic diversification and structural change, all within a balanced development programme. These intentions were, until recently however, not formulated on a comprehensive or systematic basis, but were somewhat evident from various official documents.

Given the intention of the Government of Saudi Arabia, and given the fact that oil, the major source of revenue, is a non-replaceable resource, even with immense reserves and exhaustion not imminent, rational resource allocation and utilization is required through sound planning and a clearly defined and elaborated strategy for overall and sectoral growth, with the ultimate objective of a self-sustained and self-generating economy. Most of the oil-producing and oil-exporting countries of the Middle East have adopted a planning approach for development dating back to the mid-1950s. In the pre-1970 era Saudi Arabia's allocation policies were intentionally implemented through the budgetary process, despite the non-existence of development plans. Since 1970 the Kingdom has launched three five-year development plans: the First covering 1970-5 (1390-5); the Second, 1975-80 (1395-1400); and the Third, spanning 1980-5 (1400-5). The general objectives of the plans and their performance have been presented and analysed in earlier chapters. In what follows, it is intended to analyse the prospects of the economy, the size, allocations, and policy aspects of governmental budgetary expenditures, both during the decade preceding the First Development Plan and after.

Table 8.2 represents data on annual budget estimates for the years 1961/2 to 1979/80. While distinctions between current (ordinary) and development (investment) expenditures remain obscure, and despite the fact that the estimated data may probably bear not much relation to actual revenues and actual expenditures, none the less the following general features are evident from the table:

Table 8.2: Government Budget: Estimated Annual Revenues and Expenditures, 1961/2-1979/80 (SR millions)

	1961/2	1962/3	1963/4	1964/5	1965/6	1966/7	1967/8	1968/9	1969/70	1970/1
Revenues										
Oil revenues	1,651.0	1,928.0	2,268.0	2,592.0	3,166.0	3,974.0	3,547.0	4,196.0	5,198.0	5,346.0
Other revenues	356.0	338.0	358.0	370.0	448.0	476.0	518.0	703.0	768.0	944.0
Allocation from Reserve and Development Fund	159.0	186.0	60.0	150.0	347.0	575.0	872.0	636.0	–	–
Total revenues	2,166.0	2,452.0	2,686.0	3,112.0	3,961.0	5,025.0	4,937.0	5,535.0	5,966.0	6,380.0
Expenditures										
Project budget	400.0	550.0[a]	550.0[a]	762.0[b]	1,402.0[c]	1,717.0[d]	2,147.0[e]	2,570.0	2,682.0	2,596.0
Recurrent	1,766.0	1,902.0	2,136.0	2,350.0	2,559.0	3,308.0	2,790.0	2,965.0	3,284.0	3,784.0
Total expenditures	2,166.0	2,452.0	2,686.0	3,112.0	3,961.0	5,025.0	4,937.0	5,535.0	5,966.0	6,380.0

Table 8.2 (continued)

	1971/2	1972/3	1973/4	1974/5	1975/6	1976/7	1977/8	1978/9	1979/80
Revenues									
Oil revenues	9,855.0	12,098.0	21,110.0	94,432.0	86,969.0	99,507.0	131,154.0	116,534.0	155,406.0
Other revenues	927.0	1,102.0	1,750.0	3,815.0	8,878.0	11,428.0	15,339.0	13,466.0	3,594.0
Allocation from Reserve and Development Fund	–	–	–	–	15,088.0	–	–	–	–
Total revenues	10,782.0	13,200.0	22,810.0	98,247.0	110,935.0	110,935.0	146,493.0	130,000.0	160,000.0
Expenditures									
Project budget	5,036.0	6,718.0	14,263.0	78,901.0[f]	74,379.0	74,433.0	74,866.0	84,048.0	105,680.0
Recurrent	5,746.0	6,482.0[a]	8,547.0	19,346.0	36,556.0	36,502.0[a]	36,534.0	46,952.0	54,320.0
Total expenditures	10,782.0	13,200.0	22,810.0	98,247.0	110,935.0	110,935.0	111,400.0	130,000.0	160,000.0

Notes: a. Excludes SR 151.6 million allocated for the Project Budget from the Economic Development Fund. b. Does not include SR 321 million allocated from the Economic Development Fund previously and additional SR 122 million from this Fund and the General Reserve. c. Excluding SR 259 million allocated previously for projects to be executed this year. d. Excludes SR 271 million allocated previously for projects to be executed this year. e. Excluding SR 284 million allocated previously from the Economic Development Fund. f. Includes SR 52,564 million allocated under the Second Development Plan.
Sources: SAMA, *Annual Reports*, various issues, and *Statistical Summaries*, various issues.

(1) The government budget, which estimated total expenditures, has been the main instrument of policy towards achieving the desired socio-economic objectives. From a modest sum of SR 1,195 million in 1958/9, it increased to SR 5,966 million in 1969/70 and an estimated SR 160,000 million in 1979/80. The relative share of government budget expenditure has risen from about 28.5 per cent of the GDP in 1962/3 to about 50.1 per cent in 1977/8.
(2) Even more important than the size of the budgets has been their reorientation towards development expenditures. The general policy of the government has been, as implicit in the annual budget data, to accelerate investment outlays with a view eventually to placing the economy on a self-sustained growth path. Lately (see the Second and Third Plans), this means diversification of the economy. The strategy has been the creation of infrastructure and other physical developments and the expansion of human and social developmental activities. The total budget appropriation allocation in favour of principal development agencies or departments rose from SR 691 million (or 22.2 per cent of total expenditures in 1964/5) to SR 4,732.6 million (or 43.9 per cent) in 1969/70. Again, this increased to SR 105,680 million, or just over 66 per cent of total budget appropriations, in 1979/80. In addition, allocation for projects, which in the Saudi Arabian context is the closest thing to investment expenditures or public-capital formation, increased sharply, from SR 110 million in 1959/60 to SR 2,682 million in 1969/70. Project-budget appropriation increased dramatically to SR 83,048 million in 1978/9 and accounted for 63.9 per cent of total budget appropriation for that financial period. Estimates for 1979/80 were for the upward trend to continue, with SR 105,680 million, or just over 66 per cent of total budget appropriation, destined for project expenditure.
(3) The rapid growth in government budget and the sharp increases in project budget allocation are, quantitatively, indicative of substantial developmental expenditures which have been planned in Saudi Arabia since the 1960s.

But while *ex-ante* investment has increased substantially (if one agrees with this interpretation of budgeted development expenditure), it is more important for our purpose to know (1) ex-post or actual investments and (2) the pattern and allocation of actual investment in various sectors of the economy. These two aspects inevitably involve various analytically and practically complicated issues, especially in situations in which information is lacking or is very inadequate, as is the case in Saudi Arabia. In the following section, however, the general features of the project budget are discussed first, and then a number of important sectors of the economy are examined with regard to their specific share in public budget allocation for projects, and their implications for development and government policy.

Sectoral Allocation of Development Expenditures

Table 8.3 presents data on project budget appropriations by various sectors of the economy of Saudi Arabia. Total project (development) budget appropriation during the decade 1961/70 amounted to SR 13,845.8 million. A precise distribution of the total between various sectors is extremely difficult to compute due to (1) the limitation imposed by available information, i.e. the way the budget data are presented in official publications, and (2) lack of further information on some categories of projects listed in Table 8.3. For example, two categories, 'Finance' and 'Others' accounted jointly for SR 4,449 million, or almost one-third of that decade's budget allocated to projects. The situation in the 1970s shows an even more remarkable picture. 'Finance' and 'Others' combined made up 50.1 per cent of the total project expenditures of the 20-year period 1961/80, an amount of SR 282.1 billion. But, despite their large share, these categories of project expenditures are unfortunately more of a miscellaneous nature than anything else. Also, the details are not specified in the official publications available.

Aside from the allocations made through the project budget, and the associated difficulties with the unspecified projects, substantial amounts were also appropriated for a number of ministries and departments responsible for the execution and operation of the programmes. While the distinction between developmental and general projects remains obscure, it would be more meaningful to consider these together with the allocation made from the project budget. This is not done, because of the problems involved in identifying which of the ministries' allocations are for projects and which are not.

The problems mentioned aside, the following general features of the sectoral allocation of investment resources are evident from Table 8.3.

Allocation to the transport and communication sectors have occupied a place of prime importance in the Kingdom's development budget. This policy is claimed to be consistent with the economic and social needs of a vast but sparsely populated country. This sector has accounted for SR 3,970.3 million or about 29 per cent of the total

Table 8.3: Estimated Project Expenditures, 1960/1-1979/80 (SR millions, figures in ( ) = percentage of total)

	1960/1	1961/2	1962/3	1963/4	1964/5	1965/6	1966/7
Transport and communications	79.8 (27.4)	134.5 (33.6)	175.9 (32.0)	193.9 (27.6)	443.4 (36.8)	382.0 (26.7)	538.8 (30.9)
Agriculture and water	8.4 (2.9)	25.0 (6.3)	34.3 (6.2)	86.6 (12.3)	149.0 (12.4)	160.4 (11.2)	220.0 (12.6)
Petroleum and minerals	4.2 (1.4)	5.9 (1.5)	7.5 (1.4)	23.3 (3.3)	94.6 (7.9)	38.2 (2.7)	45.7 (2.6)
Industry and commerce	0.2 (a)	0.1 (a)	1.8 (a)	8.8 (1.3)	7.9 (a)	11.1 (a)	15.8 (a)
Social services	36.2 (12.4)	32.0 (8.0)	65.7 (11.9)	105.4 (15.0)	149.0 (12.4)	215.0 (15.0)	240.6 (13.8)
Education	15.2 (5.2)	12.3 (3.1)	35.4 (6.4)	60.8 (8.7)	74.0 (6.1)	124.4 (8.7)	113.4 (6.5)
Health	11.0 (3.8)	12.6 (3.2)	11.6 (2.1)	16.0 (2.3)	23.5 (2.0)	31.2 (2.2)	28.3 (1.6)
Information	10.0 (3.4)	3.4 (a)	6.3 (1.1)	22.4 (3.2)	37.1 (3.1)	40.4 (2.8)	85.0 (4.5)
Labour and social affairs	— —	3.7 (a)	12.4 (2.3)	6.2 (a)	14.4 (1.2)	19.0 (1.3)	13.8 (a)
Finance	62.5 (21.5)	40.3 (10.1)	55.5 (10.1)	63.9 (9.1)	65.9 (5.5)	105.6 (7.4)	112.8 (6.5)
Municipalities, interior	4.2 (1.4)	50.0 (12.5)	82.5 (15.0)	130.0 (18.5)	197.3 (16.4)	267.8 (18.7)	314.1 (18.0)
Mosque, Hajj	4.5 (1.6)	7.5 (1.9)	8.7 (1.6)	12.2 (1.7)	15.6 (1.3)	19.4 (1.4)	21.7 (1.2)
Others	91.0 (31.3)	104.8 (26.2)	118.2 (21.5)	77.6 (11.1)	82.5 (6.9)	229.3 (16.1)	236.6 (13.6)
Total	291.0 (100.)	400.1 (100.)	550.1 (100.)	701.7 (100.)	1,205.2 (100.)	1,428.8 (100.)	1,746.1 (100.)

Table 8.3 (continued)

	1967/8	1968/9	1969/70	1970/1	1971/2	1972/3
Transport and communications	527.0 (23.3)	794.4 (30.7)	700.6 (26.1)	603.5 (23.5)	1,461.0 (29.0)	1,470.0 (21.9)
Agriculture and water	314.2 (13.9)	398.8 (15.4)	300.0 (11.2)	230.1 (8.9)	456.0 (9.1)	572.5 (8.5)
Petroleum and minerals	41.7 (1.8)	56.2 (2.2)	57.7 (2.2)	39.6 (1.5)	82.3 (1.6)	86.7 (1.3)
Industry and commerce	7.5 (a)	14.4 (a)	8.7 (a)	9.2 (a)	28.9 (a)	29.9 (a)
Social services	181.9 (8.0)	133.1 (5.2)	108.7 (4.1)	72.2 (2.8)	228.0 (4.5)	409.1 (6.0)
Education	76.6 (3.3)	60.1 (2.3)	33.0 (1.2)	24.9 (1.0)	125.9 (2.5)	255.1 (3.8)
Health	21.8 (a)	14.1 (a)	13.5 (a)	10.9 (a)	29.2 (a)	45.4 (a)
Information	72.4 (3.2)	50.9 (2.0)	53.5 (2.0)	28.2 (1.1)	48.8 (1.0)	82.2 (1.2)
Labour and social affairs	11.1 (a)	8.0 (a)	8.7 (a)	8.2 (a)	24.1 (a)	26.4 (a)
Finance	105.3 (4.6)	164.8 (6.4)	143.0 (5.3)	b	396.1 (7.9)	640.7 (9.5)
Municipalities, interior	269.0 (11.9)	317.2 (12.3)	252.4 (9.4)	190.1 (7.3)	533.6 (10.6)	827.5 (12.3)
Mosque, Hajj	16.4 (a)	19.0 (a)	10.7 (a)	9.4 (a)	28.2 (a)	45.7 (a)
Others	803.2 (35.4)	685.9 (26.5)	1,100.2 (41.0)	1,441.9 (55.5)	1,821.6 (36.1)	2,635.5 (39.2)
Total	2,266.2 (100.)	2,583.8 (100.)	2,682.0 (100.)	2,596.0 (100.)	5,035.7 (100.)	6,717.6 (100.)

Table 8.3 (continued)

	1973/4	1974/5	1975/6	1976/7	1977/8	1978/9
Transport and communications	2,518.4 (17.7)	5,362.9 (20.3)	15,464.1 (20.8)	19,850.6 (20.9)	12,192.5 (12.5)	11,289.8 (11.1)
Agriculture and water	855.0 (6.0)	1,053.5 (4.0)	1,718.0 (2.3)	1,721.4 (1.8)	1,511.4 (1.5)	1,854.4 (1.8)
Petroleum and minerals	136.3 (1.0)	164.3 (a)	341.5 (a)	b	b	b
Industry and commerce	46.0 (a)	114.4 (a)	586.7 (a)	1,081.0 (1.1)	488.0 (a)	337.3 (a)
Social services	644.6 (4.5)	2,071.7 (7.8)	10,461.9 (14.1)	11,105.2 (11.7)	13,014.6 (13.3)	9,153.9 (9.0)
Education	365.5 (2.6)	1,265.6 (4.8)	6,355.1 (8.5)	6,367.6 (6.7)	7,955.3 (8.1)	5,123.1 (5.0)
Health	84.1 (a)	435.1 (1.6)	2,061.6 (2.8)	1,737.0 (1.8)	1,758.3 (1.8)	1,855.0 (1.8)
Information	158.5 (1.1)	205.3 (a)	636.7 (a)	959.8 (1.0)	1,064.0 (1.1)	723.5 (a)
Labour and social affairs	36.4 (a)	165.7 (a)	1,408.5 (1.9)	2,040.8 (2.2)	2,237.0 (2.3)	1,452.3 (1.4)
Finance	1,182.5 (8.3)	1,955.3 (7.4)	7,030.1 (9.5)	3,984.8 (4.2)	3,754.3 (3.8)	3,309.5 (3.3)
Municipalities, interior	2,027.0 (14.2)	4,771.4 (18.1)	15,708.6 (21.1)	26,898.3 (28.4)	22,831.5 (23.4)	16,946.7 (16.7)
Mosque, Hajj	57.5 (a)	103.8 (a)	205.8 (a)	b	b	b
Others	6,795.7 (46.2)	10,799.7 (40.9)	22,862.3 (30.7)	30,153.2 (31.8)	43,927.2 (45.0)	58,832.4 (57.8)
Total	14,907.5 (100.)	26,397.0 (100.)	74,379.0 (100.)	94,794.5 (100.)[c]	97,719.5 (100.)[c]	101,724.0 (100.)

Table 8.3 (continued)

	1979/80	1960/1-1969/70	1960/1-1979/80	1970/1-1979/80
Transport and communications	16,615.9 (13.2)	3,970.3 (28.7)	90,800.1 (16.1)	86,829.8 (15.8)
Agriculture and water	3,112.0 (2.5)	1,696.7 (12.3)	14,781.0 (2.6)	13,084.3 (2.4)
Petroleum and minerals	b	375.0 (2.7)	b	b
Industry and commerce	3,350.5 (2.7)[d]	76.3 (a)	6,248.2 (1.1)	6,171.9 (1.1)
Social services	10,354.3 (8.2)	1,267.5 (9.1)	57,917.0 (10.3)	56,649.5 (10.3)
Education	5,771.5 (4.6)	605.2 (4.4)	34,214.8 (6.1)	33,609.6 (6.1)
Health	1,822.0 (1.4)	183.6 (1.3)	10,022.3 (1.8)	9,838.7 (1.8)
Information	634.3 (a)	381.4 (2.8)	4,922.7 (a)	4,541.3 (a)
Labour and social affairs	2,126.5 (1.4)	97.3 (a)	8,757.2 (1.6)	8,659.9 (1.6)
Finance	7,868.3 (6.2)	919.6 (6.6)	31,041.2 (5.5)	30,121.6 (5.5)
Municipalities, interior	16,944.2 (13.5)	1,884.5 (13.6)	109,563.4 (19.4)	107,678.9 (19.6)
Mosque, Hajj	b	135.7 (1.0)	b	b
Others	67,593.4 (53.7)	3,529.4 (25.5)	251,058.9 (44.6)	247,529.5 (45.0)
Total	125,938.6 (100.)[e]	13,854.8 (100.)	563,420.2 (100.)	549,565.4 (100.)

Notes: a. Less than 1 per cent. b. Included in 'Others'. c. Interestingly, total project expenditure has remained relatively constant at the 1975/6 level, since that financial year. If one recognizes expected shortfall in expenditures of SR 20,361 million, SR 22,853.5 million, and SR 18,676.3 in 1976/7, 1977/8, and 1978/9 fiscal years, respectively, then the estimated project budget for the 1976/7 totals SR 74,433.4 million, that for 1977/8 becomes SR 74,866 million, and that for 1978/9 is SR 83,047.7 million. d. Including gathering and liquefaction of gas. e. If expected shortfall of SR 20,258.6 million for 1979/80 is taken into account, project expenditures budget for that fiscal year would be SR 10,568 million.

Sources: SAMA, *Annual Reports* and *Statistical Summaries*, various issues; Ministry of Finance, *Statistical Yearbook*, various issues.

development-budget appropriation over the decade 1961-70, but its share has fallen in the 1970s to an average of 16 per cent.

Agriculture, including livestock and water resources, accounted for about only 12.3 per cent of the total budget for the decade 1960/1-1969/70. Its relative share has risen, however, from a disappointingly low level of SR 8.4 million or 2.8 per cent of the project budget in 1960/1, to over SR 398.8 million or about 15 per cent of the project budget in 1968/9, giving a 10-year average of 12.3 per cent. However, in the 1970s this sector did not do so well. Its share fell to 2.4 per cent in the 10-year period 1970/1-1979/80. This is an indication that the absorptive capacity of the agricultural sector has not expanded as rapidly as other sectors of the Saudi economy in the 1970s. Also, as is evident from the data in Table 8.3 and from subsequent discussion, the share of industry, mining, and commerce is almost negligible in the public-sector development budget. Altogether, these sectors accounted for only about 1 per cent of the total project budget appropriation in the 18-year period 1960/1-1977/8. The two years thereafter marked a change, however, as there was a tenfold increase between 1978/9 and 1979/80 as a result of expenditure on gas-gathering and liquefaction projects. The industry and commerce sector increased its share to almost 3 per cent of total project expenditures in 1979/80.[10]

An important sector for the purpose of project-expenditure analysis is social services, which consists of two development sectors: human-resource development and social development. The social-services sector, as defined in the budget, consists of education, health, information, and labour and social affairs. A startling fact which stands out clearly when the expenditure pattern in the subsector is examined, is the fall in the relative share of education in total project expenditures during the First Plan period below the level of the 1960s, of 4.4 per cent. Actually it was not until the 1975/6 financial year that planned expenditures on education exceeded this 10-year average by a significant amount. However, expenditures on education fell again as a percentage of total planned expenditures in 1978/9 and 1979/80 (Table 8.3). Investment in health facilities has followed the same pattern. Project expenditures which have been appropriated for health have been relatively very small: for example, during the four-year period 1970/1-1973/4 the amount appropriated for this purpose never reached 1 per cent of total project expenditures for any year; consequently, what happened in the 1967/8-1969/70 period was repeated. However, as will be emphasized in later chapters, both the Second and Third Plans made provision for expansion of education and health services in the Kingdom.

It should be mentioned that the budget appropriations given in Table 8.3 above include some projects which are not strictly developmental or are not for purposes of capital formation. It is also likely that the project-budget appropriation underestimated the level or the amount of development efforts made during the decade, since, in addition to the appropriations made in project budget, substantial amounts have also been allocated to the various government agencies dealing with development efforts. It is also likely that the level of expenditures indicated by development-budget appropriation will, as far as public investment is concerned, overestimate the level and degree of performance in various sectors. This, as will be stressed later, is due to the fact that actual expenditures, especially from the project budget until recently have fallen short of the amount appropriated. It would have been more meaningful to carry out sectoral analysis of government investment in Saudi Arabia in terms of actual expenditures as opposed to budget estimates. Unfortunately, data on actual government expenditures for sectors are not readily available. We may, however, discuss actual aggregate government expenditures and the share of project expenditures in relation to the estimates. This is done in the section which follows.

Fiscal and Budgetary Policy in Saudi Arabia

Three fiscal functions are usually identified in the discussion of budgetary policies: (1) the allocation function, (2) the distribution function, and (3) the stabilization function.[11]

The Allocation Function of Saudi Fiscal Measures

The allocation function of the budget involves the use of expenditure and tax structures to transfer factors of production from uses where they are least efficient or least needed, to uses where their contributions to social product are greatest. For example, budget could be used to alter the public-private goods mix if it is felt the existing composition is not right. Also, the content of military goods in the GNP could be changed depending on the social preference of the people of Saudi Arabia.

The measurement of public-private goods mix is not easy in practice. One rough approximation is the share of government consumption and investment in total GNP. In terms of resource acquisition, perhaps the share of government in gross fixed-capital formation or alternatively the ratio of actual government expenditures to the GNP are more appropriate.

Examination of Table 8.4 yields some interesting results. The share of the Saudi government in total consumption increased from 33.5 per cent in 1964 to 59.8 per cent in 1976, before falling in each of the next two years to 54.6 per cent in 1977 and 48 per cent in 1978. Government consumption has consequently not been rising as fast as total consumption in the Saudi economy. To the extent, however, that in relation to total GNP the share of the government total purchases of goods and services and of government expenditures has been falling up to 1975, as indicated in the second and fourth lines of Table 8.4, one need not be alarmed by the trend in government consumption. The recent upward trend in the share of government expenditures, if continued, would nullify this conclusion.[12]

We may, for a moment, concentrate on the behaviour of government consumption in order to find explanations for it. An interesting study has been undertaken by F.S. Al-Bashir;[13] this study, among other things, tried to explain the behaviour of government consumption using econometric techniques. It shows that government consumption is significantly a positive function of government revenues and lagged government consumption expenditures. Although the study uses appropriated and not actual budget expenditures and revenue figures, it would appear that the reasons given for such a relationship between budget appropriations and projected expenditures will tend to hold for interrelationship between actual expenditures and revenue figures. We cannot, however, say that the regression which was estimated should be used to describe the exact relationship between the actual expenditures and revenues. All that is going to be done is to make references for the actual figures, recognizing that such influences are at best very tenuous considering the extent to which actual expenditure and revenue figures have deviated from estimates recently in Saudi Arabia.[14]

It should not be surprising that government consumption in a given year, *t*, depends on previous year's consumption expenditures. When new expenditures are introduced in period *t*-1, in most government budgets, the probability of their being continued in period *t* is high. Thus government project expenditures tend to have cumulative impact on recurrent expenditures. Similarly, that actual or expected government revenues positively influence actual expenditures by the government should not be too difficult to explain in a developing country in which administrative, defence, and other non-project

Table 8.4: The Share of the Government in Selected Economic Quantities, 1964-78 (percentage)

	1964	1965	1966	1967	1968	1969	1970	1971	1972	1973	1974	1975	1976	1977	1978
Share of government in total consumption	33.5	36.2	38.8	40.0	37.5	36.1	36.9	37.2	38.3	40.3	33.1	53.5	59.8	54.6	48.0
Share of government purchases in Gross Domestic Product	a	a	a	a	26.4	27.4	26.6	21.8	20.3	18.1	8.3	17.3	33.3	a	a
Share of government in Gross Fixed Capital Formation	a	a	a	a	46.9	51.3	46.7	41.1	42.4	34.9	40.7	49.4	69.4	53.2	60.3
Share of government expenditures in Gross Domestic Product	24.3	27.7	33.8	32.2	32.2	30.8	31.1	27.5	28.8	25.1	18.7	26.1	52.7	62.6	61.7

Note: a. Data for government GFCF and share of government purchases in GDP are not available for these years to permit computation of percentages.

Sources: Computed from Gross Fixed Capital Formation (GFCF) and Gross Domestic Product (GDP) figures in SAMA, *Annual Reports*, various issues, and *Statistical Summaries*, various issues; International Monetary Fund, *Financial Statistics*; Table 5.

expenditures have the tendency to rise rapidly during the process of development to the extent that the only constraint on such expansion is revenue.

With respect to the control over accumulated capital, the government did quite well during the first four years of the Second Development Plan *vis-à-vis* the private sector. While the government's share in gross fixed capital formation had fluctuated around 44 per cent between 1961 and 1975, the average annual growth in value between 1975 and 1979 was 60.1 per cent as compared to 44.6 per cent for the economy as a whole. By 1979 the government share had increased to 62.1 per cent.[15]

Overall, the role of the government has more than kept up with the growth of the economy. As indicated by Table 8.4, the ratios of government purchases to GDP and government actual expenditures to GDP increased during the Second Plan. The most plausible explanation is the large amount of revenues that have been accruing to the government from the oil sector since prices began their upward spiral in 1973/4. The governmental policy of emphasizing the private sector in the development of the economy should somewhat reverse this trend in the 1980s.

Actual versus Estimated Government Revenues and Expenditures

The government of Saudi Arabia followed a 'balanced' budget. 'Balanced budget' is, however, not to be interpreted in the sense of equality between estimated expenditures and revenues for each year. Instead, the budget is said to be balanced if whatever deficit existing for each year is financed by drawing on development and/or reserve funds of the government. Surpluses are, on the other hand, added to reserve funds which in effect consist of accumulated budget surpluses. As Table 8.1 shows, since 1960 there has been, therefore, no occasion for the Saudi government to incur deficits significant enough to make it necessary to finance them by borrowing from the non-banking general public or from the banking system.[16]

Table 8.5 indicates that persistent surpluses were the rule in Saudi Arabia until 1977/8. The actual amount spent by the government each year fell consistently short of the amount appropriated over that period, with the exception of 1965/6. The government found it more difficult to use up allocated investible resources during the period referred to, than it did to spend for consumption purposes. Actual revenues fell short of estimated revenues in 1977/8, partially accounting for the deficit in that financial year, but it was the increasing

Table 8.5: Comparison of Actual and Projected Government Expenditures and Actual Revenue, 1961/2-1979/80 (SR millions)

	1961/2	1962/3	1963/4	1964/5	1965/6	1966/7	1967/8	1968/9	1969/70	1970/1	1971/2
(1) Total budget appropriations	2,166.0	2,452.0	2,686.0	3,112.0	3,961.0	5,025.0	4,939.0	5,535.5	5,966.0	6,380.0	10,782.0
(2) Project budget appropriations	400.0	550.0	550.0	762.0	1,402.0	1,717.0	2,147.0	2,570.0	2,682.0	2,596.0	5,036.0
(3) Actual total expenditures	1,773.0	2,223.0	2,269.0	2,887.0	4,034.0	4,299.0	4,717.0	4,928.0	5,417.0	6,294.0	8,130.0
(4) Actual project expenditures	240.0	260.0	263.0	363.0	734.0	788.0	1,704.0	1,860.0	2,163.0	2,304.0	3,374.0
(5) Estimated revenue	2,007.0	2,266.0	2,626.0	2,962.0	3,614.0	4,450.0	4,065.0	4,099.0	5,966.0	6,380.0	10,782.0
(6) Actual revenue[a]										7,954.0	11,116.0
(3) as % of (1)	81.0	90.7	84.4	92.8	101.8	85.6	95.5	89.0	90.8	98.7	75.4
(4) as % of (2)	60.0	47.3	47.8	47.6	52.4	45.9	79.4	72.4	80.6	88.8	67.0
(6) as % of (5)[a]										124.7	103.1
Actual surplus (+) or deficit (–)[a]										+1,660.0	+2,986.0
(3) as % of (6)[a]										79.1	73.1

Table 8.5 (continued)

	1972/3	1973/4	1974/5	1975/6	1976/7	1977/8	1978/9	1979/80
(1) Total budget appropriations	13,200.0	22,810.0	98,247.0	110,935.0	110,935.0	111,400.0	130,000.0	160,000.0
(2) Project budget appropriations	6,718.0	14,263.0	78,901.0	74,379.0	74,433.0	74,866.0	83,048.0	105,680.0
(3) Actual total expenditures[b]	10,159.0	18,595.0	32,038.0	81,784.0	128,273.0	138,027.0	147,400.0	
(4) Actual project expenditures[b]	4,503.0	10,125.0	19,832.0	43,304.0		66,253.0[c]	91,388.0[c]	
(5) Estimated revenue	13,200.0	22,810.0	98,247.0	110,935.0	110,935.0	145,493.0	130,000.0	160,000.0
(6) Actual revenue[b]	15,325.0	41,705.0	100,103.0	103,384.0	135,957.0	130,659.0	132,871.0	
(3) as % of (1)[b]	80.0	81.5	32.6	73.7	115.6	123.9	113.4	
(4) as % of (2)[b]	67.0	71.0	25.1	58.2		88.5	110.0	
(6) as % of (5)[b]	116.1	182.8	101.9	93.2	122.6	89.2	102.2	
Actual surplus (+) or deficit (–)[b]	+5,166.0	+23,110.0	+68,065.0	+21,600.0	+7,684.0	–7,368.0	–14,529.0	
(3) as % of (6)[b]	66.3	44.6	32.0	79.1	94.3	105.6	110.9	

Notes: a. Actual revenue figures for 1961/2-1969/70 are not available, hence the gap for this period. b. Actual project expenditures not available for 1976/77, hence the gap in (4) as a percentage of (2); actual total expenditures, actual project expenditures, and actual revenue figures not available for 1979/80, hence the gap for this period in percentages and surplus/deficit columns. c. Computed from SAMA, *Annual Report, 1979*, p. 14.
Sources: SAMA, *Annual Reports*, various issues; previous tables.

ability of the economy to absorb and the government to spend that largely accounted for the deficits in 1977/8 and 1978/9.

The ability of the government to invest has improved of late, despite administrative, technical and physical bottlenecks. The behaviour of actual-estimated ratios sustains this contention as evidenced by the comparison of actual project expenditures *vis-à-vis* project-budget appropriations. The actual-estimated ration, which in 1970/1 was 88.8 per cent, fell to 58.2 per cent in 1975/6. However, in the succeeding year the actual-estimated ratio rebounded to 88.5 per cent and was followed in 1978/9 by actual project expenditures being 110 per cent of the appropriated amount.

An analysis of the volume of actual expenditures over the First and Second Plan period reveals dramatic results. Actual project expenditures increased 40 times from SR 2,304 million in 1970/1 to SR 91,388 million in 1978/9. At the same time, overall actual expenditures were increasing 23.4 times, from SR 6,294 million in 1970/1 to SR 147,400 million in 1978/9. Table 8.6 offers the rest of the picture for the years 1971-9. Apart from 1974/5, actual project expenditures consistently have shown a growth rate higher than total actual government expenditures.

This is an interesting observation, in view of the general contention that the Saudi government has not been able to invest its surplus funds. If the rate of growth of actual project expenditures is compared with the rate at which funds which are appropriated has grown, or compared with the rate of growth of government revenue, then this is true. On the other hand, Table 8.6 definitely indicates that the Saudi government has not done as poorly as the above contention seems to imply in the area of investment.

Consequently, perhaps a more appropriate comment on the investment policy of the Saudi government is that there was too much anxiety to invest. The anxiety is reflected in the rate at which amounts appropriated for projects grew especially in the early 1970s. Such an overambition, as is often contained in development plans, inevitably creates the impression of unsuccessful implementation of programmes, and puts pressure on the physical as well as the manpower base of the economy, and may also create inflationary pressures. The doctrine of unbalanced growth, however, gives the rationale for creating bottlenecks in the form of shortages so that sufficient signals are given to the private sector in order to respond so as to fill in the gap between supply and demand. It is, however, also true that the nature and the extent of some bottlenecks and inflation may create economic, social and

Table 8.6: Growth of Government Appropriations and Actual Expenditures, 1970/1-1978/9 (percentages)

	1970/1	1971/2	1972/3	1973/4	1974/5	1975/6	1976/7	1977/8	1978/9
Total budget appropriation	69.0	22.4	72.8	330.7	12.9	0.0	a	16.7	23.1
Project-budget appropriation	94.0	33.4	112.3	453.2	–5.7	a	a	10.8	27.3
Actual total expenditures	29.1	25.0	83.0	88.4	155.3	56.8	7.6	6.8	–
Actual project expenditures	46.4	33.5	124.9	95.9	118.4	b	b	37.9	–

Notes: a. Less than 1 per cent. b. Not available.
Source: Computed from Table 8.5.

sometimes political conditions inconsistent with rapid economic development.

Fiscal Policy, Economic Stabilization and Distribution Function

The extent to which the fiscal policies of the government of Saudi Arabia have been successful in stabilizing prices in the Kingdom is difficult to say. But this issue presupposes that there have been conscious efforts by the government to follow budgetary policies aimed at abating or controlling inflation. Can the 'balanced budget' policy be interpreted as anti-inflationary policy?[17] Certainly budgeting for surpluses, *ceteris paribus*, is deflationary. And, consequently, since actual government spending has almost always fallen below actual government revenues, it may appear that the financial aspect of the government has at least not promoted inflation. However, this will be true only if the nature of inflation which has existed in Saudi Arabia was solely of the aggregate demand-pull type. And if this were so, the surplus financing of government projects would be deflationary only if Saudi Arabia had a closed economy. This is far from true; like most developing countries the Saudi economy is indeed a very open one, as discussions in Chapter 10 will try to emphasize, explain and analyse. Further, Saudi Arabia shares with other developing countries the structuralist interpretation of inflation. Consequently, although the government may budget for surplus, this may not be enough to curb the demand-pull inflation initiated and/or intensified by the effect of increased balance-of-payments surpluses on money supply and on aggregate spending. In any case, it is generally agreed that such broad anti-inflationary policies, like an overall surplus on the budget, are not effective at curbing inflationary pressures caused by supply bottlenecks and upward movement not only of salaries and wages, but also of most non-wage incomes. On the other hand, such supply bottlenecks exist in the Saudi economy.[18] A vivid example is housing-rents in the Central Riyadh, which have been sky-rocketing. While this is a natural outcome during the early stages of development, the Saudi case is serious in view of the increased wealth and reserves and increased government revenue. Also, imported labour tend to be highly paid, especially the technical and top-level manpower, thus establishing a fertile environment for cost-push inflation. One should also mention the effects which changes in the consumption pattern in Saudi Arabia might have on prices. We will have an occasion to go into greater details of inflation when we discuss the monetary and banking sector of the Saudi economy in Chapter 9.

It must be noted that the government has taken several measures aimed at reducing structural inflation. The Second Development Plan made initial reference by noting:

> The government, in keeping with its prime objective of improving the well-being of its people, has undertaken a number of measures to instigate this situation. It has eliminated a number of taxes, and reduced others, as rising oil revenues have rendered taxation for revenue purposes unnecessary. The road tax . . . and taxes on domestic petroleum products have been eliminated. Many customs duties and the 10 per cent surcharge have been eliminated, and tariffs on the balance reduced to a token 3 per cent . . . on a number of import subsidies: milk, milk products, flour, rice, sugar, meats, vegetable oils, and fats and medicines.[19]

These are certainly short-run measures for abating inflation which has been caused by increased government spending and is bound to accelerate as development continues. In recognition of the problem of high inflation which was confronting the Kingdom at the end of the First Plan and the beginning of the Second, the government undertook fiscal measures that were effective in reducing the rate of inflation. Appropriations were held constant in the second and third years of the Second Plan at the level they had been in the Plan's first year. As a result of this fiscal policy, inflation as measured by the CLI (cost of living index) peaked in the first year of the Second Plan at 31.5 per cent and by 1980 had been virtually brought under control to approximately 3.5 per cent.[20]

In addition, the government recognized the 'removal of major bottlenecks in the implementation of the [Second] Plan and on the rapid increase of supplies from both domestic and foreign resources'[21] as short-run measures to curb inflation, in addition to the recognition that, 'in the long run, increased production of goods and services and higher productivity per worker are the only effective means of achieving a high rate of growth without adverse inflationary effects'.[22]

It is important to note here that the conventional analysis of budget surplus and deficits and their implications for inflation may not be applicable to the case of Saudi Arabia. This is because of the openness of the Saudi economy and the particular role of oil as a source of government revenue.

A budget surplus does not have the same interpretation in relation to impact on prices. In an economy in which the bulk of the revenue originates from taxes on the general public, surplus could correctly be regarded as deflationary. On the other hand, in an economy like that of Saudi Arabia, such an interpretation would be erroneous since the bulk of the revenue does not originate from sources which reduce the purchasing power of the general public. Thus the relevant indicator of inflationary impact of government fiscal policy is the size of government expenditures and their composition and not the size of the budget surplus or deficits.

With respect to the distributional function, the extent of government subsidies, housing programmes, trade liberalization, etc. all go to show an indication that the objective of the government, as expressed in the Second and Third Plans, to ensure a decent standard of living for the average Saudi, is being taken seriously. However, one does not have empirical data to confirm the effectiveness of these policies in achieving redistribution of income in Saudi Arabia. So far as redistribution of income among Saudi nationals is concerned, it can be said that the present tax policy is passive since the zakat is a proportional form of tax.

Prospects for Saudi Public Finance

With the oil reserves of the Kingdom projected to last approximately 35 years, the prospect for government revenue is bright.[23] Oil revenues are likely to continue to dominate the government revenue sector despite the government's diversification policy. And to the extent that the government of Saudi Arabia continues to use tax relief as a weapon against inflation, it is even more likely that the oil sector will increase its share in the revenue of the government, especially as 100 per cent government participation in the oil industry is implemented.

However, with the increased incomes will emerge increased pressures on the Saudi government to disperse the oil revenue. The human capital, infrastructural, administrative, and technical bases of the Saudi economy will thus be stretched to their limits (maybe beyond their limits!) in the years ahead, unless the recognition of inflationary consequences of government expenditure expansion is able to instil more prudence into the fiscal measures of the government. There is no way in which the economy can absorb all the increased oil revenues. But the Saudi government need not allow itself to be coerced by writers on absorptive capacity into overinvesting in the domestic economy. Alternative direction of investment outside the Kingdom – in neighbouring Arab and Middle East countries, developing countries and in advanced countries – must be increasingly sought and considered according to some rational criteria. In this connection, the guiding principle must be to maximize the social rate of return of Saudi's investible resources within the framework of the political, cultural, social and economic aspirations of the people of Saudi Arabia.

Notes

1. G.M. Meier, *Leading Issues in Economic Development*, 3rd edn (New York, Oxford University Press, 1976). See selections in Chapter 12 for discussions of the merits and demerits of the price system and the need for development planning.

2. Vide Reginald H. Green, 'The Role of the State as an Agent of Economic Development and Social Development in the Least Developed Countries,' *Journal of Development Planning*, No. 6, 1974, pp. 15-38, for a discussion of some of these elements of development.

3. G.M. Meier, *Leading Issues*, p. 267.

4. SAMA, *Annual Report, 1976 (1397)*, pp. 45 and 150 and *Annual Report, 1979 (1399)*, pp. 45-6. This trend, however, has been changing. The 1976 figures reveal a remarkable upturn in the investment-GDP ratio to 21 per cent and the 1978 figures reveal continuing increase to 30 per cent.

5. See Chapter 2 of this volume for a detailed discussion of this source of government revenue.

6. See pp. 274-85.

7. The details on the tax system in Saudi Arabia discussed here are based on the discussion of N.A. Shilling, *Doing Business in Saudi Arabia and the Arab Gulf States* (New York, Intercrescent Publishing and Information Corporation, 1975), pp. 336-40.

8. See Chapter 6 of this volume for a discussion of these goals in the Second Plan. Chapter 12 has a more detailed discussion of tax incentives which private firms can enjoy in the Kingdom. The Third Development Plan policy intends to review all of these subsidies with the intention of eliminating a number of them.

9. Some of the well-known criteria within these hypotheses are: (1) the social marginal productivity criteria; (2) the marginal *per capita* reinvestment quotient criteria; (3) the marginal growth contribution criterion; (4) the reinvestible surplus criteria; (5) the balanced and unbalanced growth criteria; and (6) the programming techniques for resource allocation and development. For a review of these criteria see, G.M. Meier, *Leading Issues*, Chapter 7.

10. This objective of diversification of the economy is spelled out especially in the Second and Third Plans, 1975-85. Both plans, nevertheless, make provision for increased investment in manufacturing, for example, the projects in the Eastern Province.

11. Richard A. Musgrave and Peggy B. Musgrave, *Public Finance in Theory and Practice*, 2nd edn (New York, McGraw-Hill, 1973), pp. 6-7.

12. The years 1977 and 1978 witnessed a reversal of this trend with the percentage dropping to 54.6 and 48, respectively.

13. Faisal S. Al-Bashir, *A Structural Econometric Model of the Saudi Arabian Economy, 1960-70* (New York, Wiley Press, 1977), p. 63. The regression obtained by two-stage Least Square method was $C_G = -61.344 + 0.294G_R + 0.278G_{R-1}$ where C_G = government consumption and G_R = government revenue.

14. But perhaps all that is required for the inferences to be meaningful is for the estimates to be good proxies for the actual figures. Considering, therefore, that the actual and estimated figures for government revenue expenditures are

highly correlated (both actual and estimated figures have shown an upward trend), Al-Bashir's results may have been used too cautiously in this study.

15. Kingdom of Saudi Arabia, *Third Development Plan, 1400-1405/1980-1985*, Chapter 2, section 2.3.2.2.

16. The same idea has been expressed by Donald A. Wells, *Saudi Arabian Revenues and Expenditures* (Washington, DC, Resources for the Future, Inc., 1974), p. 11. It must be noted, however, that in 1955/7 the economic and financial crisis which took place forced the government to undertake deficit financing and therefore contributed to the inflation and balance-of-payments disequilibrium which characterized that period. SAMA, *Annual Report, 1960*, pp. 1-9.

17. Later on the inapplicability for the Saudi case of the conventional interpretation of budget deficits and surpluses in relation to inflation or deflation will be discussed.

18. These supply bottlenecks were greatly reduced during the Second Plan as is discussed earlier in the section on implementation in Chapter 6.

19. Kingdom of Saudi Arabia, *Second Development Plan, 1394-1400/1975-1980*, p. 45.

20. SAMA, *Annual Report, 1979*, p. 11.

21. SAMA, *Annual Report, 1976*, p. 1.

22. Kingdom of Saudi Arabia, *Second Development Plan*, p. 45.

23. *Petroleum Intelligence Weekly*, 23 May 1977, p. 4. One should note that various estimates of year of depletion have been made. They differ according to the estimated reserves used and the rate of production assumed for the future.

9 MONEY AND BANKING

Introduction

> For an open economy like that of Saudi Arabia, without exchange or import restrictions, etc., existence of a strong diversified and viable banking system is of fundamental importance for stability of the economy and for a satisfactory rate of growth without inflationary excess.[1]

This quotation stands as an ample description of the role that financial institutions can play in the development process. In addition, it must be supplemented that although money is not needed for its own sake, there appears to be a direct relationship between the degree of monetization of an economy and the level of its development. In other words, there must be some truth in the contention of some monetary economists that money yields both productivity and utility.[2] Indeed, the controversy about whether money does or does not matter vanishes when money in growth models is discussed. For example, Milton Friedman, who will argue in comparative static analysis that in the long run a change in money supply will not affect real variables, recognizes an optimum rate of growth of the money supply consistent with the rate of growth of income. Indeed, as the survey by Stein indicates, money plays a positive role in the growth of an economy. A money economy is obviously more efficient and productive than a barter economy.[3]

It is in the recognition of the productivity of money in providing information for transactions, reducing other costs associated with exchange, etc. that, historically, in early stages of development 'transaction dominating assets emerge'.[4] The emergence of these assets constitutes the beginning of money. In Saudi Arabia the fondness of the people for gold was not accidental. In ancient times Arabian people 'used and later copied the money of Athens'.[5] Indeed, 'full bodied metallic coins have long circulated in the Arabian Peninsula',[6] as will be seen in the next section.

The institution of money is only the first step towards a full-fledged financial/banking system capable of financing economic growth by generating savings and allocating them into profitable investment opportunities. In the case of Saudi Arabia, entrepreneurs may be constrained to establish firms owing to lack of funds. Thus, although in Saudi Arabia the country as a whole may experience surplus funds, it is possible for enterprising individuals to be short of funds both to expand business and to start new ones; hence the crucial role of financial institutions in the development process of Saudi Arabia. The mere establishment of financial and lending institutions or monetary and credit system is not a *sine qua non* for successful financing of development. These institutions should primarily be tailored to the conditions of the country.

In this chapter, apart from describing the monetary and banking system of Saudi Arabia, tracing the history of money and banking in the Kingdom, and analysing the working of the financial system, attempts will be made to examine efforts which have been undertaken by the government either directly or through its financial wing, to establish and develop a financial system based on the traditional beliefs and institutions prevailing in the Kingdom. In other words, we will try to answer the following question: what have been the efforts made to achieve an optimal financial system from the point of view of growth?

One must be warned against the trap which one is apt to fall into in the analysis of the role of financial institutions in a surplus-funds country, namely that the non-existence of the role of these institutions in saving accumulation makes them any less important in these countries than their counterparts are in deficit-funds countries. On the contrary, monetary/credit management assumes an even greater importance, and the role of the financial institutions in this area cannot be overemphasized. This is especially the case for the Kingdom of Saudi Arabia from the point of view of the need to distribute oil revenue throughout the Kingdom, and considering the desire of the government to develop a cadre of indigenous entrepreneurs capable of helping it achieve its diversification objective. The financial institutions of Saudi Arabia, indeed, have an important role to play. Also, the monetary policies at the head of the financial system are important mechanisms to achieving the financial harmony and stable framework within which the monetary and financial system could function to promote growth in the economy.

Monetary and Banking Development in Saudi Arabia

The history of money and banking in the Kingdom of Saudi Arabia may be broken down into three periods: (1) the period prior to the establishment of the Saudi Arabian Monetary Agency (SAMA) in 1952;

(2) the period between the establishment of SAMA and 1960 when note currency was introduced; and (3) the post-1960 era. Monetary development in the Kingdom followed the classical sequence often enumerated in monetary economics textbooks, namely, from primitive money through full-bodied metallic via token metallic to paper money.

(1) The Genesis of Money and Banking

Prior to 1952 several coins, mostly foreign, circulated in Saudi Arabia. In the ancient past many foreign coins circulated either in their original form or in their copied form using local gold and silver deposits. The modern past of this period witnessed the extensive circulation of Maria Theresa thaler and the Indian rupee.[7] The former coin, which was first issued in 1780, had a wider circulation than the latter, stretching beyond the Arabian Peninsula to East African and even to West African territories. Another full-bodied coin which circulated in this period in Saudi Arabia was the British gold sovereign. The gold coin was copied and received a very wide circulation throughout the Kingdom.

In 1927 an attempt was made to standardize the monetary units which were circulating in Saudi Arabia by the issue of a Saudi Arabian silver riyal to replace all the coins which were in circulation, except one: the British gold sovereign was used as the standard within which the riyal acquired value. And since both the gold sovereign and the silver riyal circulated side by side in the Kingdom, there emerged a bimetallic monetary standard. The bimetallic nature of the money system, like all such systems, had inherent instability. There is, for example, the problem connected with exchange rate between the two currencies, since both were full-bodied currencies and therefore their values would be subjected to prevailing prices of gold and silver. Indeed, after the establishment of the bimetallic system, supply-and-demand conditions for gold and silver changed, giving rise to increases in the price of silver relative to the price of gold. This made the silver riyal undervalued at the original exchange rate of 10 riyals to one gold sovereign. The incentive which this situation created for hoarding of silver coins (and melting them for resale at a higher value than the exchange rate of a riyal) resulted in the disappearance of the silver riyal. The government took an immediate measure by recalling the silver coins in order to prevent Gresham's Law from operating to an extent injurious to the economy.[8] It must be stressed that the changes in market conditions of silver and gold might have been caused by speculators and smugglers, perhaps after an initial external influence.

In any case, the 1927 silver riyal was replaced in 1936 by another silver riyal of a smaller size and weight. The 1936 silver riyal was of equal weight and fineness to the Indian rupee. It must be noted that this new measure only removed the tacit relationship between the silver riyal and the British gold sovereign. But exchange rate between the two coins still existed, although it was now determined by the free market and not by any official declaration. Therefore, automatic adjustment of the exchange rate between the gold sovereign and the silver riyal in accordance with the market conditions in gold and silver markets, took the burden of exchange-rate adjustment off the shoulders of the government. But to the extent that a bimetallic system still existed in the Kingdom, the problem of stability of exchange rate was not removed. What was stopped was the tendency for the riyal or the gold sovereign to vanish completely from circulation owing to changes in the relative prices of gold and silver.[9]

It will be realized that the 1936 monetary reform did nothing about the full-bodied nature of the coins which circulated in the Kingdom of Saudi Arabia. Several problems are posed by the existence of full-bodied currencies. The most obvious are those connected with the making of payments for transactions involving large amounts of money. These problems arise because of the bulkiness of the coins used in the transactions. As Young has observed, 'the riyal is a heavy coin in relation to value. For any sizeable transaction there have been problems of carrying large weights of metal and counting numbers of coins.'[10] Consequently, even at that stage of monetary development there was sufficient case for fiduciary issue, despite the fact that paper money would not have been acceptable at that moment. But the confidence which people had in the silver riyal was based on its 100 per cent metal content. It is unlikely, therefore, that if the weight were anything less than equivalent silver metal which a riyal could buy, the coin could have had the general acceptability which it enjoyed at that time. Indeed, the additional fiduciary coins which existed side by side with the silver riyal and gold sovereign, even as late as in 1952, were very small and had very narrow circulation.

With respect to banking, it is essentially a modern addition to the financial system which already existed in the Kingdom. There is certainly a positive correlation between the development of money and banking development. Until money was widely used in the Kingdom, money changers were sufficient banking institutions, although the only banking function they performed was, as their name implies, converting foreign currencies into Saudi currencies, and vice versa. Of course traditional credit institutions – money lenders – also existed.

The first bank in the Kingdom was the one established by the Netherlands Trading Society in 1926, and as oil revenues augmented the use of money, other indigenous and foreign banks were established after World War II. Banking in developing countries has traditionally been closely related to foreign trade. This is evidenced in the case of Saudi Arabia by the fact that the business of the banks established in this period (and indeed in the post-1952 period) was dominated by short-term credits to importers and activities generated by pilgrims.

(2) Development of Money and Banking in the 1952-60 Period

Until October 1952, when Saudi Arabia issued her own gold sovereign, the country had a bimetallic currency system: the British gold sovereign and the Saudi Arabian silver riyal. The latter was more convenient for smaller transactions owing to the problems of weight discussed above. On the other hand, gold coins were very convenient for large transactions since the value-weight ratio was relatively very high. In addition, there were some minor coins which contained fiduciary elements as noted above.

Some of the defects of the bimetallic system which existed in 1952 have been discussed already. In addition, the inability of the government to carry out any monetary policies was a defect of the monetary system as a whole, not necessarily of the bimetallic character of it. The government also had no mechanism to handle foreign exchange and domestic fiscal transactions. In other words, Saudi Arabia 'lacked a central bank or other authority specially charged with regulating the currency and performing fiscal agency functions.'[11] Motivated by the need to improve the financial and banking system of the Kingdom, the government invited a financial mission headed by Arthur N. Young to study the financial problems of the Kingdom and make recommendations for reforming the financial and banking system.

Before we go into the monetary reform which followed the report of this financial mission from the United States, however, it would be instructive to examine some of the special characteristics of the Saudi population and the country as a whole which invariably would tend to influence any plan for a monetary reform.

Young lists seven of these characteristics.[12] In the first place, the long history of full-bodied monies has created not only an attachment to currencies with 'intrinsic' full-metal content, but also a distrust for fiduciary currency, especially paper money. Secondly, and consequently, any monetary reform should necessarily adopt a gradualistic approach towards the process of creating the fiduciary element in the money supply. This accounts for the fact that the 1952 charter establishing SAMA contained a clause prohibiting the monetary agency from issuing paper currency.[13] The full-bodied nature of the currencies also tended to create incentive for hoarding and dishoarding whenever conditions necessitated such behaviour. Thirdly, the credit structure of the economy was rudimentary. Contractual obligations were few and tended to impede the process of monetization. A fourth characteristic was the lack of uniformity of a currency/monetary system across regions of the country, owing to the disparity in development among regions. Consequently, monetary control in the country could not be undertaken on purely aggregate level, but mainly at regional levels. On the other hand, this presupposes the availability of a central financial authority with adequate manpower resources to regionalize its activities. Fifth, the country depended on oil for both revenues and foreign exchange. This has two implications: (1) the possibility of establishing a strong monetary system backed by sufficient foreign reserves, and (2) the tendency for the monetary system to be tied to the balance of payments of the country. Lastly, there is the characteristic already referred to above: the lack of a central authority to manage the monetary system and serve as the government's fiscal agent.

Before the financial mission arrived in Saudi Arabia to study the financial system, the government had already placed an order for Saudi gold sovereigns. But apart from the issue of this local gold coin and its circulation side by side with the British gold sovereign and the silver riyal, there were several alternative currency systems which could be established or which could be recommended to the Saudi government at the beginning of 1952. For example, a single currency system like silver standard or gold standard or even sterling standard was a possibility. However, Young is of the opinion that the system in which two gold currencies (the British sovereign and the Saudi gold coin) co-existed with silver coins was the most appropriate monetary system at the time considering the attitude of the people of Saudi Arabia and the government. The introduction of the Saudi Arabian gold sovereign was considered only as a step towards a modernized monetary system.

Therefore, upon the recommendation of the financial mission, on 20 April 1952, a Royal Decree sanctioned the Charter of the Saudi Arabian Monetary Agency, and in October 1952 SAMA issued the Saudi gold sovereign. The main provisions of the charter are examined later.

The issue of Saudi gold coins and the establishment of SAMA could not remove the defect of the bimetallic system, as is evidenced by events which followed the 1952 monetary reform. An attempt to correct the instability of the exchange rate between the silver and gold coins resulting from unstable silver and gold market conditions, only created new problems of counterfeiting. The Saudi gold sovereign was of the same size and weight and fineness as the British gold sovereign. The similarity between the Saudi and British gold coins was intended to enable the local gold coin to acquire the same general acceptability and confidence which the British gold coin enjoyed, and since the latter coin was no longer being minted, the Saudi gold sovereign was meant to replace the British gold coin. In order to remove the instability which existed in the exchange rate between the silver and gold coins, the riyal-sovereign ratio was fixed at 40:1. Also attempt was made to fix the external value of the gold sovereign: a sovereign exchanged for $11.00 with the responsibility of maintaining this exchange rate in the hand of SAMA.

The Saudi Arabian gold sovereign was essentially a token coin, backed 100 per cent by gold and foreign exchange. The token nature of the coin, although it prevented hoarding, created counterfeiting problems necessitating the withdrawal of the gold coin less than two years after it was issued. With most of the British coins gone into hoards, the silver riyal became the principal currency in circulation until October 1955, when owing to a big rise in the international price of silver, silver coins began to be hoarded and the riyal was withdrawn from circulation, to be replaced with pilgrim receipts. It is not clear to what extent pilgrim receipts were the principal monetary asset in the Kingdom after October 1955 until 1960, when Saudi Arabian currency notes were issued, since both Saudi silver and gold had been withdrawn from circulation, leaving only the British sovereign coins and some minor fiduciary monetary units like the quirks. Yet the pilgrim receipts were technically only receipts and not a currency, although they served as an appropriate introduction to notes issue. It would appear that although the Saudi gold and silver coins were withdrawn from circulation in the mid-1950s, they continued to circulate until the currency notes were issued, and the coins were officially demonetized in the Kingdom in 1960. This perhaps explains why, although the pilgrim receipts were not currency, these were able to perform monetary functions until notes were issued by SAMA.

In 1960, the exchange rate of the riyal was fixed at SR 4.50 per US dollar, after the successful stabilization programme undertaken during 1958-60 which helped to restore equilibrium in the internal monetary arrangements. The monetary development in the 1950s is summarized beautifully by Ali and Hitti: 'The transition from a silver standard to a fully convertible paper currency through bimetallism, exchange control, and floating exchange rate thus took place in less than a decade – a remarkable acceleration of monetary evolution.'[14]

(3) The Period of Paper Currency – The Post-1960 Era

Although foreign paper currencies circulated in the Arabian Peninsula in the pre-1960 period, it was not until the Charter of SAMA was amended in 1960 to permit the issue of note currency that paper money became generally a characteristic of the monetary system of the Kingdom. It must be remembered, of course, that pilgrim receipts had already tested the attitude of the people towards paper currency.

This period consists of attempts by SAMA to strengthen its control over the monetary system and to establish a statistical base for the economy. It also witnessed extensive credit and monetary expansion. But at the same time it demonstrated the resistance which traditional beliefs could provide to monetization efforts in a country like Saudi Arabia. The post-1960 period is the modern era in the study of money and banking in Saudi Arabia.

The Saudi Arabian Monetary/Banking System

The structure of the Saudi Arabian financial system is summarized in Figure 9.1. At the apex of the financial structure is SAMA, which is the central monetary/banking authority. Below SAMA are the commercial banks, development financial institutions, and non-banking (or non-monetary) financial institutions, such as insurance companies.

This section analyses the modern development of these financial institutions and their roles in the economic development of Saudi Arabia.

SAMA – The Central Bank

Since its inception in 1952 SAMA has come a long way to acquiring the characteristics of a full-fledged central bank. It will be recalled from the previous section that the Charter which established this monetary agency specifically prevented it, among other things, from performing two traditional functions of a central bank, namely, issuing of currency notes, and making loans to the government.[15] In a broader context, currency-related functions and fiscal-agency functions of SAMA were unnecessarily impaired.

At present, SAMA is a 'semi-autonomous government corporation

Figure 9.1: The Structure of the Saudi Financial System

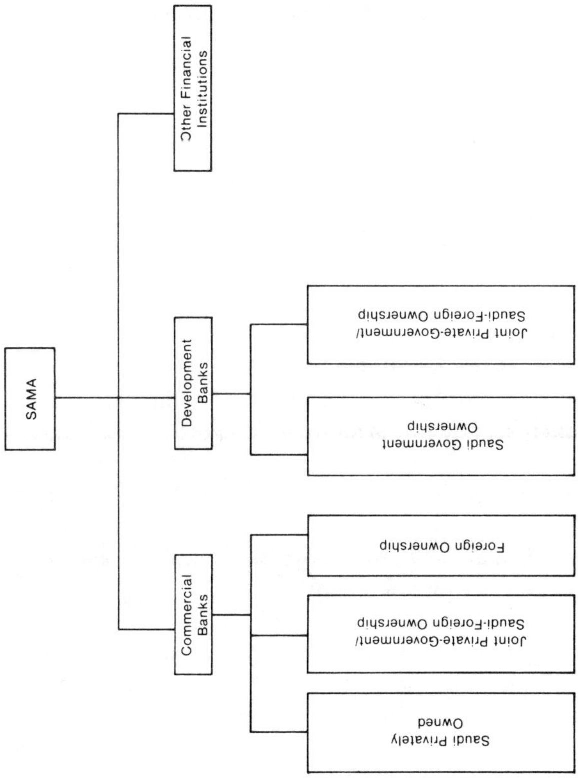

related to the Ministry of Finance'.[16] Its functions can be broken down into the following categories:

(1) Regulation of the money supply
(2) Stabilization of the external value of the riyal
(3) Supervision of banking activities and the financial system
(4) Serving as government banker
(5) Management of foreign reserves
(6) Promotion of economic development
(7) Undertaking financial and economic research

Functions (1) and (2) relate to currency affairs. The Charter of 1952 spelled out the details of these functions by providing that the following detailed functions be performed by SAMA:[17]

(a) To stabilize and maintain the external and internal value of the currency.
(b) To hold and operate any monetary reserve funds as separate funds earmarked for monetary purposes only.
(c) To buy and sell for Government account gold and silver coin bullion.
(d) To advise the Government about new coinage and handle the manufacture, shipment and issue of all coins; it being understood that coins would be issued only through and at the request of the Agency.
(e) To regulate commercial banks, exchange dealers and money changers as may be found appropriate.

The objectives of the functions were to realize the goal of creating a monetary agency which could 'strengthen the currency of Saudi Arabia and . . . stabilize it in relation to foreign currencies . . .'[18] The defect of the Charter in prohibiting the issue of notes was corrected in December 1959, when a Currency Statute amended the 1952 Charter to allow the Agency to issue paper money.[19] The paper money was fully backed by gold and currencies convertible into gold.[20] Consequently, fiduciary-note issue was not provided for either in the Charter or in the 1959 amendment. Indeed, as can be inferred from the prohibition clause, Article 7(c) makes fiduciary issue illegal. However, between 1952 and 1959 a fiduciary element might have emerged in the coin issue. The 1956-8 financial crisis necessitated an amendment to enable the government to borrow from the Agency.[21] Perhaps the full backing of the notes provision of the 1959 amendment was motivated by the successful implementation of the stabilization programme and the confidence in the ability of oil revenues to ensure a persistent and continuous large inflow of foreign exchange. As it turned out later, and perhaps as an understatement, the confidence in oil was well founded.

The fiscal-agency functions of SAMA concerned the centralization of government revenue in the Agency and the making of payments on behalf of the government from central account with the Agency. Consequently, SAMA was authorized to:[22]

(1) receive and act as depositary for all revenues including receipts from concessionaire companies, from customs, from the Haj, and from other sources, and to maintain deposit accounts under such heads as the Government through the Minister of Finance may direct;
(2) act as agent for the Government in paying out funds for purposes duly approved by the Government through the Minister of Finance.

As has been indicated earlier, the clause of the Charter prohibiting the Agency from advancing money to the Saudi government prevented it from performing the full function of a central bank as banker to the government. This also reduces the efficiency of any monetary policy, since government bonds usually constitute the bulk of credit instruments in developing economies, and since fiscal and monetary policies are almost always intertwined.[23] The relationship between the government and the Agency as envisaged in the Charter was similar to that between a commercial bank and its customers, where the customers cannot take advantage of any overdraft or loan facilities with their bank. The existence of surplus funds of the Saudi government and the country as a whole has created a situation in which the riyal is currently backed by more than 100 per cent reserves (gold and convertible currencies), and therefore, the need for fiduciary element is eliminated. The 1959 amendment demonstrates that whenever the need for fiduciary issue arises (i.e. the need to buy government bonds to finance budget deficits), quick measures would be taken in the form of amendments to rectify the situation. It must, however, be noted that such a need is presently far away in the future.

The function of SAMA as supervisor of the banking system and as regulator of the money supply presupposes that the Agency has the capability to perform those functions. In the area of regulating the banking system, it was cautious, and progress was relatively slow. One reason was that the Agency did not have sufficient qualified personnel to carry out that function. But also, the Agency was reluctant to interfere with the banking system for justifiable reasons. It is normal for a new financial authority which finds itself superimposed upon an existing foreign-dominated banking structure to shy away from its duties of regulating the activities of the institutions comprising the system. For one thing, the authority might feel inferior in banking matters.

There are two possible solutions to this inferiority complex which might be exhibited by a new central banking authority. First, the government might recruit internationally and locally recognized bankers and financial experts to man the authority, at least during the teething period. This was done in the case of SAMA. An American, Mr George A. Blowers, who was with the IMF and was also a former Governor of the Central Bank of Ethiopia, was invited to become the first governor of SAMA, with Rasem Bey Khalidi, an experienced Saudi manager of Arab Bank, as his assistant.[24] The other option is to appoint whatever qualified people are available and allow the authority to develop self-confidence gradually through a 'learning-by-doing' approach. In either case, it takes some time for it to effectively control the activities of the commercial banks and other financial institutions, and therefore initiate any meaningful monetary policies. Even with respect to the first option, the foreign management of the central financial authority will necessarily need time to learn the peculiar characteristics of the Saudi economy and its financial system before venturing into any 'fight' with the experienced members of the system.

SAMA, however, began to implement the provisions of its Charter on the banking regulations surprisingly early. In October 1952 all commercial banks were required to register with the Agency and to submit monthly reports. And in 1955 the Agency began to process foreign banks' applications to open new branches, although the final approval rested with the Ministry of Finance.[25]

After the stabilization programme was completed in 1960, SAMA broadened the scope of its activities, especially with respect to monetary and banking control. The details of banking regulations which tended to widen the regulatory function of the Agency will be analysed from the point of view of commercial banking in the Kingdom later.

Regulation of the banking and monetary system could obviously influence economic development in a positive manner if done properly. However, given that SAMA could neither directly give credits to the private sector nor invest in business ventures, the only other avenue open to it was the regulation of the lending activities of both commercial banks and development banks. Most of the latter were established by the government upon the recommendations of SAMA or upon the provisions of development plans, in the drawing up of which SAMA played no small role. The role of the Agency in this area of development promotion will be further discussed later.

With respect to management of the external resources of the Kingdom and maintaining the external value of the riyal, SAMA is the financial authority responsible for those functions. The test of SAMA's ability to stabilize the external value of the riyal came during the financial crisis of the mid-1950s when increased government borrowing from the financial authority caused the free-market rate of the riyal to depreciate considerably and become unstable. The establishment of a dual exchange-rate system by SAMA, together with other measures in the stabilization package (such as tighter control over government spending) succeeded in eliminating the public debt and stabilized the value of the riyal at SR 4.50 to US $1, a rate representing a *de facto* official devaluation of 20 per cent when compared to the original exchange rate before the crisis of SR 3.75 to $1.00. The Currency Statute (Royal Decree 6) authorized SAMA to invest foreign-exchange reserves of the Kingdom 'in foreign securities in accordance with banking practice of central banks'.[26] This was the first indication that the financial authority had been exempted from the Islamic religious requirement that banks in or belonging to Saudi Arabia should not charge interest. Decree No. 10 amended the Charter to allow SAMA to maintain a stable exchange rate of the riyal by operating in the open foreign-exchange market.

This discussion cannot conclude without recognizing the role which SAMA has played since its inception in the area of data collection. The economic and financial analysis and information contained in the *Annual Reports* and *Statistical Summaries* published by the Agency's Research and Statistics Department are ample evidence of the serious manner in which SAMA has carried out its function in this area. It would therefore appear that Article 6 of the Charter, which provides for the establishment of 'a Research Department to collect and analyse data needed to aid the government and the Agency in formulating and carrying out financial and economic policies'[27] has been adhered to by SAMA, in spite of manpower shortages. On the other hand, as the need for planning and for rapid development through the formulation of effective development strategies and policies has increased over time (and is likely to increase further in the future), the need for an efficient statistical base and sound economic and financial analysis has become even more imperative, and with it the role of the Research and Statistics Department has increased significantly, and will increase at an even faster rate in the future. In this endeavour, co-operation between this Department and the Government Statistics Department is inevitable and must be pursued to avoid duplication, especially since manpower bottlenecks in the area of data collection and analysis are very acute.

Commercial Banking

'The period following the establishment of SAMA was characterized by an expansion of commercial banking through the further establishment of both local banks and branches of foreign banks'.[28] From the single bank of the Netherlands Trading Society at Jeddah in the twenties, commercial banks in Saudi Arabia have grown to 12, with 72 permanent offices and branches in 1974.[29] It is believed that the establishment of SAMA in 1952 opened a new era in the country's banking development,[30] and augmented the growth of commercial banking in Saudi Arabia. Before the enactment of the 1952 Charter, there were only 'six foreign banks and a number of local banks and money changers in the country'.[31] Since then the number of foreign banks has grown to nine.[32]

Commercial banking practice in Saudi Arabia has been influenced by both foreign banking practices and local religious conditions. Given that the activities of traditional money changers cannot for one moment be regarded as banking business, then the commercial banking in the Kingdom was historically controlled by foreign interests. The first break with foreign domination came in 1938 when the National Commercial Bank owned by Saudi nationals was established. Another such development had to wait until 1957 when the Riyadh Bank Ltd was established. The foreign banks in the Arabian Peninsula, especially the British banks, operated according to the norms and practices of banking in the metropolitan countries. But these norms and practices may not be consistent with the interests of the domestic economy. Also, the foreign banks (and also the local banks following in the foreign banks' footsteps) have tended to concentrate on short-term commercial loans. There is no doubt that such a credit structure of commercial banks will tend to underemphasize productive sectors of the economy, the development of which will determine the success or failure of the government's diversification programmes. It must be noted that the application of foreign banking practices necessarily gives rise to this type of credit structure, since farmers and small businessmen in the manufacturing sector will invariably not have the collateral securities often demanded in, for example, the British financial market. Perhaps the banks regarded long-term loans as too risky from the point of view of rational banking, and would instead give out loans on a short-term basis to trading firms which would be able to pay back quickly after the imported goods which were financed by the banks had been sold. No wonder, even at the present time, that the 'banking market is very competitive on the lending side, with each bank seeking blue chip customers to whom to lend'.[33] It is, consequently, difficult for newcomers, small businesses, and people on low incomes to obtain loans from the commercial banks. For these reasons SAMA has created several special banks whose activities are essentially geared towards serving special groups of people and investors, either in the area of housing or other type of construction, agriculture, manufacturing, or for purely social/religious purposes.[34]

Growth of banking business in Saudi Arabia has for a long time been influenced by Quoranic teachings. The most important is the prohibition of interest payments or receiving interests (i.e. usury). This might have contributed to the sluggishness of the development of indigenous banks in the Kingdom. However, banks in Saudi Arabia have by-passed this rule by charging and paying 'commissions' instead of interests. Commissions charged for services may vary from 7 to 8.5 per cent, while commissions paid on savings accounts and time deposits range between 3.5 and 5 per cent.[35]

Aside from interest prohibition and some foreign banking practices which have inhibited the expansion of banks and credits in general in the Kingdom, there has been a conscious strategy by the monetary authority to control and regulate the activities of commercial banks. For example, there have been attempts to control the number of foreign commercial banks in the country, the regional distribution of branches of commercial banks, and the general operation of the commercial banks, in order to influence the composition of their loans and to control the total credit and thus liquidity in the Kingdom.

An important banking development from the point of view of SAMA's effectiveness in regulating the banking system is the enactment of the Banking Control Law of 1966, which had the purpose of strengthening SAMA's powers. Also it was hoped the law would encourage foreign banks to open new branches in the country. However, in the 1970s SAMA adopted a policy which has tended to prevent the creation of new banks or the opening of new ones, although recently there are indications that it intends to 'soften up' on the question of commercial-banking expansion.[36]

In any case, the Decree of 11 June 1966 gave the legal framework within which commercial banks have been operating in Saudi Arabia. The banking regulations as contained in the Banking Control Law of

1966 can be discussed under several headings. The first concerns licensing and the corporate nature of the commercial banks. The commercial banks are divided into national banks on the one hand, which are banks with head offices in Saudi Arabia, and foreign banks on the other, which have branches only in Saudi Arabia, with the parent company in a foreign country. National banks are to be licensed by the Ministry of Finance and National Economy. But the establishment of foreign banks is controlled by requiring certain conditions to be met. Also, a foreign bank cannot have deposit liabilities in excess of 15 per cent of its invested capital in its Saudi Arabian operation. This requirement serves to limit the activities of foreign banks, and it encourages such banks to have headquarters in Saudi Arabia; it should be noted also that the requirement coincides with the government's recent Saudization of banking programmes. From the point of view of monetary policy (i.e. control of liquidity in the Kingdom), this regulation permits the monetary authority to be more effective (or less ineffective) in controlling the credit-creation activities of commercial banks. This is further reinforced by the requirement that the deposit liabilities of any bank should not exceed 15 times the reserves and paid-up invested capital.[37] In the event of a violation of this regulation, the bank concerned is required to correct the situation within a month or deposit 50 per cent of the excess with SAMA. Thus an element of flexibility which is necessary at an early stage of banking development was built into this aspect of the banking-control law.

A weapon of monetary control was given to SAMA by the requirement that all commercial banks kept a minimum liquid reserve-deposits ratio of 15 per cent. Liquid reserves were defined to include the following: cash, gold and 30-day credit instruments.[38] However, SAMA's ability to manipulate the reserve ratio for the purpose of monetary and liquidity control was inhibited by the clause that it could raise the reserve requirement to 20 per cent, if this is interpreted as the upper limit to which the Agency could raise the ratio. The objectives of the deposit-reserve plus paid-up capital ratio, and the minimum reserve requirement, were to control excess liquidity and in order to avoid inflationary pressures. In practice, Saudi commercial banks have operated at levels far below the 6.7 per cent deposits-reserve plus paid-up capital ratio. In addition to the reserve requirement, commercial banks were required not to give a single loan or credit in excess of 25 per cent of their reserves and paid-up capital, the percentage to be changed to 50 at the discretion of SAMA.[39] It would seem that the objective of this regulation was to ensure equitable distribution of loans among applicants in the country.

To ensure that banks operating in the Kingdom were solvent, the 1966 Banking Control Law was amended in 1971 to require that before a bank paid any dividend, or remitted any part of its profits abroad, its total capitalized expenditures, including any accumulated losses and preliminary expenses, should have all been paid. The Banking Control Law of 1966, in summary, sought to ensure that the banking system was efficient, stable and promoted economic growth.

Other Financial Institutions

What banking regulations in Saudi Arabia have not been able to do is to allow selective measures to be used by SAMA in order to influence the allocation of credits given by commercial banks among various uses in accordance with any investment strategy. SAMA cannot enforce any measure to ensure, for example, that commercial banks increase credits to the agricultural sector or for a particular purpose such as small advances to low-income individuals.

To the extent that the activities of commercial banks are concentrated on the foreign-trade sector of the economy, especially import financing, a feasible alternative is to create quasi-governmental financial institutions capable of filling in the gaps which have been created by commercial banks' profit motive. Since 1965, therefore, a number of such development-financing institutions have been set up by the government in co-operation with SAMA. Table 9.1 gives a list of financial institutions which have been set up by the government or in which the government of Saudi Arabia has interest. The Table also gives a quick summary of the nature of the financial institutions: capital, date of creation, purposes for which they were set up, and in some cases ownership. Because of the important role which these financial institutions are expected to play in the development process, a more detailed analysis is in order.

Agricultural Development Bank (ADB). It has already been stated that commercial banks in Saudi Arabia have, traditionally, been biased towards commerce in their lending activities. Agricultural loans have been the lowest of all loans to any sector in the economy in any year in the history of commercial banking in Saudi Arabia. As later discussion of commercial-bank credit by economic activity will show,[40] since mid-1970 there has been no year in which loans granted by commercial banks for agricultural and fishing purposes were up to 0.7 per cent of total commercial bank loans.

Table 9.1: Saudi Arabian Quasi-Governmental Financial Institutions

Name	Year of operation	Capital (SR millions)	Remarks
Agricultural Development Bank	1965	500 (1975)	Provides short, medium and long-term loans for small and large-scale, public and private agricultural projects
Public Investment Fund	1971	5,800 (1976)	Provides interest-free medium and long-term loans to public sector industrial projects, including joint-ventures
Saudi Credit Bank (or Bank for People of Small Means)	1971	45 (1975)	Grants interest-free loans in amounts of SR 5,000 or less to Saudi citizens with incomes less than SR 12,000
Saudi Industrial Development Fund	1974 (March)	500	Supports industrial development in the private sector through medium and long-term interest-free loans
Credit Fund for Contractors	1974	50	Helps Saudi contractors fill the large number of tenders by granting interest-free loans to them
Saudi Fund for Development	1974 (August)	10,000	Extends assistance to friendly developing nations
Islamic Development Bank	1975		Joint Islamic Bank with 26 member-countries. Objective to participate in joint-ventures and grant loans to member countries
Saudi International Bank	1975	191.25	Merchant Bank, London. 50% SAMA; 45% Foreign; 5% Saudi banks
Saudi Investment Bank	1976	30	Multi-national joint-venture. 36% Saudi government; 64% Saudi/foreign private banks
Real Estate Development Fund	1974	9,200 (1976)	Extends medium and long-term credits to individual Saudis towards a maximum of 70% of housing-construction costs, and 50% of cost of houses by Saudi companies

In 1965, therefore, ADB was established to advance credits to both public and private agricultural activities. With an initial capital of SR 10 million, its activities have expanded and the expansion has

Table 9.2: New Loans Granted by the Agricultural Bank by Term of Loan (SR thousands)

Fiscal year	No. of loans (1)	Total value (2) = (4) + (6)	Average value per loan (3) = (2) ÷ (1)	Short-term Value (4)	Short-term Per cent[a] (5) = (4) ÷ (2)	Medium-term Value (6)	Medium-term Per cent[a] (7) = (6) ÷ (2)
1965	714	4,390	6.1	131	3	4,259	97
1966	1,833	9,927	5.4	295	3	9,632	97
1967	3,149	13,220	4.2	1,082	8	12,100	92
1968	3,732	12,000	3.2	1,542	13	10,458	89
1969	3,674	13,863	3.8	1,675	12	12,188	88
1970	4,356	16,134	3.7	3,007	18	13,127	81
1971	4,381	16,628	3.8	2,575	15	14,052	85
1972	3,865	16,558	4.3	2,266	14	14,292	86
1973	4,477	19,593	4.4	2,916	15	16,677	85
1974	5,414	36,304	6.7	3,545	10	32,759	90
1975	16,251	145,505	8.9	7,182	5	138,324	95
1976	19,702	269,433	13.7	8,244	3	261,189	97
1977	21,377	489,838	22.9	17,288	5	472,550	95
1978	20,298	585,668	28.9	43,713	7.5	541,955	92.5

Note: a. Per cent of total value loaned in given year.
Sources: SAMA, *Statistical Summary*, 1st issue, 1978, pp. 64-5; *Annual Report, 1976*, p. 116 and *Annual Report, 1979*.

necessitated the enlargement of its capital over the years to the point that almost SR 586 million was loaned in 1978. In its first year of operation outstanding credits amounted to SR 3.8 million, and within a year it had increased to SR 13.6 million – an increase of almost SR 10 million. The rapid growth in the activities of ADB can further be illustrated by examining Table 9.2. Apart from 1968 and 1972, the value of new loans given by the Bank each year has been higher than the previous year.

A more interesting characteristic of the loans given by ADB which Table 9.2 brings out is the composition of the loans (short and medium term). During the first two years of its operation the Bank's short-term loans were only 3 per cent of total loans given in each year. The percentage rose to an all-time high of 18 per cent in 1970, but since then medium-term loans have begun to recapture more than a 90 per cent share of new loans which prevailed in the formative years of the Bank.[41] Table 9.3 summarizes the nature of the loans given by ADB by giving a breakdown by purpose. It should be pointed out that engines, pumps and accessories, well drilling and casing, livestock, and installation and labour in the past have been the principal purposes for which loans have been granted. An interesting development in the composition of new loans by the Bank has been the increased share of construction in 1977 and 1978. From 6.7 per cent in 1976, this sector increased its share to just under 17 per cent in one year as a result of government emphasis upon such projects as dam construction, land reclamation and the like. Also reflected in Table 9.3 is the larger share going to tractors and agricultural machines in recent years. The leap from 3 per cent in 1972 to approximately 17 per cent in 1976, 1977 and 1978 indicates the extent of mechanization which has taken place in the agricultural sector. The results of this programme and the impact on the development of agriculture in the economy remains to be seen.

Public Investment Fund (PIF). This Fund, also known as the General Investment Fund, was established in 1971 with an initial capital allocation of SR 350 million. By 1978 loans outstanding through this agency totalled almost SR 5,900 million. The original objective for establishing this Fund was to 'finance commercially oriented productive investments of the government, industrial credit institutions, and public corporations undertaken independently or in collaboration with the private sector.'[42] PIF, since April 1974, has been given the power to participate in newly established industrial, agricultural or commercial enterprises incorporated in the country, in addition to its original

Table 9.3: New Loans Granted by the Agricultural Bank by Purpose, 1971/2-1977/8 (SR thousands)

Purpose	1971/2 Value of loans	1971/2 % of total	1972/3 Value of loans	1972/3 % of total	1973/4 Value of loans	1973/4 % of total	1974/5 Value of loans	1974/5 % of total	1975/6 Value of loans	1975/6 % of total	1976/7 Value of loans	1976/7 % of total	1977/8 Value of loans	1977/8 % of total
Engines	3,653.0	22.1	4,048.1	20.7	6,260.6	17.3	15,461.8	10.6	23,287.2	8.6	31,027.0	6.3	49,898.1	8.5
Pumps and accessories	1,986.3	12.0	2,367.6	12.1	3,988.9	11.0	10,834.1	7.4	15,198.3	5.6	22,623.9	4.6	34,794.6	5.9
Well drilling and casing	1,811.6	10.9	1,816.1	9.3	2,293.5	6.3	5,497.6	3.8	10,235.6	3.8	34,284.8	7.0	100,139.2	17.1
Vehicles	781.3	4.7	1,150.6	5.9	3,168.6	8.7	12,237.4	8.4	46,236.5	17.2	81,394.3	16.6	26,132.6	4.5
Tractors and agricultural machines	496.0	3.0	1,461.6	7.4	5,307.2	14.6	19,910.4	13.7	47,593.6	17.7	81,049.5	16.5	99,966.3	17.1
Ploughing and levelling	401.7	2.4	362.5	1.8	554.9	1.5	3,516.4	2.4	5,255.2	2.0	9,952.8	2.0	16,010.3	2.7
Fertilizers and seeds	913.9	5.5	1,172.7	6.0	1,732.4	4.8	4,337.0	3.0	6,410.0	2.4	11,891.3	2.4	19,791.4	3.4
Livestock	1,570.4	9.5	1,853.9	9.4	3,459.2	9.5	34,097.9	23.4	60,227.8	22.4	61,894.0	12.6	19,840.2	2.4
Poultry	507.1	3.1	133.0	0.7	195.3	0.5	693.8	0.5	846.8	0.3	1,797.9	0.4	1,607.7	0.3
Fodder	812.2	4.9	758.2	3.9	1,550.8	4.3	4,218.8	2.9	9,273.6	3.4	13,022.7	2.7	45,026.0	7.7
Pipes	600.0	3.6	527.5	2.7	1,204.0	3.3	3,162.2	2.2	4,438.2	1.6	8,280.8	1.7	25,034.9	4.3
Construction	534.2	3.2	613.6	3.1	1,450.9	4.0	4,442.1	3.0	18,056.7	6.7	81,550.5	16.7	109,013.9	18.6
Installation and labour	1,312.2	7.9	1,973.8	10.1	2,112.0	5.8	22,065.3	15.2	8,623.0	3.2	2,218.7	0.5	4,983.2	0.8
Fuel	270.5	1.6	301.7	1.5	459.2	1.3	835.1	0.6	559.6	0.2	560.5	0.1	844.5	0.1
Other	907.7	5.5	1,052.5	5.4	2,566.1	7.1	4,195.4	2.9	13,191.1	4.9	48,289.7	9.9	32,585.5	5.6
Total	16,558.1	100.0	19,593.5	100.0	36,303.6	100.0	145,505.4	100.0	269,433.2	100.0	489,838.4	100.0	585,668.4	100.0

Sources: SAMA, *Statistical Summaries*, 2nd issue, 1977, p. 40, and 2nd issue, 1978, p. 66; *Annual Report, 1979*, p. 157.

functions. The Fund did not begin to operate until 1973, but since then it has sought to complement the activities of Petromin, Sabic (Saudi Basic Industries Corporation), and SAUDIA airline and has participated in the Kuwaiti-based Arab Maritime Company for Petroleum Transport and the Suez-Mediterranean Pipeline Company (SUMED).

Saudi Credit (Assistance) Bank or Bank for People of Small Means (SCB). The main objective for the creation of this Bank is to grant interest-free loans to low-income citizens. The loans granted are for specified social and economic purposes. It was created in 1971 when its Charter was approved on 9 November, although it was not inaugurated until 1 December 1973. It began operations with a capital of SR 5 million to extend loans not exceeding SR 5,000 to Saudis with low incomes. Credit disbursed has since increased to SR 101 million in 1978. The Bank's charter provides for expansion of the financial resources of the body by permitting it to accept deposits from the general public.[43] There are plans to expand the activities of SCB by opening branches in major towns of the Kingdom.

Saudi Industrial Development Fund (SIDF). The SIDF was established on 20 March 1974, with an initial capital of SR 500 million. The Fund is committed to the granting of medium and long-term loans of up to 50 per cent of total requirements of new industrial projects or for renovation, expansion and modernization of existing ones. By July 1975 the Fund had approved 20 loan applications amounting to SR 127 million. And, by the end of 1975, the value of loans outstanding was one-fifth of total loans which had been extended by all specialized credit institutions.

For the period 1976-8, SIDF ranked third in total credit disbursed (behind the Real Estate Development Fund and PIF) with a total of SR 9.2 billion. Lending increased in the three years from SR 1.7 billion in 1976 to SR 2.3 billion in 1977 and to SR 5.2 billion in 1978. Of the SR 5.2 billion disbursed in the latter year, SR 3.9 billion or 75 per cent was granted to finance the expansion of private electricity companies, while the remaining SR 1.3 billion was allocated to other private-sector industrial projects.

Real Estate Development Fund (REDF). 'To encourage the private sector to build for residential and commercial purposes, the government established the Real Estate Development Fund (Royal Decree No. M/23 dated July 1, 1974).'[44] The Fund's regulations provide that (1) medium and long-term loans be granted to Saudi nationals in low and medium-income ranges for the purpose of home construction, up to 70 per cent of costs (to Saudi companies the loan would be up to 50 per cent of costs of constructing residential houses or hotels); (2) granting of loans for municipal development, and (3) granting of loans to housing projects approved by the Committee in charge of the Fund.

In August 1974 the Council of Ministers passed a resolution converting two-sevenths of any loan granted for the above purposes by the Fund into subsidy. Also, the capital of the Fund, which was initially fixed at SR 250 million, was raised to SR 2,000 million in 1975, and loan ceilings were set for owner-occupied houses at SR 300,000 and SR 10 million for buildings and housing compounds. Government-sponsored and large private-corporation housing projects would be determined in accordance with feasibility studies. REDF's capital was again raised substantially to SR 9,200 million in July 1976.[45] During the period 1976-9, total loan disbursements of REDF were SR 24.4 billion, making it the largest grantor of loans of the specialized credit institutions in Saudi Arabia.

Credit Fund for Contractors (CDC). The purpose for establishing this Fund in 1974 was to assist Saudi contractors meet the financial requirements which the proliferation of tenders resulting from the attempt to fulfil development-plan objectives bestowed upon them. CDC, with a capital of SR 50 million, provides loans to Saudi contractors which enables them to buy specific equipment, machinery and building materials. A number of this Fund's functions recently have been taken over by other institutions, making its role less important than it previously had been.

Saudi Fund for Development (SFD). This is one of the financial institutions established by the government of Saudi Arabia in which the government participates and has orientation towards external financing. SFD was established in August 1974 in response to the appeals made by developing countries for help when the 1973 and subsequent increases in oil prices put pressures on the balance-of-payments positions and development efforts of non-oil-producing developing countries. 'The purpose of this fund is to extend development assistance to friendly developing nations'.[46] The initial capital was very high: SR 10,000 million. By 10 May 1976 it had approved 49 loans to 5 Arab, 11 African, 5 Asian countries and one Latin American country amounting to a total of SR 54.1 million.[47]

Islamic Development Bank (IDB). Another financial institution with international orientation in which the Saudi government participates is IDB, which started operation immediately after its inauguration in July 1975. The bank has 26 member countries, and two new members were expected to join.[48] The objective of the bank is to grant loans to and participate in joint-ventures in member countries which are essentially Islamic.

Saudi International Bank. As part of a long-range objective to develop harmonious economic and financial interrelationships between Saudi Arabia and advanced countries, and to gain direct experience in international financial markets for Saudi nationals, the Saudi International Bank was incorporated on 22 August 1975 as a British company. Its authorized share capital was SR 191.3 million or £25 million sterling. It is a joint private-public multinational company, with SAMA the principal shareholder. SAMA holds 50 per cent of the authorized share, two Saudi-owned commercial banks (National Commercial Bank and Riyadh Bank Limited) own 2.5 per cent each, and six international banks own the remaining 45 per cent (Morgan Guaranty Trust Company of New York with 20 per cent and Bank of Tokyo, Banque Nationale de Paris, Deutsche Bank AG, National Westminster Bank and Union Bank of Switzerland each with 5 per cent).[49]

Saudi Investment Bank (SIB)

The promulgation of the Royal Decree on 23 June 1976, establishing the Saudi Investment Bank (in Arabic 'Al-Sharika Al-Masrafiyyah Al-Saudiyah Lil Istihmar') is considered an event of vital importance to the financial system of Saudi Arabia.[50] The principal objective of this Bank is to give long and medium-term loans to businesses and individuals, especially for financing new projects. It is hoped that this financial institution will contribute significantly to the industrial and agricultural development of the country and consequently help achieve the diversification objective of the government's policies.

The Bank had an initial capital of SR 30 million. In line with the recent trend in the ownership of development-finance institutions, SIB is jointly owned by the Saudi government and local and foreign private companies. The government owns 36 per cent of the capital, 29 per cent is owned by four Saudi sponsors (National Commercial Bank, Riyadh Bank, Al-Jazirah Bank and the General Organization for Social Insurance), and the remaining 35 per cent has foreign sponsorship (Chase Manhattan Overseas Banking Corporation, Commerzbank AG of

West Germany, Industrial Bank of Japan and J. Henry Schroder Wagg and Company of the United Kingdom). It appears that the reason for low government participation in the Bank was the desire that private entrepreneurs would supply needed technical assistance; foreign sponsors particularly, it was hoped, would bring along with their capital, the expert know-how needed to achieve the objectives of the bank. If this technical know-how and expertise were no motive for the establishment of the Saudi Investment Bank, then one does not see any other reason for its establishment, to the extent that existing institutions, such as SIDF, could have served the same purpose for which SIB was established.

Saudization of Foreign Banks

Recently the government of Saudi Arabia has adopted a programme to transform branches of foreign commercial banks which operate in the country into Saudi banks with foreign participation. For a start, the National Bank of Pakistan was transformed into Al-Jazirah Bank on 18 December 1976. Saudi interests in the Bank amount to 65 per cent of the controlling capital and the National Bank of Pakistan has the remaining 35 per cent. Of the 65 per cent Saudi interests, 35 per cent of total capital is owned by the government, while 30 per cent is owned by Saudi private shareholders. Therefore, the Al-Jazirah Bank is a quasi-public institution.

The second foreign commercial bank to be Saudized is a subsidiary of Algemene Bank Nederland in Holland. A Royal Decree was promulgated in 1976 approving the establishment of Al-Bank Al-Saudi Al-Hollandi to take over the Algemene Nederland Bank branches at Jeddah, Dammam and Al-Khobar. The share capital of SR 53 million is owned by Saudi interests and Algemene Bank Nederland in the proportion of 3 to 2. Like Al-Jazirah Bank, the membership of the Board of Directors reflects the ownership composition.

Since 1976 four more banks have been Saudized. These are Al-Bank Al-Saudi Al-Britani, Al-Bank Al-Saudi Al-Franci, Saudi-Cairo Bank, and most recently, the Arab National Bank. Including the two original banks (Riyadh Bank and National Commercial Bank), there are now eight Saudi banks in the Kingdom. Negotiations are under way for Saudization of the remaining foreign banks.

It would be appropriate to mention an important event in the banking and financial development of the country: the spread of clearing houses. The first was established at Jeddah on 4 October 1967.[51] This constitutes a milestone in the development of banking in Saudi Arabia.

Later, clearing houses were created in Riyadh and Dammam. It was hoped, when established, that they would facilitate the smooth and prompt handling of the volume of cheques which have been increasing rapidly. From a modest beginning of 33,584 cheques having a total value of SR 1,018.4 million during 1967/8 financial years, the number of cheques cleared increased to 1,286,057 with a total value of SR 557,153 in 1978/9. To the extent that the use of cheques may be regarded as a measure of the extent of monetization, this development could be considered an important monetary expansion.

Monetary Analysis

The previous discussions should provide the reader with the historical and institutional background necessary for appreciating the monetary analysis which is contained in the current section. There are various ways in which to carry out monetary analysis of the Saudi Arabian economy. A rigorous approach is to use an econometric model of the monetary sector of the economy and examine the structural equations contained in this sector. The implications for forecasting and policy-analysis could then be discussed. Another approach is to analyse the growth of money supply in Saudi Arabia in relation to the growth path of important economic variables such as the GNP, the rate of interest, prices, accumulated external reserves, credits, government expenditures, etc., by the use of tables and charts.

In this section we intend to combine both approaches. On the one hand some econometric results from the work of Al-Bashir are used, and on the other, the methodology of Jakubiak and Dajani is employed in the analysis of monetary/financial behaviour in the Saudi Arabian economy in the 1960s and 1970s.[52]

The financial analysis is carried out in three parts. First, seasonality of the money supply is examined. The seasonal nature of the quantity of money in Saudi Arabia appears to indicate that in the short run, demand for money influences its supply. Money supply is thus simultaneously determined in the monetary sector together with other major economic variables. Therefore, in the short run at least, money supply cannot be said to be exogenous. It would appear that in the short run, money-creating financial institutions have behaved in a passive sort of way so far as the quantity of money in the Saudi economy is concerned.

Secondly, an analysis of determinants of money supply is undertaken within the long-run framework when annual data are used. It is this part of the monetary analysis which constitutes the bulk of this section. Also, factors affecting the demand for money will be discussed and tied in with our discussion in the concluding section of the role of money in economic development in Saudi Arabia.

Seasonal Variations in Saudi Money Supply

Figures 9.2 to 9.4 will be used to analyse variations in the quantity of money in Saudi Arabia from month to month within a set of representative Hijri years. Several features which the diagrams bring out need to be emphasized.

First, over the years the seasonality has experienced a smoothing-out process. In other words, as the economy has expanded and become more and more monetized, factors which influence short-term variations in the quantity of money have tended to give way to long-run influences, a process which might be the characteristic of a rapidly expanding economy like that of Saudi Arabia. A comparison between Figures 9.2 and 9.3 supports the contention that money supply in the Kingdom has undergone dramatic changes so far as seasonal variations are concerned.

Secondly, however, the peak period for money supply, which was in Jumad II, the downturn after that Hijri month (i.e. downturn in Rajab and/or Sha'aban), and the upturn after Sha'aban, still existed in 1964/5 and 1974/5 as they existed in 1959/60.[53]

Thirdly, there has been the tendency for the graph of money supply for each year to be above the previous year's graph, with the exception of 1960/1 when it was not until the last quarter of the Hijri year (in the month of Shawwal) that the quantity of money in the Kingdom for each month exceeded the corresponding figures for 1959/60.

Further, Figure 9.4 appears to indicate that the seasonal variation of money supply is irrespective of the definition money used. The graphs for M1 and M2 in that figure remarkably run quite parallel to each other.

It is not difficult to find reasons for the seasonal variations found in the supply of money in Saudi Arabia. The peak in Jumad II can be accounted for by the fact that Jumad II is the last month of the financial year in Saudi Arabia, and also by the closely related fact that budgets are read in Rajah, each year, which is the beginning of the new financial year. As it is often the case in developing economies, ministries attempt to spend as much as possible of their appropriations during the year, so that as small a surplus as possible is returned to the general fund. In Saudi Arabia there is an even greater pressure on the ministries

Figure 9.2: Seasonality in Money Supply (M1), 1959/60-1960/1

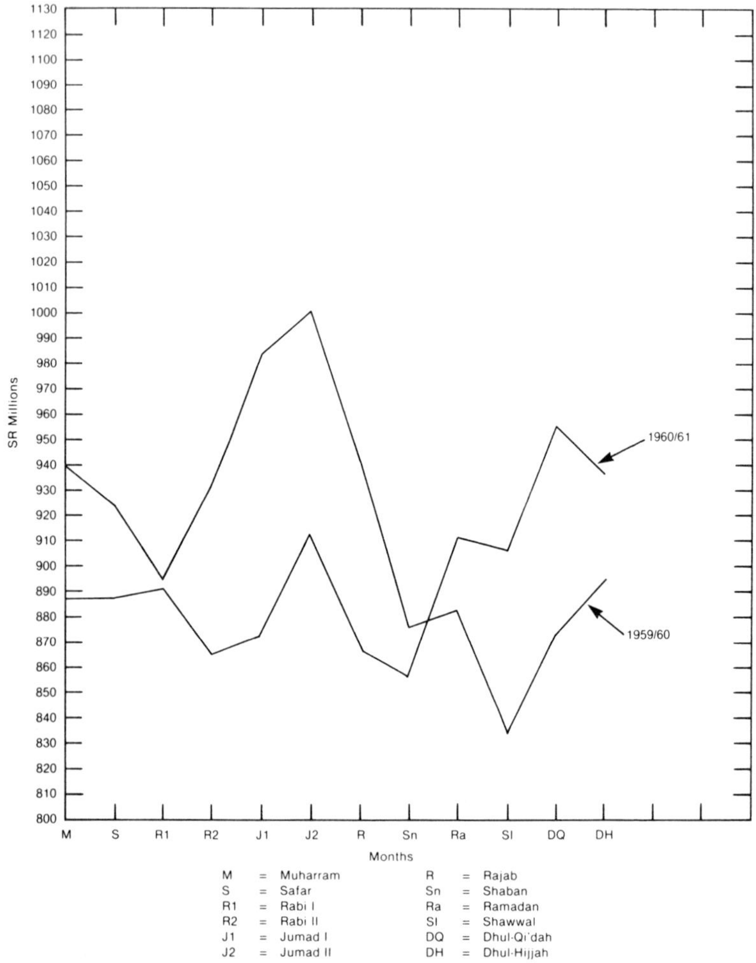

Figure 9.3: Seasonality in Money Supply (M1), 1964/5-1965/6

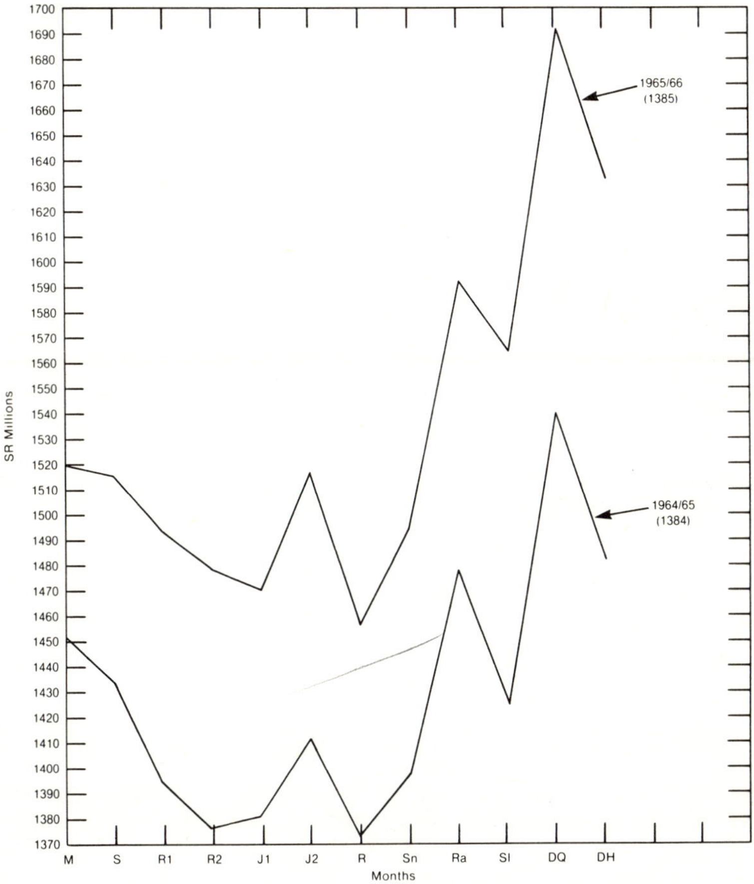

M	=	Muharram	R	=	Rajab
S	=	Safar	Sn	=	Shaban
R1	=	Rabi I	Ra	=	Ramadan
R2	=	Rabi II	Sl	=	Shawwal
J1	=	Jumad I	DQ	=	Dhul-Qi'dah
J2	=	Jumad II	DH	=	Dhul-Hijjah

Figure 9.4: Seasonality in Money Supply (M1 and M2), 1974/5

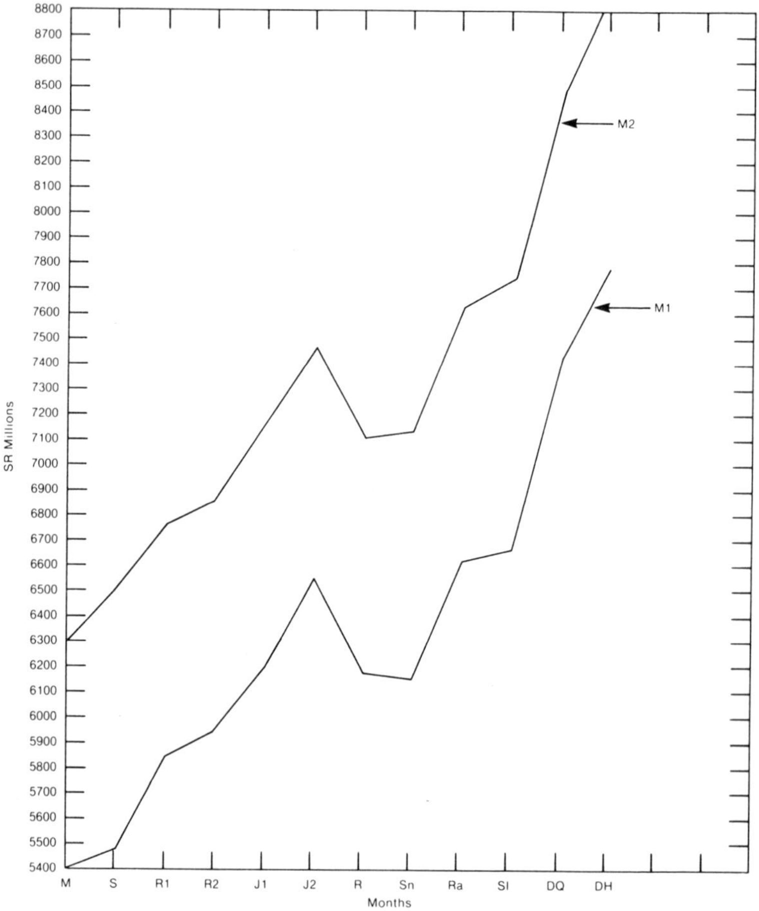

M	=	Muharram	R	=	Rajab
S	=	Safar	Sn	=	Shaban
R1	=	Rabi I	Ra	=	Ramadan
R2	=	Rabi II	Sl	=	Shawwal
J1	=	Jumad I	DQ	=	Dhul-Qi'dah
J2	=	Jumad II	DH	=	Dhul-Hijjah

to justify the estimates made during the budget of plan-preparation process. Given, therefore, that during the initial month of a fiscal year actual expenditures in a given ministry might be below a level consistent with annual budget allocation, there will be the tendency to undertake large expenditures in the last month in an attempt to 'catch up'. If one generalizes for all (or most of) the ministries and other government departments, then there would be every likelihood that government expenditures in Jumad II would be larger than any other month in the fiscal year. On the other hand, government expenditures appear to be the most important source of money supply in Saudi Arabia, as later discussions will indicate.[54] Also, the annual budget is likely to create expectations of impending wage increases in the minds of workers in government establishments. This might have a vibrating effect on other sectors of the economy, and, therefore, people might decide to hold more liquid assets or go into debt in the hope that the increased wages would permit them to retire the debt when their expectations were realized.

At the beginning of the financial year matters settle down to the level in Jumad II when government departments are under less pressure to spend. In any case, Rajab is the month for both stocktaking of the previous financial year's performance, and for preparing the ways and means for undertaking projects in the current financial year; it is a cautious month. Also the expectations of government workers, together with other households, would have died down and things would have returned to normal, except that soon the government departments begin to spend their allocations at an increasing rate, and just before and during Hijjah, liquidity goes up again.

Money Supply: Long-run Analysis

Although SAMA is the head of the monetary and financial system in Saudi Arabia, it cannot be said that it has had control, since its inception, over the quantity of money which circulates in Saudi Arabia. As later analysis will show, changes in government expenditures have been the principal determinant of money supply. To this extent, in Saudi Arabia, the distinction often made in macroeconomic textbooks between fiscal and monetary policies does not apply.[55] Indeed, apart from the financial year 1970-1, when potential budgetary deficit was financed through the imposition of income and gasoline taxes and increased import duties, increases in government expenditures have been met mainly by drawing on its reserves with SAMA.[56]

Saying that monetary and fiscal policies are one and the same thing does not, of course, imply that these policies have been consciously undertaken in Saudi Arabia. All that this means is that changes in government expenditures, whether they are due to a policy action on the part of the government or are determined by factors endogenous in the Saudi economy, have influenced the growth of money in the Kingdom.

The mechanism through which a given increase in government expenditures tends to increase money supply could be described as follows.

First, let the government at any point in time spend a given amount of money, call it G. The initial impact will be to increase the monetary base, or sometimes called high-powered money B. Let the increase in high-powered money be represented by ΔB.

The second-round effect will take place when the change in B increases money supply. It should not be assumed that even in a country like Saudi Arabia, there is a one-to-one correspondence between changes in the monetary base and money supply. The increase in B will have a multiplier effect on money supply; how big the multiplier is, however, is an empirical question. The causal relationship between changes in money supply and the monetary base can be represented by the following conventional expression:[57]

$$(1)\ \Delta M = \frac{1}{c + R - cR}\,\Delta B$$

where R is the ratio of reserves to deposits, and c is the ratio of currency to total money supply. Whereas in advanced economies, R may be a policy variable, which could be controlled by the Central Bank, this has not been the case in Saudi Arabia. It was not until 1966 that reserve ratio was specified for commercial banks and since then it has not been manipulated as a policy tool.[58] It is also our opinion that actual reserve ratio is determined by commercial banking practice in Saudi Arabia rather than by any legal requirement. In other words, as obtains in most developing countries, the minimum reserve requirement has not been an effective tool of monetary management in the Kingdom of Saudi Arabia. As Table 9.4 shows, the reserve ratios actually kept by Saudi commercial banks have been considerably in excess of the minimum legal requirement of 15 per cent.

If there is anything common to historical studies of monetary development in different countries, it is the circular-decline trend which currency-money ratio tends to follow as the economy develops and

Table 9.4: Deposits, Reserves, and Reserve Ratios of Commercial Banks, 1964-79 (SR millions)

Year	Reserves	Demand deposits (DD)	Total deposits DD + T and SD[a]	R_1[b] (%)	R_2[c] (%)
1964 Mid	157	517	783	30.4	20.1
End	199	518	853	38.4	23.3
1965 Mid	205	538	891	38.1	23.0
End	253	570	934	44.4	27.1
1966 Mid	212	619	1,042	34.3	20.3
End	246	667	1,123	36.9	21.9
1967 Mid	258	701	1,234	36.8	20.9
End	307	759	1,322	40.5	23.2
1968 Mid	317	740	1,357	42.8	23.4
End	322	804	1,469	40.1	21.9
1969 Mid	240	808	1,471	29.7	16.3
End	296	839	1,560	35.9	19.0
1970 Mid	260	812	1,609	29.6	14.9
End	321	868	1,736	40.0	18.5
1971 Mid	338	968	1,877	34.9	18.0
End	533	1,007	2,116	52.9	25.2
1972 Mid	723	1,309	2,530	55.2	28.6
End	580	1,465	2,863	39.6	20.3
1973 Mid	2,386	2,259	3,730	105.5	63.9
End	1,319	2,311	4,077	57.1	32.4
1974 Mid	2,566	3,195	5,357	80.3	47.9
End	1,959	3,711	6,340	52.8	30.9
1975 Mid	3,530	5,632	9,340	62.7	37.8
End	4,845	7,427	11,302	65.2	42.9
1976 Mid	6,038	11,012	12,584	54.8	48.0
End	7,111	13,607	15,499	52.3	45.9
1977 Mid	12,288	17,610	19,421	69.8	63.3
End	15,244	20,793	23,092	73.3	66.0
1978 Mid	18,324	27,327	30,388	67.1	60.3
End	19,334	27,764	31,897	69.6	60.6
1979 Mid	17,298	29,476	33,642	58.7	51.4

Notes: a. T and SD = time and savings deposits. b. R_1 = ratio of reserves to demand deposits. c. R_2 = ratio of reserves to total deposits.
Sources: Compiled from SAMA, *Statistical Summary*, 1st issue, 1978, pp. 38-9, *Annual Report, 1977*, p. 113 and *Annual Report, 1979*, pp. 111-12.

becomes more and more monetized. In Saudi Arabia there has been this tendency for currency-money ratio to fall since 1970, although such a circular decline cannot be observed in the 1960s. The latter could be explained by reference to the traditional orientation of the monetary system, with its built-in fear for formal methods of storing liquid wealth. However, in the 1970s, especially after the oil boom in the early years of the decade, the phenomenal expansion of cash balances created a situation in which the traditional avenues of storing liquid assets became inappropriate or too risky. Also expansion of branch-banking in the Kingdom must be given some credit for increases in bank deposits in the country.

Considering therefore, that currency-money ratio is a historical parameter which (a) can either be altered only very slowly over time, or (b) follows a well-defined path such that it cannot be regarded as a monetary policy variable, then according to expression (1) above, we are left with B as the only monetary-policy variable, to the extent that reserve ratio is also historically determined and is not influenced by SAMA's minimum requirement. However, the principal source of changes in B, high-powered money, is changes in government expenditures. Hence the assertion that monetary and fiscal policies in Saudi Arabia are identical. We can summarize the process of money-supply determination in Saudi Arabia as follows: first, government budgetary policies determine the size of high-powered money (B), then the banking habits of commercial banks and the portfolio composition of the general public determine the multiple effect which the high-powered money will have on money supply. Considering, therefore, that commercial-banking practice and portfolio composition is endogenous to the monetary system, it becomes evident that the most important aspect of long-run analysis of monetary aggregates in Saudi Arabia is the relationship between government spending and high-powered money, or (more directly) money supply.

The study by Al-Bashir[59] provides an econometric evidence on the positive relationship which exists between money supply and changes in government expenditures. The basic formulation used is

$$(2)\ M = \alpha_0 + \alpha_1 B + \alpha_2 GNP + U$$

where M is money supply defined in both the narrow and broad senses; B is monetary base, GNP is a proxy for the level of economic activity and U is an error term. Although the study experimented with lagged values for GNP as an explanatory variable, we refer to and discuss here only regression results which used current GNP as an explanatory variable. Al-Bashir obtained the following results:[60]

	R^2
$(3)\ M1 = -98.657 - 1.028B + 0.054\ GNP$	
$\qquad\qquad (0.215) \quad (0.027)$	.99
$(4)\ M2 = -341.730 + 0.605B + 0.164\ GNP$	
$\qquad\qquad (0.274) \quad (0.034)$	.99

$$(5)\ \ln M1 = -0.840 + \underset{(0.133)}{0.731} \ln B + \underset{(0.128)}{0.355} \ln GNP \qquad R^2 = .99$$

$$(6)\ \ln M2 = -2.342 + \underset{(0.133)}{0.592} \ln B + \underset{(0.128)}{0.621} \ln GNP \qquad .99$$

The above results show a positive correlation between money supply and monetary base and GNP. To the extent that monetary base is positively determined by government expenditures, the direct relationship between government expenditures and money supply is established. It must, however, be noted that in the econometric study under reference, B is supposed to capture both the effects of SAMA policies on reserves of commercial banks and changes in government expenditures. Nevertheless, since it has been earlier concluded that reserve requirements have had no effect on the lending ability of commercial banks in Saudi Arabia, it can be said that B is a good proxy for the effect of government expenditures on money supply. In terms of elasticities, the explanatory power of monetary base is also significant, as equations (5) and (6) indicate. Also note that the monetary-base elasticity of supply of M1 and M2 is positive.

The results of the study do not appear to give exclusive power to government expenditures as the determinant of money supply, since in addition to the monetary base the level of economic activity is also a significant explanatory variable in the money supply equations. However, one can find a consensus in the literature on Saudi Arabia about the impact of oil revenues, and for that matter, the impact of government expenditures on the level of economic activity. Recall from Chapter 8 that government spending is the major avenue through which oil revenue is disbursed throughout the economy of Saudi Arabia. If, therefore, the level of economic activity is positively influenced by the level of government expenditures, the dominant role of government expenditures in the money supply determination is complete.

Another approach for monetary analysis which can be adopted is the one discussed by Jakubiak and Dajani.[61] The approach involves the examination of sources of changes in money and quasi-money. The objective for discussing this alternative approach is to resolve the inconclusive atmosphere surrounding the econometric approach discussed earlier. The sources-of-monetary-changes approach, according to the joint-authors, 'identifies the rapid growth in public sector, and primarily central government net domestic expenditures . . . in Saudi Arabia as the main factor accounting for the acceleration in the rate of monetary expansion'.[62] This is so since the 'net impact' of the non-governmental sector on money supply was contractionary. Indeed, the private sector's 'balance-of-payments deficit exceeded the granting of credits to the sector'[63] for the period 1972/3 to 1974/5. But what are the empirical correlates of the following concepts used by the authors: 'central government net domestic expenditures', 'monetary impact of private sector', etc? It is in the attempt to estimate empirically these variables and utilize them in monetary analysis which make the study different from the one by Al-Bashir.

Despite the small size (three years), we do not extend the tables used by the authors to analyse factors which determine money and quasi-money in Saudi Arabia are not extended. Instead, Table 4 of that study is utilized for the purpose of our analysis.[64] Before we go into the interpretation of this table, however, let us explain the concepts referred to above. First, public-sector net domestic expenditure is defined as central-government and public-institutions spending less domestic revenues. This can roughly be approximated as total government expenditures less non-oil revenue, less foreign expenditures. The authors statistically derive it as the 'difference between net external receipts of the public sector and the increase in net public sector deposits with the banking system'.[65] Monetary impact of the private sector is: private-sector balance of payments less increase in bank claims on the private sector. This was negative for all the three financial years 1972/3-1974/5.

Table 9.5: Factors Affecting Changes in Money and Quasi-Money (US $ billions)

	1972/3	1973/4	1974/5
Changes in money and quasi-money	0.43	0.70	1.50
Government net domestic expenditures[a]	1.70	2.95	5.81
Monetary impact of private sector	–1.70	–2.11	–4.00
Bank claims on private sector (increase +)	0.03	0.39	0.62
Private sector balance of payments (deficit –)[b]	–1.10	–2.50	–4.62
Changes in net unclassified bank liabilities	–0.20	–0.14	–0.31

Notes: a. Derived as the sum of public-sector net foreign-exchange receipts, as recorded in the balance-of-payments statement and the increase in net bank claims on the public sector. b. Includes net errors and omissions of the balance-of-payments statement.
Source: H.E. Jakubiak and M.T. Dajani, 'Oil Income', p. 15, Table 4.

Table 9.5 is self-explanatory and consequently there need be only a brief analysis. Changes in money and quasi-money are derived from three main sources: net government domestic expenditures, monetary impact of private sector and net changes in other bank liabilities. The effects of the latter two on monetary changes were negative for 1972/3-1974/5. In other words, they tended to reduce the quantity of money and quasi-money in Saudi Arabia. On the other hand, government net domestic expenditures were sufficiently large to offset the negative effects of the other sources, in order to ensure expansionary effect in money supply. The dominance of net domestic expenditure of the government as a source of monetary expansion is therefore unquestionable.

A word or two on the pattern of monetary growth in the Saudi economy is in order at the concluding stage of this subsection. Monetary growth in Saudi Arabia has been phenomenal, thanks to increased government expenditures which were made possible by the removal of financial constraint on government budgetary allocations by increased oil revenues. All monetary aggregates (M1, M2, and M3) have experienced high expansion, especially since the 1973-4 oil-price increases. Tables 9.6 and 9.7 tell their own stories regarding the pattern and extent of growth in monetary aggregates in the economy. The implications of rapid increases in money and quasi-money on the economy depend on factors determining supply of goods and services and portfolio composition. Some aspects of these implications will be discussed next.

Demand for Money in Saudi Arabia

If the monetary agency has limited control over the supply of money in Saudi Arabia, it is primarily because money supply is mainly demand-determined. Reference to banking practice and the composition of liquid assets held by Saudi Arabians as determining factors of the reserve ratio and currency-money ratios, point to this situation. If that is the case, it will be interesting to find out what factors determine the demand for money in the Kingdom of Saudi Arabia. Unfortunately, this is an area where empirical studies do not exist. In lieu of such studies, we are left with deductive reasoning. A relevant question which may be asked is whether the simple Keynesian demand for money relation often used to explain the desire of people to hold cash balances as given by

(7) $Md = Md(Y, r)$

Table 9.6: Monetary Aggregates in Saudi Arabia, 1964-78[a] (monthly average)

Year	CC	DD	M1	T & SD	M2	QM	M3
1964	909.6	518.9	1,428.5	91.2	1,519.7	276.1	1,704.6
1965	985.7	549.4	1,535.1	113.8	1,648.9	346.5	1,881.6
1966	1,111.3	634.2	1,745.5	143.0	1,888.5	398.7	2,144.2
1967	1,271.3	708.0	1,979.3	208.4	2,187.7	516.0	2,495.3
1968	1,393.5	744.5	2,138.0	307.7	2,445.7	623.9	2,761.9
1969	1,491.4	805.7	2,297.1	363.0	2,680.1	686.1	2,983.2
1970	1,561.8	798.5	2,360.3	492.8	2,853.1	801.7	3,162.0
1971	1,682.2	924.5	2,606.7	638.0	3,244.7	970.1	3,576.8
1972	2,001.0	1,228.7	3,229.7	797.6	4,027.3	1,265.6	4,495.3
1973	2,540.6	1,983.1	4,523.7	846.0	5,369.7	1,530.1	6,053.8
1974	3,430.5	2,929.2	6,359.7	976.4	7,336.1	2,184.5	8,544.2
1975	5,215.5	5,341.5	10,557.0	1,542.6	12,099.6	3,450.2	14,007.2
1976	8,596.2	10,895.2	19,491.4	1,766.2	21,258.0	5,119.2	24,610.6
1977	13,395.8	17,688.0	31,083.8	2,134.2	33,218.0	6,322.8	37,406.6
1978	17,882.7	26,775.2	44,654.9	3,184.1	47,839.0	8,437.4	53,092.3

Note: a. CC = currency with non-banking public; DD = demand deposits; T & SD = time and savings deposits; QM = quasi-money; M1 = CC + DD; M2 = M1 + T & SD; M3 = M1 + QM.
Source: Computed from SAMA, *Statistical Summary, 1978*, Tables 1a to 1g.

Table 9.7: Growth of Monetary Aggregates and Government Expenditures, 1964-78[a] (percentages)

Year	CC	DD	M1	T & SD	M2	QM	M3
1964	–	–	–	–	–	–	–
1965	8.4	5.9	7.5	24.9	8.5	25.5	10.4
1966	12.7	15.4	13.7	25.7	14.5	15.1	14.0
1967	14.4	11.6	13.4	45.7	15.8	29.4	16.4
1968	9.6	5.1	8.0	47.6	11.8	20.9	10.7
1969	7.0	8.2	7.4	24.5	9.6	10.0	8.0
1970	4.7	1.7	–0.9	28.7	6.5	16.8	6.0
1971	7.7	15.8	10.4	29.5	13.7	21.0	13.1
1972	19.0	32.0	23.9	25.0	24.9	30.5	25.7
1973	27.0	61.4	40.1	6.0	33.3	20.9	34.7
1974	35.0	47.7	40.6	15.4	36.6	42.8	41.1
1975	52.1	82.7	65.0	58.0	64.9	57.9	63.9
1976	64.8	104.0	84.6	14.5	75.7	48.4	75.7
1977	55.8	62.3	59.5	20.8	56.3	23.5	52.0
1978	33.5	51.4	43.7	49.2	44.0	33.4	41.9

Note: a. CC = currency with non-banking public; DD = demand deposits; T & SD = time and savings deposits; QM = quasi-money; M1 = CC + DD; M2 = M1 + T & SD; M3 = M1 + QM.
Source: Computed from Table 9.6.

(where Md is amount of cash balances held, Y is national income, and r is the rate of interest), holds for the Saudi Arabian case. This is an important question considering that a modern money market is still a rudimentary institution in the country. Again, this is a question which could be resolved only empirically. But, despite that the inadequate data base has prevented an empirical resolution of this issue, perhaps we do not need an econometric test to be able to tell whether or not the rate of interest is an important determinant of the demand for money in an environment in which the money market is at best under-developed. Consequently, what often happens in empirical work on the monetary sector of a developing country is to ignore the rate of interest, and to specify a crude-quantity theory of money equation to describe the demand for money. This approach is appropriate if it is assumed that the rate of interest has no effect on money demand, in which case the bulk of cash balances in Saudi Arabia, for example, would be held for transaction purposes.[66] Therefore, the demand for money will depend on income. The crude-quantity theory of money thus appears to be applicable to a developing country.

A case of reference is the use of a price equation by Al-Bashir to describe 'the other side, *i.e., the demand side*, of the monety sector'[67] in Saudi Arabia. He obtained the following results from his econometric study:[68]

$$(8)\ P = 68.726 + \underset{(0.14)}{0.027\ M1} \qquad \frac{R^2}{.53}$$

where P is the wholesale price index. The above expression indicates that if money supply increases by 100 per cent, for example, the price level would go up by 2.7 per cent. This is a considerably low impact of money-supply changes on inflation in Saudi Arabia. But this is not surprising considering the proxy used for price level. Wholesale price index cannot be considered a measure of the cost of living in Saudi Arabia, or even the rate at which prices are changing in the entire economy. Two alternative indices which could be used in such a regression would be the consumer price index and non-oil GNP deflator. More will be said on inflation and money supply in the next section.

Growth of Monetary Assets, Prices, and Economic Development

Has expansion of liquidity in the Kingdom of Saudi Arabia been growth-promoting or has it inhibited growth? To answer this question precisely we need to compare the level of real economic activities as they have existed in the country, to the levels which they would have been had monetary aggregates not expanded at the rates they did in the four years between 1973 and 1977. The alternative development with and without such accelerated growth in liquidity could be obtained by breaking the span 1963-78 into two subperiods – the first to cover 1963-72 when the rate of monetary expansion was moderate, and the second subperiod to cover the post-1972 era, the period of rapid monetary expansion as previous discussions have shown. Then, the growth rates of real GNP or GDP in the two periods could be compared and inferences made as to the relationship between monetary expansion and economic development. But whether or not we find that there is a significant difference in the rate of growth of real GNP in the two subperiods, it may not be justifiable to attribute all of it to the differential monetary growth rates. For one thing, the rapid increase in monetary expansion is due to increases in oil revenue, and to the extent that the component of GNP, at current prices, originating from oil is quite large (about 57 per cent of GNP in 1978),[69] the correlation between rapid monetary expansion and rapid economic growth may not necessarily mean that the former causes the latter. Thus, unlike what some monetary economists (for example, Friedman) or econometricians (such as Sims) infer, the causality between money supply and income in Saudi Arabia may be from the latter to the former and not vice versa.[70] We must bear in mind however that this is basically a statistical problem. It is not intended to undertake any rigorous statistical proof of this conclusion. For this reason, we discuss along the following two lines: (1) the growth and composition of credits to various economic activities; and (2) the relationship between money supply and the rate of inflation in Saudi Arabia. The first will give an idea how financial resources were injected into the production sectors of the economy, and the second recognizes the negative effects which monetary expansion might have on the standard of living of the people of Saudi Arabia.

Bank Credit and Economic Activity

In an earlier part of this chapter the activities of quasi-government financial institutions which have been set up to extend credits for specific purposes, such as agriculture, construction, manufacturing, etc.,

Table 9.8: Bank Credit by Economic Activity, 1970/1-1977/8 (SR millions, figures in ( ) = annual percentage increase)

Economic activity	1970/1	1971/2	1972/3	1973/4	1974/5	1975/6	1976/7	1977/8	Average growth rate (1973/4-1977/8) (%)
Agriculture and fishing	10	10 (0)	11 (10)	20 (82)	34 (70)	38 (70)	67 (76)	93 (39)	67
Industry, manufacturing, and processing	91	112 (23)	102 (−9)	221 (117)	760 (881)	1,011 (33)	1,138 (13)	1,433 (26)	214
Mining and quarrying	38	37 (−3)	35 (−4)	24 (−31)	40 (67)	30 (−25)	36 (20)	117 (225)	51
Electricity, water, other utilities	75	83 (11)	56 (−33)	116 (107)	195 (68)	172 (−12)	224 (30)	469 (109)	160
Building and construction	249	266 (7)	302 (14)	518 (72)	1,186 (129)	1,882 (59)	2,467 (31)	2,930 (10)	62
Commerce	536	569 (6)	637 (12)	1,176 (85)	1,836 (56)	3,186 (74)	3,315 (4)	4,520 (36)	51
Transport and communications	59	27 (−54)	41 (52)	105 (156)	179 (70)	209 (17)	163 (−22)	316 (94)	63
Finance	148	121 (−18)	85 (−30)	63 (−26)	74 (17)	122 (65)	104 (−15)	225 (116)	31
Services	22	19 (−14)	37 (95)	67 (81)	84 (25)	193 (130)	203 (5)	426 (110)	70
Miscellaneous	401	375 (−6)	400 (7)	748 (87)	910 (22)	1,444 (59)	1,911 (32)	2,821 (48)	50
Subtotal	1,629	1,619 (−1)	1,706 (5)	3,058 (79)	5,298 (73)	8,287 (56)	9,628 (16)	13,350 (39)	53
Investments	65	65 (0)	115 (77)	104 (−10)	210 (102)	247 (18)	405 (64)	533 (32)	41
Total	1,694	1,684 (−1)	1,821 (8)	3,162 (74)	5,508 (74)	8,534 (55)	10,033 (18)	13,883 (38)	48

Sources: SAMA, *Annual Reports, 1977*, pp. 26, 112 and *1979*, p. 36.

were discussed. The concern now is with the composition of bank credits in Saudi Arabia; it is hoped this will prove a more practical way of analysing the effects of liquidity expansion on Saudi economic development. The analysis is based on Table 9.8, which covers the period 1970/1 to 1977/8.

Bank credits outstanding at the end of the 1971/2 financial year were below the 1970/1 level. This was caused by a decline in credits given to mining and quarrying, transport and communications, finance, services and miscellaneous. On the other hand, agriculture maintained a constant level, while industry and building construction had increased. Credit to commerce, which always has been the favourite economic activity for financial institutions, expanded the most. A striking feature in credit expansion in Saudi Arabia, as found in monetary expansion, is the rapid increase after the 1973 oil-price hikes. Between 1973/4 and 1977/8, credits rose by 58 per cent pei annum. Credits to the commerce sector, which went up by 51 per cent, made the largest contributions to the credit expansion in the five years. But this was more because of the significant weight which commerce has in total credits. The sector which had the largest increase of credit was industry and manufacturing (214 per cent), followed by services (70 per cent) and transport and communications (63 per cent). Credits to finance experienced a very low growth rate (31 per cent). The fact that credit expansion, averaged over the period 1973/4 to 1975/6, was at a more rapid pace than total-liquidity expansion (68 per cent against 60 per cent) was a healthy development. However, more recent data indicate that over the span 1973/4 to 1977/8, credit expansion declined to a 48 per cent average annual growth, which perhaps reflects the overall economic restraints placed on the Saudi economy to combat inflation during a portion of the Second Development Plan.

Money Supply and Inflation

Economic development without inflation is now a phenomenon of the past in developing countries. And in an economy in which the bulk of the income is generated from a source which constitutes an insignificant share of total economic activity in terms of employment (1.4 per cent),[71] impact is bound to be enormous, especially if it is considered that the production base in manufacturing and agriculture is very small. The crude-quantity theory of money which was discussed earlier in the chapter explains very well the cause of inflation in Saudi Arabia, except that the proxy used for the level of prices is not the appropriate one. We shall attempt to correct this here. The price index which is considered most appropriate is the cost of living index (CLI) of Saudi Arabia, although, as will be evident shortly, it also has serious shortcomings. Table 9.9 gives the cost of living index and the rate of inflation for the years 1964-78. Also, GDP deflator of the non-oil component of GDP is given in Table 9.10. The differences between these two indices is that CLI is an index of a representative basket of goods bought by urban households in the income group SR 600 to SR 899 per month. This index, therefore, covers imported consumer goods, changes in the price of which will influence CLI. On the other hand, non-oil GDP deflator is the weighted index of the value added by domestic producers other than producers of oil – this does not cover imports. The distinction between the two indices is important because the difference between them gives an indication as to the extent of imported inflation.

Table 9.9: Cost of Living Index (CLI), 1964-78[a] (1963 = 100)

	Food		Housing		Clothing		General	
	Index	RI[b]	Index	RI[b]	Index	RI[b]	Index	RI[b]
1964	103.9	3.9	103.6	3.6	102.0	2.0	102.8	2.8
1965	104.2	0.3	106.7	3.0	96.2	–5.7	103.2	0.4
1966	106.0	1.7	109.7	2.8	97.9	1.8	104.8	1.6
1967	111.4	4.8	112.1	2.2	96.2	–1.7	107.0	2.1
1968	110.0	–1.3	118.2	5.4	89.2	–6.9	108.7	1.6
1969	116.0	5.5	120.7	2.1	96.7	7.9	112.5	3.5
1970	114.6	–1.2	122.2	1.2	96.1	–0.6	112.7	0.2
1971	117.7	2.7	136.2	11.5	102.9	7.1	118.2	4.9
1972	119.7	1.7	148.5	9.0	113.2	10.0	123.2	4.2
1973	137.7	15.9	166.4	12.1	129.7	14.6	143.1	16.0
1974	163.6	18.0	231.2	38.9	146.8	13.2	173.8	21.5
1975	195.9	19.7	406.7	75.9	149.1	1.6	233.9	34.6
1976	241.0	23.0	586.3	44.2	185.0	24.1	307.7	31.6
1977[c]	292.0	21.2	599.6	2.3	202.7	9.6	342.8	11.4
1978	285.0	–2.4	562.6	–6.2	228.1	12.5	337.4	–1.6

Notes: a. The new cost of living index for urban households in the income group SR 600 to SR 899 with base year 1970 = 100 is shown in the table. However, to provide an indication of the long-term trend of prices, the provisional index numbers presented in Jumad II, 1390, for households having income of SR 600 per month (base 1963 = 100) have been linked in this table with the new cost of living index with 1970 as the base year. b. Rate of inflation (RI) is defined as $\frac{(CLI_t - CLI_{t-1})}{CLI_{t-1}} \times 100$ where CLI is the cost of living for year t and CLI_{t-1} is for the previous year. c. Six-month average.

Source: SAMA, *Statistical Summary*, 1st issue, 1978, p. 70 and 1979, p. 161.

Taking the tables individually, Table 9.9 shows that the period 1964-72 was a period of relatively stable prices. The reason for such a stability in the Saudi economy is obvious: moderate growth in money supply (see Table 9.7). On the other hand, the high level of inflation in the post-1972 era coincides with the period of high monetary expansion. From a descriptive statistics point of view, it may be stated that, whereas in the 1964-72 period annual monetary expansion of 13 per cent cushioned an average rate of inflation of 2.4 per cent, in the period 1973-8 liquidity expansion of 51.8 per cent per annum generated an annual rate of inflation of 18.9 per cent. It must be pointed out, however, that the government's deflationary policies have begun to take effect. The rate of inflation actually declined (–1.6 per cent) in 1978.[72]

In addition, there is something to say for the structuralist explanation of inflation in the case of Saudi Arabia. This can be seen in the differences in the rate of inflation for the separate components of the basket of goods which the general price index refers to. Especially, the recent phenomenal increases in the index for housing which has a weight of 25 per cent must be noted. Urban housing industry has experienced demand pressures owing to the rural-urban migration which has taken place in Saudi Arabia, and industry concentration brought about by the oil boom. Consequently, pressures on housing which generate big increases in rents, etc., have had spill-over effects on other components of the representative basket. It was a fall in rents and the prices of a number of other commodities that accounted for the decline in the CLI in 1978.

Table 9.10 confirms the inflationary impact of monetary expansion in Saudi Arabia, although the rate of inflation indicated by the non-oil GDP deflator is milder than the one described by CLI. A comparison of columns 4 and 5 in Table 9.10 brings this out. The explanation for the difference is what we have implied earlier by reference to imported inflation. It would appear that in the two years 1974/5 and 1975/6, the contribution of imports to the rate of inflation in Saudi Arabia has been substantial, having raised CLI above the non-oil GDP deflator by about 35 and 30 points, respectively for these years (based on 1969/70 constant prices).

Whereas the non-oil GDP deflator cannot tell us much about the cost of living for the average Saudi, the cost of living index, with its narrowly defined income base is not an adequate indicator of the cost of living either. In the first place, the income base of CLI is too high – SR 600 to 899 per month (or \$170 to \$255 at SR 3.52 = \$1). It excludes the basket of goods and services which many of the population buy; it indicates only the medium-income group of a single urban centre, i.e. Riyadh. Thus, CLI is not representative enough.

Table 9.10: Non-oil GDP, Deflator, and Cost of Living Index (CLI), 1969/70-1978/9[a] (prices in SR billions)

Year	Non-oil GDP Current prices	Non-oil GDP 1969/70 prices	Deflator	CLI[b] (1970 = 100)
1969/70	8.1	8.1	100.0	100.0
1970/1	8.9	8.6	103.4	104.9
1971/2	9.9	9.2	107.6	109.3
1972/3	12.5	10.6	117.9	127.0
1973/4	16.6	12.1	137.2	154.2
1974/5	23.7	13.7	173.0	207.6
1975/6	39.5	16.2	243.8	273.0
		1974/5 prices		
1974/5[c]	28.1	28.1	100.0	207.6
1975/6[c]	47.3	33.7	140.4	273.0
1976/7[c]	67.7	39.3	171.9	304.2
1977/8[d]	88.2	44.8	196.9	299.4
1978/9[d]	109.6	50.9	215.1	e

Notes: a. Saudi Arabian statistics in the 1979 publications were recomputed on a different basis from those obtaining in earlier publications. The overlap for the years 1974/5 and 1975/6 are given for comparative purposes. b. CLI based on calendar (annual) year. c. Revised; excludes import duties. d. Preliminary; excludes import duties. e. Not available.
Sources: SAMA, *Statistical Summaries*, 1st issue, 1978, pp. 71, 74-5, 76-7, and 1979, p. 162; *Annual Report, 1979*, pp. 4 and 54.

Therefore, regarding the inflationary impact of monetary expansion on the standard of living of the people of Saudi Arabia, and for that matter the effect of the oil boom on the welfare of the people, the data on prices do not give us sufficient information to be definite about any conclusions. However, since the cost-of-living index as currently calculated is more likely to be higher than it would be for a lower-income category and for rural communities (considering the behaviour of prices in the housing industry and the weight given to it in total consumption), one may tentatively at least conclude that CLI tends to overestimate the rate of inflation in Saudi Arabia. From the point of view of non-oil income, it would appear that real GDP has been increasing in Saudi Arabia consistently, as Table 9.10 indicates. Further, in the light of several government policies regarding food subsidies, outright financial grants to poor-income families, subsidized housing construction, etc., the standard of living of the average Saudi is likely to rise substantially in the future.[73]

Notes

1. SAMA, *Annual Report, 1968/69 (1388/89)*, pp. 24-5.
2. The debate over productivity and utility of money is a current monetary issue. For a sophisticated discussion of this, see Karl Brunner, 'A Survey of Selected Issues in Monetary Theory', *Review of Economics and Statistics*, March 1971, pp. 5-25; M. Friedman, *The Optimum Quantity of Money* (Chicago, Aldine, 1969); B. Pesek and T. Savings, *Money, Wealth and Economic Theory* (New York, Macmillan, 1967); D. Lavhari and D. Patinkin, 'The Role of Money in a Simple Growth Economy', *American Economic Review*, September 1968; J. Stein, 'The Optimum Quantity of Money', *Journal of Money, Credit, and Banking*, November 1970; H. Johnson, 'Inside Money Outside Money and the Wealth Effect: A Review Essay', *Journal of Money, Credit, and Banking*, February 1969.
3. Jerome Stein, 'Monetary Growth Theory in Perspective', *American Economic Review*, March 1970, pp. 85-106.
4. Karl Brunner, 'Survey of Selective Issues', p. 7.
5. Arthur N. Young, 'Saudi Arabian Currency and Finance', *Middle East Journal*, Summer and Autumn 1953, p. 361.
6. Edo, *Currency Arrangements and Banking Legislation in the Arabian Peninsula*, International Monetary Fund document DM/74/86, August 1974, p. 1.
7. A.S. Edo, *Currency Arrangements*, p. 1.
8. Gresham's Law is a process in which 'bad' money drives out 'good' money from circulation as the latter is kept by individuals.
9. From 1945 to October 1952 the exchange ration between the two coins on the market varied between 89 and 40 3/4 riyals per sovereign with the riyal value tending to appreciate against the sovereign. M.E. Edo, *Currency Regulations*, p. 3.
10. A.N. Young, 'Currency and Finance', p. 369.
11. Ibid., p. 370.
12. Ibid., pp. 369-70. We give a summary of the characteristics here and also some implications from them.
13. See the appendix to this chapter for the text of the charter.
14. Anwar Ali and Said Hitti, 'Monetary Experience of an Oil Economy', *Finance and Development*, December 1974, p. 225.
15. See appendix to this chapter, Article 7 of the Charter.
16. N.A. Shilling, *Doing Business in Saudi Arabia and the Gulf States* (New York, Intercrescent Publishing and Information Corporation, 1975), p. 349.
17. Article 4 of the Charter.
18. Article 2(a) of the Charter.
19. Royal Decree No. 6, 1959. Reference is M.E. Edo, *Currency Arrangements*, p. 32.
20. M.E. Edo, *Currency Arrangements*, p. 15.
21. J.O. Ronall, 'Banking Regulations in Saudi Arabia', *The Middle East Journal*, Summer 1967, p. 401.
22. See appendix to this chapter.
23. See, for example, the groundbreaking article by L.A. Metzler, 'Wealth, Saving and the Rate of Interest', *Journal of Political Economy*, June 1951, pp. 96-116.

24. A.N. Young, *Currency and Finance*, pp. 375-6.
25. The Minister of Finance passes upon the applications in the light of comments by SAMA. See Ronall, 'Banking Regulations', p. 400.
26. M.E. Edo, *Currency Arrangements*, p. 15.
27. See appendix to this chapter.
28. J.O. Ronall, 'Banking Regulations', p. 400.
29. R. Knauerhase, *The Saudi Arabian Economy* (New York, Praeger Publishers, 1975), p. 250. For a list of banking and other financial institutions, see N.A. Shilling, *Doing Business*, pp. 352-3 and 279-80.
30. J.O. Ronall, 'Banking Regulations', p. 402.
31. M.E. Edo, *Currency Arrangements*, p. 23.
32. That is before the Saudization policy affected the National Bank of Pakistan in 1975, SAMA, *Annual Report, 1976*, p. 29. See also N.A. Shilling, *Doing Business*, pp. 352-3 and 379-80.
33. N.A. Shilling, *Doing Business*, p. 351.
34. These special financial institutions are discussed later in this chapter.
35. N.A. Shilling, *Doing Business*, p. 351.
36. For example, R. Knauerhase, *Saudi Arabian Economy*, p. 250, has observed that in 1975 SAMA issued licences for the establishment of 12 additional branches to be open in the near future.
37. N.A. Shilling, *Doing Business*, p. 351.
38. R. Knauerhase, *Saudi Arabian Economy*, p. 253.
39. N.A. Shilling, *Doing Business*, p. 351. This regulation tended to discourage the banks from making industrial loans.
40. See Table 9.8.
41. Short and medium terms are not defined, however.
42. SAMA, *Annual Report, 1975*, p. 34.
43. Ibid., p. 33.
44. Ibid., p. 35.
45. SAMA, *Statistical Summary*, 1st issue, 1977, p. 7.
46. SAMA, *Annual Report, 1976*, p. 33.
47. Ibid.
48. SAMA, *Statistical Summary*, 1977, p. 8.
49. SAMA, *Annual Report, 1975*, p. 37.
50. SAMA, *Annual Report, 1976*, p. 32.
51. SAMA, *Annual Report, 1966/67 (1386/87)*, p. 15.
52. F.S. Al-Bashir, *A Structural Econometric Model of the Saudi Arabian Economy: 1960-1970* (New York, Wiley, 1977); H.E. Jakubiak and M.T. Dajani, 'Oil Income and Financial Policies in Iran and Saudi Arabia', *Finance and Development*, December 1976, pp. 12-15. The econometric analysis in this section is not rigorous.
53. See Figures 9.2 and 9.4.
54. For extra evidence on the significant contribution of government expenditures on money supply, see H.E. Jakubiak and M.T. Dajani, 'Oil Income'.
55. F.S. Al-Bashir, *A Structural Econometric Model*, p. 14, supports this contention. It may further be noted that several monetary economists recognize the interdependence between these policies. See, for example, W.L. Silber, 'Fiscal Policy in IS-LM Analysis: A Correction', *Journal of Money, Credit, and Banking*, November 1970, pp. 461-72.
56. Note that apart from 1955-7, budgetary deficits had not been significant enough to necessitate borrowing from the private sector of the economy.
57. See, for example, Fred R. Glahe, *Macroeconomics: Theory and Policy*, 2nd edn (New York, Harcourt, 1977), p. 149.
58. F.S. Al-Bashir, *A Structural Econometric Model*, p. 17. The reserve ratio

was fixed at 15 per cent by the 1966 Banking Regulation as discussed earlier in this chapter.

59. F.S. Al-Bashir, *A Structural Econometric Model*, pp. 14-20.

60. Ibid., pp. 17-18. The figures in parentheses are standard errors of corresponding coefficients.

61. H.E. Jakubiak and M.T. Dajani, 'Oil Income'.

62. Ibid., p. 13.

63. Ibid.

64. Ibid., p. 15. This table is referred to as Table 9.5 of this chapter.

65. Ibid., p. 13.

66. It must be noted, however, that transaction demand for money is now considered to be influenced by the rate of interest in developed economies. Vide W.J. Bamoul, 'The Transactions Demand for Cash: An Inventory Theoretic Approach', *Quarterly Journal of Economics*, November 1952, pp. 545-56, and J. Tobin, 'The Interest Elasticity of Transactions Demand for Cash', *Review of Economics and Statistics*, August 1956, pp. 241-7.

67. F.S. Al-Bashir, *A Structural Econometric Model*, p. 20. Italics added for emphasis.

68. Ibid.

69. SAMA, *Annual Report, 1979*, p. 165.

70. See M. Friedman and A.J. Schwartz, *A Monetary History of the United States, 1867-1960* (Princeton, Princeton University Press for the National Bureau of Economic Research, 1963); C.A. Sims, 'Money, Income and Causality', *American Economic Review*, September 1972, pp. 540-52; also, F.S. Al-Bashir, *A Structural Econometric Model*, p. 17, makes a similar assertion.

71. F.S. Al-Bashir, *A Structural Econometric Model*, p. 22.

72. The policies include rationalization of government spending and increases in supplies due to the removal of physical bottlenecks. See SAMA, *Statistical Summary*, 1st issue, 1978, p. 4.

73. See Chapter 8. The Third Development Plan calls for the review and elimination of many of these subsidies.

Appendix

Charter of the Saudi Arabian Monetary Agency

I Creation and Objects

(1) There is hereby created according to these regulations an institution to be called Saudi Arabian Monetary Agency, the main operating office in which it shall start its functions to be in Jeddah. It shall have branches and agencies in the places where required.

(2) The objects of the Agency shall be:

(a) To strengthen the currency of Saudi Arabia and to stabilize it in relation to foreign currencies, and to avoid the losses resulting to the Government and the people from fluctuations in the exchange value of Saudi Arabian coins whose rates have not so far been fixed in relation to foreign currencies which form the major part of the Government's income.

(b) To aid the Ministry of Finance in centralizing the receipts and expenditures of the Government in accordance with the items of the authorized budget and in controlling payments so that all branches of the Government shall abide by the budget.

II Capital

(3) The Agency shall have an authorized capital equivalent to 500,000 gold sovereigns (calculated at $12.00 and equivalent to $6,000,000). The Government shall provide the entire capital of the Agency. At least two-thirds of the capital shall be paid in prior to commencement of operations. Paid-in capital shall include the value of a building or buildings and equipment which the Government may provide.

III Operations

(4) The Agency shall have the following functions in relation to currency:

(a) To stabilize and maintain the external and internal value of the currency.

(b) To hold and operate any monetary reserve funds as separate funds earmarked for monetary purposes only.

(c) To buy and sell for Government account gold and silver coin and bullion.

(d) To advise the Government about new coinage and handle the manufacture, shipment and issue of all coins; it being understood that coins would be issued only through and at the request of the Agency.

(e) To regulate commercial banks, exchange dealers and money changers as may be found appropriate.

(5) The Agency shall aid the Ministry of Finance in centralizing the receipts and expenditures of the Government in accordance with the items of the authorized budget and in controlling payments so that all branches of the Government shall abide by the budget. To that end the Agency shall have the following functions:

(a) To receive and act as depository for all revenues including receipts from concessionaire companies, from customs, from the Haj, and from other sources, and to maintain deposit accounts under such heads as the Government through the Minister of Finance may direct.

(b) To act as agent for the Government in paying out funds for purposes duly approved by the Government through the Minister of Finance.

(6) The Agency shall establish a Research Department to collect and analyse data needed to aid the Government and the Agency in formulating and carrying out financial and economic policies.

(7) The Agency shall not charge any profits on its receipts and payments and shall not act in any manner which conflicts with the teachings of the Islamic Law. The Agency shall not undertake any of the following functions:

(a) Paying or receiving interest.

(b) Receiving private deposits.

(c) Making advances to the Government or to private parties.

(d) Engaging in trade or having an interest in any commercial, industrial or agriculture enterprise.

(e) Buying or holding fixed property except what the Agency reasonably needs for its operations.

(f) Issuing currency notes.

IV Direction and Administration

(8) The Agency shall be under the control of a Board of Directors which shall be generally responsible for its efficient administration and operation and shall have such powers as are necessary and appropriate to the end. The Board of Directors may make such rules and regulations as it may consider necessary and appropriate to the conduct of the work of the Agency in accordance with this charter. In the event that changes in this charter are found necessary, the Board of Directors shall recommend them to the Government through the Minister of Finance.

(9) The Agency in the name, 'Saudi Arabian Monetary Agency', shall be a corporation with continuing succession. The Agency is authorized to take such action as may be necessary and appropriate to give effect to this charter including, but without thereby limiting its authority, authority to make contracts, to

acquire and hold and pledge assets, and to incur such liabilities as are necessary and appropriate to the conduct of its operations.
(10) The Board of Directors shall consist of a President, a Vice-President, a Governor of the Agency, and two other members. These shall be appointed by an order of His Majesty the King upon nomination by the Minister of Finance.
(11) The Minister of Finance shall nominate the Governor of the Agency and obtain an order for his appointment from His Majesty the King. The Governor shall not be removed from office except by an order from His Majesty the King.
(12) The Agency shall render to the Government through the Minister of Finance monthly reports of its operations. The Agency shall be subject to audit by auditors appointed by the Government.

10 INTERNATIONAL TRADE

Introduction

It has become self-evident that the logical nexus among the economies of Saudi Arabia, Western industrialized countries, and the world in general is *trade*. As the world's third-largest oil producer endowed with approximately one-fourth of the world's proven oil reserves, Saudi Arabia is the world's leading exporter of crude and now commands a primary position in the international economy. The significance of that position will undoubtedly increase along with the increase in the global demand for energy resources. One cannot overstate the value of a working partnership with the Kingdom of Saudi Arabia, founded on the principles of mutual economic co-operation and benefit, nor its implications for the future. This 'special relationship' with the United States, and increasingly with Western Europe, may be applied in a broader context to both the developed and developing countries of the world. The fountainhead of this relationship may well be the development plans of Saudi Arabia, which call for extremely large expenditures. The Second Plan's $149,500 million is to be exceeded by the $235,000 million scheduled to be spent during the Third Plan. Whether or not the Saudi government will be able to spend this overwhelming amount by 1985 remains to be seen,[1] but, nevertheless, the Western industrialized nations have a significant stake in the growth and development of the Saudi economy.

International trade, predicated upon the export of oil, is the backbone of the Saudi Arabian economy. The oil sector alone accounts for about 60 per cent of the country's gross domestic product, more than 85 per cent of government revenues, and approximately 99 per cent of Saudi Arabia's foreign exchange. It is indeed 'wide-open' in terms of the role of the foreign sector in the economy. If we examine the dependence of the economy on foreign trade by the ratio of total trade/GNP, Saudi Arabia reveals figures nearly nine times greater than a closed economy such as that of the USA (see Table 10.1). (For the purpose of comparison we have included Kuwait as a similar surplus-fund economy dependent upon the foreign sector.) There are, however, problems inherent in such overdependence upon one sector of the economy, which results in an extreme dualistic pattern of development. We shall see later how the Kingdom is attempting to deal with these problems.

Table 10.1: Importance of Trade

	1969	1970	1971	1972	1973	1974	1975	1976	1977	1978
Saudi Arabia	(SR millions)									
Exports	9,086	10,302	15,189	19,862	30,012	85,862	114,461	120,284	140,321	139,544
Imports	4,851	4,990	5,205	6,303	8,272	15,293	27,257	42,863	62,699	81,856
Total trade	13,937	15,292	20,394	26,165	32,284	100,975	141,718	163,147	203,020	221,400
Gross National Product (GNP)	12,727	13,574	17,241	20,588	32,062	50,758	73,682	97,612	139,947	185,384
Trade/GNP	1.095	1.127	1.183	1.271	1.194	1.989	1.923	1.671	1.451	1.194
Kuwait	(dinars millions)									
Exports	628	706	983	1,108	1,766	2,993	2,613	2,914	2,918	–
Imports	286	273	278	266	331	519	738	1,085	1,760	-
Total trade	914	979	1,261	1,374	2,097	3,512	3,351	3,999	4,678	–
Gross National Product (GNP)	840	909	1,151	1,200	1,771	3,170	3,450	–	–	–
Trade/GNP	1.008	1.007	1.096	1.145	1.184	1.108	0.971	–	–	–
USA	($ billions)									
Exports	46.5	53.9	56.0	62.5	87.5	113.0	129.0	141.7	150.6	175.8
Imports	49.2	54.5	61.0	72.7	89.4	120.1	119.2	148.3	178.3	206.7
Total trade	95.7	108.4	117.0	135.2	176.9	233.1	248.2	290.0	328.9	382.5
Gross National Product (GNP)	935.5	982.4	1,063.4	1,171.1	1,306.6	1,412.9	1,528.8	1,702.2	1,899.5	2,127.6
Trade/GNP	0.102	0.110	0.110	0.115	0.135	0.165	0.162	0.170	0.173	0.180

Source: International Monetary Fund, *International Financial Statistics*, September 1977, pp. 220, 304, 370, and September 1980, p. 3.

Trade and Development

In spite of the capital surpluses derived from the oil sector, Saudi Arabia still faces many of the real challenges of development. International trade, the importance of which will be demonstrated in our discussion of the Saudi balance-of-payments position, theoretically enables a country to export those commodities in which it has a comparative advantage in production in exchange for goods and services produced abroad at lower costs. Saudi economic expansion induced by trade is based on interdependence and specialization, the benefits from which may be reaped by all partners involved. Given certain constraints in the case of Saudi Arabia, the greater the returns from trade, the greater are the benefits of economic growth and progress towards economic development. As was demonstrated by the figures of Table 10.1, trade plays quantitatively a major role in the Saudi economy. In addition to the static gains from trade such as foreign-exchange savings, transactions within the foreign sector will provide certain 'dynamic benefits'[2] such as capital goods, technical and managerial skills and services, and other infrastructure requirements, the fulfilment of which is indispensable to Saudi Arabian economic development. In other words, international trade is the 'engine of growth' that will inevitably provide the motive power for Saudi Arabian economic development. This chapter will be concerned with the structure and composition of trade in Saudi Arabia, as well as the direction of that trade with the rest of the world. One should keep in mind the particular gains from trade and the effect of these gains on the Saudi economy, as well as the extremely significant impact of Saudi trade on the international economy in general.

Balance of Payments

A brief listing of the Saudi Arabian balance-of-payments position is perhaps in order to further examine the role of the foreign sector in the Saudi economy (see Tables 10.2 and 10.3). An examination of these figures should be divided into two relevant time periods: the first being that period to 1970 (Table 10.2), when the major oil companies in effect controlled the oil industry; and since 1970 (Table 10.3), when the oil-producing countries asserted their control over the production and marketing of petroleum at the Teheran conference.[3]

Current-account receipts for the first period increased from SR

Table 10.2: Balance of Payments Estimates, 1963-78 (SR millions)

	1963	1964	1965	1966	1967	1968	1969	1970	1971	1972
Current account										
Receipts	5,198	5,299	6,030	7,632	7,880	8,960	9,284	10,971	17,610	18,149
Exports, f.o.b.[a]	4,923	4,864	5,576	7,132	7,263	8,276	8,546	10,107	16,647	16,809
Pilgrimage	180	239	256	266	284	324	423	459	485	686
Miscellaneous	95	126	198	234	333	360	315	405	478	654
Payments	4,460	4,608	5,589	7,038	7,475	9,509	9,819	10,688	13,605	9,533
Imports, c.i.f.	1,440	1,773	2,259	2,830	2,912	3,838	4,018	4,010	4,226	5,488
Investment income[b]	2,106	1,787	2,048	2,799	2,776	3,168	3,303	4,099	6,488	677
Travel	176	198	243	302	374	428	468	554	649	793
Govenment expenditures[c]	243	315	342	365	621	1,215	1,251	1,206	1,232	1,243
Other services[d]	495	535	697	742	792	860	779	819	1,010	1,332
Current account surplus (+) or deficit (–), (receipts less payments)	+738	+639	+441	+594	+405	–549	–535	+283	+4,005	+8,616
Capital account										
Direct investment (– indicates inflow)	–50	–63	–243	–342	–167	–81	–22	–14	–490	–1,488
Other capital (+ indicates outflow)[e]	–427	+272	+251	+663	+476	+5	–116	–199	+850	+4,156
SAMA foreign assets (+ indicates increase)	+1,066	+401	+554	+341	–124	–419	–442	+392	+3,542	+5,207
Commercial banks net foreign assets (+ indicates increase)	+149	+27	–121	–68	+220	–54	+45	+104	+103	+741

Table 10.2 (continued)

	1973	1974	1975	1976	1977	1978[g]
Current account						
Receipts	24,621	125,207	107,195	141,803	163,496	147,903
Exports, f.o.b.[a]	22,542	118,585	97,761	127,824	144,284	127,476
Pilgrimage	956	1,832	1,968	2,427	2,911	3,516
Miscellaneous	1,124	4,790	7,466	11,552	16,301	16,911
Payments	15,241	42,764	56,927	91,499	119,998	151,233
Imports, c.i.f.	7,576	13,490	24,282	43,987	60,709	82,800
Investment income[b]	1,517	17,672	7,463	11,581	14,380	14,073
Travel	1,050	1,317	2,238	3,568	4,992	7,580
Government expenditures[c]	2,991	7,468	18,988	26,556	31,831	37,596
Other services[d]	2,107	2,817	3,956	5,796	8,086	9,184
Current account surplus (+) or deficit (–), (receipts less payments)	+9,380	+82,443	+50,268	+50,315	+43,498	–3,330
Capital account						
Direct investment (– indicates inflow)	–226[f]	–2,812	–4,431	–5,698	–3,755	–4,180
Other capital (+ indicates outflow)[e]	+4,422	+41,452	+23,547	+40,518	+40,044	+11,866
SAMA foreign assets (+ indicates increase)	+5,235	+43,486	+30,685	+13,706	+2,425	+2,144
Commercial banks net foreign assets (+ indicates increase)	–51	+317	+467	+1,789	+2,784	–13,160

Notes: a. On the basis of market prices. b. Including non-monetary gold. c. Including aid granted by Saudi Arabia. d. Including Tapline expenditures abroad. e. Including errors and omissions. f. Net of participation payment to Aramco. g. Provisional.

Sources: SAMA, *Statistical Summary*, 1st issue, 1975, pp. 62-3, 1st issue, 1976, pp. 86-7, and *Annual Reports*, 1977, p. 141 and *1979*

5,198 million in 1963 to SR 10,971 million in 1970. This is a rise of 11.6 per cent per annum which may be attributed almost entirely to the 11.3 per cent per annum average rise in the value of exports over the same period. The payments side of the current account for the first period relevant to our discussion exhibited an increase from SR 4,460 million in 1963 to SR 10,688 million in 1970, i.e. a 13.7 per cent average increase per annum. This is, of course, in large part due to the 16.4 per cent average rise in the value of imports over this period. However, here is where we must look beyond the simple balance of trade. It can be seen from the balance-of-payments estimates in the two tables that the Saudi economy demonstrated a current-account surplus in all but three years over the period 1963-78, the most recent being the latter year. The current-account deficits in 1968 and 1969 are indeed significant, since they were probably a prime motivating factor behind the change in existing arrangements between the Saudi government and the oil companies a year later.[4] The current-account deficits of SR 549 million and SR 535 million for 1968 and 1969, respectively, may be largely attributed to the doubling of government expenditures abroad over those of 1967. Included under these expenditures is foreign aid granted by Saudi Arabia to other Arab states, the need for which was accelerated by the 1967 Arab-Israeli conflict.

The second period relevant to this brief historical discussion extends from 1970 to 1978. Current-account receipts for this period increased an average of 70.4 per cent per annum over the eight-year period 1970-8, while the value of exports increased an average of 71.8 per cent per annum over the same period. It should be noted that this average includes the approximately fourfold rise in the value of exports accruing from the sharp rise in oil prices in 1974, along with the 18 per cent decrease in the total value of exports in 1975 and the 12 per cent decrease in 1978. These decreases were due principally to the fall in production of the oil sector – largely a result of conservation measures on the part of the industrialized nations, and the persistent global recession in temporarily decreasing aggregate foreign demand for Saudi oil. The 1978 drop in oil exports from the Kingdom can also be attributed to a decrease in Saudi oil output brought on by technical factors and policy decisions relevant to conservation of production.

In the period 1970-3, Saudi Arabia exhibited a growth in current-account surpluses from SR 283 million to SR 9,380 million, respectively. This trend may be traced to the greater expansion of the oil sector surplus than the non-oil-sector deficits.[5] It should, however, be noted that any significant current-account surplus did not occur until

1971, when the growth rates of oil production began to accelerate relative to the modest growth of the previous decade. These production increases were, of course, integrally related to the agreements on pricing made by the Organization of the Petroleum Exporting Countries (OPEC) at the Teheran Conference the previous year.

In addition, the substantial growth in current-account surpluses for 1970-3 would have been still greater had it not been for the substantial rise in investment-income payments in the 1970s (Table 10.2). The significant amounts after 1973 can be attributed to government compensation to oil companies for participation arrangements.[6]

The rise in oil prices in 1974 resulted in current-account receipts more than four times total receipts for 1973. These additional oil revenues increased the current account of 1973 by a factor of almost nine, to SR 82,443 million, in spite of the fact that imports and non-oil payments continued to rise at increasingly rapid rates. In sum, the overwhelming rise in oil revenues has been the mainstay of the Saudi economy and the singular cause of current-account surpluses since 1970 (with the exception of 1978). At the same time, the levels of the surpluses have been affected, and will continue to be influenced to a greater degree in the future, by the increasingly rapid rise in Saudi imports. The expansion of the Saudi import market may be attributed to the government's diversification policy, present needs in response to the implementation of development plans, the increased purchasing power within the domestic economy, and the growth of the oil-sector acquisition of capital equipment for both the petroleum and petrochemical industries. This growth in import demand is reflected in the private, as well as the public sector of the economy. The structure of the overall Saudi Arabian balance-of-payments position has been summarized in a recent IMF survey:[7]

> The structure of Saudi Arabia's balance of payments reflects the typical characteristics of an oil economy, i.e., predominance of the oil sector in financial developments and a limited home production base. The net surplus of the oil sector accrues almost entirely to the public sector in the form of government oil revenues and is injected into the domestic income stream through the government's domestic expenditures. Given the free and open Saudi Arabian economy and the limited supply of domestically produced goods and services, a major part of private sector income is translated quickly into demand for foreign goods and services. Non-oil current account receipts are small, with the exception of the recent growth in

investment income on external assets, and recorded net capital movements (excluding the oil sector) have also been relatively small in recent years. (It should be noted that the total external surpluses of the public sector are reflected in increases in foreign assets of SAMA.) In this situation, the overall balance between the net surplus of the oil sector is against the net-deficit of the non-oil private sector and government direct foreign exchange expenditures which have recently increased substantially.

Table 10.3: Total Annual Oil Exports, 1970-9 (millions of barrels)

Year	Crude	Refined
1970	1,174.2	207.9
1971	1,528.2	193.9
1972	1,988.0	207.2
1973	2,557.0	212.4
1974	2,891.7	210.6
1975	2,409.4	175.3
1976	2,939.6	205.8
1977	3,142.1	188.4
1978	2,812.7	178.4
1979	3,218.5	178.4

Sources: SAMA, *Statistical Summary*, 1st issue, 1978, p. 43, and *Annual Report, 1979*, p. 20; Kingdom of Saudi Arabia, Ministry of Petroleum and Mineral Resources, Economics Department, *Petroleum Statistical Bulletin, 1979*, pp. 31-2.

The Structure of Trade

Composition of Exports

Saudi Arabian exports consist almost exclusively of crude and refined petroleum. Total crude exports increased from 1,174.2 million barrels in 1970 to 2,812.7 million barrels in 1978, while total exports of refined oil decreased from 207.9 million barrels to only 178.4 million barrels over the same period (see Table 10.3). After the 1973 OPEC price adjustment, total revenues from these exports increased by more than five times over 1973 revenues to SR 80,136 million in 1974.[8] Global economic recession and conservation measures adopted by most of the Western consumer nations effectively stifled demand for Saudi oil exports in 1975, causing a cutback in production to 2,409.4 million barrels crude and 175.3 million barrels refined, or a 17 per cent decrease over 1974 production levels. In spite of this drop in output, total oil-export revenues rose nearly 14 per cent in 1975 to SR 91,150.51 million. Crude exports began increasing again in 1975 and continued this trend throughout 1977. A drop occurred in 1978 as a result of technical factors in the Kingdom. While exports of refined petroleum have slowed down to pre-1970 levels as a result of increased domestic-consumption requirements, the Third Development Plan calls for the expansion of domestic and export refinery capacity. The increased domestic consumption is evidenced by the fourfold rise in domestic consumption/production ratios of refined petroleum products from 5.2 per cent in 1962 to 20.3 per cent in 1975.

Direction of Exports

The pattern of Saudi Arabian export relationships changed somewhat in the 1970s. While Western Europe historically has been the primary recipient of Saudi exports (i.e. oil), receiving better than one-half of total export value in the early part of the decade, this percentage dropped to 40 in 1977 and 37 in 1978. Conservation efforts in response to higher prices and the coming on stream of North Sea oil are factors in this decrease, as well as the adjustments in purchasing patterns of other major oil importers caused by the changing production situation in the region. Asian states, including those in East and Southeast Asia, have increased considerably their purchase of Saudi exports, still ranking second to Western Europe in 1977 and 1978, but a much closer second with 31 per cent and 34 per cent in those two years, respectively. Japan has been and remains the number-one importer of Saudi Arabian crude, receiving 21 per cent (of total export value) in 1970 and 20 per cent in 1978 (see Table 10.4).

The USA maintained a 3 to 5 per cent share of the Saudi export market through the decade until 1976, when it dramatically increased its market share to almost 10 per cent in 1977 and 15 per cent in 1978. The primary reason for this increase was the Saudi price level coupled with oil-export cutbacks from Iran. Significant increases in market shares have also occurred in the developing states of the Western hemisphere, such as the Bahamas, Brazil, the (Netherland) Antilles and Trinidad. These increases are reflected in the figures for the Western hemisphere as a whole.

While the USA ranked as only the tenth largest importer of Saudi petroleum in 1976 – having purchased less than 5 per cent of the total export value in that year – the loss of Iranian oil supplies and output cutbacks by several OPEC nations (as a move to shore-up prices and for conservation purposes) caused a dramatic change. Saudi Arabia is now the foremost exporter of petroleum to the USA. Some 16.4 per cent of the US total petroleum requirements, both directly and indirectly, were

Table 10.4: Direction of Exports, 1970-8 (value SR millions)

Region/Country	1970	1971	1972	1973	1974	1975	1976	1977	1978
Western hemisphere,[a] of which:	591	1,707	2,523	4,678	17,155	14,810	21,275	28,291	29,636
United States	98	590	1,129	1,625	4,417	4,031	6,377	14,575	21,771
Europe[b]	4,820	8,286	12,580	17,466	65,141	45,420	55,598	60,538	51,538
Common Market (EEC), of which:	3,333	7,437	10,422	14,308	53,528	37,645	45,592	50,625	42,894
Belgium	248	351	275	595	4,351	3,090	3,480	5,237	3,990
France	692	1,662	2,111	3,061	14,570	11,290	15,582	14,704	14,776
Germany	222	578	736	1,102	5,541	3,659	4,238	4,435	3,779
Italy	1,179	1,767	2,547	3,322	11,050	7,894	8,587	11,182	9,360
Netherlands	993	1,569	2,708	3,111	3,259	5,291	6,951	8,123	6,018
United Kingdom	828	1,510	1,846	2,651	11,755	6,271	6,618	6,491	4,678
Other European,[c] of which:	660	949	2,158	3,158	11,614	7,709	9,930	9,912	8,641
Spain	466	543	1,220	1,830	8,139	5,205	5,704	5,579	5,468
Middle East, of which:	609	806	839	1,266	4,135	3,574	4,209	5,756	4,900
Bahrain	512	646	616	770	2,804	2,249	2,548	3,370	4,900
Asia, of which:	3,339	4,414	5,532	8,219	31,973	31,135	41,074	47,162	46,947
Japan	2,323	2,783	3,444	4,940	20,135	20,483	27,097	29,080	27,881
Africa	474	759	425	586	1,157	1,154	1,246	926	853
Oceania	309	254	214	245	1,129	1,480	1,682	2,154	1,746
Others[d]	765	977	650	848	5,533	6,839	10,170	8,383	2,622
Total	10,907	17,303	22,761	33,308	126,223	104,412	135,154	153,209	138,242

Notes: a. Including Latin America. b. Including exports to Eastern Europe. c. Other Western European. d. Mainly bunker fuel exports.
Sources: SAMA, *Statistical Summaries*, 1st issue, 1973/4, pp. 60-1; 1st issue, 1975/6, pp. 84-5; 1st issue, 1978, pp. 60-1; *Annual Report, 1979*, pp. 152-3.

received from Saudi Arabia in 1976 and more than 18 per cent in 1977.[9] Furthermore, this situation is likely to continue in the near future, given the present political situation in the Middle East.

Composition of Imports

The Saudi import position reflects the dynamic processes of development which the economy is experiencing. The total value of imports rose approximately 30 times over the period 1960-78. In the span 1968-78, total imports (c.i.f.) have grown from SR 2,578 million to SR 69,180 million – a 27-fold increase (see Table 10.5). The largest increases have occurred since 1973, with successive annual growth percentages of 52.9, 41.0, 46.1, 107.0, 68.3, and 33.9 during the 1971-8 period. The sharp rise in the value of imports for these years may be attributed in part to inflationary price trends.[10] However, a large portion of the increase in the total value of Saudi imports must be attributed to the satisfaction of development requirements for the First and Second Development Plans and an increase in the marginal propensity to import in the private sector, leading to an expansion in volume of imports.[11]

The private sector has averaged over 76 per cent of the total value of imports since 1973. In 1977 and 1978, almost 22 per cent and 17 per cent, respectively, of the total import value went to the public non-oil sector. The oil sector accounted for 2.3 per cent and 5.4 per cent in the same two years. The share of the private sector climbed steadily during the Second Plan from approximately 68 per cent in 1975 to almost 78 per cent, reflecting the government's emphasis on the private sector as a force in the Kingdom's development.

With respect to the actual composition of imported goods, the leading market has been in machinery, transportation equipment, and electrical appliances. The total in this category increased from SR 846 million in 1968 to an estimated SR 28,880 million in 1978. The second-largest import category through 1978 was 'miscellaneous', rising from SR 343 million in 1968 to SR 13,142 million in 1978 largely as a result of increased imports of glassware, precious/semi-precious stones, precision instruments and sound equipment. In third place through 1978 was building materials, reflecting the Second Development Plan emphasis on construction. Foodstuffs have been a substantial import category, ranking fourth, with vegetable products, prepared items (such as beverages and tobacco) as well as dairy products being important. Chemical products have commanded the smallest share of total imports.

Table 10.5: Composition of Imports, 1972-8 (SR millions)

	1972	1973	1974	1975	1976	1977	1978
Live animal and animal products	310	441	441	642	925	1,465	2,057
Vegetable products	496	661	911	934	1,478	1,647	2,730
Animal and vegetable fats, oils and products	61	58	72	100	147	224	296
Prepared foodstuffs (beverages, vinegar, tobacco)	354	526	598	625	986	2,029	2,719
of which: sugar	80	113	151	119	148	202	217
flour	82	77	153	256	366	315	430
Mineral products	97	113	325	324	919	1,827	2,192
of which: cement	35	45	184	169	589	1,334	1,511
Products of chemical and allied industries	244	399	442	668	900	1,739	2,234
Artificial resins, plastics, cellulose esters, rubber, synthetic rubber	114	162	242	376	624	1,171	1,496
Raw hides and skins, furs and articles thereof	15	25	32	50	101	201	277
Wood and wood products (charcoal, cork, etc.)	78	146	224	372	1,535	2,138	2,058
of which: wood	75	139	209	349	505	1,998	1,845
Paper-making materials, cardboard and articles thereof	66	113	177	604	254	566	771
Textile and textile articles	344	696	955	1,291	2,170	3,496	4,178
Footwear, headgear, umbrellas, artificial flowers, articles of human hair and fans	40	51	108	77	120	242	270

Table 10.5 (continued)

	1972	1973	1974	1975	1976	1977	1978
Articles of stone, plaster, asbestos, ceramic, glass and glassware	54	76	196	189	513	1,460	3,247
Pearls, precious/semi-precious stones, precious metals, articles and imitation jewellery	67	79	89	429	1,374	1,906	1,659
Base metal and articles of base metals	477	772	1,071	1,383	3,586	7,650	9,588
Machinery, mechanical appliances, electrical equipment and parts thereof	973	1,512	1,995	2,883	7,454	13,961	19,844
Transport equipment	712	1,023	1,691	3,063	5,632	6,607	9,036
of which: cars (including buses, trucks, pickups)	366	432	1,294	2,070	3,309	5,100	5,562
Optical, photographic, measuring, precision and medical instruments, clocks, musical instruments, sound records and reproducers and parts thereof	138	230	356	516	1,139	1,714	2,653
Arms, ammunition and parts thereof	2	2	20	17	171	182	44
Miscellaneous manufactured articles	66	112	202	275	571	1,216	1,818
Works of art, collection pieces and antiques	–	–	1	5	92	221	13
Total	4,708	7,197	10,149	14,823	30,691	51,662	69,180

Source: SAMA, *Annual Report, 1979*, pp. 150-1.

Although imports of foodstuffs have been rising steadily in absolute terms, there has been a downward trend in their relative shares of total imports. This, and the tendency towards increasing imports of manufactured goods, machinery, and transport equipment, seem to indicate that imports will be primarily directed towards secondary and tertiary economic activities in response to the needs of the oil industry and the major infrastructural construction programmes for the development of utilities, highways, airports, communications networks and other facilities.

This shift in the composition of imports is exhibited very often in developing economies. As the increase in oil revenues leads to growing prosperity, the quantity of foodstuffs demanded by the economy is increasing, but at decreasing rates.[12] The relative shares of foodstuff imports to total imports has declined from 31.6 per cent in 1970 to 24.2 per cent in 1973 and to 11.3 per cent in 1978. An examination of private-sector imports paid for through commercial banks is further evidence of this shift in import composition (see Table 10.6). These figures provide a relatively close proxy to actual trends. While the share of foodstuff imports has declined from 29.7 per cent in 1970 to an estimated 15 per cent in 1978, the share of capital goods[13] has been rising at increasing rates. These trends are in line with the government's efforts to shift resources from consumption to development.

Table 10.6: Private-sector Imports Paid for Through Commercial Banks, 1974/5-1978/9 (SR millions)

	1974/5	1975/6	1976/7	1977/8	1978/9
Total foodstuffs	2,381	2,510	2,665	3,813	4,651
Total non-foods	8,606	14,017	20,103	24,187	26,440
Textiles and clothing	729	1,263	1,616	2,036	2,492
Building materials	827	1,261	2,500	2,626	3,280
Motor vehicles	1,926	3,297	4,196	4,341	4,017
Machinery and appliances	2,221	3,828	5,237	6,781	6,695
Other goods	2,903	4,368	6,554	8,403	9,956
Total	10,987	16,527	22,768	28,000	31,091

Source: SAMA, *Annual Report, 1979*, p. 46.

Sources of Imports

The major sources of Saudi Arabian imports in 1978 were Western Europe, the USA and Japan (see Table 10.7). The rapid growth of

Table 10.7: Sources of Imports, 1968-78 (value in SR millions)

	1968	1969	1970	1971	1972	1973	1974	1975	1976	1977	1978
USA	571	622	569	615	917	1,407	1,735	2,538	5,739	9,621	14,434
Europe	807	1,281	1,150	1,295	1,438	2,079	2,696	4,669	10,844	19,424	31,323
Common Market (EEC)	721	1,120	979	1,116	1,228	1,721	2,542	3,784	8,327	15,624	24,742
of which: Belgium	57	82	65	91	88	172	308	243	512	832	1,234
France	65	123	88	79	108	156	180	332	821	1,728	2,668
Germany	174	267	313	289	294	458	612	1,017	2,538	4,320	7,467
Italy	115	177	143	161	191	198	280	578	1,504	3,168	4,945
Netherlands	119	170	140	169	198	256	403	430	1,135	2,278	3,011
UK	192	301	231	328	345	466	492	1,147	1,815	3,182	5,093
Othei Western Europe,	48	108	102	102	117	198	266	768	2,189	3,430	5,607
of which: Switzerland	15	50	44	52	49	100	118	419	1,094	1,510	1,952
Eastern Europe	37	52	69	77	93	161	139	117	328	370	974
Middle East,	554	629	636	810	1,009	1,625	2,836	3,647	7,296	7,243	2,739
of which: Bahrain	30	44	47	79	92	152	238	201	640	762	156
Jordan	44	64	46	41	50	49	100	135	620	429	264
Kuwait	42	46	63	86	136	252	445	722	2,690	2,300	359
Lebanon	267	334	363	474	579	867	1,547	1,537	739	1,165	1,064
Syria	49	53	51	55	97	207	330	681	2,019	1,816	326
Asia,	463	625	611	712	1,025	1,641	2,487	3,152	5,673	10,468	17,612
of which: India	47	93	102	69	84	93	194	153	329	601	805
Japan	234	348	314	414	676	1,133	1,616	2,267	3,731	5,981	10,659
Pakistan	55	44	31	48	50	68	120	153	236	238	322
Africa,	145	152	127	152	216	225	272	321	366	451	710
of which: Somalia	106	97	87	105	141	115	110	173	166	122	304
Oceania	31	62	95	66	86	183	89	104	128	310	537
Others	8	5	10	17	17	36	34	392	536	3,868	1,341
Total	2,578	3,377	3,197	3,668	4,708	7,197	10,149	14,823	30,691	51,662	69,180

Sources: SAMA, *Statistical Summaries*, 1st issue, 1973/4, pp. 60-1; 1st issue, 1975/6, pp. 84-5; 1st issue, 1978, pp. 60-1; 1st issue, 1979,

Saudi imports that we have already examined has not been accompanied by any distinct changes in the positions of the suppliers of these imports. Nevertheless, Western Europe has dramatically increased its share from 36 per cent in 1970 to 45 per cent in 1978.

Most notable of these European nations have been West Germany, the UK, and Italy, which have ranked in that order since 1975. The USA supplied an average of just over 19 per cent of Saudi import demand between 1970 and 1978; the American share was raised to almost 21 per cent in the latter year. Behind the USA, the second-largest, single nation-supplier in the 1970s was Japan. Its share expanded from 9.8 per cent to 15.4 per cent of the Saudi import market in 1978.

Regional Middle Eastern trade accounted for slightly over 14 per cent of Saudi imports between 1970 and 1978, with Lebanon being the most regular supplier from year to year.

In Table 10.8, the balance-of-trade category of the current account of Saudi Arabia has been calculated for selected countries for which there are adequate export-import data for the period 1968-78. In 1978 West Germany and the UK were the only nations with which Saudi Arabia had a net deficit. Since 1974, when the terms of trade were most favourable to the Kingdom as a result of the massive 1973-4 oil-price hikes, various forces have been in operation relative to the balance of trade. While the tendency has been for surpluses to deteriorate with increased Saudi demand for imports in the public sector because of economic development needs, and in the private sector due to rising standards of living, the demand for oil from certain nations (such as Japan, France, and the USA) has kept the balance largely in favour of Saudi Arabia. Future increases in the price of oil exports will likely slow the rate at which Saudi Arabian surpluses dwindle.

Outlook for the Future

Since 1974 Saudi Arabia has claimed the world's second-largest position in international reserves, behind the Federal Republic of Germany. These reserves were valued at US $30 billion in 1977 (see Table 10.9), an overwhelming status in international liquidity as a result of the Kingdom's oil revenues and the consequences of its limited ability to absorb this wealth through domestic consumption and investment. Saudi reserves may be compared to $39.7 billion for West Germany and $19.4 billion for the USA in 1977. What do these surplus funds, along with Saudi requirements for economic development, portend for future trade?

Table 10.8: Net Balance of Trade with Selected Major Saudi Suppliers, 1968-78[a] (SR millions)

Country	1968	1969	1970	1971	1972	1973	1974	1975	1976	1977	1978
USA	−278	−369	−470	−26	212	218	327	1,493	638	4,954	7,337
Japan	1,740	1,873	2,009	2,369	2,768	3,808	16,796	18,216	23,366	23,099	17,222
UK	397	477	597	1,183	1,501	2,185	10,207	5,124	4,803	3,309	−415
Federal Republic of Germany	205	−25	−91	289	442	644	4,105	2,642	1,700	115	−3,688
Netherlands	414	534	853	1,400	2,510	2,855	2,835	4,861	5,816	5,845	3,007
Italy	821	763	1,036	1,606	2,356	3,124	12,331	7,316	7,083	8,014	4,415
France	317	292	604	1,583	2,004	2,904	13,672	10,958	14,761	12,976	12,108
Belgium	143	214	183	260	187	423	4,015	2,847	2,968	4,405	2,756

Note: a. A minus sign preceding a figure indicates that Saudi imports from the supplier exceeded Saudi exports to that country.
Sources: SAMA, *Statistical Summaries*, 1st issue, 1973/4, pp. 60-1; 1st issue, 1975/6, pp. 84-5; 1st issue, 1978, pp. 60-1; *Annual Report, 1979*, pp. 152-3; International Monetary Fund, *International Financial Statistics*, September 1977.

Table 10.9: International Liquidity of Saudi Arabia, 1970-8 (US $ millions)

	1970	1971	1972	1973	1974	1975	1976	1977	1978
Foreign exchange	520	1,291	2,347	3,707	13,424	21,355	24,337	27,212	16,730[a]
Reserve position in the IMF[b]	23	36	36	40	725	1,838	2,563	2,691	2,470
Gold	119	117	117	130	132	126	125	131	207
Total international reserves	662	1,444	2,500	3,877	14,285	23,319	27,025	30,034	19,407[a]

Notes: a. Plus $5,300 million foreign-exchange cover as of March 1978. b. IMF = International Monetary Fund.
Source: International Monetary Fund, *International Financial Statistics*, January 1978 and December 1979.

Various projections of Saudi Arabia's ability to absorb real goods and services have been made, based upon the growth of the Kingdom's economy.[14] This concept of absorptive capacity has been defined as 'that amount of investment or that rate of gross domestic investment expressed as a proportion of GNP that can be made at an acceptable rate of return . . .'[15] It has become evident that the future of Saudi Arabian economic development will be focused upon its ability to expand its absorptive capacity and, subsequently, the ability to import goods and services. According to a US Department of Treasury study, the major constraints upon the achievement of the Second Plan's objective of increasing imports by 30 per cent per year consisted of manpower shortages, particularly skilled and semi-skilled labour, and the inefficiency of air and sea ports.[16]

While facilities for importing to the Kingdom were inadequate during the early 1970s, substantial expansion in the Second Plan period increased port capacity to 130 berths in 1980 from the 24 in operation in 1975. As an example of this expansion effort, the Gulf port of Dammam raised its port capacity more than fourfold to 12.7 million deadweight tons in 1980.[17]

The Treasury Department study predicted a moderate rate of import growth to 1980, thereafter accelerating sharply once the major constraints were overcome, to an estimated SR 61,422 million (17.4 billion in constant 1974 dollars) by 1985.[18] It is apparent from the figures in Table 10.7, however, that this study underestimated the ability of the Saudi economy to absorb imports, for the total imports in 1978 had already exceeded the 1985 projection.

In the mid-1970s, it was estimated that the total value of imports in 1980 and 1985 would be based on the assumption that the Saudi economy was capable of sustaining a growth rate of 9 per cent in real terms to support the targeted 30 per cent annual import growth.[19] These increasing import trends, of course, depend upon the speed of implementation of planned projects. With respect to the composition of these future imports, it has been suggested that:

> Growth in import demand over the medium term will clearly be very substantial, but within this framework, the extent to which future economic development will be primarily geared to import substitution clearly implies that imports of foodstuffs (particularly processed), together with textiles and clothing and building materials, will decline in relative importance over the next decade whereas those of capital goods, intermediate products and industrial

raw materials will all increase at above average rates. Such trends will represent a continuation of those in recent years.[20]

In a 1976 study prepared for the US Department of State, Saudi import projections were based upon the absorptive capacity of the country and a 'particular oil revenue scenario'.[21] In addition to the physical constraints of population, manpower and infrastructure, other obstacles to the expansion of domestic absorptive capacity involved what at that time was seen as questionable implementation of the Second Development Plan and the various changes in policies affecting oil output and marketing. However, a somewhat more optimistic view of the effect of these factors on the future level of imports was subsequently presented:

> Lack of skilled manpower and other bottlenecks will probably hamper efficient operation and utilization of Saudi Arabia's infrastructure well into the 1980s. A more serious problem is the short-run inadequacy of infrastructure, causing delays and leading to cost overruns in construction projects for the development plans. However, these factors are not expected to prevent Saudi Arabia from experiencing a high rate of economic growth or continuing to increase imports rapidly.[22]

The results of this particular study predicted a 14.4 per cent average annual growth rate of imports until 1980, thereafter slowing down to 4.7 per cent per year through 1985. Relative shares of imports of major trading partners were expected to remain generally the same as in the past.[23] Results now available through 1978 indicate that imports increased at a 64 per cent average annual rate between 1975 and 1978 (46.1 per cent, 107 per cent, 68.3 per cent, and 33.9 per cent, respectively, for the years involved) and that the source of imports shifted slightly in the direction of Western Europe, Japan and the USA. Further, the projections of planners for the 1980-5 span are for imports to grow at a 7 per cent annual figure.

As an indicator of future imports, a study was conducted using an econometric model developed by Faisal Al-Bashir.[24] This model was employed with data presented in the CACI study pertaining to projections for the Saudi Arabian oil industry. A 10 per cent annual GDP growth rate which was the objective of the Second Development Plan was utilized, and an assumption was made that this rate of growth was reflected in a proportional rise in personal income. The results were that imports would reach SR 39,226.4 million in 1980 and SR 45,272.1 million by 1985. The estimates revealed an average annual increase of just over 29 per cent from the 1975 actual level of imports to the projected 1980 figures. This percentage compared very favourably to the stated objective of the Second Plan to increase the level of imports by 25 to 30 per cent per year.

As indicated in Table 10.8, actual imports for 1978 were SR 69,180 million, 76 per cent more than the projected figure for 1980. Moreover, imports increased at an average of 64 per cent annually between 1975 and 1978 compared to planners' estimates of less than half that rate. It is obvious that the economy was able to overcome the previously mentioned constraints and to have a considerable expansion in absorptive capacity, so that imports could increase so markedly.

With the restricted growth projections for the Third Development Plan, import growth is projected to return to its historical trend of approximately 7 per cent average annual increase. However, as import markets continue to develop in the Saudi economy, the reciprocal relationship between growth and trade will become increasingly evident. Furthermore, to the extent that surplus oil revenues exceed absorptive capacity, which we have just shown to be reflected in the level of that country's imports, Saudi Arabia's position in international reserves and foreign exchange will continue to grow. The relative size of that position will continue to determine Saudi Arabia's role as a major force in international financial markets.

Saudi Arabia and the International Economy

To achieve the fundamental objectives of economic diversification and a reduction in dependence upon the oil sector, the government of Saudi Arabia has stated that fiscal management will be guided in part by the 'fulfilment of the Kingdom's international obligation and the promotion of international cooperation and monetary stability'.[25] It is within this policy, stated in the spirit of enlightened self-interest, that we must assess the role of the Kingdom in the international economy.

The quadrupling of oil prices in 1974 effectively launched the international reserve position of this country from a moderate level of $3.9 billion to about $14.3 billion by the end of 1974 and to $30 billion in 1977 (see Table 10.9). This rise in the price of oil, of course, generated through OPEC, was to have 'serious implications for the world's balance of payments and world economic order in terms of real incomes and the international monetary system'.[26]

There are various factors involved in determining the levels of future Saudi Arabian surplus funds, the most important being:[27]

(1) volume of oil exports,
(2) government revenues per barrel,
(3) volume and price of non-oil imports,
(4) magnitude of grants and foreign aid,
(5) return on external investments.

With respect to the first two factors, it appears that these may or may not affect levels of Saudi expenditures and consequently affect the levels of surplus funds, depending upon the time frame in which we are working. In the past we have seen that expenditures have tended to follow revenues quite closely, although projected magnitudes and rates of change of government revenues and expenditures for the next decade may prove to be quite different.[28] Let us clarify this point by studying the situation brought about in 1975. For the many reasons we have stated previously, world oil consumption fell by nearly 3 per cent in 1975 over 1974 levels of consumption.[29] While Saudi export revenues subsequently fell 18 per cent due to the decline in export volume, total imports increased in value by more than 85 per cent and international reserves *also* rose by more than 63 per cent. It appears that historical experience (for example, the 1950s balance-of-payments crisis) has left a significant impact upon the government of Saudi Arabia 'to maintain high levels of foreign exchange and short-term assets to guard against adverse effects from a decline of petroleum revenues'.[30] The point to be drawn from this example is that, while the volume of exports may be a significant factor involved in determining surplus funds in the *long term*, it appears that the Kingdom has adequately insured itself against short-term dislocations by maintaining a strong position of international liquidity. While a discussion of the future demand for Saudi petroleum is clearly beyond the scope of this brief chapter, suffice it to say that we can see no reason for a significant decline in the industry until domestic reserves are depleted.[31]

The relationship between economic growth and the volume of imports, as well as the underlying concept of absorptive capacity being a determinant of the effectiveness of that relationship was, of course, mentioned in the previous section. However, the price of future Saudi imports will also affect the future levels of international reserves.

Table 10.10 displays the export price indices of the 14 industrialized countries which are also the major suppliers of goods to Saudi Arabia, as well as the export price index of Saudi Arabian oil. Following the major price increase for crude oil which occurred in 1973-4, it is apparent that the subsequent increases in the price of that commodity have not quite kept pace with the prices of those goods imported by Saudi Arabia. The export price index for the 14 major suppliers increased by 24 per cent over the three-year span (1976-8), while the price index was rising by 17 per cent for Saudi Arabian exports. Consequently, if future price trends remain at parity while Saudi demands for imports continue to rise faster than the global demand for oil, this will lead to a reduction in the Kingdom's reserve position and will also alleviate the international balance-of-payments deficit with these countries.

Table 10.10: Export Price Index, 1972-8

	(1970 = 100)				(1975 = 100)			
	1972	1973	1974	1975	1975	1976	1977	1978
14 industrial countries[a]	114	136	171	191	100	101	109	124
Saudi Arabia	131	179	637	685	100	107	115	117

Note: a. The 14 industrial countries are: USA, Canada, Japan, Austria, Belgium, Denmark, France, Germany (Federal Republic), Italy, Netherlands, Norway, Sweden, Switzerland, and UK.
Source: International Monetary Fund, *International Financial Statistics*, September 1977, p. 37, and December 1979, p. 48.

Thus, in reference to the international balance-of-payments problem with Saudi Arabia, Yoon S. Park has presented a 'dynamic-adjustment model for the world economy' in which he states that the ultimate solution to balance-of-payments adjustment is to raise the overall absorptive capacity of the oil exporters.[32] This can only be achieved through expansion of trade with Saudi Arabia and the promotion of economic development in that country.

The present and future size of grants and foreign aid will not only further utilize these surplus capital funds, but is also likely to offset the severe economic dislocations that have particularly affected the non-oil developing countries.[33] Foreign aid of all types granted by Saudi Arabia has risen from $220.9 million in 1972 to $5,664.0 million in 1975 (2.7 per cent and 13.8 per cent of GDP, respectively).[34] Saudi Arabia now claims to be the largest contributor to Third World development.[35] Included among the various financial organizations established in recent years for the purposes of extending soft loans and grants are the Saudi Development Fund, Islamic Development Bank, Arab Bank for Economic Development in Africa, Arab Investment Company, and the Arab Fund for Economic and Social Development. Other institutions to which the Kingdom has been a major contributor include the World Bank and International Monetary Fund's Oil Lending Facility, as well as the so-called 'Witteveen Fund' for financing balance-of-payments deficits. While in the past much of this aid has been only regionally distributed within the Arab world, the Saudi government now appears to be diversifying its development assistance into other areas of the world. At the 1977 Afro-Arab Summit Conference in Cairo it was announced that Saudi Arabia would contribute more than $1 billion in aid to African countries through the Arab Bank for Economic Development in Africa.

The last point in this discussion of Saudi Arabia's international reserve position concerns the nature of investible capital surpluses and the returns on those investments. Perhaps the greatest fear to rise out of the 1974 energy crisis had to do with the huge transfer of funds to Saudi Arabia, which amounted to no less than an immediate redistribution of world income from the oil importers to the oil exporters. Furthermore, what the Saudis were to do with these surplus funds would have the most serious implications for international financial institutions and the international monetary system as we know it today. Concern over these assets, which were held primarily in short-term deposits in the Eurodollar banks, nearly led to panic when a few large Eurobanks collapsed. (These failures were, however, due to reasons other than 'petrodollar' flows.) 'Recycling' of these surplus funds became a major topic of debate and various schemes were suggested to enable developing as well as developed countries to finance their balance-of-payments deficits with the OPEC nations as a whole, and particularly Saudi Arabia.

A major crisis in the international monetary system was obviously averted, perhaps due to the fiscal responsibility of the Saudi government and their firm policy commitment to stability in the international monetary system. The government of Saudi Arabia is attempting instead to invest these funds in long-term financial and capital assets as a means of ensuring the Kingdom's economic growth in the future. As oil is a non-renewable resource, Saudi Arabia is clearly making an attempt to protect its future without sacrificing the economic stability of the world. Furthermore, it is in the best interest of the Western industrialized nations to provide adequate investment outlets, as well as a favourable climate for the promotion of long-term investment by OPEC countries.

Notes

1. Refer to Chapters 5, 6 and 7 on development planning in Saudi Arabia.
2. Gottfried Haberler, 'International Trade and Economic Development', National Bank of Egypt Fiftieth Anniversary Commemorative Lectures, Cairo, 1959.
3. The Teheran Conference was held in February 1971. Refer to Abdul Amir Kubbah, *OPEC, Past and Present* (Vienna, Petro-Economic Research Centre, 1974).
4. Ramon Knauerhase, *The Saudi Arabian Economy* (New York, Praeger Publishers, 1975), p. 145.
5. International Monetary Fund (IMF), *Saudi Arabia: An Economic and Financial Survey* (Washington, DC, IMF, March 1976), p. 45.
6. For a detailed discussion of oil sector transactions, refer to Chapter 2.
7. International Monetary Fund, *Saudi Arabia: An Economic and Financial Survey*, p. 48. According to a study by Morgan Guaranty Trust Company published in *World Financial Markets*, April 1978, the current-account surplus in Saudi Arabian balance of payments was expected to decline sharply by 1980. This forecast was based upon static oil revenues evidenced by the OPEC decision in late 1977 to effectively 'freeze' prices until 1979 which, along with rising demand for imports by the Kingdom, would result in deteriorating terms of trade and, according to the Morgan Guaranty study, the current-account surplus (excluding official transfers) might approach $6.8 billion in 1979 and $4.7 billion in 1980. The rapid price escalations in 1979 and 1980 in OPEC oil threw this projection off sharply, indicating another of the pitfalls in estimation for financial developments in Saudi Arabia and, indeed, all the major oil-exporting nations.
8. It is important to note that export figures published by SAMA are based on the volume of exports reported by the oil companies and valued at posted prices, which usually exceeds the actual price paid. Thus, these reported statistics may not be an entirely accurate statement of total foreign-exchange earnings.
9. United States, Department of the Interior, Bureau of Mines, in Federal Energy Administration, *Monthly Energy Review*, January 1977 and January 1978.
10. The IMF export price indices of the major Saudi suppliers displayed an average increase of 25 per cent in 1974 and 12 per cent in 1975. International Monetary Fund, *International Financial Statistics*, September 1977.
11. SAMA, *Annual Report, 1976*, p. 36.
12. This is a practical explanation of the consumers' Engel curve. According to this curve, the quantity consumed of good X is increasing, but at a decreasing rate.

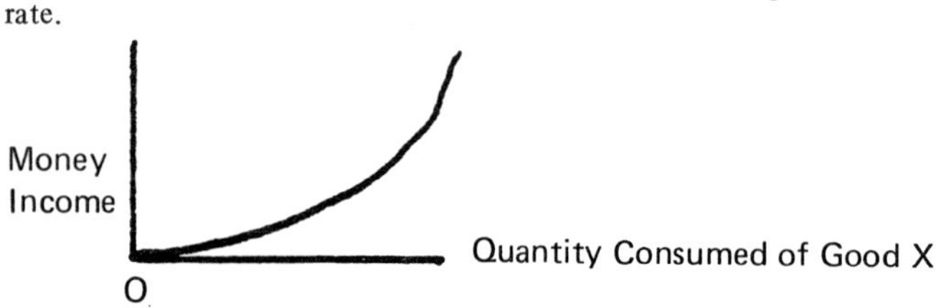

13. Capital goods for this estimate include building materials, motor vehicles, and machinery and appliances. Although some of these items may be considered consumer durables, it is, nevertheless, an indication of the shift.

14. For a detailed discussion, refer to the Appendix to this volume, 'Economic Development and Absorptive Capacity'.

15. John H. Adler, *Absorptive Capacity: The Concept and Its Determinants* (Washington, DC, The Brookings Institution, June 1965).

16. US, Department of Treasury, *The Absorptive Capacity of OPEC Countries* (Washington, DC, Government Printing Office, November 1976), p. 11. Substantial progress was made in port capacity during the Second Development Plan. Further expansion during the Third Plan should accommodate projected imports for the 1980-5 period.

17. Kingdom of Saudi Arabia, Ministry of Planning, *Third Development Plan, 1400-1405/1980-1985*, Chapter 7, section 7.2.4.4, p. 410. Port capacity and tonnage are given in deadweight tons (dwt), with 1 dwt = 1.016 metric tons.

18. US, Department of Treasury, *The Absorptive Capacity*, p. 6.

19. Henley Centre for Forecasting, *Middle East Economic Prospects: Forecasts* (London, Henley Centre for Forecasting, 1975), p. 238. In retrospect, this projected rate of growth was perhaps unrealistic, particularly as the Third Plan's projected growth rate is for about 3 per cent, *Third Development Plan, 1400-1405/1980-1985*, Chapter 1, section 1.1.1.3, pp. 18, 20.

20. Henley Centre for Forecasting, *Economic Prospects*, p. 224.

21. CACI, Inc., *Medium-Term Ability of Oil-Producing Countries to Absorb Real Goods and Services* (Arlington, Virginia, CACI, Inc., March 1976). Appendix I to this chapter has details of this scenario.

22. Ibid., vol. 2, pp. 14-31.

23. It appears from present levels of exports and recent developments in the Saudi economy that the Department of Treasury study established the most valid projections of future Saudi import levels, while the Henley Centre forecast remains significantly overestimated, and the CACI study perhaps underestimated the potential of the Kingdom to adapt to rising oil revenues, increasing domestic demand, and the ability of the Saudi people to alleviate, at best in part, existing infrastructural bottlenecks. See appendix II of this chapter for additional comments and a comparison of other projections.

24. F.S. Al-Bashir, *A Structural Econometric Model of the Saudi Arabian Economy: 1960-1970* (New York, Wiley, 1977). The process of selecting the functions and the actual data may be found in the appendices to this chapter.

25. Kingdom of Saudi Arabia, Ministry of Planning, *Second Development Plan, 1395-1400/1975-1980*, p. 88.

26. Yoon S. Park, *Oil Money and the World Economy* (Boulder, Colorado, Westview Press, 1976), p. 45.

27. Ibid.

28. Donald A. Wells, *Saudi Arabian Revenues and Expenditures* (Washington, DC, Resources for the Future, Inc., 1974).

29. The following year (1976) saw a 6.6 per cent *increase* in the level of world oil consumption.

30. Donald A. Wells, *Revenues and Expenditures*.

31. Even the most conservative estimates project free-world oil demand to rise by about 3 per cent annually in 1980-90. See US, Library of Congress. Congressional Research Service, *Project Interdependence: U.S. and World Energy Outlook Through 1990* (Washington, DC, Government Printing Office, 1977).

32. Yoon S. Park, *Oil Money*, p. 55.

33. Saudi foreign aid is detailed in the next chapter.

34. SAMA, *Annual Report, 1976*, p. 11.

35. Dr. Farouk Akhdar, 'Saudi Arabia-United States: Between Interdependence and Cooperation', address to the Conference on World Affairs, University of Colorado, Boulder, Colorado, April 1977.

Appendix I: Projections for the Saudi Arabian Oil Industry

	Production (million b/d)	Consumption (million b/d)	Exports (million b/d)	Capacity (million b/d)	Reserves (billion barrels)	Saudi Arabia ($10/ barrel)
1970	3.799 A	0.042 A	3.783 A	4.000	86.0	1.214 A
1971	4.769 A	0.047 A	4.716 A	5.100	91.0	1.885 A
1972	6.012 A	0.052 A	6.012 A	6.150	92.0	2.745 A
1973	7.610 A	0.060 E	7.550 E	7.800	97.0	4.340 A
1974	8.490 A	0.080 E	8.400 E	10.000		22.573 A
1975	7.200 E	0.100 E	7.100 E	11.500	110.0	25.676 A
1976	8.500 P	0.125 P	8.350 P	11.700	120.0	31.025 P
1977	9.500 P	0.147 P	9.350 P	11.900	117.0	34.675 P
1978	11.000 P	0.170 P	10.800 P	12.100	113.5	40.150 P
1979	12.000 P	0.200 P	11.800 P	12.300	110.3	43.800 P
1980	12.500 P	0.225 P	12.255 P	13.500	106.0	45.625 P
1981	13.000 P	0.250 P	12.745 P	13.700	101.8	47.450 P
1982	13.500 P	0.280 P	13.210 P	13.800	96.5	49.275 P
1983	13.500 P	0.310 P	13.180 P	13.900	92.0	49.275 P
1984	13.500 P	0.345 P	13.145 P	14.000	87.6	49.275 P
1985	13.500 P	0.377 P	13.110 P	14.000	82.5	49.275 P

Source: CACI, Inc., *Medium-Term Ability of Oil-Producing Countries to Absorb Real Goods and Services*, vol. 3, p. B-16.

Appendix II

Two import functions are derived in Faisal S. Al-Bashir's model in *A Structural Econometric Model of the Saudi Arabian Economy, 1960-1970*, p. 73:

	Equation	R^2
OLS	$M = -388.056 + .212\ Y_0 + .277\ Y_{P1}$	.99
	$(.122) \quad (.270)$	
2SLS	$M = -497.695 + .074\ Y_0 + .577\ Y_{P1}$	.98
	$(.152) \quad (.331)$	

where Y_{P1} = personal income in millions SR
Y_0 = gross income from oil in millions SR.

Whereas Al-Bashir advocates the use of the two-stage regression equation, we found that the OLS equation was better for forecasting, in spite of the fact that the RMSE for OLS was significantly greater than 2SLS. The OLS equation places greater emphasis on the oil sector than the two-stage equation, which is certainly borne out statistically in the Saudi Arabian economy. Consequently, the results obtained are presented in appendix III, which follows.

Appendix III[a]

T	Plan[b] $\bar{M}$ OLS	$\bar{M}$ Actual[c]	CACI[d] $\bar{M}$ OLS	CACI[e] $\bar{M}$ 'Best'	$\bar{M}$ USDT[f]	$\bar{M}$ Henley[g]
1974	19,495.0	10,149.0				
1975	22,220.8	14,823.0				
1976	26,566.2	30,691.0	26,542.6			
1977	29,671.8	51,662.0	29,620.1			
1978	34,182.3	69,179.7	34,097.3			
1979	37,365.8		37,241.6			
1980	39,226.4		39,056.1	32,168.5	26,512.5	194,425.0
1981	41,136.4		40,586.6			
1982	43,100.5		42,122.2			
1983	43,756.6		42,295.2			
1984	44,478.3		42,473.6			
1985	45,272.1		42,657.6	38,885.0	61,509.0	282,800.0

Notes: a. All values are in SR millions. b. Predicted imports using Al-Bashir's OLS import equation, projections for the Saudi Arabian oil industry listed in appendix II, and a GDP growth rate of 10 per cent per annum. F.S. Al-Bashir, *A Structural Econometric Model*. c. Actual imports for 1974-8 from SAMA, *Statistical Summaries*, 1977 and 1979. d. Predicted imports using Al-Bashir's OLS import equation, projections for the Saudi Arabian oil industry listed in appendix II, and a GDP growth rate of 9.3 per cent for 1976-80, and 3.1 per cent for 1981-5 (based on CACI, Inc., *Medium-term Ability of Oil-Producing Countries to Absorb Real Goods and Services*.) e. The 'Best' estimates from CACI, Inc., *Medium-Term Ability*. f. Estimates from US, Department of Treasury, *The Absorptive Capacity of OPEC Countries*. g. Estimates from Henley Centre for Forecasting, *Middle East Economic Prospects: Forecasts to 1985*.

11 SAUDI ARABIAN FOREIGN AID

Introduction

In the early 1970s, the world experienced economic instability which was evidenced by a 'slowdown of economic growth in the industrial countries, high prices for commodities, food and fertilizers, rising inflation and interest rates, and general uncertainty in world monetary and trade relations'.[1] The immediate effects of these problems were severely felt in the Third World. Although some of these developing nations were able to cope with these problems through increasing the prices of their export commodities such as oil, the majority were unable to adjust to the situation. Among the consequences of these problems were the inability of the developing countries to repay their debts and the slowdown of capital transfers to them. This created severe balance-of-payments liquidity crises and caused a disturbing effect on creditor-debtor relationships.

Since these developing countries were so dependent on foreign-capital transfers, their economic growth was in jeopardy. An alternative source of capital transfer was necessary to help these nations maintain a reasonable rate of growth which would help in generating returns that could be used for repayment of both new and old debts. On the other hand, the sudden rise in oil prices in the early 1970s led to an increase in revenues so dramatic that the Saudi Arabian economy was unable to utilize and invest all these funds efficiently due to its relatively low absorptive capacity.

To the above situation, the Kingdom responded with a plentitude of commitments involving substantial transfers in various forms of development aid. Before considering the amounts of aid provided by Saudi Arabia and the countries which received this aid, it may be appropriate to discuss the meaning of economic aid, the forms it takes, and the objectives behind it.

Definition and Objectives of Foreign Economic Aid

In economic literature there prevails no consensus on the meaning of foreign economic aid. Some economists confine aid only to grants which are not to be paid back.[2] The United Nations defines economic aid as 'the flow of grants and long-term loans in cash and kind'.[3] Still others have defined development aid as 'cooperation with a foreign state or autonomous political unit with the object of assisting that state or autonomous political unit in furthering its economic growth and social progress'.[4] For our purpose, aid will include, in addition to grants and long-term loans contained in the UN definition, capital investments and other transfers for humanitarian purposes.

Theoretically, the reasons for extending aid may fall into four categories: (1) the political motive; (2) the cultural motive; (3) the economic motive; and (4) the humanitarian motive. For Saudi Arabia these motives should be considered in the light of the position that Saudi Arabia occupies with respect to the Arab world, the Moslem world, and the rest of the developing world. The political and cultural-religious motives behind Saudi aid to Arab countries is attributable to the fact that Saudi Arabia plays a major role in the Arab world.[5] It shares with the rest of the Arab countries close affinities in language, religion, background and history. In addition, the Saudis have been considered as a moderating political force in the Arab world. The continuation of this role by Saudi Arabia requires social and economic stability in the region, which, in turn, is essential for orderly economic development. Indeed, social and economic stability takes on an added impetus as the 1980s open with the Gulf witnessing instabilities in Iran and with the Iran-Iraq conflict.

Moreover, Saudi Arabia is a labour-deficient country. To execute its development plans it has to rely heavily on expatriate, especially skilled labour. This could be considered a rational motive for Saudi aid to labour-surplus Arab countries such as Egypt and North Yemen. Furthermore, economic co-operation between the Arab oil-producing countries, of which Saudi Arabia is the main member, and the non-oil states, is of great potential benefit to both groups. Co-operation enlarges the size of the market and reduces marketing uncertainty, hence encouraging the exploitation of economies of large-scale production which in turn permits specialization and contributes to more efficient allocation of resources.

One may also interpret Saudi aid to the non-oil-producing Arab countries as an attempt to close the gap in the standard of living between the oil and non-oil countries which was magnified by the sudden increase in oil revenue in 1973 and 1979. This may reflect the belief of the Saudis in the moral principle of relative egalitarianism as a prevailing attitude in the Islamic society.

The objectives of Saudi aid to non-Arab Moslem countries are not very much different from those mentioned above. Saudi Arabia contains the two holy sites (Mecca and Al-Medina) for the Islamic world. It also assumes the leadership of the Islamic society. Therefore, the strong relationship of Saudi Arabia to the Moslem nations is similar to the ties with the Arab countries.

The motives for providing economic assistance to developing countries outside the Arab and Islamic worlds may be attributed to the fact that Saudi Arabia was, and still is, a developing country. Thus, it feels a responsibility towards these countries which have suffered long from colonialism, poverty, deprivation and backwardness. Moreover, aid to these developing countries could indirectly benefit the Arab world by gaining Third World support for the Arab position in the Middle East crisis.

Saudi Arabia's Entry into the Donor List

When it began accumulating large oil-revenue surpluses in the 1970s, Saudi Arabia moved to transfer substantial amounts of concessional aid to developing countries. These funds disbursed by the Kingdom increased dramatically in 1974 and 1975 before peaking in 1976 at \$2.407 billion; after 1976 the total declined slightly in the following year and substantially in 1978 to \$1.455 billion (Table 11.1). Following several years of an almost open-handed approach to fulfilling assistance requests from practically all comers, the Kingdom became more selective in its lending, such as loans to help prop up nations with close relations to Saudi Arabia, or whose plight was severe.

Viewed in the context of a world in recession, the 1978 Saudi aid figure was still sizable enough that, by the end of the year, the Kingdom was able to rank second behind the USA in absolute total aid disbursed. This high ranking was a climb from the fifth position that Saudi Arabia had occupied as recently as 1974, when four industrialized, developed nations – the USA, West Germany, France, and Japan – preceded the Kingdom.

As a percentage of GNP, Saudi concessional foreign aid in 1978 was 2.76, a drop from the previous year's 4.3 per cent and 1976's 5.73 per cent (Table 11.1). This 1978 percentage was lower than three other OPEC members (United Arab Emirates, Kuwait and Qatar) but still far above the 0.22 per cent (1977) of the USA and the 0.31 per cent (1977) of the 17-member Development Assistance Committee of the Organization for Economic Cooperation and Development (OECD).[6] If

Table 11.1: Concessional Aid of OPEC Members (disbursements, net in $ millions)

Country	1973 Amount	1973 % of GNP	1974 Amount	1974 % of GNP	1975 Amount	1975 % of GNP	1976 Amount	1976 % of GNP	1977 Amount	1977 % of GNP	1978[a] Amount	1978[a] % of GNP	1979[a] Amount	1979[a] % of GNP
Algeria	25.4	0.29	46.9	0.37	40.7	0.28	53.6	0.33	46.7	0.24	44	0.18	45	0.14
Iran	1.9	0.01	408.3	0.88	593.1	0.13	752.5	1.13	251.2	0.30	278	0.33	21	0.03
Iraq	11.1	0.21	422.9	3.98	218.4	1.65	231.7	1.44	56.0	0.29	172	0.76	861	2.94
Kuwait	345.2	5.72	622.5	5.72	976.3	8.12	615.3	4.36	1,443.0	10.09	1,268	6.35	1,099	5.14
Libya	214.6	3.32	147.0	1.23	261.1	2.31	93.6	0.63	109.6	0.62	169	0.93	146	0.58
Nigeria	4.7	0.04	15.3	0.07	13.9	0.05	82.9	0.25	64.4	0.16	38	0.08	28	0.05
Qatar	93.7	15.62	185.2	9.26	338.9	15.62	195.0	7.95	194.3	7.83	106	3.65	251	5.60
Saudi Arabia	304.9	4.04	1,029.1	4.46	1,997.4	5.40	2,407.1	5.73	2,400.8	4.30	1,470	2.76	1,970	3.15
United Arab Emirates	288.6	15.96	510.6	7.57	1,046.1	14.12	1,060.2	11.02	1,229.4	10.67	690	5.60	207	1.58
Venezuela	17.7	0.11	58.8	0.20	31.0	0.11	102.8	0.33	51.5	0.14	109	0.28	83	0.18
Total	1,307.8	1.42	3,446.6	1.96	5,516.9	2.71	5,594.7	2.27	5,846.9	1.96	4,344	1.35	4,711	1.28

Note: a. Provisional.
Source: Organization for Economic Cooperation and Development (OECD), *Development Cooperation 1979* (Paris: OECD, 1979) and Robert McNamara, address to the joint World Bank-International Monetary Fund meeting, Washington, DC, 30 September 1980 in *Middle East Economic Survey*, supplement, 20 October 1980, p. II and 7 July 1980, p. I.

all disbursements of both bilateral and multilateral and concessional and non-concessional assistance are tabulated, as seen in Table 11.2, the percentage of the Kingdom's GNP expended in this fashion rises even further to 4.86 per cent and 2.78 per cent in 1977 and 1978, respectively.

Table 11.2: Total Net Flows (Disbursements) from OPEC Members, 1973-8[a] ($ millions)

	1973	1974	1975	1976	1977	1978[b]
Algeria	29.8	51.4	42.2	66.6	73.1	55.2
Iran	4.9	739.4	936.1	807.3	315.5	333.4
Iraq	11.1	440.2	254.4	254.7	135.2	211.1
Kuwait	555.7	1,187.1	1,712.2	1,875.7	1,864.6	1,150.8
Libya	403.8	263.2	362.8	363.2	287.0	548.9
Nigeria	5.7	134.8	347.5	176.8	35.7	7.7
Qatar	93.7	217.9	366.7	240.3	265.9	133.6
Saudi Arabia	334.9	1,622.1	2,466.7	2,817.3	2,709.7	1,746.7
United Arab Emirates	288.6	749.4	1,206.6	1,144.5	1,395.2	761.4
Venezuela	17.7	483.4	473.8	392.2	510.5	346.7
Total	1,745.9	5,888.9	8,169.0	8,138.6	7,592.4	5,295.6
	As percent of Gross National Product					
	1973	1974	1975	1976	1977	1978[b]
Algeria	0.34	0.41	0.29	0.41	0.38	0.23
Iran	0.02	1.59	1.79	1.22	0.38	(0.40)
Iraq	0.21	4.15	1.92	1.59	0.70	0.96
Kuwait	9.21	10.90	14.23	13.28	13.04	6.10
Libya	6.25	2.21	3.21	2.45	1.62	3.01
Nigeria	0.05	0.60	1.31	0.52	0.09	0.02
Qatar	15.62	10.90	16.90	9.79	10.65	4.61
Saudi Arabia	4.43	7.02	6.67	6.70	4.86	2.78
United Arab Emirates	15.96	11.12	16.29	11.89	12.11	6.63
Venezuela	0.11	1.66	1.75	1.26	1.43	0.85
Total	1.89	3.35	4.01	3.30	2.54	1.59

Notes: a. Total flows from OPEC states to other developing countries include both concessional and non-concessional and bilateral and multilateral assistance.
b. Provisional.
Source: *Middle East Economic Survey*, 4 February 1980, p. VI.

The above figures represent only the official aid, which may not include the unannounced assistance and aid for humanitarian purposes, such as earthquake and flood relief.[7] The magnitude of the Saudi assistance reflects the Saudi concern for the economic growth of developing countries: an important factor for the economic stability of the world. This concern is evidenced by the huge Saudi contribution to the International Monetary Fund (IMF) which reached $2.9 billion in 1977.[8] This amount was aimed at expanding the IMF Oil Facility programme through 'Special Drawing Rights' (SDRs).

In March 1977 the Foreign Minister of Saudi Arabia announced at the First Arab-African Conference in Cairo that Saudi Arabia had pledged to grant $1 billion to African development assistance.[9] This was one of the largest single infusions of aid granted to developing countries in history. Added to the $433 million pledged at the Conference by other Arab oil-producing countries, the amount was believed to be even higher than the African nations themselves had anticipated. Among the purposes of this assistance were the following:

> To encourage national and international financial organizations, to increase their technical and financial assistance to feasibility studies for development and infrastructure projects in Africa, and to prepare these projects for financing.[10]

Saudi Development Fund

Lending Conditions and Creditworthiness

The Saudi Development Fund (SDF), also called the Saudi Fund for Development, was established on 26 August 1974, and capitalized at SR 10 billion, which is equivalent to about $2,900 million.[11] The Saudi Council of Ministers was authorized to increase the capital of the Fund when and if necessary. The objective of the SDF was to contribute to development projects in the developing countries through extending loans. In conducting the Fund's operations, four financial aspects are considered: (1) the creditworthiness of the project in terms of the size of the loan, and the ability of the recipient country with respect to repayment; (2) the importance of the project for which the loan is extended and its priority and integration with the other economic projects of the recipient country; (3) the appropriateness of the project studied from both the economic and technical viewpoints; and (4) the ability of the recipient country to finance the portion of the project which is not financed by the Fund. This concern about the project's worthiness is vital to the success of the SDF and its continuation. In addition, this policy would be useful should the Fund decide to borrow from local or international markets.

In providing the loan, the SDF should make sure that the project is sound both economically and socially. Limits have been set as to the share and the total amount which can be supplied – no more than 5 per cent of the Fund's capital or 50 per cent of the total cost of the project should be extended. In addition, loans advanced to a single country should not exceed at any time, 10 per cent of the SDF's authorized capital. Despite these restrictions, an element of flexibility was provided. The Council of Ministers was authorized to override any of the above stipulations if necessitated by the circumstances. Apparently, these conditions are aimed at stressing the responsibility of the borrower and stimulating participation by local capital. The Fund's 50 per cent restriction on its share of financing could have the advantage of safeguarding the institution from assuming too heavy a commitment which might result in concentration on depth rather than scope.

An essential condition was that the loan should be spent entirely on the agreed-upon project and that the borrower should provide the Fund with progress reports concerning the project and its financing by other institutions. In addition, the loan agreement should include a guarantee by the borrower: (1) to facilitate all the financial operations of the Fund in the recipient country; (2) not to impose directly or indirectly any restrictions on the movements of the currency or documents relating to the loan; (3) to exempt the Fund's income and operations from taxes; and (4) to exempt all the Fund's assets and income from any measures of nationalization, confiscation and seizure. These conditions were seemingly dictated by the relatively unstable economic and political conditions that the developing countries in general, and Middle Eastern countries in particular, have experienced.

Between the commencement of operations in February 1975 and the end of 1977, 61 loan agreements with 29 countries were signed. Funds committed were \$1.6 billion, with over half of that amount extended in 1977. Total disbursements came to some \$248 million (\$188 million in 1977). The geographical distribution ranged from Korea and Taiwan to Brazil. Half the commitments were to Arab nations, over one-third to Asian countries, and 3 per cent to Latin American recipients. The poorer developing countries obtained almost three-quarters of the total.

Aid has emphasized transportation, with roads, railroads, ports and the Suez Canal accounting for more than 40 per cent of commitments. Electricity, industry and agriculture each obtained over 10 per cent. This sectoral distribution is indicative of the high priority attached to infrastructure investment, upon which development of the recipient economies is so heavily premised.

In the future the Fund intends to focus on the least-developed regions within the recipient countries, the goal of which is to attempt to impact upon the poorest segment of the population. Education, health and social development – largely bypassed until 1978 – were to receive greater emphasis.[12]

In 1978 some 29 loan agreements totalling $765 million were signed; disbursements in that year were about $200 million for the newly initialled agreements and those previously agreed upon. Overall, it appeared that the Fund was disbursing about 25 per cent of its accumulated commitments. In 1979 the SDF concluded nine agreements for a commitment of $259.2 million (SR 870.9 million).[13]

There are several aspects of SDF assistance, indeed of Saudi aid generally, which should be noted. Many of those features which distinguish Saudi economic assistance from that extended by the industrial donors also can be ascribed to OPEC and other Arab aid activities. First, SDF loans contain a high 'grant' element. Although the credits are repaid, the lending terms are considered 'soft' when compared with those prevailing in commercial credit markets. The low interest rates (usually around 3 per cent), long maturities (about 15-20 years), and grace period (frequently of 5 years) lead to the designation of 'soft' loans. The grant element, then, would be the difference between the loan terms of the SDF (or those in the Kingdom's bilateral, government-to-government credits) and that prevailing in international commercial credit at the time of the loan. If the substantial fluctuation in and high prime-interest rates within the industrialized nations in the late 1970s and early 1980s is kept in mind, the grant element in Saudi lending is significant.

Moreover, the multilateral agencies through which the Kingdom channels much of its aid – the OPEC Special Fund (renamed the OPEC Fund for International Development), the Arab Fund for Economic and Social Development, the World Bank-affiliated International Development Association, the International Fund for Agricultural Development, the Islamic Development Bank, as a sampling – similarly extend loans with a high degree of grant element. Thus, in assessing aid from SDF and Saudi assistance bilaterally or through other multinational agencies, the quality of such aid, in addition to the quantity and proportion it represents of the Kingdom's GNP, is sizable. Moreover, unlike the predominant share of industrialized-country aid, Saudi (and Arab/OPEC) assistance is not tied to purchases of products manufactured in the donor nation. US aid is now upwards of 90 per cent 'tied'.

SDF Aid to Arab Countries

Table 11.3 offers a selected listing of loans extended by the SDF to Arab nations for the period 1973-80. As indicated by their brief description, these projects – without exception – are developmental and/or infrastructural in nature. To manifest the priority assigned by the Fund to the purpose of its assistance and the effect of such assistance on the development process of the recipient, it is helpful to review briefly in somewhat greater detail some of the loans and projects supported by the Fund.

For many years Egypt has been a major recipient of Arab aid and investment. SDF loans to Egypt amounted to $113.6 million in 1975, $110 million the following year, and $50 million in 1977. The first of these credits (some $48.5 million) was earmarked for reopening of the Suez Canal, closed as a consequence of the 1967 Middle East war. This vital waterway is an important link in international trade, not only of dry goods and products but for oil tankers. A reopened Canal reduces the sailing time between Europe and Asia by two weeks and initially increased the Egyptian income by as much as $286 million.[14] The canal is a major foreign-exchange earner for the economy. The Saudi share was 18 per cent of the total cost of the project.

A second loan in 1975 of just over $65 million went to the second stage of the railway development project. Carrying out this scheme was a vital undertaking for a nation such as Egypt, where the population has been growing steadily and where agriculture forms a significant sector of the economy necessitating transportation for both workers and products. As is clear from Table 11.3, other loans extended to Egypt were for similar developmental projects such as cotton ginning, highway construction and the like.

In August 1976 Syria received a $75.3-million SDF loan.[15] The projects benefiting from this credit included: $25.6 million for the expansion of the port of Tartus; $24.1 million for the expansion of Latakia port; some $14.2 million for financing construction of a military hospital; and $11.4 million for the construction of a major highway linking Damascus with the Lebanese border. This latter project was also partially financed by the World Bank-affiliated International Development Association (IDA). The four undertakings just noted once again indicate the emphasis of the Fund on the infrastructural aspects and needs of the borrowing country.

The loan granted to Tunisia in the first year of the SDF's operation (1975) amounted to $30.3 million for the improvement and

Table 11.3: Selected List of Saudi Development Fund Aid to Arab Countries, 1975-80

Country/Year	Loans ($ millions)	Description of projects for which loans were extended
Algeria		
1977	45.5	Tijet Port
Bahrain		
1977	45.5	Power station
Egypt		
1975	48.5	Reopening and development of Suez Canal
	65.1	Second stage of railway development project
1976	25.6	Development of cotton ginning
	23.0	Telephone project connecting Cairo with Ismailia, Port Said and Suez
	61.5	Heliopolis-Helwan highway project
1977	50.0	Deepening and widening of Suez Canal
	7.2	Electricity
Jordan		
1977	22.9	Expansion of Aqaba Port
1978	75.5	Water and electricity
1980	11.6	Improvement of 21 kilometre stretch of Hijaz railroad
Morocco		
1977	31.0	Wadi Al-Gharb irrigation
1978	34.7	Al-Massira dam
	34.7	Jarf Lasfar Port
Yemen Arab Republic (North Yemen)		
1976	25.5	Various development projects
	38.0	Construction of Dhamar-Rada road
	10.0	Development of grain silos
	14.5	Second stage of Sana'a water and drainage system
1977	3.5	Purchase of scientific instruments for secondary schools
	3.5	Telecommunications and agricultural projects
	20.0	Electricity projects
	25.0	Hodeida electricity project
1978	29.4	Tai'z water and sewerage project
	25.9	Second stage Hodeida power project
	15.1	Sana'a water and sewerage project
	11.3	Grain silos construction
1980	16.2	Second stage central electrification project, including turbines with 150-MW capacity
	11.1	Grain silos
Oman		
1977	48.1	153-km road network and administrative and social centres
People's Democratic Republic of Yemen (South Yemen)		
1977	34.3	Housing and electricity

Table 11.3 (continued)

Country/Year	Loans ($ millions)	Description of projects for which loans were extended
Sudan		
1975	28.2	Al-Rahd irrigation project
1976	36.0	Construction of Port Sudan-Kasala road and an airport at Port Sudan
1977	93.5	Purchase of educational facilities; telecommunications; highways; ports
1980	22.4	245-km highway linking southern Sudan with Kenya's Rift Valley
Syria		
1976	93.8	Expansion of ports; construction of hospital and highway
1978	46.1	Development of Tashrin University (Latakia)
	14.7	Transit lounge at Damascus International Airport
	10.4	Highway, Damascus to Al-Masnah on Lebanese border
Tunisia		
1975	30.3	Development of Greater Tunis project
1977	56.3	Engineering School; water supply
1978	70.2	Sidi Sa'd dam at Kairouan

Sources: *Middle East Economic Survey*, selected issues, 1975-80; Saudi Development Fund, *First Annual Report* (March-July 1975); various issues of *Okaz* newspaper.

enlargement of the sewerage system in the city of Tunis. A major objective of the project was the reduction in the contamination level in the sewerage water so that it could be utilized for irrigation purposes.

An example of the type of project supported in Jordan was the 1977 credit of $22.9 million earmarked for the expansion of the port of Aqaba on the Red Sea. Aqaba serves as the only outlet to the sea for that nation; hence, it plays a critical role in trade and transport for the entire economy. The project receiving SDF funding in 1980 was linked to improvement of the Hijaz railroad in the south of Jordan. Aspects of the scheme included the purchase of diesel locomotives, housing units and a communications network along the line. With this loan, SDF credits to Jordan reached more than SR 384 million ($115.6 million) for the partial financing of six development projects.[16]

In recent years Sudan has increasingly drawn Arab investment and aid. It has enormous agricultural potential and, unlike its neighbour to the north, Egypt, is not beset by overpopulation. The end of the civil war, which plagued Sudan through much of the late 1960s and early 1970s, has been supplanted by a period of stability. Moreover, optimistic oil reports in 1980 seem to indicate that Sudan's petroleum reserves may prove substantial. One of the world's largest sugar plants – the Kenana Sugar Company – stands as an example of the regional investment in Sudan. Of the total shares of 330 million Sudanese pounds ($412.5 million), just over 34 per cent is held by the government of Sudan, over 33 per cent by the state of Kuwait, almost 12 per cent ($48.9 million) each by the government of Saudi Arabia and the multinational Riyadh-based Arab Development Corporation.[17]

The emphasis on development of agriculture and agribusiness in Sudan can be seen as well in the thrust of projects supported by the SDF. In 1975 Sudan received a $28.2 million-credit for the Al-Rahd irrigation project. This undertaking would water an area of 121,400 hectares, thus increasing the crops of cotton, sugar cane, peanuts and vegetables. It was expected that the project would triple the income of 16,000 families, provide seasonal jobs for about 90,000 workers and permanent employment for about 2,300, and increase the foreign-exchange flow to Sudan by $72 million annually. The Saudi contribution constituted 12 per cent of the total cost of the project. A second loan extended in 1976 for $36 million was for the construction of the Port Sudan-Kasala road. For the development of a country with a vast area like Sudan, road construction holds a high priority. This specific project would link the agricultural area in Kasala with Port Sudan on the Red Sea, facilitating the flow of imports and exports. Also in the transport sector falls the 1980 credit (in conjunction with the SDF loan to Kenya) to link the Rift Valley in Kenya with southern Sudan. As with so many infrastructure projects, the loan's terms are 'soft' – 3 per cent interest, 20-year maturity, and a 5-year grace period.[18] It is also worth noting that a 1977 loan went to the purchase of educational facilities. By assisting in the modernization of the education system an invaluable input into the development of required human resources was supported. Inadequate manpower, either in numbers or training, has proved consistently to be a bottleneck to economic development throughout much of the Arab world.

The Yemen Arab Republic or North Yemen is the closest neighbour to the south of Saudi Arabia and the second largest nation in the Arabian peninsula. Yemenis form the largest single group of non-indigenous workers in the Saudi labour force. Due to the relative scarcity of natural resources and other factors, North Yemen is considered one of the least-developed Arab countries. Its terrain is varied, rising from low coastal plains to rugged mountains, making transportation and integration of the economy through infrastructure development paramount. To date, North and South Yemen are the only two non-oil states in the Arabian peninsula. The Saudi desire for ongoing peninsular stability is seen as being advanced by a policy aimed at reducing the contrast between the region's 'have's' and 'have not's'. Thus, the Kingdom's financial support for North Yemen's development – both through government-to-government loans (see Table 11.4) and SDF credits – along with the undeniable need by North Yemen for economic assistance, explain the large number of loans to that country. Given the scope of Saudi aid activities, in 1978 a North Yemen-Saudi Joint Co-ordination Aid Programme was established.

Table 11.4: Selected List of Saudi Governmental Aid to Arab League Countries, 1974-80

Country/Year	Loans and grants ($ millions)	Purpose
Algeria		
1980	15.0	Earthquake victims
Egypt		
1974	100.0	Rebuilding Suez Canal towns damaged during October 1973 war
	300.0	Rebuilding Suez Canal areas
1975	7.7	Construction of Islamic university in Assuit
1976	800.0	(Pledge) to assist Egyptian economy
Jordan		
1976	215.0	To finance Jordan Five-Year Plan
1980	10.0	Flood and heavy snow-damage repair
Lebanon		
1980	38.1	First instalment of $114.3-million annual contribution to five-year, $2-billion Arab aid programme agreed upon at the November 1979 Tunis summit
Yemen Arab Republic (North Yemen)		
1975	82.0	Budget support
	30.0	Electricity projects
	146.0	Road construction
	15.0	Grain mills and silos
	13.7	Drilling artesian wells
	4.3	Flood aid
1977	101.6	Budget support
1978	101.6	Budget support
1979	101.6	Budget support
	4.8	Compensation for higher prices paid for imports of Saudi oil

Table 11.4 (continued)

Country/Year	Loans and grants ($ millions)	Purpose
Oman		
1975	100.0	Development projects
Somalia		
1975	11.5	Famine and drought assistance
1979	20.0	Grant
1980	10.0	Budget support
People's Democratic Republic of Yemen (South Yemen)		
1976	100.0	Development assistance
Sudan		
1974	200.0	To finance industrial and agricultural projects
1978	2.9	Flood relief
1980	11.0	Exploration for minerals (zinc, silver, copper, gold and chromium)
Syria		
1975	200.0	(Pledged) for weapon purchases
	219.9	For various development projects
1977	50.0	Economic assistance
Tunisia		
1979	7.0	Expenses of Arab Summit conference
	13.0	Economic development purposes
Djibouti		
1977	10.0	Economic assistance

Source: *Middle East Economic Survey*, various issues, 1974-80.

Road construction understandably has been given high priority in Yemeni development plans. During 1976 the SDF extended one of its four loans to North Yemen that year for the Dhamar-Rada road project. The $38 million earmarked for that undertaking is the largest SDF credit to a single project in North Yemen and ranks among the most sizable of all the Fund's loans. Large-scale infrastructural projects, particularly electricity and water and drainage systems, received the lion's share of SDF lending (Table 11.3). In December 1977 it was announced that the SDF would finance approximately one-sixth (or $570 million) of North Yemen's first five-year development plan (1978-83). These funds were for six major projects related to electric power generation, development of water resources, sewerage systems and road networks.[19]

Although Oman is one of the Arab oil producers, its oil revenues are modest when compared with that of other Middle Eastern and North African petroleum states. The Fund's 1977 loan of $48.1 million went toward the construction of a 153-kilometre road network and for the construction of administrative and social centres in the Sultanate.

Some $100.4 million lent to Morocco went for three major development projects: Al-Massira dam, Jarf Lasfar port and the Wadi Al-Gharb irrigation works. The objective was to enhance the agricultural productivity of the country through regulation of water supply and to increase the import-export capacity of the nation.

SDF Aid to Non-Arab Countries

Table 11.5 offers an idea of the extent and type of aid extended by the Fund to the non-Arab countries from 1975 to 1980. SDF credits, some reviewed briefly here, are extended with an eye to the potential effect of the supported projects on the development of each recipient. Non-Arab regional nations, specifically Pakistan and Turkey, have received sizable Fund credits.

Table 11.5: (continued)

Country/Year	Loans and grants ($ millions)	Description of projects for which loans were extended
Bangladesh		
1977	50.0	Railroad renovation
1979	30.0	Limestone and mining project at Jaipurhat
Cameroon		
1977	29.9	Hydroelectric dam project
1979	3.6	Tshanshi-Foudair highway
Comoros Islands		
1979	14.5	70-km of roads on Islands
Congo		
1976	28.0	Railway project
Gambia		
1977	6.6	Development of Yundum Airport
Ghana		
1977	29.9	Electricity projects
India		
1976	107.0	Power projects
Indonesia		
1976	70.0	Fertilizer plant in South Sumatra
1977	50.0	Road project in East Java
Kenya		
1978	25.0	Expansion of Nairobi water network system
1980	22.4	245-km road linking Rift Valley Province with southern Sudan

Table 11.5 (continued)

Country/Year	Loans and grants ($ millions)	Description of projects for which loans were extended
Liberia		
1978	11.0	Thermal power plant
	9.0	Bridge across St. Paul River and road linking it to mining region of Bomi Hills
Malaysia		
1975	76.6	Medical school; technical university; reclamation and resettlement projects
1979	30.4	Establishment of scientific institutes; levelling and landscaping
Mali		
1975	2.25	Assistance for drought and development projects
1976	6.0	Assistance for drought and development projects
1977	5.0	'Urgent' development projects
	15.0	Development assistance
	15.0	Sankorami River dam construction
Mauritania[a]		
1976	51.5	Steel plant
Pakistan		
1976	32.1	Mirpur Mathelo fertilizer project
1979	90.2	Thermal power station at Pipri near Karachi
	48.8	Tarbila dam project
	31.2	Fertilizer plant construction at Mirpur Mathelo
	14.7	Port Qasim project
	10.3	Purchase of diesel locomotives for Pakistan Railways
1980	60.0	Repairs and modifications of Tarbila dam
Rwanda		
1976	5.4	Kigali road project
Senegal		
1976	36.0	Dhakar-Thias motorway
1978	3.9	First stage of 2,500-hectare land reclamation scheme in Anaby River basin
Somalia[a]		
1976	72.6	Sugar cane factory
1980	10.6	For establishment of a national university
South Korea		
1976	44.2	Highway and port projects
Taiwan		
1976	53.0	Taiwan highway projects
1977	30.3	Railway electrification
1978	30.0	Automatic telephone system
Turkey		
1980	250.0	Railway modernization; power lines and

Table 11.5 (continued)

Country/Year	Loans and grants ($ millions)	Description of projects for which loans were extended
		lignite power plant mixing yard; other public-sector (especially energy) projects (amount negotiated in 1979 with disbursements made upon submission of projects by Turkish government)
Uganda		
1975	31.0	Development projects
	18.0	Agricultural and livestock projects

Note: a. Members of the League of Arab States.
Sources: *Middle East Economic Survey*, selected issues, 1975-80; Saudi Development Fund, *First Annual Report* (March-July 1975).

Agricultural products constitute 85 per cent of Uganda's exports and about 90 per cent of the population is employed in the agricultural sector. It thus has become a major goal to diversify the agricultural sector away from overdependence on two products, cotton and coffee. It was planned that the $49 million loaned to Uganda would help to achieve this target, providing the country with an additional annual inflow of foreign exchange of about $13 million and making the nation self-sufficient in terms of meat and dairy products by the year 1985. SDF loans represent 45 per cent of the total cost of the projects.

The loans extended to Malaysia totalled $76.6 million and were to support the following three projects: (1) $17.7 million for a technological university project. This institution will contribute to the nation's development through the training of a sorely needed skilled labour force; (2) the $16 million for a medical school at Kibanga University is aimed at improving the medical services throughout the nation; (3) the reclamation and resettlement projects supported by a $43-million SDF loan are expected to prepare 160,260 hectares for cultivation and help resettle about 78,000 farmers. This could result in a substantial improvement in the agricultural sector.

Indonesia, one of the largest and most populated Islamic countries, is also a member of OPEC. Despite its oil revenues, Indonesia's financial requirements for development are enormous and it remains a borrower in international credit markets. Of the $130 million loaned by the Fund to this nation, some $70 million was to finance a fertilizer plant in South Sumatra. The productive capacity of the facility will be 1,725 tons per day and it will provide Indonesia with its fertilizer requirements. The second credit of $50 million supported a road project in East Java. This scheme will provide better transportation for about 31 million people in Java, indicating the potential effect of the project on the social and economic development of that province.

The drought which descended on sub-Saharan Africa in the mid and late 1970s not only delayed development but led to widespread famine. Mali was one of the most severely hit nations. Thus, a high priority was assigned not only to drought relief but to projects related to water regulation, resettlement, livestock, and building materials (such as cement). SDF credits from 1975 through 1977 totalled $43 million.

The $28-million loan to the Congo supported that nation's railway system, to increase the capacity of the network by 36 per cent and improving transportation not only for the Congo, but with the neighbouring states of Chad, Cameroon and Central Africa.

As seen in Table 11.5, SDF loans granted to Gambia, Cameroon, Ghana, India, Comoros Islands, Kenya, Liberia, Bangladesh, Pakistan, Rwanda, Senegal, Somalia, South Korea, Taiwan and Turkey similarly were in support of transportation-sector projects (railways, airports, roads, bridges, ports), water and power generation (dams, electricity projects), and to a lesser extent, for industrial and agro-industrial schemes (mining, fertilizers, sugar-cane refinery facility). Such infrastructure projects are vital but because they are not usually immediately profit making – rather 'building blocks' for further development in industry and agriculture – the return on the investment takes place over a long period. Commercial financing for such undertakings is difficult to locate, and then the higher interest rates prevailing from such sources make the project costs ever higher. The SDF falls into the tradition of a number of multinational agencies and other aid/development bodies in becoming an important source of reasonable financing for crucial infrastructure projects in the Third World.

Saudi Governmental Aid

Governmental Aid to Arab League Countries

Table 11.4 illustrates some of the assistance given directly through the Saudi government from 1974 to 1980.[20] Although the Kingdom's aid began earlier, the year 1974 was chosen as this period witnessed substantially increased oil-generated revenues, enabling the nation to raise its assistance to incredible levels.

It is clear from Table 11.4 that among Arab League members Egypt was an early, heavy recipient, followed by North Yemen, Syria, Jordan and Sudan.[21]

The first $100 million offered to Egypt in 1974 was a grant to assist in rebuilding the Suez Canal towns damaged during the October 1973 war. During a state visit by the late King Faisal in August 1974, Egypt was granted another $300 million in immediate aid designated again for the reconstruction of the Suez Canal area. The $800 million of 1976 constituted 40 per cent of the Saudi share in the Arab Assistance Fund for Egypt which was established in August of that year. The fund was managed by a Riyadh-based agency called the Gulf Organization for Development in Egypt (GODE). The other participants in the Fund were Kuwait (30 per cent), Qatar (15 per cent), and the United Arab Emirates (15 per cent).[22]

The implications of the relatively strong emphasis of aid programmes to Egypt can be explained easily. Of the major Arab nations, Egypt suffered the most in the 1967 and 1973 Middle East conflicts. The loss was severely felt in the Suez Canal area and was worsened by the closing of the Canal, so vital to the traffic in the region in both dry-cargo transport and the tanker fleets moving oil to the West. In addition, Egypt is the most populous Arab state; it has been a major reservoir of skilled labour for Saudi Arabia and other parts of the Arab world. Aside from these considerations, the stability of Egypt has been considered vital to the security of the entire Arab world.

The circumstances of Syria, another large-scale recipient shown in Table 11.4, are in some respects similar to those of Egypt. Both countries have suffered from two major wars, which have involved occupation of their territories and substantial draining of their economies.

Sudan and North Yemen have been significant recipients of Saudi bilateral governmental assistance in areas of humanitarian aid, development projects in agriculture, industry, infrastructure, and budgetary support. Often the governmental assistance is supportive of the same or related projects which have received SDF loans.

Government Aid to Non-Arab League Nations

In addition to SDF activities, the recipients of Saudi governmental assistance to non-Arab League states ranged from some of the most developed nations (such as Germany, Japan and France and entities within the USA) to underdeveloped, recently independent countries such as Niger. With respect to the developing bloc – Pakistan, Bangladesh, Malaysia, as a sampling – given in Table 11.6, this form of aid can be viewed much in light of what has been noted regarding the rationale and purpose for SDF lending and of government assistance to Arab League states.

Table 11.6: Selected List of Saudi Governmental Aid to Non-Arab League Countries, 1974-80

Country/Year	Loans and grants ($ millions)	Purpose
Bangladesh 1974	10	Flood aid (grant)
Federal Republic of Germany 1980	2.6	Direct and indirect credits
France 1974	200	Loan from SAMA (10 years), at 10 per cent, recycling petrodollars
Hong Kong 1979	0.3	Mosque renovation
Iran 1978	10	Tabas earthquake victims (grant)
Ireland 1976	300	Loan (5 years), at 9.2 per cent, guaranteed by EEC
Italy 1980	10	Earthquake assistance (grant)
Japan 1974	1,000	Loan from SAMA (5 years), at 10 per cent, recycling petrodollars
Malaysia 1975	85	Development projects
Malta 1974	5	Interest-free loan repayable in 20 years
Niger 1975	10	Drought assistance (grant)
1978	5	Islamic University of Niger
Nigeria 1977	5	Islamic University of Nigeria
Pakistan 1975	100	Interest-free loan for industrial projects
	10	Earthquake assistance (grant)
South Korea 1975	70	Development projects (repayable over 25 years)
Turkey 1977	5	Earthquake assistance (grant)
Turkish of Cyprus 1975	5	Economic assistance
United States 1975	100	Loan to AT&T (American Telephone & Telegraph), repayable over 6 years at 8.4 per cent
1980	300	Loan to IBM (SAMA placement of notes), 10.8 per cent, average life 5.5 years, redeemed within 7 years
Yugoslavia 1979	2.5	Renovation of Sarajevo mosque

Source: *Middle East Economic Survey*, various issues, 1974-80.

However, some questions might be raised regarding the purpose of loans to the industrialized, developed countries. One answer offered is 'that the world must have a stable, international economy based in part upon the existence of a strong and viable industrial world' and 'that these . . . considerations are, of course, as important to Saudi Arabia as to others'.[23] International economic stability can best be achieved through the meeting of a requisite level of both industrial and Third World needs. In addition to the argument of greater global stability, the loans to industrial nations, or more specifically to institutions in these countries, may be looked upon as secured investments aimed at yielding reasonable returns. In short, this assistance offers an outlet for surplus oil-generated capital into profitable investments rather than exposing accumulated funds to uncertainties inherent in currency fluctuations.

Saudi Aid to Institutions and Agencies

Much Saudi assistance is channelled through multinational institutions. As shown by Tables 11.7, 11.8 and 11.9, the word 'institution' is not used here to mean strictly development-finance bodies; it covers as well some charitable and religious organizations. The recipients listed in Table 11.7 are a sampling only. For example, in the four years from 1977 to 1980, Saudi Arabia has been the largest annual donor to the United Nations-sponsored World Food Programme.[24] Moreover, the purchase of World Bank bond issues by SAMA has been substantial over the past half decade; the issue cited in Table 11.7 is offered as an example in part because, prior to this purchase, SAMA has held to a maximum of 15 per cent only of any World Bank issues taken.[25] This would seem to indicate a change toward a larger Saudi role in petro-dollar recycling.

Other aid represents Saudi contributions to the international agencies as the International Monetary Fund's Oil Facility and the OPEC Fund along with its specialized agency the International Fund for Agricultural Development; these assistance entities will be given further examination due to their relative importance and the magnitude of aid involved. Along with the Arab/Islamic specialized programmes receiving Saudi contributions, all these bodies and institutions to which the Kingdom contributes stand as concrete evidence of the often-expressed Saudi concern with world economic stability.

International Monetary Fund Oil Facility

This body was established in 1975 when the IMF made arrangements with 11 countries to finance the Fund's Special Drawing Rights (SDRs) to assist nations with balance-of-payments difficulties resulting from higher oil prices. The total amount committed by these states in 1975 was SDR 2.860 billion, distributed as follows: Australia, 50 million; Belgium, 100 million; West Germany, 300 million; Iran, 410 million;

Kuwait, 200 million; Netherlands, 200 million; Nigeria, 200 million; Norway, 50 million; Saudi Arabia, 1 billion; Switzerland, 150 million; Venezuela, 200 million. The Saudi share exceeded one-third of the total amount of the Fund. However, by mid-1977, the Saudi contribution was believed to have amounted to 2.9 billion SDRs or $3.5 billion.[26] Recipients of IMF Facility assistance included nations on every continent. The objective was to ward off the more serious financial consequences which resulted from the quadrupling of crude-oil prices in 1973-4. However, since 1976 this type of assistance in foreign trade financing has increasingly fallen under the aegis of the OPEC Fund.

Table 11.7: Selected List of Saudi Aid to Non-Arab, Non-OPEC Institutions, 1975-80

Institution	Contribution ($ millions)	Disposition of aid
Asian Development Bank		
1975	50.0	Loan from SAMA
International Monetary Fund (IMF)		
1975	1,200.0	Oil facility SDRs
1977	1,700.0	Oil facility
Islamic Conference Organization (ICO)/ Islamic Solidarity Fund (ISF)		
1975	14.99	Islamic News Agency; ISF; Islamic Philanthropic Society (Makased, Beirut); construction of Islamic mosques, schools, and centres in Australia
1977	28.0	ISF for development projects in Islamic countries; Islamic News Agency; Jerusalem Fund
1978	38.7	ISF; Jerusalem Fund; Islamic universities of Uganda and Niger; Islamic News Agency; Islamic Waqfs Fund
1979	54.8	Islamic Conference; $30 million addition to ISF's capital for scientific research and Islamic universities, natural disaster relief, mosques, schools and hospitals, Jerusalem Fund, Islamic missions, celebration of the Hijra 15th century
United Nations Educational, Scientific and Cultural Organization (UNESCO)		

Table 11.7 (continued)

Institution	Contribution ($ millions)	Disposition of aid
1975	5.6	To finance educational projects (grants); interest-free loans for educational programmes
United Nations Relief and Works Agency (UNRWA)		
1975	.6	
1976	1.2	
1977	1.2	
1978	10.2	Regular annual $1.2-million payments plus two special contributions
1979	3.5	Regular contribution plus $2.3-million special contribution
1980	5.0	Regular contribution plus $3.8-million special contribution
United Nations World Food Programme		
1976	50.0	
1980	55.0	For fourth consecutive year, Saudi Arabia was largest donor to the World Food Programme
World Bank		
1980	401.6	SAMA purchase of 28.6 per cent of German mark 700-million bond issue arranged by German banks

Source: *Middle East Economic Survey*, various issues, 1975-80.

The OPEC Fund

In 1976 the Saudi Council of Ministers approved the contribution of $152 million to the OPEC Fund established in January of that year by OPEC member states. By the beginning of 1977 $205.5 million had been contributed by the Kingdom, with a further $200-million 'replenishment' paid in 1977.[27] Table 11.8 indicates that over one-quarter of both the pledged and paid contributions to the OPEC Fund as of year-end 1979 was from Saudi Arabia. In 1980 the OPEC Finance Ministers approved a second $800-million replenishment, thus raising the Fund's resources to $2.4 billion. The replenishment formula called for a Saudi payment of $200.16 million (25.27 per cent of the total), followed by Venezuela (14.15 per cent), Kuwait with 9.1 per cent, Nigeria with 6.57 per cent, and Iraq and Libya with 5.05 per cent each.[28] Later in that same year at the May Finance Ministers' meeting,

Table 11.8: Contributions to OPEC Fund (for International Development) by OPEC Members as of 31 December 1979 (US $ millions)

	Pledged contributions					Paid contributions				
	IFAD[a]	Net[a]	Total[a]	IMF gold sales profits	Total contri-butions	IMF Trust Fund[b]	IFAD[b,c]	Invest-ment account and 1976 budget	Loans and tech-nical assis-tance	Total
Total	435.500	1,143.000	1,578.500	63,905	1,642.405	63,905	290.000	10.500	401.953	769.049
Algeria	10.000	30.000	40.000	–	40.000	–	6.667	0.270	11.556	18,492
Ecuador	–	2.000	2.000	–	2.000	–	–	–	0.230	2.000[d]
Gabon	0.500	1.500	2.000	–	2.000	–	0.500	0.014	0.565	2.000[e]
Indonesia	1.250	3.750	5.000	–	5.000	–	1.250	0.034	1.646	2.930
Iran	124.750	295.250	420.000	–	420.000	–	41.583	2.569	82.790	126.942
Iraq	20.000	20.000	40.000	10.190	50.190	10.190	20.000	0.512	2.507	33.209
Kuwait	36.000	108.000	144.000	6.092	150.092	6.092	36.000	0.971	40.725	83.787
Libya	20.000	60.000	80.000	0.964	80.964	0.964	13.333	0.539	23.006	37.842
Nigeria	26.000	78.000	104.000	–	104.000	–	17.333	0.701	29.575	47.609
Qatar	9.000	27.000	36.000	1.858	37.858	1.858	6.000	0.242	10.342	18.442
Saudi Arabia	105.500	300.000	405.500	12.539	418.039	12.539	70.333	2.695	114.907	200.474
United Arab Emirates	16.500	49.500	66.000	1.393	67.393	1,393	11.000	0.445	18.764	31.602
Venezuela	66.000	168.000	234.000	30.870	264.870	30.869	66.000	1.510	65.342	163.721

Notes: a. International Fund for Agricultural Development = IFAD; IFAD and other contributions pledged according to Resolution No. 1 (1977) of the Ministerial Committee on Financial and Monetary Matters (including an additional amount pledged by Ecuador).
b. Contributions to International Monetary Trust (IMF) Fund are paid in name of member countries. c. Including $140,959.500 paid in promissory notes. d. Including prepaid amount of $1,770,162. e. Including prepaid amount of $921,341.
Source: OPEC Fund, *Annual Report 1979* (Vienna: OPEC Fund, 1980).

approval was given for an additional increase of $1.6 billion which would bring the Fund's total resources to $4 billion. At that same session the OPEC Fund's conversion to the OPEC Fund for International Development was finalized.[29]

Table 11.9: Sample of OPEC Fund for International Development Loans Ratified 24 October 1980

Recipient	Amount ($ millions)	Interest (%)[a]	Maturity (years)	Grace period (years)	Purpose
Bangladesh	21.0	0	20	5	Energy project
Congo	8.0	4	20	4	Rail transport system
India	20.0	0	20	5	Energy project
Laos	1.5	0	15	5	Programme support
Maldive Islands	1.0	0	10	3	Balance of payments
Senegal	5.0	4	20	4	Textile project
Thailand	8.0	4	20	5	Energy project
Tunisia	6.0	4	20	4	Highway project
South Yemen (Yemen Arab Republic)	4.0	0	20	5	Water project

Note: a. Additional service charge of 0.75 per cent except for the Maldive Islands service charge of 0.5 per cent.
Source: *Middle East Economic Survey*, 3 November 1980, p. II.

The purpose of the OPEC Fund has been to provide financial assistance to developing countries. It was created to complement the bilateral and multilateral arrangements through which OPEC states have extended financial support to the rest of the Third World. The aspects deserving the Fund's assistance included balance-of-payments support, financing of development projects and programmes, and for operations carried out by international development agencies (as, for example, technical assistance through the United Nations Development Programme). The loans provided by the Fund carry low, and frequently no interest and are repayable for upwards of 20 years with a five-year grace period. A small annual service charge (half to three-quarters of 1 per cent) is assessed on loans. Such arrangements and terms result in a grant element amounting to 70 per cent of the loan.[30]

Initially, heavy emphasis was placed on balance-of-payments support; in 1977 about 70 per cent of committed loans were earmarked for this purpose. In subsequent years the trend has been steadily toward project/programme lending, so that in 1979 65 per cent of total loans were for projects rather than balance-of-payments support.[31] Thus the name change effected in 1980 stresses the direction of the fund role more into international development than trade (import) financing.

Between 1976 and the end of 1979 the cumulative value of grants and loans committed by this Fund was $1.2 billion, of which 46.5 per cent ($554 million) already had been disbursed.[32] In the year 1979 alone this body committed $265.8 million of which $138.5 million was in project loans, $74.3 million in balance-of-payments lending, $20 million in technical-assistance grants, and some $33 million to the Trust Fund administered by the International Monetary Fund in which only Iraq, Kuwait, Qatar, Saudi Arabia and the United Arab Emirates participate. A breakdown of the project loans saw 73.8 per cent going to Asian nations, 20.2 per cent to African recipients, and 6 per cent to Latin American countries. Sectoral distribution of supported projects fell heavily in that of power (42 per cent), followed by transportation (28 per cent), and agriculture and agro-industries (13.4 per cent). These credits reflect the stated OPEC policy to assist in financing, locating and developing of indigenous energy resources in the developing countries in order to reduce their dependence on imported oil. The continuation of this emphasis in lending is apparent in Table 11.9, which gives details of the nine loans ratified at the OPEC Fund for International Development (OFID), 30 October 1980, board meeting. Including the agreements formalized at that time, OFID's commitments had reached $1.5 billion, including $910 million in loans to 76 developing nations with the remainder in grants and contributions to other international development agencies.[33]

Saudi Contributions to Joint Arab/Islamic Development Projects

Table 11.10 illustrates the joint Arab and/or Islamic projects to which Saudi Arabia is a major contributor. The extent of these various entities' activities can be seen in Table 11.11. Some of these projects and bodies are aid institutions directed toward the development process in the Arab, African and Islamic countries (examples of these are the Arab Bank for Economic Development in Africa – ABEDA – and the Islamic Development Bank – IDB). Others are wholly Arab undertakings, most of which are commercial companies seeking profitable opportunities in the Arab world. Although the primary concern of these enterprises is return on investment, their positive contribution to the socio-economic development of the Middle East region should not

Table 11.10: Saudi Contributions to Joint Arab and/or Islamic Development Bodies

Institution	Date of establishment	Headquarters	Capitalization ($ million)	Saudi share ($ million)	Purpose
The Arab Bank for Economic Development in Africa (ABEDA)	Feb. 1974	Khartoum	231	50	Provision of soft loans for medium and small-sized projects in co-operation with other international lending agencies.
Arab Fund for Economic and Social Development (AFESD)	June 1973	Kuwait	357	65.8	To finance the social and economic development projects in Arab countries.
Islamic Development Bank (IDB)[a]	Aug. 1974	Jeddah	910 (may be raised to 2,500)	91	To support economic and social development of member countries and Muslim societies individually and collectively.
The Arab Company for Investment (ACI)	June 1974	Riyadh	300	45	To investment in productive projects in such fields as agriculture, industry, transportation and services.
Arab Company for Petroleum Investment	July 1974	Dammam	343	62	To finance petroleum projects and other supporting projects with emphasis on Arab joint projects.
Arab-African Technical Assistance Fund (AATAF)	Jan. 1974	Cairo	25	3	To provide both Arabs and Africans with technical assistance related to economic, social, and scientific development.
Oil Fund for African Countries		Khartoum	220	50	To extend loans to African countries for their oil purchases, repayable in 25 years with a grace period of 10 years, and annual interest of 1%.
United Arab Maritime Co.	Jan. 1976	Kuwait	630	122	To perform maritime transportation.
Arab Tanker Company	Jan. 1973	Kuwait	500	60	Maritime transportation of hydrocarbonic materials.

Table 11.10: (continued)

Institution	Date of establishment	Headquarters	Capitalization ($ million)	Saudi share ($ million)	Purpose
Arab Pipeline Company	Dec. 1973	Alexandria	400	60	Construction and operation of oil pipelines to transfer oil from the Suez Gulf to Mediterranean
Saudi-Egyptian Industrial Investment Co.	May 1975	Cairo	100	50	To establish and operate industrial projects in Egypt
Arab Weaponry Co.	April 1975	Cairo	1,040	260	To establish and develop Arab weaponry
Saudi-Egyptian Co. for Reconstruction	May 1975	Cairo	50	25	Real-estate operations, including construction, purchase and sale
Arab Co. for Livestock Development	Feb. 1975	Damascus	175	35	All operations related to livestock, including manufacturing, transportation, and marketing of livestock products and feed
Arab Mining Company	Feb. 1976	Amman, Jordan	350	70	Oil exploration, extraction, and supporting operations
Gulf Organization for Industrial Counselling	Feb. 1976	Doha, Qatar		17% of annual budget	Industrial co-operation and co-ordination among member countries
Arab Company for Medical Industry	May 1975	Cairo	175	35	Production and marketing medical products
Arab Company for Building and Repairing Vessels	Dec. 1973	Manama, Bahrain	200	16	Building, repairing and maintenance of ships and other maritime transportation means of hydrocarbons

Note: a. Membership includes both Arab and non-Arab Islamic countries.
Source: 'Development Strategy in Saudi Arabia', a working paper presented to the Fourth Conference for Industrial Development in the Arab States, held in Baghdad in October 1976, published by Industrial Studies and Development Centre.

Table 11.11: Total Net Flows Committed by Arab/OPEC Multilateral Institutions, 1974-8 ($ millions)

Institution	1974	1975	1976	1977	1978
Arab Fund for Economic and Social Development (AFESD)	127.2	200.7	336.5	365.3	1.3
Arab Fund for Technical Assistance to Arab and African Countries (AFTAAAC)	–	–	0.5	4.1	6.8
Arab Bank for Economic Development in Africa (ABEDA)	–	–	79.6	77.0	72.8
Gulf Organization for Development in Egypt (GODE)	–	–	250.0	1,495.0[a]	100.0[a]
Islamic Development Bank (IDB)	–	–	–	120.2	240.0[a]
Islamic Solidarity Fund (ISF)	–	–	6.0	8.0[a]	8.0[a]
Organization of the Arab Petroleum Exporting Countries (OAPEC) Special Account	79.0	–	37.1	–	–
OPEC Special Fund[b]	–	–	42.7	243.0	155.0
Special Arab Aid Fund for Africa (SAAFA)[c]	80.3	71.6	56.5	13.2	–
Others[d]	41.4	70.1	207.2	400.0[a]	450.0[a]
Total	327.9	342.4	1,016.1	2,725.8[a]	1,033.9[a]

Notes: a. Estimate by the Organization for Economic Co-operation and Development Secretariat. b. Renamed in 1980 the OPEC Fund for International Development. c. SAAFA merged with ABEDA in 1977. d. Arab African Bank; Arab International Bank; Arab Investments Company; Arab Petroleum Investments Corporation (Apicorp).

Source: *Middle East Economic Survey*, 4 February 1980, p. VII.

be understated.[34] They tend to augment the regional availability and mobility of capital, thus resulting in a more efficient allocation of a vital and scarce factor of production.

Another noticeable point in Table 11.10 is that some of these investments are directed toward petroleum-based industries. The other projects form joint industrial and agricultural projects which can be considered serious attempts to establish sound economic bases for the prosperity of the Arab world as a whole. They also provide a diversification means for the region's resources and might thereby be seen as lessening the vulnerability of oil-producing countries with single-product economies.

A continent in the throes of development, decolonization, nation-building, and severe climatic setbacks such as drought, Africa is none the less rich in human potential and natural resources. Between 1975 and the end of 1979 ABEDA had provided $571 million in loans to 50 projects in 36 countries. This ABEDA lending has acted as a catalyst to stimulate the flow of additional investment into the continent. Between 1974 and 1979 Arab aid to Africa averaged between $700 million and $800 million per annum, a total of around $5 billion, most of which emanated from the Arab oil producers. Of the $4.367 billion cumulative aid to Africa at the end of 1979, $2.838 billion was pledged by seven Arab nations and the balance from the ABEDA; the Special Arab Aid Fund for Africa (SAAFA) accounted for $533 million, the Technical Assistance Fund for Africa some $5.9 million, $158 million from the Islamic Development Bank, a sum of $320 million from the OPEC Fund, the Arab-African Bank accounted for $23 million, the Islamic Solidarity Fund about $11.5 million, and the IMF Oil Facility channelled $473 million. About 70 per cent of this assistance was granted at preferential terms with a grant element of 25 per cent. The distribution within the continent saw almost half going to West Africa, East Africa received some 40 per cent, and 23 per cent (including a portion of East and West African distribution) went to the seven Sahel countries – those sub-Saharan nations most seriously damaged by prolonged drought.[35]

The oldest multilateral Arab-aid institution is the Kuwait-headquartered Arab Fund for Economic and Social Development (AFESD). Its original capitalization of $357 million (Table 11.10) has been raised several times; its subscribed capital (but not fully paid up) at the beginning of 1980 was $1.469 billion (Kuwaiti dinars 400 million). The cumulative value of AFESD loans approved from 1973 to 1979 (79.5 per cent of its subscribed capital) involved participation in

52 projects in 14 nations.[36]

A major multinational body which receives sizable financial participation from Saudi Arabia is the Jeddah-based Islamic Development Bank (IDB). In 1979 alone this agency was involved in 33 agreements (largely in foreign-trade financing), representing a commitment of \$269.7 million and thus ranking it first among Arab, OPEC and Islamic aid institutions.[37] Composed of 34 countries in Africa, the Middle East and Asia which have large or predominantly Moslem populations, its non-Arab League members include Afghanistan, Bangladesh, Cameroon, Chad, Guinea, Indonesia, Malaysia, Mali, Niger, Pakistan, Senegal, Turkey, Uganda and Upper Volta.[38] As of December 1977, after little more than a year of operations, the Saudi contribution had reached \$232.6 million (Islamic dinars 200 million) or over 26 per cent of the Bank's total subscriptions of \$886.8 million (Islamic dinars 762.5 million). The IDB loans fall into four general categories: (1) to the least-developed member countries for infrastructure; (2) equity financing in industries such as cement, textiles, and petroleum; (3) foreign-trade (import) financing; and (4) technical assistance for effecting feasibility studies of potential projects.[39] As of 11 July 1980, the total value of IDB loans to and investment in member states totalled \$1.139 billion for 155 projects and transactions since October 1975.[40]

For example, among the transactions approved by the Bank's Board at its 7 May 1980, meeting were: (1) \$40 million to Algeria for intermediate industrial goods; (2) \$20 million to Bangladesh for crude oil from Saudi Arabia and the United Arab Emirates; (3) \$7 million to Mali for aviation fuel; (4) \$20 million to Pakistan for crude oil from Saudi Arabia and the United Arab Emirates; (5) \$20 million to Somalia for crude oil from Iraq; (6) \$18.5 million to Sudan for refined petroleum products from Kuwait; (7) \$11 million to Tunisia for raw and woven cotton from Pakistan, Senegal, Syria and Turkey.[41] This is an excellent instance to indicate the emphasis on import financing by the Bank. IDB equity investments have been increasing, including those of \$5.24 million in the Sudan Development Corporation and \$4.2 million in an Upper Volta gold-mining project. On a Saudi resolution, the Bank's capital was raised in mid-1980 from \$1.3 billion (Islamic dinars 1 billion) to \$1.9 billion (Islamic dinars 1.5 billion).

As an example of the activities of joint Arab investment companies in which Saudi Arabia participates, the operations of the Arab Company for Investment can be described briefly (see Table 11.10). Set up in 1974, the principal shareholders are the governments of Saudi Arabia, Kuwait, Sudan, Qatar, United Arab Emirates, Bahrain, Syria, Iraq,

Jordan, Tunisia, Morocco, Libya and Oman. By the close of 1979 this enterprise had invested SR 955 million ($286.8 million) in development projects in the Arab world of which SR 255 million ($76.6 million) were in the form of equity participation in 20 projects and the remaining SR 700 million ($210.2 million) had been extended in long-term loans.[42]

The Impact of Saudi Foreign Aid on Regional Development

The Arab world is characterized by uneven distribution of factors of production. The states that enjoy an abundance of capital, such as Saudi Arabia and most of the Arab oil producers, often suffer from a lack of both the skilled and unskilled labour necessary for execution of their development plans. By contrast, states for which labour surpluses constitute acute economic and social problems, such as Egypt, North Yemen and the like, suffer from a shortage of capital. This problem of shortages and surpluses also manifests itself clearly in the agricultural sector.

Some nations like Sudan and, to a lesser extent, Syria have tremendous potential capabilities for providing the entire region with a large share of its food needs and other agricultural products, but they lack the capital required for carrying out the necessary expansion of that sector. Capital-surplus states, such as Saudi Arabia and Kuwait, are confronted with water constraints which strictly limit agricultural output. Though not exclusive, these examples are sufficient to shed enough light on the problem of uneven distribution of resources in the region which can be considered one of the main obstacles retarding economic development in the Arab world. There, concerted efforts by all Arab states are urgently needed to diminish this problem.

With respect to the movement of labour, the main obstacle has been the frequent political disruptions which could be attributed to the economic and political instability of the area. The Saudi policy of pursuing greater regional stability has been enhanced by the Kingdom's substantial economic assistance. The Saudi development plans and programmes have speeded up the movement of labour, especially between Saudi Arabia, the largest labour importer, and other Arab states such as Egypt and North Yemen. Encouraging the movement of labour will not only help the labour-deficit countries carry out their development and industrial projects, but will also result in more capital transfers to the labour-surplus nations. The immediate result of this is, of course, the lessening of the gap in the unequal distribution of two critical factors of production: labour and capital.

The emphasis on the agricultural sector is evidenced by the SDF loans extended for the purposes, such as the Al-Rahd irrigation scheme in Sudan, cotton ginning in Egypt, grain silos in North Yemen, and the Al-Massira dam and Al-Gharb irrigation projects in Morocco.

Saudi contributions to joint Arab projects represent another serious effort to encourage capital movement in the region. As shown in Tables 11.10 and 11.11, the purposes of these joint undertakings indicate the attempts to diversify the sources of income in the region through region-wide investment and thereby lessen the Kingdom's heavy dependence upon oil revenues by a steadily growing inflow of investment income.

Though not complete, the factors discussed above may form the starting point on the course of full regional development. And if it is true that 'economic integration should not be visualized as "all or nothing" ',[43] the Saudis have done their fair share to make regional development a reality.

Conclusions

This chapter has attempted to provide a survey and analysis of Saudi foreign aid since 1974. Although Saudi assistance started as early as the 1950s, the substantial increase in oil revenue enabled Saudi Arabia in 1978 to occupy the second position on the list of donors to developing countries. Prior to the establishment of the SDF in 1974, Saudi assistance was extended on an *ad hoc* basis with little possibility for extensive economic evaluation of the projects for which aid was provided. The creation of the SDF as a specialized, bilateral lending agency indicates the Saudi emphasis on the development aspects of the recipients, although the SDF has not become the sole body through which aid is channelled. Many donor countries have moved to increase the level of their aid through multinational agencies. This has been true also for Saudi Arabia through its contributions to and purchase of bond issues of the International Monetary Fund and the World Bank, as well as the Arab Fund for Economic and Social Development and the Islamic Development Bank, among other entities. In the case of the World Bank issues, there is an investment aspect in addition to employing that agency as an aid channel. And, of course, utilizing multinational bodies has the benefit of well-qualified staffs and procedures already in place, not to mention a reduction in the possibility for friction arising between donor and recipient countries in bilateral aid arrangements.

The most recent Saudi commitment – and a critical one for the International Monetary Fund – was to assist this financially beleaguered agency with a loan of almost $10 billion. Announced in March 1981 by the Managing Director of the 141-member IMF, the credit will be divided into two annual payments of 4 billion SDRs (special drawing rights) equivalent to $4.9 billion each. A tentative agreement might extend the loan to yet a third year for an additional $4.9 billion. With this massive credit, Saudi Arabia received increased voting strength from 1.74 per cent to 3.5 per cent, as well as a permanent seat on the 22-member board of directors. The Kingdom now ranks sixth in voting strength among the IMF members, after the United States (20.78 per cent), Great Britain, Germany, France and Japan.

Moreover, estimates in 1981 of the total level of Saudi aid to developing countries for the preceding year (1980) was on the rise again, to upwards of $5 billion.[44]

It has been seen that the extension of assistance to the Kingdom's neighbours – as well as beyond the Arab world – is motivated by a rather broad spectrum of reasons. Political motivations have included the promotion of security and stability within the Middle Eastern region, while economic reasons for giving aid cannot ignore the potential for certain reciprocal efforts on the part of developing nations to assist the Kingdom in the future. Moreover, the extension of assistance cannot help but enhance the promotion of export sales and the development of markets for Saudi products in coming years.

Lastly, the absorptive-capacity constraints in the Saudi economy have led to the accumulation of surplus capital funds. The assistance programmes have offered a beneficial means of utilizing those funds, often with an investment quality to the aid.

There do exist humanitarian and qualitative motives in the Kingdom's assistance directed toward the development of the Third World. Saudi Arabia has been a major voice in global forums and institutions, such as the Conference on International Economic Co-operation (CIEC) or the North-South dialogue, calling for renewed efforts among the developed, richer nations to assisted the less-developed countries of the world. These efforts are seen as building a bridge towards global economic stability.

Notes

1. Organization for Economic Cooperation and Development, 'Debt Problems of Developing Countries', *OECD Observer*, March-April 1975, p. 27. (Hereafter the Organization for Economic Cooperation and Development will be cited as OECD.)

2. Frederic Benham, *Economic Aid to Underdeveloped Countries* (London, Oxford University Press, 1976), p. 24.

3. United Nations, Economic and Social Council, *International Economic Assistance to Underdeveloped Countries in 1956/57*, Report of the Secretary General, 26th session (E.3131 and ad. 1), 3 June 1958, p. 74.

4. William Gustaaf Zeylstra, *Aid or Development, The Relevance of Development Aid to Problems of Developing Countries* (Leyden, A. Wijthoff, 1975), p. 16.

5. Ragaei El Mallakh and Mihssen Kadhim, 'Arab Institutionalized Development Aid: An Evaluation', *The Middle East Journal*, Autumn 1976, pp. 478-9.

6. OECD, *Development Cooperation, 1978* and *1979* (Paris, OECD, 1978 and 1979); *OECD Observer*, November 1978.

7. For example, Saudi Arabia authorized $10 million in relief to Italian earthquake victims in December 1980; *Middle East Economic Survey*, 22 December 1980, p. II. (Hereafter *Middle East Economic Survey* will be cited as *MEES*.) Other instances of disaster aid and/or government-to-government assistance of a specialized nature include, as a partial listing: $10 million for earthquake aid to the Tabas area of Iran (*MEES*, 2 October 1978, p. 8); in September 1978 flood relief of $2.9 million to Sudan (*MEES*, 2 October 1978, p. 8); some $10 million to assist in repair flooding and heavy snowfall damage in Jordan (*MEES*, 31 March 1980, p. II); and $4.8 million extended to North Yemen to compensate for higher oil prices paid by that nation for imports of Saudi oil (*MEES*, 29 October 1979, p. II).

8. *MEES*, 6 June 1977, p. 12.

9. *MEES*, 14 March 1977, p. 9.

10. Ibid.

11. Saudi Development Fund, *First Annual Report* (March-July 1975).

12. *OECD Observer*, November 1978, pp. 24-5.

13. *Middle East Economic Digest*, July 1980, p. 83 and *MEES*, 11 February 1980, p. IV. (Hereafter *Middle East Economic Digest* will be cited as *MEED*.)

14. Saudi Development Fund, *First Annual Report* (March-July 1975), p. 10.

15. *MEES*, 30 August 1976, p. 4.

16. *MEES*, 28 April 1980, p. III.

17. *Financial Times*, 27 February 1982, p. 32. The Kuwait Fund for Arab Economic Development has been a relatively large lender to Sudan, particularly in cultivation of sugar cane and sugar-refining schemes.

18. *MEES*, 8 September 1980, p. I.

19. *MEES*, 12 December 1977, p. 9.

20. Bilateral government-to-government aid sometimes is unannounced or announced, but few details are given. This use of this aid form appears to be slackening somewhat, with greater employment of the structured SDF and multinational agencies.

21. This does not include the 'crisis' aid given annually to the countries involved in the 1967 Middle East war.

22. *MEES*, 30 August 1976, p. 8. GODE's activities were suspended in the late 1970s as a result of Egypt's policy differences on settlement of the Arab-

Israeli problem.

23. Dr. Farouk Akhdar, 'Saudi Arabia-United States: Between Interdependence and Cooperation', plenary address to the 30th Annual Conference on World Affairs, University of Colorado, Boulder, April 1977, p. 4.

24. *MEES*, 14 April 1980, p. II.

25. *MEES*, 14 July 1980, p. II.

26. *MEES*, 6 June 1977, p. 12.

27. John Law, *Arab Aid: Who Gets It, For What and How?* (New York, Chase World Information Corporation, May 1978), p. 151 and *MEES*, 5 March 1976, p. 10.

28. *MEES*, 21 January 1980, pp. 1-2 and 2 June 1980, p. 1. In line with its past level of commitments, Iran would have contributed an amount equal to Saudi Arabia; however, due to its instabilities and financial problems, Iran's replenishment share was set at 7.125 per cent of the total. Other OPEC members' shares were: Algeria, 2.3 per cent; Qatar, 2.27 per cent; Indonesia, 0.31 per cent; Ecuador and Gabon, 0.13 per cent each.

29. *MEES*, 2 June 1980, p. 1.

30. OPEC Special Fund, *Basic Information* (Vienna, OPEC Special Fund, December 1976), pp. 4-5.

31. *MEES*, 23 June 1980, p. III. The annual average for 1977-9 was 52 per cent for project and 48 per cent for balance of payments.

32. Ibid., pp. I-IV.

33. *MEES*, 3 November 1980, p. II.

34. Ragaei El Mallakh and Mihssen Kadhim, 'Arab Institutionalized Development', pp. 477-8.

35. *MEES*, 24 November 1981, pp. II-III and 15 December 1980, p. I.

36. *MEES*, 11 February 1980, p. IV. The value of AFESD lending accounted for 15 per cent of the total value of commitments of all Arab, OPEC and Islamic aid-extending bodies at this point in time.

37. Ibid., pp. III-IV.

38. From the Arab League membership, IDB countries include Algeria, Bahrain, Egypt, Jordan, Kuwait, Lebanon, Libya, Mauritania, Morocco, Oman, the Palestine Liberation Organization, Qatar, Saudi Arabia, Somalia, Sudan, Syria, Tunisia, United Arab Emirates, Yemen Arab Republic (North Yemen) and the People's Democratic Republic of Yemen (South Yemen).

39. *MEES*, 24 April 1978, pp. 8 and ii.

40. *MEES*, 21 July 1980, p. I.

41. *MEES*, 19 May 1980, pp. I-II.

42. *MEES*, 5 May 1980, p. III.

43. Ragaei El Mallakh, 'Planning for Economic Integration in the Arab World', unpublished paper.

44. *New York Times*, 24 March 1981, p. 4.

12 BUSINESS TRENDS AND POTENTIAL

Business Activities

Prospects for Private-sector Participation

The Second Development Plan issued in 1975 first put forth the goal of economic diversification away from near-total dependency on the oil sector. The private sector was to be encouraged to participate in capital investments and only 'where the size of investment is large and beyond the capacity of private individuals, [that] the government itself undertakes capital investment'.[1]

Half a decade later, in 1980, the same goal of diversification remained one of the fundamental objectives for the long-term economic development of the Kingdom and a key aspect of the strategy for the 1980-5 period. The productive sectors, including agriculture, industry and mining were to be emphasized, with the development to be primarily undertaken by the private sector with the government's role to be that of support for the non-public sector in its tasks.[2]

This support was to take the form of providing information on the opportunities for investment in the productive sectors of the economy. The information would accrue from increased emphasis on economic feasibility studies and programmes of applied research. Further government support would come from the completion of infrastructure and the provision of services related to maintenance, marketing and transport where needed to support productive industries.[3]

Perhaps the most important role reserved for the government was that of setting priorities for investment during the Third Plan. Considered by government planners to be among the most critical areas for investment in the 1980-5 span by the private sector were: large-scale mechanized agricultural projects; projects which introduce appropriate and new economic technologies; and maximization of the value added from crude-oil production through the development of hydrocarbon-based industries.[4]

As a result of rapid economic growth, the Kingdom had its total value of imports rise from SR 1.155 billion (1961-2) to SR 69.180 billion in 1978. Imports increased over the period 1973-8 by 58.2 per cent average annual figure, reaching the amount of SR 69,180 million in the latter year. A high propensity to import was projected to be maintained in the Third Plan period as well. Intentions of planners were for the import growth rate to stabilize at about 7 per cent per annum. Import composition for the five-year span was expected to be influenced by a rise in components and products substituting for labour.[5]

The trends in the gross domestic product (GDP) also exemplify the growth in Saudi Arabia's economy. Since the discovery of oil in the 1930s, the petroleum sector has dominated the economy. Oil's share of GDP in the fiscal year 1974/5 (at current prices) was 79.8 per cent and private non-oil output was 13.1 per cent. Through the implementation of the Second Plan, the oil sector decreased to 57.1 per cent in 1978/9 while the private non-oil sector had risen to 23.1 per cent.[6]

Table 12.1: Real Gross Domestic Product (Annual Growth Rates) (in percentages)

	1975/6	1976/7	1977/8	1978/9	Third plan projections
Gross domestic product	8.6	14.8	5.9	7.6	3.3
Oil sector	1.1	13.2	−0.5	1.8	1.3
Non-oil sector	19.8	16.9	13.8	13.7	6.2
Private	17.8	18.9	13.9	14.1	–
Public	23.9	12.9	13.5	12.9	–

Sources: SAMA, *Annual Report, 1979*, p. 1 and *Third Development Plan*, Table 1-4, p. 20.

Table 12.1 portrays the annual growth rates of real GDP and points out that the non-oil sector (public and private) grew by rates of at least 13.7 per cent annually during the Second Plan while the oil sector was increasing at very low rates per annum with the exception of one year – 1976/7 – when the rise was 13.2 per cent. Third Plan projections are for the petroleum sector to grow by only a 1.3 per cent annual rate while the non-oil sectors will expand by a larger (but more modest than in the Second Plan) rate of 6.2 per cent. The data would indicate, then, a still lower share for oil and a higher one for non-oil private output. While oil will continue to dominate the economy, all indications are that the diversification efforts as provided for in the Second and Third Plans will bear fruit. Opportunities for business in the non-oil private sector are thus likely to grow in the foreseeable future.

Opportunities under the Third Development Plan

While one of the largest areas for business opportunity in the 1970s was in construction and related fields, such as engineering and architectural services, the publication of the Third Plan in May 1980 indicated that this sector would receive less emphasis during the 1980-5 period. Spending on infrastructure would be 35 per cent of total expenditures instead of half the total as in the Second Plan. By comparison, investment in productive activities would be up from 25 per cent to 37 per cent of total spending.

However, indications are that this intention of moving away from spending on construction may be difficult to translate into actuality, and that the building boom is far from over (see Table 12.2). Numerous projects carried over from the Second Plan will still be on-going well into the Third Plan. Stress on regional and rural development will require considerable outlays for construction. The SR 21,104.4 million ($6,386.7 million) allocated to public works will include considerable infrastructure spending as well as amounts included in other overall sectoral allocations. Much construction remains to be done in education, industry, water and electricity, health, communications and transport, and housing (see Table 12.3). The construction sector should continue to provide opportunities through the Third Plan period and beyond.

Table 12.2: Non-oil Private-sector Second Plan Growth Rates (annual rates of real growth, in per cent)

	Average annual plan projections	1st-year actuals 1975/6[a]	2nd-year actuals 1976/7[a]	3rd-year actuals 1977/8[b]	4th-year actuals 1978/9[b]
Non-oil private sector	13.4	17.8	18.9	13.9	14.1
Agriculture	4.0	4.0	5.0	6.0	–
Manufacturing	14.0	8.2	13.6	8.7	–
Construction	15.0	34.5	25.3	10.5	–
Transport, communications, storage	15.0	22.6	22.1	22.7	–

Source: SAMA, *Annual Report, 1979*, p. 60.

This is not to say that the construction industry is without problems or bottlenecks. Manpower is perhaps the foremost of these bottlenecks as indicated by its receiving top priority as an area of concern during the Third Plan. Expatriate workers who are vital to the construction as well as other sectors of the economy are limited to a projected 0.2 per cent annual increase during the 1980-5 Plan period; this can be compared with the approximately 48 per cent annual increase in the Second

Plan. The number of Saudi workers is projected to rise by 1.9 per cent per annum in the Third Plan, the same rate of increase as that between 1975 and 1980. Overall employment in the Kingdom is scheduled to rise by 1.2 per cent in the Third Plan as compared to 12.8 per cent per annum during the preceding half-decade. This manpower bottleneck must be considered in any business undertaking in Saudi Arabia.

Table 12.3: Third Plan Sectoral Projects Involving Construction

Sector	Cost (SR millions)	Targets	Projects
Education			
Male	52,473.0	1,027,369 students	Dormitories costing SR 15,140 million; housing SR 1,600 million; new colleges SR 718 million; medical complexes SR 1,700 million; staff quarters SR 5,500 million
Female	23,989.0	613,648 students	
Universities	24,709.0	73,490 students with 37,000 graduating in 1980-5 span	
Health/social services			
Health facilities	34,884.8	36 hospitals	
Communications/transport			
Telephones	28,907.0	1,177,000 lines, 885,000 subscribers	
Roads	37,764.3	28,085 km	
Railways	4,499.0	641 km	
Ports	23,782.0	46.8 million tons/year with 145 berths	
Industry			
General Petroleum and Mineral Organization (Petromin)	27,684.0	Annual output to rise 500 per cent	1985 output increase; local refineries from 120,000 b/d to 640,000 b/d; export refineries from 580,000 b/d to 1.33 million b/d; lube oil from 500,000 barrels/year to 2 million barrels/year; storage from 9.6 million barrels to 22.75 million barrels; oil product pipelines from 112,000 b/d to 511,000 b/d; crude-oil pipelines from 51,000 b/d to 2.2 million b/d
Saudi Basic Industries Corporation[a]	25,564.0	Industrial complexes	Jubail: 1 steel mill, 1 fertilizer plant, 6 petrochemicals plants; Yanbu; 1 petrochemicals plant
Industrial estates	2,006.8		Other planned industries: glass, cement, industrial gas, car parts,

Table 12.3 (continued)

Sector	Cost (SR millions)	Targets	Projects
			metallurgy, building materials, farm products, animal feed concentrates
Grain silos/ flour mills	4,802.7		
Water and electricity			
Water projects	13,377.0	816,000 m^3/day	Riyadh drinking water cost SR 4,525 million, capacity raised from 280,000 m^3/day by 200,000 m^3/day from Al-Wasia in 1982 and 300,000 m^3/day from Jubail; Taif and Al-Hada capacity doubled from 17,500 m^3/day from Wadi Tarabah; 37 dams and 250 water networks installed; construction of 29 desalination plants with electricity output of 1,985 MW
Desalination	39,602.0		
Electricity	52,585.2	15,320 MW generating capacity	
Housing and public works	21,204.4	35,853 homes	Diplomatic living area constructed in Riyadh replacing embassies near Jeddah at a cost of SR 1,800 million
Total project and recurrent expenditure[b]	783,000.0		

Notes: a. Saudi Basic Industries Corporation is abbreviated as Sabic. b. This original total allocation includes expenditures for Judiciary, Agriculture, projects in Health/Social Services, and Communications/Transport not cited in this table.
Source: Kingdom of Saudi Arabia, Ministry of Planning, *Third Development Plan, 1400-1405/1980-1985*, various tables and chapters.

Competition in the construction industry in the Kingdom is brisk. As of 1977 European-owned or managed firms represented 51 per cent of all the activity in Saudi Arabia. They accounted for 40 per cent of all contractors active. The Saudis followed with 25 per cent of the total volume of construction, while US firms carried 15 per cent and the Asian and Middle Eastern contractors had 9 per cent.[7]

Because competition is keen, with no shortage of bids and offers, the government prefers dealing with foreign companies whose reputations have been well established and whose people are known locally. Time is another consideration. If bids are relatively close, the shortest completion time is preferred.[8] Another aspect to consider is the local variables that must be included in contract and bidding calculations. These involve knowledge of the existing work rules, religious customs, and the effects of climate.[9]

A noteworthy development pertaining to Saudi business opportunities which was expressed in the Third Plan involves the concept of 'Saudization'. This principle provides for priority in the awarding of contracts to be given to Saudi contractors. When contracts are awarded to foreign contractors, there will be a stipulation that some of the work must be subcontracted to Saudi companies. In order to facilitate the policy, it is intended that very large projects be split up rather than awarded as a single package.[10]

The Saudization policy was intended to reduce the dependence on expatriate manpower and to distribute more of the benefits of development to the citizenry. Contractors that provide for 'Saudization' in their programmes and have well-articulated policies for it will be given preference.[11]

For almost any commercial or contracting activity, a joint venture is recommended. (Appendix A of this chapter outlines the practical steps involved in licensing of a company under the foreign capital investment regulations.) The 1979 Foreign Capital Investment Law offers incentives for certain types of projects, among them (1) tax exemption for from five to ten years, (2) duty-free import of plant and equipment, and (3) low land purchase prices on governmental industrial estates, all of which are provided upon the granting of an operating licence. Additionally, financing of up to as much as 50 per cent of the project costs may be forthcoming from the Saudi Industrial Development Fund. The projects being sought as development schemes falling under the auspices of the Foreign Capital Investment Law are: productive industrial-development undertakings, health-development projects, productive agricultural-development schemes, services and contracting.

Those projects falling into the first classification are those industrial undertakings involved with the conversion of raw materials into manufactured or semi-manufactured goods, from the semi-manufactured to the final, completed product, or the supply, bottling or packing of the finished products. Among those projects considered in the health-development category are the creation, management and operation of hospitals, clinics and similar health units. The acceptable agricultural projects would be those dealing with agricultural resources (such as the production of fruit, vegetables, cereals, nurseries, greenhouses, crop seed and fodder), animal resources (cattle, sheep, poultry, apiaries and dairy output), and marine resources (fishing and the creation of fish farms).

Foreign participation acceptable in the services sector is wide ranging from banking to hotel and tourism, training, maintenance, environmental protection, transport, loading and unloading, publicity, publishing, advertising, computers, and the establishment of large-scale workshops and cold-storage centres, shopping and trading centres, and workshops with a high level of advanced technology. Finally, the contracting projects are defined as effecting work on a specific undertaking at a set fee (such as civil engineering in construction of roads, ports, prefabricated buildings, airports, and the like, electrical engineering related to electricity generation, supply and distribution, and mechanical-project contracting for such items as water-desalination facilities and factories). Flexibility has been built into the law by allowing for amendment by the Foreign Capital Investment Committee or a decision by that committee for acceptance of a development project not included in the law.[12] This new set of guidelines has been prepared with an eye to fulfilling the Third Plan's goal of stimulating the private sector to participate in the economic diversification of the Saudi economy, including the involvement of foreign capital in a number of new private-sector development projects.

The most-favoured organization for most contracting ventures has been the limited liability company, similar to a partnership and more closely related to French law than either US or UK law. It is estimated that between 90 and 95 per cent of companies in the Kingdom involving foreign participation as of 1980 were of this form.[13]

Minimum capital acceptable to the Ministry of Industry and Electricity, one of the key agencies, was about SR 1 million ($300,300) as of 1980. This was interpreted as proof of a company's serious intent to participate in the development of the nation. Besides sufficient capital, a Saudi agent was essential, in order to have an acceptable level of local representation.[14]

As with participation in projects in many countries, there is no guarantee of quick profits even though all procedures are followed according to protocol. Long lead times are involved in setting up any type of operation. Negotiations in typical contracting ventures involving foreign and Saudi companies are concluded at a different pace in each instance.

The diversification of the Kingdom's petroleum-related industry is being undertaken by the General Organization for Petroleum and Minerals (Petromin); that body was discussed earlier in greater detail in Chapter 2. Petromin has a 10-year, $15 billion programme (see Table 12.4) which attempts to expand production of petroleum products within Saudi Arabia in addition to utilizing the energy resource which oil and gas represent to generate heavy industry. As examined elsewhere, important aspects of this programme are the Jubail and Yanbu petroleum-based industrial complexes. Thus, the area of opportunity for private business is in the expansion of petrochemicals, industrial gases, glass, metallurgy and other energy-intensive industries. In addition to investing directly in these ventures, management, engineering and marketing services are also needed and encouraged.

As a result of the diversification goal embodied in the Second and Third Plans, the non-oil-related industries are heartily encouraged. In this sector the objectives stated by the Saudi government include: (1) to increase the domestic economy's capacity to produce at competitive costs a wide range of products for domestic as well as for the export market; (2) the industrial exploitation of the substantial comparative advantages arising from low-cost energy, raw materials from hydrocarbon-related industry, minerals, agricultural and fishing resources; (3) widening and deepening the Kingdom's access to modern technology; (4) to encourage fuller utilization of capacity in the private manufacturing sector; (5) to increase productivity through closer approach to optimal size of plants; (6) to secure a regional and balanced development of industry; (7) to reduce dependence on expatriate workers by national skill creation through the development of general and technical education and on-the-job training of national workers; and (8) to promote interlinkage among industries.[15]

Due to the small population base in Saudi Arabia, most of the non-oil industries established are on a limited scale. In 1972 the manufacturing sector was dominated (as it currently is), in terms of employment and number of enterprises, by establishments producing on a small scale for the consumer market. Of the total 9,360 manufacturing establishments, 8,979 (or 96 per cent) employed less than 10 persons and 8,221 establishments (or 88 per cent) employed 1 to 4 persons.[16] In addition, 65 per cent of the total manufacturing industries responsible for 37 per cent of the gross value of output were in the consumer market such as food processing, textiles, clothing, leather and leather products. The demand for consumer goods is expected to increase as a

Table 12.4: Second Development Plan, Major Development Projects, Hydrocarbon-based Industry, 1975-85

Programme and project	Investment ($ millions)	Capacity
Eastern Region		
Gas-gathering and treatment	4,571	45.3 million m^3/day
Petrochemical complex (4 total, 3 initiated 1975-80)	2,571	@ 500,000 metric tons/year ethylene equivalent
Lube oil refinery	583	107,000 b/d
Export refineries (2)	1,314	@ 250,000 b/d
Fertilizer plants (4 total, 2 initiated 1975-80)	400	@ 110,000 metric tons/year ammonia; 250,000 metric tons/year urea
Aluminium	371	210,000 metric tons/year
Steel mill	1,571	3.5 million metric tons/year
Subtotal	11,380	
Western Region		
Crude pipeline to west	1,514	2.4 million b/d
NGL pipeline to west	343	356,000 b/d
Export refinery	600	250,000 b/d
Petrochemical complex	643	500,000 metric tons/year (ethylene equivalent)
Subtotal	3,100	
Grand total	14,480	

Source: *The Second Development Plan*, Table IV-18, p. 182.

Table 12.5: Industrial Licences Issued and Implemented, 1975-8

Activity	Issued: No. of licences	Issued: Capital (SR millions) Paid-up	Issued: Capital (SR millions) Authorized	Issued: Employment	Implemented: No. of licences	Implemented: Capital (SR millions) Paid-up	Implemented: Capital (SR millions) Authorized	Implemented: Employment
Food and beverages	184	927.5	2,407.1	7,318	111	524.1	1,793.3	5,213
Textile, clothing, leather products	24	200.1	334.2	2,167	11	46.7	132.8	1,144
Wood products	21	89.1	236.2	1,620	16	73.8	160.7	1,365
Paper products, printing	39	125.0	313.9	1,912	23	73.0	185.5	1,303
Chemical products, including petrochemicals, rubber, plastics	137	548.6	1,385.4	4,158	78	316.5	738.3	2,318
Construction materials, china, ceramics, glassware	374	3,937.9	8,864.2	25,347	262	2,509.3	5,685.1	16,634
Metal products	253	1,076.1	3,212.4	16,287	147	515.9	1,354.6	7,502
Other products	3	20.8	26.2	125	2	12.4	17.8	102
Total	1,035	6,925.1	16,779.6	58,934	650	4,071.7	10,068.1	35,581
National	758	4,919.1	11,331.6	35,602	467	3,009.7	7,210.1	22,859
Joint venture	277	2,006.0	5,448.0	23,332	183	1,062.0	2,867.0	12,722

Source: SAMA, *Annual Report, 1979*, p. 75.

result of the large expatriate community as well as urbanization and a growing Saudi middle class. It should be noted that the Saudi consumers insist on high-quality products.

Some areas for greatest expansion result from increased demand for household furnishings, extending from large and small appliances including refrigerators, ranges and washing machines (especially those which conserve water and electricity) to rugs, drapes, floor coverings and furniture. In addition, there is an increasing demand for office furnishings and office equipment, including communication systems.[17] Table 12.5 indicates the recent trends in the types of industrial undertakings.

Other areas in the consumer market which should not be overlooked are products related to recreation. As the middle class in Saudi Arabia enlarges, there is more money available for the purchase of recreational equipment and more time to enjoy it.

Table 12.6: Sabic's First-phase Industrial Programme

Project/Types of products	Annual production capacity (metric tons)
Petrochemicals	
Ethylene	2,000,000
Low-density polyethylene	708,000
High-density polyethylene	196,000
Ethylene glycol	650,000
Styrene	295,000
Ethylene dichloride	454,000
Crude industrial ethanol	281,000
Caustic soda	377,000
Methanol	1,300,000
Polyisoprene	300,000
Fertilizers	
Urea	1,000,000
Metallurgical	
Iron and steel	2,650,000
Sponge iron	800,000
Steel billets	850,000
Reinforced wire rods and bars	1,000,000
Aluminium	
Aluminium ingots	225,000

Source: SAMA, *Annual Report, 1979*, p. 80.

Finally, attention should be given to the massive development projects in the initial or planning stages which will involve joint ventures with foreign companies. As briefly sketched in Table 12.3, Petromin and Sabic are primarily involved in the hydrocarbon-related industrial undertakings. Sabic, while not limited to petroleum-based projects, has put forward a substantial first-phase industrial programme (Table 12.6), much of which is also included in the Third Plan. In the petrochemical classification, a number of enterprises are under way.

Located at Jubail will be the Sabic/Pecten Arabia Ltd (belonging to Shell Oil Company) project costing in the neighbourhood of $4 billion. The output of ethylene from this plant will act as a feedstock for the Sabic/Exxon project. Production from the Sabic/Pecten scheme will be 656,000 metric tons of ethylene, 295,000 metric tons of styrene, 454,000 metric tons of ethylene dichloride, 281,000 metric tons of crude industrial ethanol, and 355,000 metric tons of caustic soda annually.[18]

The Sabic/Exxon joint venture, also sited at Jubail, will produce 240,000 metric tons of low-density polyethylene per year. Costs of this project are approximately $1 billion.[19]

A third joint venture is the Sabic/Mobil project at Yanbu to produce 450,000 metric tons of ethylene, 200,000 metric tons of low-density polyethylene, 200,000 metric tons of ethylene glycol, and 91,000 metric tons of high-density polyethylene annually. Joint ventures, as this one, have a high degree of technology transfer. On this project alone, a number of Saudi engineers are receiving training in the USA.[20]

Other petrochemical projects under consideration are joint ventures between Sabic and Dow Chemical Company, Celanese-Texas Eastern, Mitsubishi and a Japanese consortium of Mitsubishi and C. ITOH. The undertaking with Dow would be located at Jubail and would have a production capacity of 440,000 metric tons of ethylene, 200,000 metric tons of low-density polyethylene, and 300,000 metric tons of ethylene glycol annually. It is expected that Dow will provide the technology and engineering designs for the project. The venture with Celanese-Texas Eastern will also be at Jubail with a production target of 700,000 metric tons of methanol per year. The Japanese government will likely participate, along with other companies from that country, in the Mitsubishi project under study. The plant, if established, would have an annual output of 450,000 metric tons of ethylene equivalent. The Japanese consortium of Mitsubishi and C. ITOH would include others such as W.R. Grace (USA), with the project located at Jubail. The goal is for production of 600,000 metric tons of chemical-grade methanol annually. In conjunction with this latter project, a number of Saudi engineers are receiving training at Mitsubishi plants in Japan.[21]

The metallurgical projects under Sabic's purview include two, one with Korf-Stahl of West Germany and the other still under study. The iron and steel joint venture with Korf involves construction of an integrated steel complex at Jubail. Estimated to cost about SR 2 billion and scheduled for completion in 1984, the project will produce 800,000 metric tons of sponge iron and 850,000 metric tons each of steel billets and reinforced iron bars and wire rods (although output of the latter may be expanded). The second project for which a feasibility study has been completed would be an aluminium-smelting plant with a capacity of 225,000 metric tons of aluminium ingots per year and other secondary products.[22] Although these projects will rely, at least in the foreseeable future, on imported raw materials, the presence of low-cost energy in this energy-intensive industry makes such undertakings feasible.

Having massive feedstocks in its petroleum resources, fertilizer production is a natural choice in Saudi industrialization. Thus, Sabic is involved in this third area of activity. An interim joint-venture agreement was signed between Sabic and Taiwan Fertilizer Company to investigate the feasibility of a project to produce 500,000 metric tons of urea for export. In the negotiation stage for a joint venture, Sabic has under consideration the establishment of another urea project with an annual output of 500,000 metric tons, thereby doubling urea production.[23]

As pointed out earlier, Sabic has since its establishment in 1976 also been involved in non-hydrocarbon-based industries, particularly in the development of basic-metal industries. Other agencies involved in industrialization in the non-oil sector include the Grain Silos and Flour Mills Organization (GSFMO), which, like Sabic, is a government corporation. Created in 1972, GSFMO is concerned with the construction and operation of grain silos, and flour and animal-feed concentrate mills. The Saudi Consulting House (SCH) came into being in 1977 and was formerly known as the Industrial Studies and Development Centre. This government corporation works closely with the Ministry of Industry and Electricity and other government agencies on technical and market research. A fourth governmental agency with special authority in non-hydrocarbon-based industrialization is the Royal Commission for Jubail and Yanbu. As covered in detail elsewhere, this Commission is empowered to provide sites and infrastructure for basic-metal industry and secondary industry parts at Jubail and Yanbu as required. The remaining two bodies noted in the Third Plan for this type of industrialization are the Saudi Industrial Development Fund (SIDF) and the Ministry of Industry and Electricity itself. SIDF is the governmental, industrial lending agency which, since 1974, has provided loans to private-sector industrial projects. The Ministry is held accountable for the implementation of governmental industrial policy and the regulation of industry, including the licensing of projects as well as the provision of industrial estates.[24]

Investment Climate

The government of Saudi Arabia 'realizes that the objectives of industrial development may be more effectively attained if the business community bears in the long run the responsibility of implementing projects'. In addition, 'the government aims at encouraging and expanding' the private sector in making possible its objectives.[25] The areas in which the government has given support to the creation of a business sector and problems particular to its development follow.

Taxation

Tax incentives have been established to encourage domestic and foreign investment. As set out in the Foreign Investment Code, projects approved as 'assisting the country in economic development' are tax-exempt for five years from the date of production, given that there is local capital participation of not less than 25 per cent. Due to the broad definition of an enterprise assisting in the economic development of the country, most foreign joint ventures with Saudis which are approved and correctly registered are able to qualify for the tax holiday.

Saudi citizens and companies are exempt from taxation on personal and corporate income.[26] Only foreign shares of Saudi companies and foreign companies are required to pay income tax. However, Saudi individuals, partnerships, corporations and legal entities such as trusts and endowments, are subject to pay zakat, a religious tithe. Zakat is an annual tax assessed on all profits, revenues, capital gains and real property at 2.5 per cent. It is collected by the government and is administered through the Ministry of Labour and Social Affairs for the relief of the poor.

Although wholly Saudi-owned companies are not required to submit an audit, in the case of a Saudi/foreign joint venture an annual audit is required. Thus, the payments of both the foreign company tax and zakat for these enterprises are determined by the results of the audit.[27]

For companies (regardless of the type of entity) engaged in a joint venture with Saudis or which are wholly foreign owned, income taxes are determined on a graduated basis as follows: income of SR 100,000 or less, 25 per cent; income of SR 100,001 to 500,000, 35 per cent; income of SR 500,001 to 1,000,000, 40 per cent; over SR 1 million, 45 per cent.[28]

Taxable income is determined from profits on income derived from operations within the Kingdom, dividends of Saudi enterprises paid to non-Saudis, and the full share of non-Saudi silent partners in the net profits of partnerships. Gross revenues, less expenses, equal income for taxation purposes. Expenses are defined as: (1) all normal and essential expenses required by the trade or business which are paid during the year, including a reasonable amount for employees' salaries and any awards that may be given for personal services; (2) expenses related to trade or business; (3) rental of properties in connection with trade or business; (4) any losses that may be suffered by the trade or business that have not been recovered in any way; and (5) a reasonable amount against depreciation of properties employed in business.[29]

Expenses do not include head office administrative costs – only expenses related specifically to a company's operations in Saudi Arabia. A 'reasonable amount' allocated to depreciation is determined by the government on a fixed basis with no accelerated depreciations allowed. The fixed amounts can be adjusted upward only in exceptional cases.[30]

Companies which are required to pay income taxes are obligated to do so by the fifteenth day of the third month of the year following that year covered by the financial statement.

On 15 May 1975, a Royal Decree abolished personal income taxes on wages and salaries earned by foreigners in Saudi Arabia, although partnerships are still taxed as individuals at rates ranging from 5 to 30 per cent on incomes of SR 16,000 and up. Thus, partnerships are assessed taxes at lower rates than corporations.

While not obligated to pay personal income taxes, salaried employees are required to pay a surtax of 2 per cent for the highway fund, if earning more than SR 400 per month. Other forms of taxation include a contribution to the social insurance fund amounting to 8 per cent of the gross earning of employees which the firm must pay if employing 20 or more persons. These contributions are tax deductible.

Labour

Saudi Arabia, like other Gulf nations, is constrained by a shortage of manpower to meet rapid development requirements (Table 12.7). Through professional and technical-training programmes established by the government, incentives to the private sector to train personnel, and requirements in the Labour Code to train and improve skills of employees, the Saudi government is working toward meeting manpower needs. Nevertheless, the government realizes that in the near term, skilled and semi-skilled labour will continue to be imported because of development goals. As discussed earlier, the importation of foreign workers is to be reduced during the Third Development Plan. Combined with a relatively low rate of increase for Saudi workers, this restriction upon foreigners may be a constraint upon more ambitious economic development.

Table 12.7: Estimated Manpower Distribution in Various Occupational Groups (thousands)

Occupational groups	1975 Saudi	1975 Non-Saudi	1980 Saudi	1980 Non-Saudi
Managers and officials	7.4	6.3	8.7	12.4
Professionals	48.4	15.7	52.9	23.5
Technicians and sub-professionals	25.0	31.4	33.4	81.3
Clerical	67.5	31.4	99.6	121.8
Sales	82.3	47.1	97.2	112.6
Service	105.2	47.1	134.5	145.2
Operatives	40.0	25.1	57.1	51.4
Skilled workers	70.1	47.1	93.5	101.9
Semi-skilled	170.0	62.8	265.0	162.5
Subtotal	615.9	314.0	841.9	812.6
Unskilled	244.0	–	296.4	–
Farmers	311.2	–	281.0	–
Bedouin	114.9	–	98.7	–
Subtotal	670.1	–	1,518.0	–
Grand total	1,286.0	314.0	2,359.9	812.6

Source: The Industrial Studies and Development Centre (ISDC), *A Guide to Industrial Investment in Saudi Arabia*, 5th edn (Riyadh, ISDC, 1977), p. 95.

A work permit is required for all foreign nationals and this regulation is administered through the Ministry of Labour and Social Affairs. The current policy concerning labour importation is that the foreign national must possess a skill needed by the employer which an available Saudi national does not possess (see Appendix C of this chapter for greater details on basic regulations).

In addition to the work permit, all workers are required to have a labour contract to ensure the rights of both the employer and employee. The contract must include the conditions of employment, date of termination, if any, and end-of-service indemnities. At the end of the contract period, whether specified or unspecified, the employee is entitled to severance pay amounting to half a month's salary for each of the first five years of service and one month's pay for each subsequent year, with the last rate of pay as the base. In addition, an employee is also eligible for severance pay if: he is called to military service; a female worker resigns because of marriage or childbirth; or the worker is leaving his job as a result of a *force majeure* beyond his control.[31] Upon resignation of an employee who has given prior notice, the severance pay will fall between one-third and the full amount or in accordance with the employment period.

These payments are applicable to all employees whether Saudi or expatriate, management or labour. In lieu of the severance pay, an employee may choose an indemnity or retirement plan that includes more benefits.

An employer is exempt from severance pay obligations if the employee has: (1) assaulted a supervisor; (2) failed to fulfil contract obligations; (3) been proven guilty of a dishonest act; (4) misrepresented himself to obtain employment; (5) been hired on probation and not found satisfactory; (6) had excessive absence (defined by law); or (7) disclosed secrets concerning the employer's activities.[32]

In addition to providing for termination payments, the Labour Code also provides for protection of workmen against hazards and diseases from work-related activities, working hours, a variety of social services, and settlements of labour disputes.

Although medical insurance is provided free by the government, the Labour Code maintains that additional medical services be provided for employees. The work area must be sanitary, with proper lighting and ventilation. The working hours consist of an eight-hour day, six-day week, except during the month of Ramadan when the work day is reduced to six hours. When the work time exceeds the 48-hour week, overtime pay at a rate of the normal wage plus 50 per cent is to be paid.

The Labour Code also specifies vacation time and sick leave. Employees after one year of service are entitled to 15 days paid vacation which increases to 21 days after 10 years of continuous employment. Paid holidays of 10 days a year and paid sick leave up to 30 days full and 60 days with three-fourths pay are stipulated in the Labour Code.

If a firm employs more than 500 people it may be required to provide recreational facilities, shops, children's schools, mosques, and adult educational programmes.

Western firms have not found it difficult to comply with the provisions of the Labour Code. Many large companies have previously established a 40-hour week and grant over the specified ten days of holidays. Other legal requirements are similar to Western practices; therefore, management is familiar with the laws and norms.

Labour disputes are handled through the Ministry of Labour, although mutual agreements between employer and employee are preferred. If a settlement is not obtainable the grievance can be turned over to the appropriate regional judicial commission.

Due to the shortage of manpower at the managerial and administrative level, firms often hire Western expatriates for decision-making positions. It can be very expensive for a firm to relocate and recruit top-level executives to Saudi Arabia, as Table 12.8 indicates.

Trade Regulation

The trade policy of Saudi Arabia exemplifies the philosophy of free competition which flows throughout the economy. Such a liberal trade policy is not consistent with most other developing countries, but it is made possible through the Kingdom's stable economy, relative dependence on imports, and substantial supply of foreign exchange.

This commitment to a free-trade policy was recently reaffirmed by the Minister of Industry and Electricity. He stated that the Kingdom's development strategy was premised upon expanding export-oriented oil and gas-related industries, along with encouragement of the private sector to establish import-substitution industries. However, the Minister Dr. Algosaibi stressed that the Ministry does not automatically grant protection for domestic industries. Before such requests are approved, the companies involved must prove their production is large enough to meet between 40 and 50 per cent of local demand, that both the price and quality of their products are acceptable to the consumers, and that the firm has been in operation for a year or more.[33]

There are a few exceptions to the free-trade stance. Certain imports, such as liquor and pork products, are forbidden due to religious and social customs. The trade policy, specifically the tariff regulations, has been established to promote domestic industries and, in some cases, does so through protection. If imports compete with locally produced items a duty may be placed on them at a rate of between 15 and 20 per cent. In most instances, duties run from 0 to 3 per cent. An example is machinery and raw materials imported for use by local firms (including joint ventures with foreign participation), which are exempt from duties. In addition, signatories[34] of the Agreement to Facilitate Trade and Exchange and to Organize Transit between Arab League States

Table 12.8: Average Monthly Costs for Riyadh or Jeddah (expatriate family of four, early 1977; cost of living index for 1977 and 1978)

Item	Amount	Cost of living index (1970 = 100) 1977	1978
Housing	SR 35-70,000 per year, 2-bedroom apartment[a] SR 120-170,000 per year, 3 bedroom villa[a]	490.67	460.39
Food	SR 2,300 per month	254.83	248.68
Clothing and footwear	SR 300 per month[b]	210.94	237.34
School fees	SR 1,125 per month	–	–
Car (purchase, insurance, petrol, maintenance)	SR 1,000 per month	–	–
Medical expenses	SR 800 per month (includes only normal medical care)	–	–
Electricity and water	SR 300 per month[c]	–	–
Servant	SR 1,500 per month (maid from Africa – least expensive servant available)	–	–
General cost of living index		304.17	299.40

Notes: a. Unfurnished, no appliances or utilities. b. Ordinarily, clothing needs will be purchased outside the Kingdom. c. In Jeddah, water can cost SR 300 per month alone, doubling the total.
Sources: N.A. Shilling, *Doing Business in Saudi Arabia and the Arab Gulf States* (New York, Intercrescent Publishing and Information Corporation, 1975), supplement (1977), p. 111 and SAMA, *Annual Report, 1979*, p. 162.

receive some preferential duty treatment. With the Arab League states, Saudi Arabia participates in the economic boycott against Israel.

When duties are assessed they are done so at the cost, insurance, and freight (c.i.f.) value. Imports which enter Saudi Arabia are unloaded into customs warehouses and do not become the responsibility of the importer but, instead, that of the shipping company until clearing customs. They can be stored in the customs warehouses at no charge for 10 days.

The government, in an attempt to relieve bottlenecks, has revised and reduced the required number of import documents and also has changed from the system in which two dozen signatures were required, to a system needing only two or three signatures. An additional requirement for importers is that letters of credit must be margined by 25 per cent with the importer's local bank.

Export controls are also very liberal. Export income is not regulated by the government, and export licences are not required. The re-exportation of imports subsidized by the government and exports to Israel and South Africa are prohibited.

Legislation and Procedures

When exporting to Saudi Arabia, the market would centre around four prospective clients: the Arabian American Oil Company (Aramco), Petromin or other similar semi-autonomous government agencies as Sabic, the private sector and government bodies *per se*.

Aramco and Petromin each has its own purchasing department in which quality goods are given first priority. The government agencies must be dealt with personally where the lowest bidder receives the offer, other things being equal. The private sector is growing rapidly, and it also considers quality to be an important factor.

All markets in Saudi Arabia are characterized by a few distinguishing features: (1) little brand loyalty; (2) quality often determined by price; (3) top and bottom-line products sell more quickly than medium-range goods; (4) presentation of goods, i.e. packaging and display, are an important factor to sales; and (5) rapid delivery time will gain sales.[35]

Agents are an important aspect with regard to selling products in Saudi Arabia. The government requires that the importing activities, including distribution and commercial sales, be conducted through Saudi firms. One such agent is a commission agent who carries on functions similar to an indent agent in Western countries. The main activities of a commission agent include arranging orders for products from Saudi merchants at a commission. In addition, there are wholesalers and shipping agencies which act, respectively, as distributors and agents of foreign transport firms.

Another type of agent which can be advantageous for a foreign company is a tender-agent to act as liaison with Saudi purchasers as well as arranging and submitting bids. As the preparation of tender-bids (i.e. bids for supply and project contracts) is a lengthy process, a local agent with direct contacts can speed the process.

The tender-rules have been revised to allow the government more freedom to negotiate with the bidders, if it is felt that the low bid is unacceptable. As an immediate result, Saudi Arabia was able to reduce a microwave contract with Western Electric, a branch of American Telephone and Telegraph (AT&T), by SR 500 million when Western Electric was originally 30 per cent higher than the low bidder. The new tender-ruling also provides for the direct purchase of spare parts to help reduce costs, in addition to a major change in the procedures which allows government agencies to put bidders through a screening process and then invite a limited number to tender.[36]

The reason behind some of these changes dates back to the problems the government had regarding overpricing of bids. The result has been to turn to lower and medium-technology services available from Asia. One of the cancelled bids was from eight companies for electrification projects, as cost estimates greatly exceeded the government's own official estimates. Dr. Algosaibi, Minister of Industry and Electricity, stated: 'We would rather live with candlelight than pay these prices. We could have moved all these people in some of these areas to Geneva and it still would have been cheaper than providing them with electricity here.'[37]

Saudi officials have stated that inflation, contract requirements and working conditions are responsible for increasing the expected costs of various projects, but that the gross overpricing of several firms is due to the desire for excessive profits. Officials have acknowledged that they might have to pay 20 to 50 per cent more than the current world prices for the quality and speed they demand, although they do not agree to pay 200 to 300 per cent more.

Major Bottlenecks

Bottlenecks that impede the development projects in the public sector and the economy as a whole naturally have an impact on the expansion of the private sector and the flow of imports into the economy. Two major bottlenecks of the mid-1970s – transportation infrastructure and inflation – appear at this point in time to have been largely corrected.

As mentioned in the discussion of the Second Development Plan, considerable success was achieved in expanding port capacity in the Kingdom during 1975-80 so that the delayed unloading of ships would not impede construction and development. Also accomplished during the Second Plan period was an abatement of the high rate of inflation that was threatening real development in the country. Government fiscal policy was a major factor in reducing the rate of inflation to an acceptable level. It is anticipated by planners that inflation during the 1980-5 Third Plan can be maintained at a tolerable rate of approximately 10 per cent.

Looming very evident as the major constraint in the upcoming 1980-5 span is manpower. While this problem is not new to the Kingdom with its relatively small labour force, the vast number of foreign workers imported during the Second Plan has resulted in planners providing for very limited growth in the number of expatriate workers during the Third Plan.[38] This manpower bottleneck will necessarily be a limiting element for business in the foreseeable future, but at the same time it will allow for certain opportunities for training and education-related enterprises.

Housing likewise is a sector with vast construction potential, but appears as a bottleneck. First and Second Plan objectives were not entirely met so that construction well into the Third Plan will be directed toward catching up. Increasing demand for modern housing from the domestic population as the standard of living improves will combine with expatriate demand for housing, to cause prices to continue to rise. The Third Plan calls for 730,000 new units to be constructed,[39] but until the construction plans can be realized, the government will continue several policies now in place to combat immediate problems. They include: (1) the requirement of firms with government contracts continuing at least three years and valued at SR 100 million or more and with employees of over 50 persons, to provide their own housing and office facilities; (2) establishment of the Saudi Real Estate Company to construct high-rise buildings and promote urban development programmes; (3) freezing the rental of increased office space to government agencies for the purpose of expansion; (4) creation of a prefabricated-housing programme with special banking facilities available to developers; and (5) limiting rent increases to 5 per cent in 1975, a freeze on increases in 1976, a 15 per cent increase in 1977, and controlled rises thereafter.

Hotel accommodation, like housing, had until recently been in scarce supply. However, rapid construction during the Second Plan has resulted in the first signs of overcapacity in Jeddah, Riyadh and Dammam/Al-Khobar. Occupancy rates in 1980 were lower than in 1979 in most of the deluxe hotels in those cities and still lower in the Eastern Province.[40]

Finally, some observers have talked of what they consider a high degree of indecision, particularly on projects often of a joint-venture nature.[41] It must be pointed out, however, that these are frequently massive projects involving major commitments of funds and resources. For example, the petrochemical industries carry implications for oil-output policy. The commitment of a certain level of associated natural gas (produced in conjunction with crude oil) as a feedstock required for efficient operation of petrochemicals and fertilizers industries is tied, then, to a certain level of oil production. Moreover, decision-making and procedural apparatus improve with experience. As a developing country, Saudi Arabia is gaining this experience and at a rate much more rapid than most.

Foreign business enterprises in Saudi Arabia are influenced not simply by Saudi restrictions, regulations or bottlenecks, but also by the existence of certain elements within the foreign companies' countries. The USA offers one example.

Between 1975 and 1980 the US share of Saudi imports hovered around 20 per cent; however, unlike its chief competitors, there was virtually no growth. From $4.4 billion in 1978 to $4.9 billion in 1979, the import total from the USA was expected to reach $6 billion in 1980 – a slightly diminished share relative to the main industrial rivals.[42]

The reason lies not so much in the strength of foreign competition as it does in self-imposed Congressional and bureaucratic limitations, such as the US foreign-tax law, the Export Administration Act, tight monitoring of anti-boycott legislation, the Foreign Corrupt Practices Act, and general misconceptions about Saudi Arabia in government and business. Staffing of US companies abroad is made difficult by tax laws that impose taxes on overseas employees for salaries, incentives, bonuses, health insurance, cost-of-living allowances, and additional earned income. Eight of the primary industrial competitors of the United States – Japan, West Germany, the UK, Italy, France, South Korea, Canada and Sweden – with minor exceptions, exempt their overseas employees from these taxes.

Anti-boycott provisions of the Export Administration Act are a source of problems to US businesses. Large corporations with ample legal advice are often able to deal with this constraint while smaller and medium-sized businesses have greater difficulty.[43]

While certain US government departments are working to encourage exports from the USA,[44] other government departments examine companies' books scrupulously for signs of the slightest infringement of the Foreign Corrupt Practices Act or other legislation. The atmosphere of mutual understanding necessary for sound business relations can be marred with the prevalence of such sentiment.

Misconceptions about Saudi Arabia by those with little or no overseas experience is a detriment to increased business opportunities in the Kingdom. Mistaken attitudes regarding Saudi customs and restrictions need to be rectified before opportunities can be explored.

American businesses cannot attribute all of their exporting and business activity problems to their government. US prices are often not competitive and the Saudi government has recently become more cost-conscious as the change in tender-bidding procedures demonstrates.

This is not to say that opportunity does not exist for US business in Saudi Arabia. Saudis regard American products as quality items, which is an important element to the potential US exporters. In some areas the USA has a reputation for experience and quality, as in petroleum and its related fields, petrochemicals, engineering and agricultural equipment.

US government activities have also contributed to the promotion of trade and business between the two countries. In addition to the Department of Commerce and the American Embassy in the Kingdom, the Saudi Arabian-US Joint Commission on Economic Cooperation (JEC), which was established to provide technical assistance, has developed into an avenue for US business opportunity by supplying information and being a source of good will.

Conclusions

Saudi Arabia is enjoying an unprecedented period of development in which diversification of its economic base and expansion of infrastructural facilities require the material and expertise of the industrialized world. At the same time the industrialized bloc is dependent upon the flow of petrodollars back into its economy. Thus, there is a need for co-operation and a stream of information between the West and Saudi Arabia which the business community can help to provide.

The Third Plan is expected to provide numerous opportunities for medium-sized companies, particularly in communications and service industries. Joint-venture enterprises with Saudi partners will also have much potential in such areas as building supplies, construction and maintenance equipment, business and educational equipment and systems, transportation, water resources, electric power equipment and health-care services and systems.

Marketing appears to be the catalyst to success in the Saudi market. With the increased familiarity for products and methods carried home by the considerable number of Saudi students who have studied abroad, marketing efforts by firms doing business in Saudi Arabia should be facilitated. And, of course, exhibitions remain a medium for providing familiarity with product lines and services.

The bottlenecks in the Saudi economy could create constraints to investment objectives, just as they could hinder the efforts of the government to achieve development targets incorporated in the Third Plan. In spite of these bottlenecks and the expected obstacles to project-implementation which investors might encounter when working in any foreign country, Saudi Arabia represents an excellent opportunity for investment and a promising market for the export of goods and services.

Ultimately, the transfer of technology should prove to be the critical key to the continued development of Saudi Arabia. While the rush to development has been fuelled by the utilization of the nation's vast, yet non-renewable resource of petroleum, the primary thrust of that development is to achieve a self-sustaining and adequately diversified economy.

Notes

1. The Industrial Studies and Development Centre (ISDC), *Guide to Industrial Investment in Saudi Arabia*, 4th edn (Riyadh, ISDC, 1974), p. 20.
2. Kingdom of Saudi Arabia, Ministry of Planning, *Third Development Plan, 1400-1405/1980-1985*, Chapter 3, section 3.1.1.2, p. 76. (Hereafter this source will be cited as *Third Development Plan*.)
3. Ibid.
4. Ibid., p. 77.
5. Ibid., Chapter 3, section 3.6.2, p. 107.
6. Saudi Arabian Monetary Agency (SAMA), *Annual Report, 1399/1979*, p. 54. (Hereafter this source will be cited as SAMA, *Annual Report, 1979*.)
7. Chase World Information Corporation, *Mideast Markets*, 10 October 1977, p. 12.
8. 'The Boom Continues', *Saudi Business & Arab Economic Report*, 27 October 1977, p. 1. This weekly publication of the Jeddah-based Saudi Research & Marketing, Inc., with offices in the United States, Europe, Middle East, and

Japan, is an example of the information sources now available on current Saudi economic and business trends. Reports, interviews, listing of new companies and tenders make it a valuable resource.

9. An example of the sources for in-depth information is that by David M. Wallace (of the Arabian American Oil Company), *Construction Costs in Saudi Arabia*, distributed by the Commerce Action Group for the Near East (CAGNE) of the United States Department of Commerce.

10. *Third Development Plan*, Chapter 3, section 3.1.3.4, p. 86.

11. *Middle East Economic Digest*, special report, July 1980, p. 14. (Hereafter this source will be cited as *MEED*.)

12. *Middle East Economic Survey*, 10 November 1980, pp. II-III. (Hereafter *Middle East Economic Survey* will be cited as *MEES*.)

13. *MEED*, special report, July 1980, p. 31.

14. Ibid.

15. Industrial Studies and Development Centre, *Guide to Industrial Investment*, 4th edn, p. 29.

16. 'The Development of Manufacturing Industry in Saudi Arabia', *Arab Report and Memo*, 25 April 1977, p. 14.

17. US Department of Commerce, *Commerce America*, 1 August 1977, p. 33.

18. SAMA, *Annual Report, 1979*, p. 78 and *New York Times*, 24 March 1981, p. 4.

19. Ibid.

20. Ibid.

21. SAMA, *Annual Report, 1979*, pp. 78-9.

22. Ibid.

23. Ibid.

24. *Third Development Plan*, Chapter 4, section 4.6.3.2, p. 229.

25. Industrial Studies and Development Centre, *Guide to Industrial Investment in Saudi Arabia*, 4th edn, p. 30. Full text appears in Appendix B to this chapter. This position as noted earlier, was reaffirmed as a basic economic principle in the Third Development Plan.

26. Kuwaitis, Bahrainis and Qataris have been treated as Saudis for tax purposes.

27. N.A. Shilling, *Doing Business in Saudi Arabia and the Arab Gulf States* (New York, Intercrescent Publishing and Information Corporation, 1975), p. 339.

28. Industrial Studies and Development Centre, *Guide to Industrial Investment in Saudi Arabia*, 5th edn (Riyadh, ISDC, 1977), p. 110.

29. US Department of Commerce, *Overseas Business Reports*, December 1975, p. 20.

30. The rates are based on the useful life of the asset on an annual fixed instalment basis, as determined by regulation no. 12025/2/1 of 22 January 1973. The following are examples of a few depreciation rates: office and showroom furniture and fittings, 10 per cent; office equipment, 15 per cent; air conditioners, 25 per cent; trucks, 25 per cent; earth-moving equipment, 7.5 per cent; generators, 5 per cent; fixed machinery, 7.5 per cent; small tools, 20 per cent; specialized industrial machinery, depending on category, 7.5 to 12 per cent. N.A. Shilling, *Doing Business in Saudi Arabia*, p. 340.

31. Industrial Studies and Development Centre, *Guide to Industrial Investment*, 5th edn, p. 101.

32. N.A. Shilling, *Doing Business in Saudi Arabia*, p. 369.

33. *MEES*, 9 March 1981, pp. 6-7.

34. Iraq, Jordan, Lebanon, Saudi Arabia, Egypt, and Yemen Arab Republic (North Yemen).

35. N.A. Shilling, *Doing Business in Saudi Arabia*, p. 365.

36. See Appendix D of this chapter for a detailed account of tender-bid changes.
37. Chase World Information Corporation, *Mideast Markets*, 28 February 1977.
38. For details, see Chapter 7, *Third Development Plan*.
39. Ibid., Chapter 7, section 7.4.8.1, p. 448.
40. *MEED*, special report, July 1980, p. 37.
41. Louis Turner and James Bedore, *Middle East Industrialization* (New York, Praeger, Publishers for the Royal Institute of International Affairs, 1979), pp. 21-2.
42. *MEED*, special report, July 1980, p. 89.
43. Ibid.
44. Bureau of Labor statistics in the USA show that in 1979, exports to Saudi Arabia accounted for nearly 150,000 US jobs.

Appendix A

Licensing Information

Legal counsel is suggested as the following steps in the procedure can be complicated.

(1) Instructions and forms are available from the Ministry of Industry and Electricity, Foreign Capital Investment Committee (Riyadh); English translations of the forms obtainable from the Industrial Studies and Development Centre (Riyadh). Three copies of the following must be submitted to the Ministry of Industry and Electricity: (a) completed application form; (b) either a feasibility study (manufacturing) or cost analysis (service projects); (c) copies of contracts or memorandum of association between Saudi and foreign partner; (d) all other documents are required in application forms.
(2) In the process of application review by the Foreign Capital Investment Committee, the following aspects are considered: (a) determination that the project is viable; (b) determination as to whether project can be classified as a development undertaking; (c) Committee recommendation of approval for licence; (d) final action by the Minister of Industry and Electricity, based upon the Committee recommendation.
(3) The contract or memorandum of association between the Saudi and foreign partner must be determined as legally conforming to the regulations for companies by the Department of Companies; that Department informs the applicant if the memorandum is acceptable or requires modification.
(4) Public registration of the approved memorandum is required in: (a) the commercial register of the Notary Public Department with appropriate filing and (b) through publication in a local newspaper or, if the new enterprise is a limited liability company, joint partnership or stock company, the memorandum must be published in the official gazette, *Umm al-Qura*.
(5) Commercial registration is somewhat more involved. Two applications for registration (one for commercial registration and the other for inclusion in the Companies' Register) are sent to the Department of Companies and Registration of the Ministry of Industry and Electricity. Documents needed are: (a) letter requesting registration; (b) stamped copy of memorandum of association indicating its recording by the Notary Public Department; (c) example of publication of the notarized memorandum in the newspaper or gazette (preceding

section); (d) certified bank statement proving deposit of funds for the firm's capitalization (required for limited-liability companies only).
(6) The next step is registration of the company by the Department of Companies in the Companies' Register, thus completing the application process. A partner of the firm is required to sign the application form at the office of the Department of Companies (Riyadh) with final forwarding of the application form to the Commercial Registration Office.
(7) At the Commercial Registration Office the company is registered and issued a commercial registration number, with a copy of the registration certification given to the company. Registration fee in 1980 was SR 100 ($33).
Source: *MEED*, special report, July 1980, p. 33.

Appendix B

Industrial Policy and Incentive Measures

In its desire to achieve the maximum economic and social benefits for Saudi nationals from industrial development, and in order to familiarize the ministries and government departments and the business community within and outside the Kingdom with the basic policy of the Government regarding industrial development, the main principles of the industrial development policy of the Kingdom were announced in 1394 [1974] as stated below:

(i) The Government aims at encouraging and expanding manufacturing industries, including agricultural industries, which can effectively contribute to the increase of national income, to raising the standard of living and of employment and to diversification of the economy of the Kingdom. For diversifying the economy, the Government will work towards the adoption of plans which, beside increasing the national income, will reduce the effect of outside economic disturbances on the Kingdom and diversify the opportunities open to the increasing abilities and technical capabilities of the people of Saudi Arabia.
(ii) In view of the fact that the economy of the Kingdom is based on competition between the private commercial and industrial enterprises, the Government realizes that the objectives of industrial development may be more effectively attained if the business community bears in the long run the responsibility of implementing industrial projects. Accordingly, businessmen who are prepared to take the risks of success and failure, motivated by prospects of profit, will enjoy the full support of the Government during all stages of preparation, establishment and operation of industrial projects which are beneficial for the Kingdom. The Government is also ready to supplement the efforts of businessmen in the private sector by establishing, financing and participating in the management of the large industrial projects of those requiring wide technical experience and which the private sector cannot undertake alone.
(iii) The Government considers that competition serving the interests of local consumers is the best means of influencing the business community in the industrial field towards beneficial manufacturing and market-oriented projects.
The Government also considers that competition is the most effective means for selecting the investment schemes which suit the market requirements, for encouraging low-cost production and for fixing fair prices for both consumer and producer. However, the Government will not permit harmful foreign competition, such as dumping.
(iv) To ensure that businessmen who are ready to participate in the industrial development of the Kingdom are acquainted with the information required for identification, implementation and successful operation of feasible projects, the

Government shall, from time to time, familiarize them with the industrial and feasibility studies and other useful information that may be available. The Government shall also provide existing industrial establishments with the services available in the management and technical fields.

(v) In order to encourage businessmen to invest in projects of prospective benefit to the national economy, the Government is prepared to offer encouraging and financial incentives to all industrial sectors so as to make it possible for every well-conceived and well-managed project within this sector to realize reasonable profits for the investors. The Government will grant the same incentives to all projects set up within the sector, it being understood that these incentives shall be given in accordance with the regulations without delay.

The incentives may include the following:

(a) Provision of loans and participation in equity capital under encouraging conditions;
(b) assisting businessmen in the formation and organization of new industrial companies;
(c) provision of assistance in the selection of industrial projects, in the preparation of their economic feasibility studies and in evaluating them;
(d) extending operational assistance (technical and financial);
(e) exemption of imported equipment and primary materials from customs duties;
(f) exempting the share of the foreign partners from taxes on the profit of the company as provided in the Foreign Capital Investment Statute;
(g) giving preference to local producers in government purchases;
(h) imposition of protective customs tariffs on competing imports;
(i) providing accommodation in industrial areas;
(j) granting subsidies for training Saudi employees; and
(k) providing assistance for the exportation of products.

(vi) To enable organizing the assistance granted by the Government to industry and make it more effective, and appreciating the necessity of providing an atmosphere of security to industrial investors ensuring that they would realize the hoped-for benefit from the projects set by them in the light of the available market demand, the State is adopting the principle of licensing of industrial projects which exceed a specified size of invested capital, employment or production capacity, it being understood that an application for licence shall not be refused except for practical considerations relating to the supreme national interest or to the national economy.

(vii) When the Government establishes large and important industrial projects which the private sector cannot undertake, it shall make efforts for the private sector to participate in them as much as possible. In such cases and in cases where the Government participates in the capital of private projects to supplement the investments of the private sector in them, it is the policy of the Government – in respect of industries other than those relating to national security – to sell the shares owned by it to the public in due course if this serves the public interest.

In the cases in which the Government finds it necessary to assume the responsibilities of management of an enterprise because of the inability of the businessmen to operate it, the Government will hand back these responsibilities to the businessmen as soon as possible. In all cases the policy of the Government is that it shall be a partner and not a competitor of the producers in the private sector.

(viii) The Government shall do its utmost to avoid imposition of quantitative restriction or of control on prices as means for implementing its industrial policy. The Government shall not impose restrictions except in the cases in which competition cannot have an effective role, as in the case of commodities which by

their nature are characterized by monopoly.
(ix) The Government recognizes the right of the business community in the industrial field to select, utilize and manage the economic resources, including industrial workers, in so far as this does not contravene statutes in force, in order to raise the productive efficiency of industry to the maximum.
(x) The Government welcomes foreign capital as well as foreign expertise and invites their participation in the industrial development projects in cooperation with Saudi businessmen. The Government, recognizing the benefits to the industrial development of the Kingdom of the entry of foreign capital accompanied by administrative and technical capability and ability for international marketing, assures investors that it will always avoid imposing any restrictions on the entry and exit of money to and from the Kingdom and that it shall continue its policy based on the respect of private ownership in the Islamic Law (Shari'a).
(xi) The Government shall provide the public utilities and make the basic arrangements necessary for the setting up of economically feasible industries. Appreciating the dependence of industry on the general development of the Kingdom, the Government will promote the growth of all economic sectors in order to make available for the producers suitable local resources in sufficient quantities and increase purchasing power of consumers within a framework of an evergrowing national economy.
Source: Industrial Studies and Development Centre, *Guide to Industrial Investment in Saudi Arabia*, 4th edn, pp. 29-33.

Appendix C

Rules for the Organization of Labourers Exempted from Recruitment Regulations

(1) All workers exempted from recruitment regulations, whether in the Kingdom or coming here to work unsolicited, must obtain a work permit in which they are registered as 'worker' without the need of being connected with guarantors of their work unless the two parties demand a work guarantee or unless the nature of the work makes it (guarantee) necessary.
(2) The said workers will be allowed to work in commercial establishments owned by Saudis or are licensed under the foreign capital investment law.
(3) The first clause covers skilled workers who are working in (other people's) shops for their own account but the work permit must include the word 'worker' while being issued for them.
(4) The said worker must fill in the form for the application for a licence which contains general information about his professional life in the Kingdom and other pertinent details.
(5) Passport and Civil Affairs Departments must not issue such workers residence visas unless they have valid work permits. In other cases those departments will continue to implement laws in existence.
(6) The Ministry of Labour and Social Affairs shall organize the method of issuing work permits for the said workers on condition that this be completed in six months. The Ministry may put the workers in categories and give one or more time limits for them to obtain work permits with priority given to new arrivals and to those whose residence visas have expired.
(7) Establishments under any name or designation are not allowed to hire workers exempt from recruitment regulations except under written contract of labour and the workers must immediately sign contracts with their employers.

(8) As to workers who are not employed permanently by an establishment or employer but who travel around to carry out temporary work for the public, they and their employers must sign contracts if the work assigned takes more than a week to complete. If the duration of the work is less than a week, either side may demand a contract.
(9) An employer must keep the passport of a worker in his custody and must give it back to him only at the end of the contract or if the passport validity expires or in other cases where the employer is convinced of the need to give the employee back his passport. The number, date, place of issue and residence number in the passport must be included in the work contract.
(10) An employer must inform the governorate of his city or town of any violation of the above regulations committed by a worker in his employ.
(11) Employers violating any of the above rules will face a fine of SR 2,000 to 10,000 and/or a prison term of two to six weeks. A worker violating the law will be deported and not allowed to return to the Kingdom for three years.
(12) In every governorate a committee will be formed including representatives of the governorate, labour office, passport department, and security department, to look into violations of the above laws and suggest punishment in accordance with the preceding clause. The committee shall meet at the governorate's headquarters.

In areas where there are no labour or passport offices the committee shall include representatives of the other departments only.
(13) Punishment meted out by the committee must be signed by the governor or whoever he appoints as deputy.
(14) A governorate must provide the passport office with a copy of the deportation order against a worker and the office must then inform the Foreign Ministry of the case so that the worker may not return to the Kingdom before the lapse of the period mentioned in clause 12.
(15) Fines collected under these rules will be given to the Social Security Fund mentioned in article 207/2 of the Labour Law.
(16) The governorates must publish punishment decisions in the local newspapers.
(17) The Information Ministry must publish these regulations by all available media and the Ministry of Labour and Social Affairs must inform the employers and workers of their content so that they may abide by them.
(18) These regulations shall be published in the Official Gazette and become operative on publication.
Source: 'Labour Regulations Updated,' *Saudi Business & Arab Economic Report*, 3 November 1977, p. 8.

Appendix D

Tender Draft Regulations

The following is a summary of the more important provisions of the new government tender draft regulations:

(1) In all dealings with government, priority shall be given in the first place to Saudi individuals and establishments and in the second place to Saudi-foreign joint-venture firms in which the Saudi interest amounts to 50 per cent or more of the capital of the firm.
(2) For government purchases preference is to be accorded to Saudi-manufactured products, if available, even if their quality and specifications are below those of similar foreign goods.
(3) Government purchases and contract work are to be secured at fair prices not exceeding prevailing prices.

(4) Bids are to be invited through notices published at least twice in the official gazette or by letters sent to firms invited to bid in the event of restricted tenders. Offers, which are to be submitted in either sealed or open envelopes depending on the tender, should be accompanied by a preliminary guarantee amounting to 1 per cent to 2 per cent of the value of the contract. Such guarantees are not required in the case of direct purchases or open bids.
(5) Government purchases and contract work whose value does not exceed SR 1 million may be secured directly from suppliers or contractors upon the approval of the Minister or the Head of the Department concerned. The Minister may delegate his authority for such direct purchases if the total value does not exceed SR 500,000.
(6) The committees examining tenders may negotiate with the lowest bidder or other bidders in cases of: (a) significantly inflated cost estimates as compared to market prices, with a view to reducing the estimates; (b) the inclusion in the offers of the lowest bidders of certain reservations, so as to secure the withdrawal of all or some of the bidder's reservations. In the event that such reservations are unreasonable and the bidder refuses to withdraw them, then the committee shall negotiate with the next lower bidder.
(7) Tenders and offers may be cancelled if the need for them is no longer deemed necessary, or if the committee is of the opinion that the bid prices, conditions and specifications are unsuitable even after negotiation.
(8) The prerogative for approving direct purchases or contract work whose value exceeds SR 3 million lies with the Minister or the Head of the Department concerned, and for smaller amounts with the Under Secretary of the Ministry or his replacement. Such authority may be delegated to lower-ranking officials depending on the position of the official concerned.
(9) In the conclusion of contracts with the government, the contractors must provide a final guarantee equivalent to 5 per cent of the value of the contract. Such guarantees are not necessary in cases of contracts involving consulting work, direct purchases and purchases of spare parts. The value of the guarantee may also be reduced gradually in cases of operation or maintenance contracts on condition that the required guarantee must not be less than the value of the remaining part of the contract.
(10) The government may pay the contractor, upon signature, an advance payment amounting to 20 per cent of the value of the contract in return for a letter of guarantee equivalent to the said amount.
(11) Contractors are subject to the payment of a fine for late delivery amounting to a maximum of 4 per cent of the value of supply contracts and 10 per cent of the value of contracts involving operation and maintenance and consulting work, unless such delays are due to *force majeure*, accidents or other reasons beyond the control of the contractor.
Source: *Middle East Economic Survey*, 9 May 1977, pp. 5-6.

APPENDIX: ECONOMIC DEVELOPMENT AND ABSORPTIVE CAPACITY

Conceptual Framework

Economic development and absorptive capacity are two amorphous concepts in development economics literature. It is, however, not only in the difficulty of defining these concepts that they share similarities. Indeed, the problem of absorptive capacity could be interpreted as constraints on economic development when the two concepts are appropriately defined.

Defining the Concepts

The difficulties in defining economic development, like those associated with the definition of economics, have given rise to several approaches to explaining the meaning of economic development. One approach is to describe what 'economic development is not'.[1] Economic development is then contrasted with total development, economic independence, industrialization and economic growth. More specifically, economic development is either a subset of total development, or contains industrialization, or intersects with economic growth.

A second approach is to go right ahead and say what economic development is, and in this case, a long list of definitions or items which constitute economic development is given.[2]

Yet another approach is to refrain from formal definition of the concept altogether and instead discuss the problems and determinants of economic development. This approach might be based on one of three implied assumptions: (1) that the concept is generally understood and consequently its meaning is taken for granted; (2) that the meaning is so amorphous that no attempt should be made to define it; or (3) that the discussion of the problems, the determinants and other aspects of economic development would make the meaning of the concept clear. A favourite discussion which then follows is to contrast poor countries with rich countries and detail the characteristics of underdevelopment, the implication often drawn being that the study of the problems and institutions of developing nations give meaning to the conceptual framework for economic development.[3]

Rather than bore the reader with detailed examination of these approaches, working definitions of these concepts will be given, subject only to the qualification that there are other definitions. Economic development is defined as a process whereby the real *per capita* income of a country increases over a long period of time within an acceptable structure of income distribution.[4] An operational definition which is often quoted in the discussion of absorptive capacity is the one given by Adler. It may be defined as 'that rate of gross domestic investment expressed as a proportion of GNP that can be made at an acceptable rate of return, with the supply of cooperant factors considered as given'.[5]

Issues Raised by Working Definitions

Several issues are raised by these working definitions. An obvious question is whether they are appropriate for the study of economic development and absorptive capacity in Saudi Arabia.

Whereas the shortcomings of the use of the economic aggregate, real income *per capita*, as a measure of the welfare of a people are implied in the conceptual and practical difficulties encountered in estimating GNP, the important issue is whether, even if these difficulties could be assumed away, one can say the GNP really gives a correct measure of the level of income in an economy in which the bulk of income is generated from a single export commodity.

Also, since GNP includes that part emanating from oil exports, supposing that in any given year 70 per cent of it is generated from this source, is it correct to interpret all oil GDP as constituting income for the economy in that year? If the bulk of the government revenue generated from oil is kept with the Central Bank, is this part of the revenue income to the country? Or is GNP equal to the value-added of non-oil economic activities, plus total government expenditures, less domestic government revenue? Further, an expenditure approach to national-income accounting treats balance-of-payments surplus ((X–M), where X is exports and M is imports), as an addition to income. Thus, another way to pose the question is whether that part of the surplus which is kept with the Central Bank should be considered as an addition to GDP. One way to go about the problem is to interpret the surplus as potential consumption and investment expenditures, and therefore from the growth point of view it is income.

For how long must increases in real income *per capita* take place in order to call them development? Or from the Saudi Arabian point of view, if for example growth rate is not sustained in the future owing to exhaustion of oil, can we say there has been economic development? The answer to the latter question depends on what is meant by the future and what level of growth rate one wants to sustain. In any case, in the light of the large proven oil reserves of the country, and to the extent that capital accumulation which the oil revenue will be able to generate during the oil boom era will be utilized in such a way as to sustain reasonable growth of real income *per capita* during the period when oil will be no more, perhaps this issue about economic development is irrelevant in Saudi Arabia. However, a crucial element of the development process in oil-producing countries is to diversify the economies so that when oil is no more, sustainable economic growth could be achieved.[6] This is an indication that in these countries the role of oil in their economies is recognized from a long-term perspective.

The problem of diversification is another way of stating the problem of absorptive capacity. Obviously, domestic gross investment in the crude-oil industry constitutes a small proportion of total funds available for investment, and therefore the relevant aspect is the gross domestic investment in non-oil industries at an acceptable rate of return. The sluggishness in the growth of co-operant factors retards the rate of increase of this part of gross domestic investment, poses problems for diversification of the economy and provides a constraint on the extent to which the economy can absorb oil revenues.

In addition to the issues related to GNP, the definition of absorptive capacity has other problems. It is debatable whether gross investment is the only relevant expenditure to consider when avenues for spending oil revenue are sought. However, one could easily replace gross investment with 'productive expenditures', to cover all expenditures which the policy-makers deem important to the development efforts of the country. On the other hand, the term 'gross investment' could be retained provided it is recognized that expenditures which contribute directly or indirectly to the creation of both physical and human resources are considered investment expenditures. For the rest of this appendix, 'gross investment' is going to be used in the broadest sense possible unless otherwise specified.

Tied to the issue of how to treat oil revenue in the calculation of national income is the Western notion that most of the oil-producing countries are rich, since they have high *per capita* income and 'surplus funds'. Whereas to the outsider the excess of financial resources over the domestic capacity to absorb is a 'surplus', it is not interpreted that way by economists and development policy-makers in these countries. To them, whatever 'surplus' which exists is temporary, since oil is not a renewable resource. Therefore, considering that Saudi Arabia, for example, has a limited productive base (in terms of arable land or accumulated physical capital), the so-called surplus funds have long-term demand. Consequently, from far-sighted and development points of view, the excess of funds over the current domestic demand is not a 'surplus'. Hence the objective of Saudi development policies to diversify the economy by means of appropriate investment strategies.[7]

To conclude this section, it must be emphasized that investing at an 'acceptable rate of return with the supply of co-operant factors considered as given', is as important an aspect of the development process in Saudi Arabia as the more dynamic problem of increasing the supply and the productivity of these factors.

Analytical Framework

It would be an oversimplification to express the complicated process of economic development (whatever the term means) by a few mathematical or econometric relations, no matter how ingenious the formulation may be. Economic development involves a process that is partly socio-political and institutional, which, unlike some economic aggregates, defies quantification. In order to undertake a meaningful analysis of this complicated process, however, one could push the multi-dimensional nature of the process to the background, and for the sake of simplicity restrict oneself to a few socio-economic indicators or magnitudes. This section, therefore, has the task of explaining the broad determinants of economic development and, for that matter absorptive capacity, by means of a simplistic model.

Determinants of Economic Development and Absorptive Capacity

Assuming that the rate of growth of population is given, the main determinant of economic development is the growth of national income which is generally determined by the capacity of the economy to produce. This capacity or output is often expressed in the form of an aggregate production function, which may be written, from the point of view of development economics, as:

$$(1) \quad Y = f(K, L, R, T, E, W, S)$$

where Y is production capacity of the economy, K is the stock of capital, L is the amount of labour, R is natural resources, T is the level of technology, E is entrepreneurship, W is the weather and other geographical conditions, and S is an amorphous factor which serves as a proxy for socio-economic and political factors which influence the productivity in the economy.[8] It must be noted here that the use of such an aggregate production function, and the resultant derivation of the determinants of economic development from such a function, as we have done, presupposes the assumption that production capacity or GNP is the most important factor in assessing economic development. Controversies over the measurement of welfare of a society should warn us that this assumption may not be true. But so far as other factors, which together with national product make up the welfare of a country, move in the same direction as national product, the latter is a good proxy for the total welfare of the people. Consequently, the process of economic development could be interpreted as a process through which Y is made to grow at the fastest rate possible by means of increasing the quantity and quality of K, L, R, T, E, and making the weather, geographic, social and political environment conducive to the expansion of production capacity. The rate of economic growth, then, is a function of the rate of growth of the factors on the right-hand side of relation (1) above, in both quantitative and qualitative senses.

One will not, therefore, disagree that the rate of economic growth is always limited by the lack of or relative shortage of the above-mentioned factors. Which are more significant is, however, an issue which can be resolved only by studies on individual countries. The answer to this question will depend on the conditions prevailing in the country being analysed, and even for the same country it will depend on the time frame with which one is concerned.

Now what factors are responsible for limited absorptive capacity? They are basically of two types: (1) factors relating to the supply of economic inputs; and (2) institutional factors.[9] The first group concerns such constraints on development as lack of knowledge, skill, managerial experience and general shortage of manpower, the non-availability of arable land for agriculture, and other factors which limit the size and quality of any factor of production. Other 'institutional factors' could be listed as inefficient political machinery to undertaken development planning, land-tenure system, social stratification, underdeveloped economic institutions such as inadequate financial system, poor economic and social infrastructure, and general attitude towards economic development.

An examination of the catalogue of factors limiting absorptive capacity will indicate that they are not different from those which inhibit the growth of production capacity. In other words, lack of or sluggishness in the growth of any of the arguments in the aggregate production function expressed in relation to function (1) above, except capital, constitutes limitation on the absorption of financial resources. Capital is exempted because in a country in which foreign exchange is in abundance, capital accumulation is assumed to be limited only by the amount of co-operant factors. It is our contention that economic development in Saudi Arabia involves the process of expanding the capacity of the economy to absorb oil revenues over time.

Theoretical Foundations

An attempt will now be made to provide a theoretical foundation for the role which has been assigned capital formation and savings in the development process. And to the extent that surplus funds are sources of savings, a theoretical basis is also provided for the role of surplus funds in the economic development of a country like Saudi Arabia. The role in this case will be subject to the absorptive capacity of the country. Although in both neo-classical and Harrod-Domar growth models capital is made an 'engine' of growth, the emphasis on planning and the use of input-output models in developing countries tend to make the latter theory easier to use in explaining determinants of growth of output and consequently of development in these countries.[10] Also, the Harrod-Domar model is simpler than the neo-classical growth model in terms of exposition and comprehension. Consequently, we use the Harrod-Domar growth model as our theoretical basis. Indeed, this model has underlain all approaches based on capital-output ratio for estimating capital requirements for projects and for the economy as a whole.

In this subsection, two things are proposed: first will be the presentation of a growth model which will not only help us analyse the role of capital and consequently the surplus funds in economic development, but will also provide a theoretical basis for the analysis of constraints which inelastic supply of co-operant factors could have on economic development. Secondly, an investment theory which, given that the financial resources are in excess of domestic requirements, could underlie an investment strategy aimed at maximizing the net social return is presented.

The Harrod-Domar Growth Model. Expositions of the Harrod-Domar model often begin with the following Leontief-type production function:

$$(2)\quad Y = \min\left(\frac{K}{a}, \frac{L}{b}\right)$$

where Y is total output, K is capital stock, L is the effective labour force (which includes a factor for labour-augmenting technical change), a is the capital-output ratio, and b is the labour-output ratio. Then, given other equations and assumptions, mathematical manipulation is undertaken to derive the following growth requirements for total output:

(3) $\dot{Y} = \frac{s}{a}$

(4) $\dot{L} = n + \gamma$

where s is the rate of savings, n is the rate of growth of labour, the dot over a letter indicates the rate of growth of the variable represented by that letter, and γ is the rate of labour-augmenting technical change.

Relation (2) indicates that output is equal to either the product of the capital-output ratio and the capital stock or labour force multiplied by its productivity, *whichever gives the smaller output*. Given the productivity of both capital and labour, the rate of growth of the quantity of capital or the amount of labour available could put a constraint on output. From the point of view of economic growth, the growth of output is limited by the growth of capital if labour is in abundance. Relation (3) describes this situation. It is often referred to as the warranted growth rate, which is the rate of growth of output warranted by the rate of capital accumulation. On the other hand, the growth of output cannot be greater than the rate at which labour force is growing. This is expressed by relation (4) which is called the natural rate of growth.

The warranted rate of growth illustrates the role that capital accumulation (and consequently surplus funds) can play in economic development, whereas the natural rate of growth relation emphasizes the case in which capital or financial resources is no problem but co-operant factors such as labour are in short supply.

From a more dynamic point of view, one can visualize instances in which the labour productivity could increase so as to expand the utilization of surplus funds for capital formation, i.e. to increase absorptive capacity. This aspect of analysis becomes even more realistic if labour is replaced in relation (2) by a variable, Z, which covers all inputs other than capital, i.e. co operant factors. In this case the natural rate of growth or what we may call the 'effective rate of growth' is the rate at which total production would be permitted to grow by the rate at which the co-operant factors are expanding. Thus, whereas in a capital-shortage economy output is likely to grow at the 'warranted' rate, and therefore this may be the achievable target, the 'natural' or 'effective' rate is the relevant variable which the policy-makers should aim to increase in a capital-surplus but labour-shortage economy such as that of Saudi Arabia.

With respect to the so-called 'knife-edge'[11] case of Harrod-Domar theory, one may say that equilibrium at full employment of all resources need not be the objective of the government of Saudi Arabia provided that effective stabilization policies could be used to prevent the rate of inflation from becoming unacceptable. In any case, since there exist alternative avenues through which increased savings due to expanded oil revenues could be utilized (for example, foreign capital accumulation), it is conceivable to devise an investment strategy (or a set of strategies) which would keep savings and investment in equilibrium while at the same time making them consistent with the rate of growth of output at a level equal to the 'natural' rate. The long-run policy then is to maximize the utilization of surplus funds among various domestic and external alternatives so that the 'natural' rate of growth is made to increase over time – in this way absorptive capacity will be expanded. A theory which can underlie such an investment strategy is the subject of our next discussion.

An Investment Theory for a Surplus Funds Country. It is our belief that a modified version of the present value theory of investment could be applied to the problem of investing oil revenues – both domestically and externally.

Let $R_t, R_{t+1}, \ldots R_{t+n}$ represent the estimated net stream of social returns which would accrue to an investment project, and C_t be the initial cost. Then the present social value of the project (PSV) is

$$(5)\quad PSV = C_t + R_t + \frac{R_{t+1}}{1+r} + \ldots + \frac{R_{t+n}}{(1+r)} n$$

where r is an appropriate social rate of discount, and n is the life-span of the project. The values of R will of course depend on the economic, social and political factors influencing the evaluation of the project, including subjective factors.

Assuming that there is a way in which the net social returns could be estimated, then the next issue is on what rate of discount to use in arriving at the present social value of the project. Obvious candidates are the domestic rate of interest, rate of return on private investments in Saudi Arabia and foreign rates of interest. The heterogeneity of foreign rates of interest makes a choice among them difficult. An alternative will be to have a representative foreign rate of interest which would preferably be a weighted average of all foreign rates conceivable. Let such a rate be designated as r*. It is our contention, then, that if the stream of net social returns and the initial costs of domestic projects are discounted by the appropriate foreign rate of interest, we will arrive at present social values which take into account the fact that foreign investments are alternatives to domestic investment. The present social value of a typical project, then, could be represented by the following:

$$(6)\ PSV^* = C_t + R_t + \frac{R_{t+1}}{1 + r^*} + \ldots\ldots + \frac{R_{t+n}}{(1+r^*)}{}^n$$

Of course, the foreign, social rate of interest would be adjusted by planners or policy-makers to reflect political and economic uncertainties which exist in the foreign countries. It is, however, true that the smaller is r*, the bigger is PSV* of an investment project, and therefore the greater the chance for these projects to have a positive present social value. This conclusion stems from the fact that domestic and foreign investment are substitutes.

When all projects which can be conceived of by policy-makers have had their present social values calculated, the idea then is to invest in all ventures which show positive, present social values. Considering that there is an absorptive capacity constraint, it is likely that the total of such investments in any given period (say a year or a plan-period) will fall short of total investible funds available to the country. The difference between the amount which could be effectively invested domestically and the total amount of foreign exchange, should then be invested abroad.

Figure A.1 summarizes the investment theory which has been examined. VV represents the present social-value curve for domestic projects; it can be regarded as the domestic-demand curve for investible funds which is measured on the horizontal axis. Now, supposing that within a period of time, the estimated investible funds of an oil-producing country is Qt, then given the schedule of demand for domestic investment, Qd–Qt is the amount of Saudi funds which could profitably be invested abroad without sacrificing feasible domestic projects.

The position and shape of the demand curve for domestic investment

Figure A.1: Demand for Oil Revenues and Surplus Funds

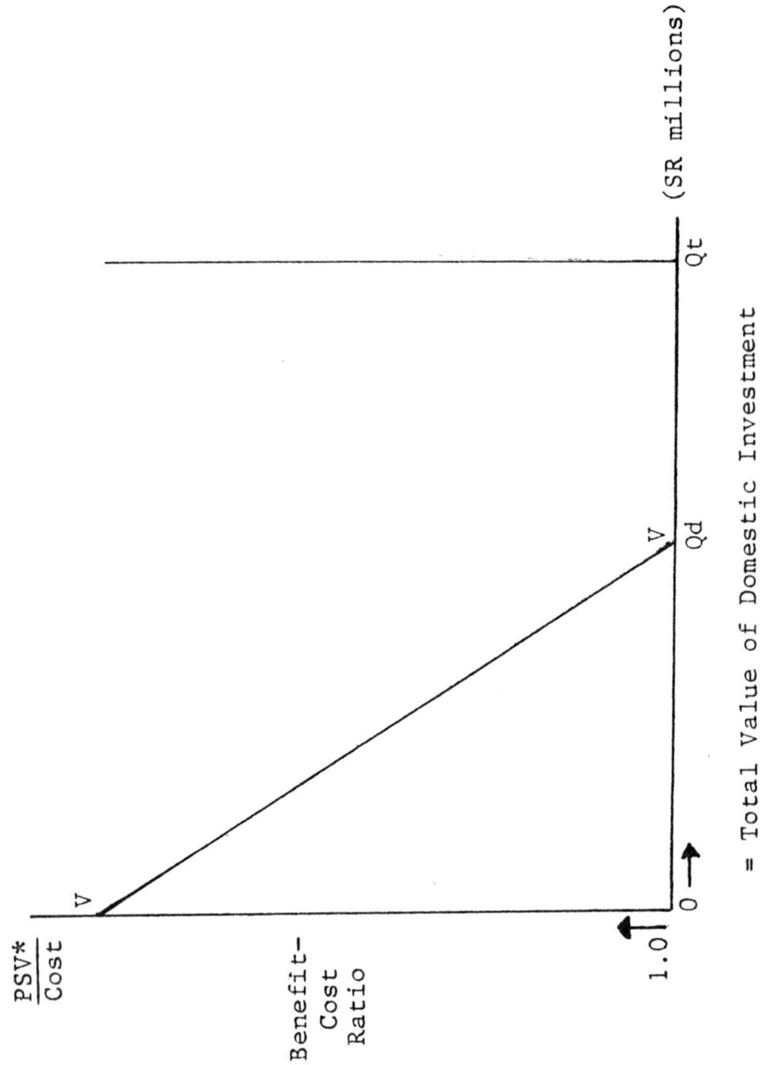

are determined by the social rates of returns of the various investment projects in the domestic economy, which depend on the discount rate used and on the size and nature of the stream of returns which accrue to the various projects. Over time, VV is likely to shift, either inwardly (signifying a reduction of domestic projects which have positive present social value, i.e. a reduction in absorptive capacity), or outwardly. However, the shift of VV need not result solely from changes in the domestic investment atmosphere. Whenever the investment environment in foreign countries becomes less conducive, for example as a result of increased uncertainty about exchange-rate policies, etc., this must be reflected in the lower rate at which domestic projects are discounted to arrive at their present social values. Thus, projects which hitherto did not have positive, present social values may become profitable, shifting curve VV to the right. Given that total investible resources are constant, the share of foreign investment in the total investment of the country will fall. In the real world and in the dynamic sense, however, both the demand for domestic-investment curve and total-investible-funds curve are likely to shift to the right. The objective of the policy-makers of a country then is to try to shift curve VV as much as possible if they are faced with the situation in which Qt shifts to the right consistently. Of course there is another policy which has been overlooked: that of taking measures to shift Qt to the left. This involves reducing the production of oil. It is suggested that the decision on that must be based on a rational assessment of the expected rate of return on a barrel of crude oil which is kept in the ground *vis-à-vis* a barrel which is extracted. Policies which are likely to shift the demand for domestic-investment curve, VV, are those which (1) attempt to expand absorptive capacity, and (2) aim at removing or reducing constraints on economic development. Hence there is a practical application of the investment theory discussed.

Economic Development and Absorptive Capacity in Saudi Arabia

Economic Development

The modern history of economic development in Saudi Arabia falls into two periods: the period prior to 1971, and the period after that year; 1971 marks the beginning of substantial current-account surpluses in the balance of payments of the Kingdom. The second period is, of course, characterized by the oil boom which gave rise to the problem of absorptive capacity. It must be noted that the first period experienced some surpluses on current account. Yet they were not substantial enough to pose the problem of absorptive capacity.

Therefore the periods shade into one another. Although discussion in this section has a bias towards the second period, it would appear that most of it has relevance to the first period as well.

Table A.1: GDP at Current Prices, 1967-75

	Oil		Non-oil		Total	
Year	SR millions	Rate of growth	SR millions	Rate of growth	SR millions	Rate of growth
1967	6,890.5	–	6,252.0	–	13,142.5	–
1968	7,794.4	13.1	6,862.2	9.7	14,656.6	11.5
1969	8,254.5	5.9	7,449.8	8.6	15,704.3	7.1
1970	9,347.2	13.2	7,805.4	4.8	17,152.6	9.2
1971	14,055.5	50.4	8,525.6	9.2	22,581.1	31.6
1972	18,373.1	30.7	9,484.2	11.2	27,857.3	23.4
1973	28,095.2	52.9	11,992.4	26.4	40,087.6	43.9
1974	82,692.0	194.3	16,623.0	38.6	99,315.0	147.7
1975	110,462.0	33.6	23,749.0	42.9	134,211.0	35.1
1976	115,522.0	4.6	39,531.0	66.5	155,053.0	15.5

Sources: SAMA, *Annual Report, 1392-1393/1972-1973*, Table 27, pp. 112-13 and *Statistical Summary*, 2nd issue, 1977 (1393), Table 28, pp. 66-7. Oil, non-oil figures and percentages were computed from these sources.

The rate of economic growth in Saudi Arabia has not only fluctuated from year to year, but it has been different for the two periods under consideration. As should be expected, the economy grew at a higher rate in the post-1970 period than in the pre-1971 era. Table A.1 gives details of the behaviour of GDP in both absolute terms and from the point of view of growth rate. Given that, and that the annual rate of inflation in the two periods averaged 1.8 and 16.2 per cent, respectively, the real GDP in the two periods grew at respective rates of 7.5 and 40.2 per cent per annum.[12] It is clear, therefore, that despite the problem of absorbing the large oil reserves domestically, the Kingdom has enjoyed an accelerated growth of wealth, even if the misconceptions about the measurement of income which have been earlier discussed will not permit one to state that there have been similar developments in real incomes. Nevertheless, the problem of absorptive capacity is real, at least from the short-run perspective. The discussion must now therefore shift towards the practical aspect of this problem.

Estimates of Absorptive Capacity of Saudi Arabia

Few people will deny that Saudi Arabia, since 1971, has consistently had foreign reserves which are above the level needed to finance expanded imports and to enable the Saudi Arabian Monetary Agency to keep the value of the Riyal stable. On the other hand, the accumulation of foreign reserves by oil-producing countries has implications for the world monetary order, especially the international liquidity and economic growth of the advanced countries. To the extent, therefore, that the concept of absorptive capacity is tied to that of surplus funds, and hence to the world monetary order, etc., it is only right that the absorptive capacities of OPEC countries be estimated. The estimation of the absorptive capacity of Saudi Arabia has an even greater significance, since she is not only the principal exporter of oil in the world, but also has the largest known reserves. Also, for the purpose of internal development of the Kingdom, a good estimate of her capacity to absorb oil revenues is vital. In particular, a knowledge of a forecasted level of maximum domestic utilization of oil revenues will aid the development of a rational investment and production strategy for the overall development of the economy.

To our knowledge, seven attempts have been made since 1973 to estimate the absorptive capacity of the Kingdom of Saudi Arabia.[13] These are (1) a study by the Royal Dutch/Shell, (2) a Department of Commerce study, (3) the testimony of T.R. Stauffer of Harvard before the Joint Economic Committee, (4) a World Bank Preliminary Report on Oil Prices, (5) a study by C.A. Gebelein of Shell Oil Company, (6) a paper by John N. Bridge, and (7) a Department of State study on 'Medium-Term Ability of Oil-Producing Countries to Absorb Imports'. The proliferation of studies on Saudi Arabia's ability to absorb oil revenues within a period of three years is not coincidental. It is an indication both of the increased interest shown in the country since the energy crisis of 1973 and an evidence of the concomitantly important role which the Kingdom has come to play in the world energy market and the international monetary system.

Most of the studies have been based on projected capacity to import. This methodology assumes that the principal use of foreign exchange derived from oil exports and royalties, etc., is for imports. In this case, an income elasticity of imports is estimated for the country and, given a projected rate of growth of GNP, future import requirements are then forecasted. The definition of absorptive capacity which underlies such a methodology is no doubt too narrow.[14]

Of all the studies, perhaps the one which adopts the most sophisticated approach is the study by Gebelein.[15] The idea here is to define absorptive capacity in terms of total expenditures by the Saudi government, and to try as much as data would permit to identify the factors which limit the growth of these expenditures and quantify them. Thus we have a classical case of maximization of an objective function subject to a set of constraints. The objective function is total expenditures identity which is a summation of various expenditure categories of the government: defence, aid, etc. The constraints in the model obviously consist of the levels of the co-operant factors: (1) skilled labour, (2) technical knowledge, (3) managerial and entrepreneurial expertise, (4) adequate financial and planning institutions, and (5) socio-cultural and political factors.[16] The solution of the constrained maximization problem need not occupy us here.[17] What is important for our purpose is to note that it produces a model which describes the relationship between absorptive capacity and the constraints. If the parameters of this model can be estimated, then assuming that a method for forecasting the exogenous variables in the model can be found, it becomes a simple matter to estimate the absorptive capacity for future years. Consequently, forecasts for available labour in Saudi Arabia were made for the years 1974, 1975, 1980, 1985 and 1990. Then, given the structural models relating government expenditures to required labour, estimates of absorptive capacity of the Kingdom for these years were undertaken.[18] Table A.2 gives these estimates, at both constant and current dollars.

Table A.2: Domestic Absorptive Capacity of Saudi Arabia

Year	Administrative	Defence	Infra-structure	Arms	Partici-pation	Absorptive capacity $	Absorptive capacity Index
(Millions 1970 $)							
1974	614	418	3,088	416	700	5,236	100.0
1975	682	496	3,396	442	140	5,156	98.5
1980	943	1,010	9,834	594	100	12,481	238.4
1985	1,304	1,805	14,769	700	0	18,577	354.8
1990	1,804	3,256	22,931	832	0	28,822	550.5
(Millions $[a])							
1974	836	569	4,201	566	952	7,124	100.0
1975	1,002	729	4,990	650	206	7,576	106.3
1980	2,036	2,181	21,231	1,282	216	26,946	378.2
1985	4,137	5,727	46,849	2,219	0	58,931	827.2
1990	8,407	15,175	106,881	3,876	0	134,339	1,885.7

Note: a. The dollar figures were obtained by assuming an 8 per cent annual rate of inflation based on 1974 dollars, resulting in very conservative estimations.
Source: C.A. Gebelein, *Estimation of Saudi Arabian Capacity to Absorb Oil Revenues* (Houston, Shell Oil Company, 1974), Tables 9 and 10.

These estimates of absorptive capacity for Saudi Arabia do not take into consideration the capacity of the Saudi governmental machinery to implement projects. As was observed in Chapter 8, actual expenditures (both project and recurrent) have always fallen short of budget appropriations in the 1970s. Using the assumption that in the 1974-80 period only 50 per cent of project-expenditures appropriations would actually be spent, and that that would rise to 70 per cent for the 1985-90 period, the revised forecasts of absorptive capacity can be made.[19] Table A.3 compares the revised and original forecasts.

Table A.3: Revised and Original Estimates of Absorptive Capacity

	1970 $				Current $			
	Original		Revised		Original		Revised[a]	
Year	$ million	Index	$ million	Index	$ million	Index	$ million	Index
1974	5,236	100.0	3,692	100.0	7,124	100.0	5,023	100.0
1975	5,156	98.5	3,458	93.7	7,576	106.3	5,081	101.2
1980	12,481	238.4	7,564	204.9	26,946	378.2	16,330	325.1
1985	18,577	354.8	14,147	383.2	58,931	827.2	44,877	893.4
1990	28,822	550.5	21,944	594.4	134,339	1,885.7	102,280	2,036.2

Note: a. The revised current-dollar estimates were computed using the price index derived from Table A.2.
Sources: From Table A.2 and C.A. Gebelein, *Estimation of Saudi Arabian Capacity to Absorb Oil Revenues*, p. 35.

It would appear that even the most conservative forecast which can be derived from these two tables predicts that between 1974 and 1990, Saudi Arabia's capacity to absorb oil revenues would jump from $3.7 billion to about $22 billion, an increase of almost 600 per cent.[20] If these estimates are compared with those of other studies, the most conservative forecast of Gebelein turns out to paint a very optimistic picture of the Kingdom's absorptive capacity. For example, the Department of State estimates that between 1975 and 1985 Saudi Arabia's ability to absorb oil revenues would increase by 215 per cent,[21] whereas the estimate in Table A.3 (column 4) projects a six-fold increase during the same period.

The differences between the estimates in the tables above and those of other studies can be explained by the nature of the methodology adopted by each study. Most of the other studies use total imports as a proxy for absorptive capacity, whereas in a broader sense total expenditures (including those on imports) is the objective variable with which Gebelein's study is concerned.

One may of course be interested in the contributions of various expenditure sectors in the absorptive-capacity determination for Saudi Arabia. The reader is free to figure the relative roles out for himself from Table A.2. When asked to make a choice between the original and revised estimates in Table A.3, it is suggested that the revised figures should be preferred to the original estimates since they give a more realistic position of Saudi Arabia's ability to utilize her oil wealth. One more choice has to be made: that between constant and current-dollar estimates. From the point of view of the role of surplus funds in international monetary arrangements and the importance of imported inflation in Saudi Arabia's pricing system, the current-dollar figures ought to be selected.

Conclusion

In this concluding section we intend to discuss some of the uses to which an estimate of absorptive capacity of Saudi Arabia could be put. An obvious one is to estimate surplus funds of the Kingdom, given estimates of oil revenue. Unfortunately, we do not know of any systematic attempt made to estimate the oil revenues of Saudi Arabia over a long period. Thus, instead of making our own estimate of oil revenues, we leave this as it is in the hope that anyone who is interested in estimating surplus funds for the Kingdom would make use either of the absorptive capacity estimates discussed in this appendix or the methodologies discussed. As a guideline, however, estimates of oil revenues should involve factors affecting OPEC pricing policies, production policies in Saudi Arabia, international pressures on the Saudis to maintain certain levels of production, and the long-term production strategies for development in Saudi Arabia. These and other topics were treated earlier in this book.

It must be noted that the estimates of surplus funds of Saudi Arabia, and for that matter of OPEC countries, *per se*, are not as helpful to individual advanced countries as the international distribution of the surplus funds and the direction of trade of the OPEC countries. Hence the Department of State's study concentrates on the direction of estimated imports of OPEC countries.[22] Therefore OPEC countries' imports from the USA could be estimated from estimates of absorptive capacities. Also, recently there has been a slackening of Arab investments in the USA.[23] Thus, although the level of surplus funds might be constant from year to year, or may indeed be falling, this does not necessarily imply that the effect on the international monetary order is neutral. If the circular fall of Arab investments in the USA continues, and if it is not offset by increased imports from the USA, it is likely to put pressure on the dollar, and given the role of the dollar in international payments, this is not a healthy development for the world monetary order.

Notes

1. G.M. Meier, 'Misconceptions of Development – Note', in G.M. Meier (ed.), *Leading Issues in Economic Development*, 3rd edn (New York, Oxford University Press, 1976), p. 5.
2. C.P. Kindleberger and B. Herrick, *Economic Development*, 3rd edn (New York, McGraw-Hill, 1977), p. 1.
3. See, for example, B. Higgins, *Economic Development: Problems, Principles and Policies*, revised edn (New York, Norton, 1968).
4. G.M. Meier, *Leading Issues*, p. 7. The income distribution portion is not Meier's.
5. J.H. Adler, *Absorptive Capacity: The Concept and Its Determinants* (Washington, DC, The Brookings Institution, 1965), p. 5. Adler's views also are offered in R. El Mallakh *et al.*, *Capital Investment in the Middle East: The Use of Surplus Funds for Regional Development* (New York, Praeger Publishers, 1977), p. 14.
6. For example, one of the important goals of Saudi development plans is to diversify the economy to make it less dependent on the oil sector.
7. An investment theory which may be employed to minimize the effects of limited absorptive capacity in the development process is presented in the next section.
8. A good discussion of how aggregate production function is used as a framework within which to introduce the analysis of growth process can be found in H.J. Bruton, *Principles of Economic Development* (Englewood Cliffs, New Jersey, Prentice-Hall, 1965), Chapter 2.
9. For a detailed discussion of general determinants of absorptive capacity, see C.A. Gebelein, *Estimation of Saudi Arabian Capacity to Absorb Oil Revenues* (Houston, Shell Oil Company, May 1975), pp. iii-v; M. Kadhim, 'The Strategy of Development Planning and the Absorptive Capacity of the Economy: A Case Study of Iraq' (PhD dissertation, University of Colorado, Boulder, 1974), pp. 334-7; J.N. Bridge, 'Financial Constraints on Absorptive Capacity and Investment Policies in the Arab World', in R. El Mallakh and C. McGuire (eds), *Energy and Development* (Boulder, Colorado, International Research Center for Energy and Economic Development, 1974), pp. 69-79.
10. A good selection of articles on modern growth theories can be found in J.E. Stiglitz and H. Uzawa, *Readings in the Modern Theory of Economics* (Cambridge, Mass., Massachusetts Institute of Technology Press, 1969). In particular, Part 1 contains the basic growth models, including E.D. Domar, 'Capital Expansion, Rate of Growth, and Employment' and R.F. Harrod, 'An Essay in Dynamic Theory' which deal with the Harrod-Domar model, while two other readings by R.M. Solow, 'A Contribution to the Theory of Economic Growth' and T.W. Swan, 'Economic Growth and Capital Accumulation' are expositions of the neo-classical growth theory.

11. An intuitive explanation of this concept is that in case the warranted and the natural growth rates are not equal, the economy can be in perpetual disequilibrium, i.e. for example, if s/a is greater than n, as is likely to be the case for Saudi Arabia, chronic inflation can result.

12. We have opted to use current prices figures for GDP because it is felt that the method used to calculate GDP at constant prices as published by SAMA and IMF *Financial Statistics* underestimates the real GDP originating from oil. For the same reason, the rate of inflation used to arrive at real growth rates is that calculated from the consumer price index, instead of the GDP deflator.

13. The first four studies have been cited in C.A. Gebelein, *Estimation of Saudi Arabian Capacity to Absorb Oil Revenues*; J.N. Bridge, 'The Absorptive Capacity of the Saudi Arabian Economy, 1970-1980', paper, Department of Economics, University of Durham, England, 1974; CACI, Inc., *Medium-Term Ability of Oil-Producing Countries to Absorb Real Goods and Services* (Arlington, Virginia, CACI, Inc., March 1976).

14. However, such a definition is implied in discussion of absorptive capacity in Chapter 10. This narrow definition of the concept is acceptable here since the relevant expenditure category is expenditure on imports.

15. Gebelein's study has appeared in several forms. The original and most detailed is *Estimation of Saudi Arabian Capacity to Absorb Oil Revenues*; an abridged form in some portions but extended to certain other oil-producing Arab countries was 'Forecasting Absorptive Capacity for Oil Revenues: Practical Techniques for Policy Analysis', paper presented to the annual meeting of the Western Economic Association, San Diego, California, June 1975; the paper was published in R. El Mallakh and C. McGuire (eds), *U.S. and World Energy Resources: Prospects and Priorities* (Boulder, Colorado, International Research Center for Energy and Economic Development, 1977).

16. C.A. Gebelein, 'Forecasting Absorptive Capacity for Oil Revenues: Practical Techniques for Policy Analysis', in *U.S. and World Energy Resources: Prospects and Priorities*, p. 107.

17. The mathematical solution can be found in C.A. Gebelein, *Estimation of Saudi Arabian Capacity to Absorb Oil Revenues*, section 5.

18. Ibid.

19. Ibid., p. 35.

20. Revised estimates at 1970 dollars. Columns 4 and 5 of Table A.3.

21. CACI, Inc., *Medium-Term Ability of Oil-Producing Countries to Absorb Real Goods and Services*, Table 12, pp. 14-39.

22. Ibid.

23. 'Arab Investments in U.S. Slacken', *New York Times*, 25 November 1977, pp. A1, A10.

SELECT BIBLIOGRAPHY

Books

Adam, Said M.A. *A Report on the Development of Planning Organization in Saudi Arabia* (Saudi Arabia, June 1965)
Adler, John H. *Absorptive Capacity: The Concept and Its Determinants* (Washington, DC, The Brookings Institution, 1965)
Al-Bashir, Faisal S. *A Structural Econometric Model of the Saudi Arabian Economy, 1960-1970* (New York, Wiley Press, 1977)
Benham, Frederic. *Economic Aid to Underdeveloped Countries* (London, Oxford University Press, 1976)
Bruton, H.J. *Principles of Economic Development* (Englewood Cliffs, New Jersey, Prentice-Hall, 1965)
Burrows, J.S. and Domenish, T.A. *An Analysis of the United States Oil Import Quota* (Lexington, Mass., D.C. Heath & Company, 1970)
CACI, Inc. *Medium-Term Ability of Oil-Producing Countries to Absorb Real Goods and Services* (Arlington, Virginia, CACI Inc., March 1976)
El Mallakh, Ragaei. *Economic Development and Regional Cooperation: Kuwait* (Chicago, Illinois, University of Chicago Press, 1968)
—, Kadhim, Mihssen and Poulson, Barry. *Capital Investment in the Middle East: The Use of Surplus Funds for Regional Development* (New York, Praeger Publishers, 1977)
— and McGuire, Carl (eds) *Energy and Development* (Boulder, Colorado, International Research Center for Energy and Economic Development, 1974)
Friedman, Milton. *The Optimum Quantity of Money* (Chicago, Illinois, Aldine, 1969)
— and Schwartz, A.J. *A Monetary History of the United States, 1867-1960* (Princeton, New Jersey, Princeton University Press for the National Bureau of Economic Research, 1963)
Glahe, Fred R. *Macroeconomics: Theory and Policy*, 2nd edn (New York, Harcourt, 1977)
Henley Centre for Forecasting. *Middle East Economic Prospects: Forecasts* (London, Henley Centre for Forecasting, 1975)
Higgins, B. *Economic Development: Problems, Principles and Policies*, revised edn (New York, Norton, 1968)
Hirst, David. *Oil and Public Opinion in the Middle East* (London, Faber

and Faber, 1966)
Jacoby, Neil H. *Multinational Oil* (New York, Macmillan Publishers, 1974)
Kindleberger, C.P. and Herrick, B. *Economic Development* 3rd edn (New York, McGraw-Hill, 1977)
Knauerhase, Ramon. *The Saudi Arabian Economy* (New York, Praeger Publishers, 1975)
Kubbah, Abdul A. *OPEC: Past and Present* (Vienna, Austria, Petro-Economic Research Centre, 1974)
Labkicher, Ray, *et al. Aramco Handbook* (Dhahran, Saudi Arabia, Arabian American Oil Company, 1960)
Law, John. *Arab Aid: Who Gets It, For What and How?* (New York, Chase World Information Corporation, May 1978)
Levy, Walter J. *Saudi Arabia's Approaching Choice* (London, Walter J. Levy, July 1976)
Lewis, W. Arthur. *Development Planning: The Essentials of Economic Policy* 1st edn (New York, Harper and Row, 1966)
— *Some Aspects of Economic Development* (Accra, Ghana Publishing Corporation, 1969)
Meier, G.M. (ed.) *Leading Issues in Economic Development* 3rd edn (New York, Oxford University Press, 1976)
Musgrave, Richard A. and Musgrave, Peggy B. *Public Finance in Theory and Practice* 2nd edn (New York, McGraw-Hill, 1973)
Nordhaus, William D. and Tobin, James. *Economic Growth* (New York, MBER Fiftieth Anniversary Colloquium V, 1972)
Nyrop, Richard F. *et al. Area Handbook for Saudi Arabia* 3rd edn (Washington, DC, American University, Foreign Area Studies, 1977)
Park, Yoon S. *Oil Money and the World Economy* (Boulder, Colorado, Westview Press, 1976)
Pesek, B. and Savings, T. *Money, Wealth and Economic Theory* (New York, Macmillan, 1967)
Sherbiny, Naiem A. and Tessler, Mark A. (eds) *Arab Oil: Impact on the Arab Countries and Global Implications* (New York, Praeger Publishers, 1976)
Shilling, N.A. *Doing Business in Saudi Arabia and the Arab Gulf States* (New York, Intercrescent Publishing and Information Corporation, 1975)
Stiglitz, Joseph E. and Uzawa, Hirofumi. *Readings in the Modern Theory of Economics* (Cambridge, Mass., Massachusetts Institute of Technology Press, 1969)
Tanzer, Michael. *The Political Economy of International Oil and the*

Underdeveloped Countries (Boston, Mass., Beacon Press, 1969)
Turner, Louis and Bedore, James. *Middle East Industrialization* (New York, Praeger, Publishers for the Royal Institute of International Affairs, 1979)
Waterbury, John and El Mallakh, Ragaci. *The Middle East in the Coming Decade: From Wellhead to Well-Being?* (New York, McGraw-Hill, 1978)
Wells, Donald A. *Saudi Arabian Revenues and Expenditures* (Washington, DC, Resources for the Future, Inc., 1974)
Zeylstra, William G. *Aid or Development, the Relevance of Development Aid to Problems of Developing Countries* (Leyden, A. Wijthoff, 1975)

Journals, Articles, Papers, Addresses, Dissertations, Newspapers and Periodicals

Akhdar, Farouk. 'Saudi Arabia – United States: Between Interdependence and Cooperation', an address delivered to the Conference on World Affairs, University of Colorado, Boulder, Colorado, April 1977
Al-Awadi, Y.A. 'OPEC Surplus Funds and the Investment Strategy of Kuwait', PhD dissertation, University of Colorado, Boulder, Colorado, 1975
Algosaibi, H.E. Ghazi, 'The Strategy of Industrialization in Saudi Arabia', *Journal of Energy and Development*, Spring 1977
Ali, Anwar and Hitti, Said. 'Monetary Experience of an Oil Economy', *Finance and Development*, December 1974
Alireza, Ali A. Sheikh. Speech before the National Foreign Trade Council at the Waldorf Astoria Hotel, New York, 16 November 1976
Al-Madani, Abdel R. and Al-Fayez, Muhamed, 'The Demographic Situation in the Kingdom of Saudi Arabia', *Population Bulletin*, Amman, Jordan, United Nations Commission for Western Asia, January and July 1976
American-Arab Association. *Bulletin of the American-Arab Association*
Asiel, M.A. 'Public Finance and Economic Development in Saudi Arabia, 1960/61-1973/74'. Paper presented at the University of Colorado, Boulder, Colorado, August 1974
El Mallakh, Ragaei. 'Industrialization in the Arab World; Obstacles and Prospects', in Naiem A. Sherbiny and Mark A. Tessler (eds) *Arab Oil: Impact on the Arab Countries and Global Implications*. (New

York, Praeger Publishers, 1976)
— and Kadhim, Mihssen. 'Arab Institutionalized Development Aid: An Evaluation', *Middle East Journal*, Autumn 1976
Financial Times, London, daily
Gebelein, C.A. 'Estimation of Saudi Arabian Capacity to Absorb Oil Revenues', Shell Oil Company, Houston, Texas, May 1974 (mimeographed)
— 'Forecasting Absorptive Capacity for Oil Revenues: Practical Techniques for Policy Analysis', paper presented to the annual meeting of the Western Economic Association, San Diego, California, June 1975
Ghanem, Shukri. 'OPEC: A Cartel or a Group of Competing Nations?', in Ragaei El Mallakh and Carl McGuire (eds) *Energy and Development* (Boulder, Colorado, International Research Center for Energy and Economic Development, 1974)
Haberler, Gottfried. 'International Trade and Economic Development', National Bank of Egypt Fiftieth Anniversary Commemorative Lectures, Cairo, Egypt, 1959
Jakubiak, H.E. and Dajani, M.T. 'Oil Income and Financial Policies in Iran and Saudi Arabia', *Finance and Development*, December 1976
Johnson, H. 'Inside Money, Outside Money and the Wealth Effect: A Review Essay', *Journal of Money, Credit, and Banking*, February 1969
Kadhim, Mihssen. 'The Strategy of Development Planning and Absorptive Capacity of the Economy: A Case Study of Iraq', PhD dissertation, University of Colorado, Boulder, Colorado, 1974
Los Angeles Times, interview with Sheikh Ahmad Zaki Yamani, 9 January 1978
Madani, Ghazi Obaid. 'An Analysis of the Capital Expenditures of the Saudi Arabian Firm', PhD dissertation, University of Arizona, 1972
Metzler, L.A. 'Wealth, Saving and the Rate of Investment', *Journal of Political Economy*, June 1951
Mideast Markets, New York, Chase World Information Corporation, weekly
Middle East Economic Digest, London, Middle East Economic Digest Ltd, weekly
Middle East Economic Survey, Nicosia, Cyprus, Middle East Petroleum and Economic Publications, weekly
New York Times, daily
Oil and Gas Journal, Tulsa, Oklahoma, Petroleum Publishing Company, weekly

Okaz, Jeddah, Saudi Arabia, daily (in Arabic)
Petroleum Economist, London, Petroleum Press Bureau Ltd., monthly
Petroleum Intelligence Weekly, New York, weekly
Pindyck, Robert S. 'OPEC Oil Pricing, World Energy Markets, and U.S. Energy Policy', (mimeographed)
Ronall, J.O. 'Banking Regulations in Saudi Arabia', *The Middle East Journal*, Summer 1967
Saudi Business and Arab Economic Report, Jeddah, Saudi Arabia, Saudi Research and Marketing, Inc., weekly
Saudi Report, Houston, Texas, Saudi Research and Marketing, Inc., weekly
Sherbiny, Naiem A. 'Arab Oil Production in the Context of International Conflicts' in Naiem A. Sherbiny and Mark A. Tessler (eds) *Arab Oil: Impact on the Arab Countries and Global Implications* (New York, Praeger Publishers, 1976)
Silber, W.L. 'Fiscal Policy in IS-LM Analysis: A Correction', *Journal of Money, Credit, and Banking*, November 1970
Sims, C.A. 'Money, Income and Causality', *American Economic Review*, September 1972
Stearn, E. and Tims, W. 'The Relative Bargaining Strengths of the Developing Countries', in Ronald G. Ridker (ed.), *Changing Resource Problems of the Fourth World* (Washington, DC, Resources for the Future, 1976)
Stein, Jerome. 'Monetary Growth Theory in Perspective', *American Economic Review*, March 1970
— 'The Optimum Quantity of Money', *Journal of Money, Credit and Banking*, November 1970
Stolpher, W.F. 'Comprehensive Development Planning', *East African Economics Review* I, New Series (December 1964). Reprinted in Gerald M. Meier, *Leading Issues in Economic Development*, 3rd edn (New York, Oxford University Press, 1976)
Suraisry, Jobarah E. 'Petromin: Its Activities and Role in the Development of the Economy of Saudi Arabia', University of Colorado, unpublished paper, 1977
Taher, Abdulhady H. 'The Middle East Oil and Gas Policy', *Journal of Energy and Development*, Spring 1978
Tobin, James. 'The Interest Elasticity of Transactions Demand for Cash', *Review of Economics and Statistics*, August 1956
Young, Arthur N. 'Saudi Arabian Currency and Finance', *Middle East Journal*, Summer and Autumn 1953

Official Sources, Governments and International Agencies

Arab Report and Memo.

Arabian American Oil Company. *Annual Reports*, Dhahran, Saudi Arabia, Arabian American Oil Company

International Monetary Fund. *International Financial Statistics*, (Washington, DC, International Monetary Fund, 1977-on)

— *Saudi Arabia: An Economic and Financial Survey*, Washington, DC, International Monetary Fund, 26 March 1976

Kingdom of Saudi Arabia. Industrial Studies and Development Centre, 'Development Strategy in Saudi Arabia', working paper presented to the Fourth Conference for Industrial Development in the Arab States, Baghdad, Iraq, October 1976

— *Guide to Industrial Investment in Saudi Arabia*, 4th and 5th edns (Riyadh, Saudi Arabia, Industrial Studies and Development Centre, 1974 and 1977)

— *Survey of Industrial Projects Established After 1390 A.H. (1970)* (Riyadh, Saudi Arabia, Industrial Studies and Development Centre, 1972)

— *Survey of Manufacturing Establishments* (Riyadh, Saudi Arabia, Industrial Studies and Development Centre, 1976)

Kingdom of Saudi Arabia. Ministry of Finance and National Economy, Central Bureau of Statistics, *Statistical Year Books*

— Central Department of Statistics, *Survey of Manufacturing Establishments* (1973 and revised edn 1976)

Kingdom of Saudi Arabia. Ministry of Petroleum and Mineral Resources, Economics Department, *Petroleum Statistical Bulletin, 1979*

Kingdom of Saudi Arabia. Ministry of Planning, *The Second Development Plan, 1395-1400/1975-1980*

— *The Third Development Plan, 1400-1404/1980-1985*

Kingdom of Saudi Arabia. Royal Commission for Jubail and Yanbu, *Jubail and Yanbu Industrial Complexes (A Conspectus)*, February 1977

Kingdom of Saudi Arabia. Royal Decree No. 50, 4 January 1961

Kingdom of Saudi Arabia. Saudi Arabian Monetary Agency (SAMA), *Annual Reports*

— *Statistical Summary*

Kingdom of Saudi Arabia. Saudi Development Fund, *Annual Reports*

Organization for Economic Cooperation and Development (OECD), *Development Cooperation, 1978* (Paris, OECD, 1978)

— *Development Cooperation, 1979* (Paris, OECD, 1979)
— *OECD Observer*
Organization of the Petroleum Exporting Countries Special Fund. *Basic Information* (Vienna, Organization of the Petroleum Exporting Countries Special Fund, 1956)
Royal Embassy of Saudi Arabia. *Industrialization of Saudi Arabia: Strategy and Policy* (Washington, DC, Office of the Commercial Attache, Royal Embassy of Saudi Arabia, 1976)
United Nations. Department of Economic and Social Affairs of the Secretariat, *Selected World Demographic Indicators by Countries, 1950-2000*, ESA/P/W
United Nations. Economic and Social Council. *International Economic Assistance to Under-developed Countries in 1956/57*, Report of the Secretary General, E.3131 and ad. 1, 3 June 1958
United Nations. Industrial Development Organization (UNIDO), *Industrial Development Survey* (New York, United Nations, 1970)
United Nations. *Statistical Yearbook, 1978*
United States Department of Commerce, *Commerce America*
— *Overseas Business Reports*
— *World Area by Commodity Groups* (Washington, DC, Government Printing Office, 1977)
United States Department of the Interior. Bureau of Mines, cited in Federal Energy Administration. *Monthly Energy Review*, January 1977 and 1978
United States Department of State. Policy Sciences Division, *Medium-Term Ability of Oil-Producing Countries to Absorb Real Goods and Services*. Volume 2 of research findings (Washington, DC, Government Printing Office, 1976)
United States Department of Treasury. *The Absorptive Capacity of OPEC Countries* (Washington, DC, Government Printing Office, November 1976)
United States Library of Congress. Congressional Research Service, *Project Interdependence: U.S. and World Energy Outlook Through 1990* (Washington, DC, Government Printing Office, 1977)

INDEX